THE TIDES OF CHANGE

THE TIDES OF CHANGE

Peace, Pollution, and Potential of the Oceans

ELISABETH MANN BORGESE and
DAVID KRIEGER, Editors

MASON / CHARTER

NEW YORK 1975

For Sybil
who gave me life
and has returned to the sea
D. K.

First Edition

COPYRIGHT © *1975 by Elisabeth Mann Borgese and David Krieger*

Printed in the United States of America

Library of Congress Cataloging in Publication Data

Borgese, Elisabeth Mann, comp.
 The tides of change.

 Selected papers of convocations and research projects
sponsored by Pacem in Maribus in preparation for the
United Nations Conference on the Law of the Sea.
 Includes bibliographical references and index.
 1. Maritime law--Addresses, essays, lectures.
2. Marine resources and state--Addresses, essays,
lectures. 3. Ocean bottom (Maritime law)--Addresses,
essays, lectures, I. Krieger, David, joint comp.
II. Pacem in Maribus (Organization) III. United
Nations Conference on the Law of the Sea. IV. Title.
JX4408.B67   341.7'62   74-23260
ISBN 0-88405-082-3

The problems of the sea require an *oceanic* solution—huge, deep, magnificent, even astonishing in its novelty. No temporary expedient will be appropriate to the complex and challenging issues that the sea poses to the contemporary mind.

Ambassador Reynaldo Galindo-Pohl
Permanent Mission of El Salvador
to the United Nations

It is in the interest of all that the Conference on the Law of the Sea, which will be one of the most important in the history of the United Nations, should succeed. Failure would create conditions in which international tensions would be exacerbated and the existing disparities between the affluent and indigent widened. The international community faces one of its severest tests. We have to succeed only because we cannot afford to fail.

Ambassador H. Shirley Amerasinghe of Sri Lanka
President, UN Conference on the Law of the Sea

Contents

Introduction   x

Part I. ECONOMIC POTENTIAL OF THE OCEANS

Introduction   2
1. An Economic View of Marine Problems   4
   Bertrand de Jouvenel

2. An Ocean Development Tax   33
   John Eatwell, John Llewellyn, and Roger Tarling

3. Mater Omnium: Automated Energy and Material Wealth
   from the Sea   48
   Irving Kaplan

Part II. ARMS CONTROL AND OCEAN SURVEILLANCE

Introduction   78
4. Prospects for Arms Control in the Oceans   80
   Sven Hirdman

5. A Legal Regime for Arms Control and Pollution Control in
   the Oceans   100
   John P. Craven

6. Arms Control in the Oceans: Active and Passive   110
   Elizabeth Young

7. An International Multipurpose Surveillance System   121
   Bjørn Egge

Part III. THE DEVELOPMENT OF THE MEDITERRANEAN

   Introduction   142
8. The Pollution of the Mediterranean   144
   Lord Ritchie-Calder

9. Mediterranean and Black Sea Fisheries   166
   S.H. Holt

10. Mediterranean Tourism: Some Geographic Perspectives   179
    Amiram Gonen

11. Military Force in the Mediterranean   198
    Berislav Badurina

12. A Mediterranean Council to Combat Pollution   211
    Elisabeth Mann Borgese

Part IV. THE DEVELOPMENT OF THE CARIBBEAN

   Introduction   220
13. Historical Patterns of Caribbean Communication   222
    Thomas Mathews

14. The Oil Potential of the Caribbean   239
    K.O. Emery and Elazar Uchupi

15. A Sea-Level Canal in Panama   254
    Ira Rubinoff

16. Pacem in Maribus in the Caribbean   264
    Reynaldo Galindo-Pohl

17. A Caribbean Community for Ocean Development   278
    David Krieger

Part V. SCIENTIFIC RESEARCH IN THE OCEANS

Introduction   304
18. Scientific Research in the Ocean   306
    Paul M. Fye

19. Conditions for Ocean Research   310
    Warren S. Wooster

20. Pacem in Maribus: Statement on Oceanic Research   318

Part VI. AN OCEAN REGIME

Introduction   322
21. New Institutions for Ocean Space   324
    Arvid Pardo

22. Key Issues in the Third United Nations Conference on the
    Law of the Sea   328
    H. Shirley Amerasinghe

23. A Constitution for the Oceans   340
    Elisabeth Mann Borgese

24. Recommendations from Pacem in Maribus IV to the United
    Nations Committee on the Peaceful Uses of the Sea-Bed   353

Introduction

The oceans are, in man's terms, an incredible expanse. It is only from beyond the earth that they may be viewed in their entirety. They make up more than two-thirds of the earth's surface. From the shore, the oceans simply fade into the horizon; as man has ventured farther and farther from shore, this horizon has moved ahead until at last it has returned to close the circle of our globe.

Men once believed that the horizon was the end of a flat earth. How our world view has changed. We now find ourselves traveling on a delicately suspended bobble in an immense universe. But for all this change, man remains proverbially "at sea" in his ability to bring order to the planet that has nurtured him.

For centuries men have held to the concept of freedom of the seas. Yet in spite of their greed, they have not until recent years made claims on the ocean beyond a narrow offshore strip of three miles. The oceans were traditionally a medium for transportation and communication and for fishing; they were not considered a source of wealth in and of themselves. This view has changed radically since World War II.

In 1945 President Truman issued a proclamation in which he noted that experts were of the opinion that new sources of petroleum and other minerals "underlie many parts of the continental shelf off the coasts of the United States of America, and with modern technological progress their utilization is already practicable or will become so at an early date."* He

*The full texts of historical documents referred to in the Introduction are found in S.

proclaimed United States jurisdiction and control over the natural resources on its continental shelf. The way was thus paved for a new "land grab," only this time, the land was beneath the sea.

The international response to Truman's proclamation was twofold. In 1958 the First Conference on the Law of the Sea universalized the Truman proclamation by adopting the Geneva Convention on the Continental Shelf. The shelf was defined as extending to a depth of 200 meters or beyond that, "to where the depth of the superjacent waters admits of the exploitation of the natural resources of the said areas." The convention allowed the coastal state to exercise jurisdiction over the continental shelf thus defined for the purposes of exploration and exploitation. In effect, this gave the coastal states open-ended rights to jurisdiction and exploitation of their adjacent seabeds. All they needed was the technology to get at them.

While the Truman proclamation and Geneva Convention on the Continental Shelf were concerned only with the seabed and its resources, a number of developing nations, lacking wide shelves, went further by claiming jurisdiction over the superjacent waters as well. In the Declaration of Santiago in 1952, Peru, Chile, and Ecuador claimed jurisdiction over their adjacent seas and seabeds to a distance of 200 miles from shore. They argued that it is "the duty of each Government to prevent the said resources from being used outside the area of its jurisdiction so as to endanger their existence, integrity, and conservation to the prejudice of peoples so situated geographically that their seas are irreplaceable sources of essential food and economic materials."

The substance of the Santiago Declaration was reaffirmed by the Declarations of Santo Domingo and Yaounde of 1972, claiming coastal state jurisdiction over resource exploration and exploitation within a zone extending 200 miles from shore. There can be little doubt that such an extension of jurisdiction will be recognized by the Conference on the Law of the Sea in 1974 and 1975. The implications of such an extension for the entire concept of the ocean regime have not yet been fully explored. Drastic curtailment of the economic potential of the seabed beyond the limits of national jurisdiction does, however, render the idea of a seabed regime obsolete. What we now need is a regime for ocean space and resources.

In 1967 Ambassador Pardo of Malta proposed that the agenda of the 22nd General Assembly include a "declaration and treaty concerning the reservation exclusively for peaceful purposes of the seabed and ocean floor underlying the seas beyond the limits of present national jurisdiction and the use of their resources in the interest of mankind." The item was placed

Houston Lay et al (eds.), *New Directions in the Law of the Sea*, Vols. I, II. New York: Oceana Publications, Inc., 1973.

on the General Assembly agenda and led to the creation of a 35-member Ad Hoc Committee on the Peaceful Uses of the Sea-Bed and Ocean Floor Beyond the Limits of National Jurisdiction, which was subsequently expanded to 91 members. The committee proposed and had adopted by the General Assembly several significant measures, among which was a Declaration of Principles, adopted by the Twenty-Fifth General Assembly on December 17, 1970. The Declaration of Principles described the seabed area beyond the limits of national jurisdiction as "the common heritage of mankind" and prohibited any state from claiming or exercising sovereignty over any part thereof; the declaration also called for the establishment of an international ocean regime which would be responsible for governing the exploitation of the resources of the area for the benefit of all of mankind.

In addition to adopting the Declaration of Principles, the General Assembly also passed a moratorium resolution, prohibiting development of the seabed and ocean floor beyond the limits of national jurisdiction before the establishment of an international ocean regime and declared the current decade the First International Decade of Ocean Exploration. In the years since Ambassador Pardo raised the issue of the need for international controls over ocean resources, the international community has clearly made progress toward this goal. The culmination of this activity is the Law of the Sea Conference, which began in late 1973, and held its first substantive session in Caracas, Venezuela, in the summer of 1974. The shape of the ocean regime which emerges—and we are optimistic that one will emerge —may be of critical importance to the well-being of the entire globe in the future.

There seems to be general recognition among the nations that the peace, pollution, and potential of the oceans are now at stake.

Peace. The Twenty-fifth General Assembly of the United Nations adopted a Treaty on the Prohibition of the Emplacement of Nuclear Weapons and Other Weapons of Mass Destruction on the Seabed and Ocean Floor and in the Subsoil Thereof. But the arms race in the oceans has been intensified since the signing of the treaty. As land-based weapons systems become more vulnerable to detection by satellites and high-flying spy planes, the second-strike potential of the superpowers is driven into hiding in the opaque depths of the seas. The military uses, the industrial uses, and the conservation of the oceans as a reservoir of life are on a collision course. Constructive thinking is needed to prepare for a more rational order in the seas.

Pollution. Ninety-one nations have adopted a Convention on the Dumping of Wastes at Sea. The convention prohibits the dumping of radioactive materials, chemical and biological warfare agents, and most elements that find their way into the food chain. But the pollution of the oceans is going on apace. Ship-borne pollution is only a minor part of the havoc man is wreaking from land, atmosphere and ocean floor. About a million different substances are introduced into the oceans every day. Of these, the effects of only about 300 have been studied to any degree; we know little about the interactions of these substances in the ocean environment—how they affect the life cycles of marine flora and fauna, how many of them get into the food chain and back to man.

What we do know is that about 500,000 tons of lead and DDT find their way into the ocean through rivers and the atmosphere every year. We also know that a half milligram of DDT may reduce by 70 percent the photosynthesis capacity of algae—on which all life depends.

Potential. Under the present anarchic, free-for-all system, with its built-in wastes and conflicts, fisheries are declining. Heedless overfishing and reckless pollution are reducing the quantity and quality of fish stocks. Conservation measures are clearly inadequate and are frustrated by the lack of effective international regulation and management. Yet if such regulation and management were provided, the amount of food from the oceans could be increased to a degree unimaginable even a few years ago. Not only could the oceans be improved as a "hunting ground," but wide stretches could be turned into "pastures"; species could be improved by special breeding, the size of fish, increased; the survival rate raised tenfold, even a hundredfold —considering that, in nature, only about one in a thousand eggs matures into a grown fish and that, by culturing fish larvae and young fish beyond a certain critical point, this ratio could be increased almost indefinitely. The productivity of waters could be increased by pollution controls, combined with the introduction of algae or artificial upwellings. The science and technology are available to perform this "blue revolution," whose nutritional impact on the poor nations might be far greater than that of the "green revolution." What is lacking is law and management.

Offshore drilling today accounts for about 20 percent of the world's total production of oil. It is estimated that this will rise to 50 percent during the next 20 years or so. We are at the beginning of a revolution in mineral mining in which the oceans will play an important role. The recovery of manganese nodules from the deep ocean floor of the Pacific Ocean and the industrial processing of manganese, nickel, cobalt, and other metals in practically unlimited quantities is just the beginning. Modern marine geology, which with the discovery of sea floor spreading and continental drift, has revolutionized our understanding of the earth and its history, can be used to identify the most likely sites of mineral treasures, not only on the continental shelves, but on the slopes of the mid-ocean ridges, the deep-ocean floor, and in hot brines. The value of ocean transportation and communication is increasing with the number and size of ships and tankers, carrying as much as 500,000 tons or more of deadweight, and the development of superports and underwater storage facilities. The importance of the oceans for recreation industries and for human habitats, whether underwater or on artificial islands, is growing. Factories are being moved onto the sea; oil refineries are being put on manmade platforms; new sources of energy—from tides and thermo-gradients—are coming into use; airports are being moved onto artificial islands.

At present, there is no law to regulate these new and challenging uses of the oceans. The existing international machinery is inadequate and the existing law of the sea is obsolete.

If the use of the sea is unregulated, the intensification of old uses and the addition of many new ones will create problems that are too big to be handled by any one nation, problems which are transnational in scope and which must be regulated internationally. This is the great challenge now before the Conference on the Law of the Sea. The conference must generate a treaty establishing a new kind of international organization for the rational management of ocean space and resources and for the harmonization of the multiple uses of the oceans.

In coming to grips with this complex task, the conference must deal with a number of fundamental problems, some of which transcend the oceans—problems of international relations and organization, such as relations between the developed and the developing nations. The concept—adopted by the twenty-fifth General Assembly, that the resources of the area beyond the limits of national jurisdiction are the common heritage of mankind and must be used for the benefit of all peoples, with special consideration for the needs of the developing nations—is germane to a fundamental rethinking of development strategy, which must no longer be based on aid and the humiliating division between donor and recipient, but on sharing resources which are the common heritage of all nations. That such a rethinking of development strategy is in the making is indeed indicated by current discussions on the "energy crisis" and the changing relationship between "producers" and "consumers." The concept of the common heritage of mankind and its translation into political and economic terms are dealt with in the first and last parts of this volume.

The Conference on the Law of the Sea must deal with disarmament and arms control in the oceans, a task made more challenging by the novel fact that many of the technologies and institutional arrangements essential to the monitoring and control of pollution in the oceans inevitably have an arms-control effect, with consequences for either which have not yet been much studied. This facet of the ocean regime is dealt with in Part II.

The ocean ecosystem is huge, the largest and most continuous on earth;

at the same time, it is highly diversified. While some principles are applicable on a global basis, others call for special adaptations to regional circumstances and requirements. Climate, geology, hydrology, anthropology, and history have cooperated in giving to different ocean regions a different character, which raises different problems. The Conference on the Law of the Sea will have to articulate the emergent global regime into regional subsystems. While none of these subsystems would likely be viable by itself, given the interconnectedness of all ocean areas and the interaction between water and atmosphere, no global system can be viable without such articulation into regional systems. The universal must be harmonized with the particular. The ecological and economic infrastructures of various ocean basins and regions must be defined in order to bring about suitable legal and managerial superstructures. Samples of such studies are found in Parts III and IV.

Given the enormous importance of science in the development and preservation of the oceans, the conference must define not only a new science policy for the oceans, but it must devise new instruments for making science policy which can bridge the gap between science and politics. Part V deals with some of the problems facing the marine scientist in the changing political context.

These are just a few of the problems, but they should be sufficient to indicate that what is needed is a new kind of international organization, one encompassing politics, science, and industry and one interlinking national and international competences, an international organization that may well become the prototype of international organization in the 21st century. If we succeed in solving certain basic problems with which we are faced in the oceans, we may apply the solutions to other areas of technology, with transnational implications such as the management of outer space and satellite technology, the management of energy technologies, and the management of weather control and modification technologies. All of these are involved in any comprehensive management scheme for the oceans. They may give rise to a network of international management systems based on the principle that not only the oceans but the earth and its resources are the common heritage of mankind, a system of world communities which will cement world peace in a way not known in past centuries.

Pacem in Maribus is an international and interdisciplinary organization dedicated to the creation of an ocean regime that will realize the full potential of the oceans for the benefit of mankind, while preventing ocean pollution and maintaining peace. To this end, Pacem in Maribus has held five major convocations in Malta, as well as a series of regional conferences. Pacem in Maribus convocations, sponsored by the International Ocean Institute in Malta, have brought together scientists, diplomats, politicians, and lawyers from around the globe to discuss the problems of the oceans from different perspectives. These meetings have been notable for their cross-fertilization of ideas and their expression of farsighted views which have been not so farsighted as to lose their practicality in the world of men and nations. With the assistance of the United Nations Development Programme, private foundations in the United States and Europe, and the support of individual members, Pacem in Maribus has sponsored a series of research projects on regional and functional aspects of the big-ocean problem. The content of this volume, which is the second in a series (the first was published by Dodd, Mead and Co. in 1972 under the title, *Pacem in Maribus*), is drawn both from the projects and the convocations during the period 1971–1973. All of the work was done in preparation for the Conference on the Law of the Sea, a conference, which may well turn out to be the most important event in international relations of the last half of this century.

The tides act upon the earth. In the same way, the oceans are now acting upon the international system of nations. The current emphasis on the disparity and insecurity of man is being gradually eroded by the tides of change. If man is to survive, the new system must emphasize the harmony and cooperative potential of mankind. This system is being conceived in the oceans where the development of new technologies, the lure of new riches, and the threat of new ruin have demanded its first realization.

Santa Barbara, Calif.   ELISABETH MANN BORGESE
December, 1973   DAVID KRIEGER

PART I

ECONOMIC POTENTIAL OF THE OCEANS

The three articles in Part I have been selected from three research projects sponsored by the International Ocean Institute between 1971 and 1973. Professor de Jouvenel's study was undertaken in response to a Resolution of the Social and Economic Council of the United Nations, requesting governmental and nongovernmental entities to assist the Secretary General in his assessment of the economic potential of the oceans. Professor de Jouvenel's chapter looks realistically into the future, in several respects. Writing in 1971, he foresaw the contours of the "energy crisis" and the role of the "multinationals" in it. He also foresaw the extension of national jurisdiction over resource exploitation in the oceans and the effect this would have on the basic concept of a seabed regime. By emptying it of its economic potential, it would bereave it of its political significance as well.

Irving Kaplan is a clinical psychologist in San Diego. California, and formerly a technological forecaster for the U S Navy. Messrs. Eatwell, Llewellyn, and Tarling are all economists at Cambridge University.

The article on the ocean development tax is taken from a much larger, technical study by a team of economists at Cambridge University. This study would restore economic potential to the oceans by considering ocean space as a whole and by assessing the revenue potential of all uses of ocean space and resources to the international community.

The concept of an ocean development tax was first proposed by Pacem in Maribus II in July 1971. It was subsequently introduced in the United Nations by Canada and taken up by various delegations. (See also, the reference later in this volume by Ambassador Galindo Pohl of El Salvador [p. 276].) The full text of this study on an ocean development tax has been circulated among the members of the UN Sea-Bed Committee as an official document by the Secretary General in July 1973.

Dr. Kaplan's article is part of a comprehensive project undertaken by the International Ocean Institute in cooperation with the Center for the Study of Democratic Institutions, the Pugwash Conference, and the International Institute for Systems Analysis, on *Energy Policies and the International System.* Written in 1971, the article predicts the end of an economic era based on fossil fuel energy and the transition to a new, more integrated, economy based on fusion energy, from a fuel, deuterium, which, for all practical purposes, is illimitable and free. It is not yet possible to predict which energy source will power the world of the future. What can be predicted is that we are nearing the end of fossil fuel-based energy and that new technologies will produce energy that will be more abundant, far cheaper, without geographical limitation, but potentially far more dangerous to the earth's ecosystem. The political, economic, social, and ecological consequences of this transition—which is the real crux of the present "energy crisis"—will be dramatic. It can also be predicted that the oceans will play a far greater role as a site and source of energy production than they do today.

The total value of current ocean production is only 2 to 3 percent of the total world gross national product (however that is measured), but the potential of the oceans is far greater than that. It is likely that we shall witness a large-scale shift from land-based production to ocean-based production in the coming decades.

Bertrand de Jouvenel is Professor at the Sorbonne in Paris and is one of the world's most distinguished futurologists. He is the author of many books and the editor of the magazine *Prévisions et analyses*.

CHAPTER 1

An Economic View of Marine Problems

BERTRAND DE JOUVENEL

How has it come about that the sea, after being exploited by mankind for millenia, has suddenly become a *new* sort of theme? The primary cause of this important innovation is that a new perspective has been identified. The sea has always figured in the human mind as a fluid mass supporting sailing vessels and containing an astonishing variety of marine life. Navigators have long known that this aqueous mass was supported by a floor which geology later made an object of investigation. The ocean floor was not traditionally included in ordinary thought except perhaps as a subject for poetry or as a kind of cemetery for submerged ships and cities. Incipient awareness of the potential of submerged "soils" as exploitable land is "discovery" in the most literal sense; what was hitherto covered and hidden is now observed directly.

Deep-sea exploration by the Piccards and the Cousteaus had enchanted us with underwater seascapes and the ballets of their inhabitants, but modern research of a different sort reveals the deeps rich, for example, in petroleum and natural gas. With the discovery of such wealth, the problem of a new regime for the seas is posed.

The series of events that is supposed to culminate in an international agreement on a new regime for the sea was initiated by a declaration in 1945. This declaration was the first to deal a blow to the age-old regime and was animated solely by concern for the mineral wealth of the marine depths.

Translated from the French by James Albritton and John Wilkinson.

4

Many other preoccupations might well have justified a new look at the old regime and intervention in the new, but those preoccupations are of secondary importance chronologically, and the attention given them has been minimal; we will thus begin historically.

The Truman Proclamation and the Continental Shelf

The point of departure was President Truman's proclamation of September 1945, stating that the United States government considered the natural resources on and under the continental shelf, measured three miles from the coastline, to be under U.S. control and jurisdiction. The term *continental shelf* thus entered into diplomatic language. (There was at that time undoubtedly a not inconsiderable agitation in the world's chancelleries to find the term's meaning.)

Marine geologists had used *continental shelf* to mean the shallow, submersed base, an extension of dry ground, out to the edge, at which there is a slope (known as *continental*). At the base of this slope, a zone of detritus stretches gradually to the ocean depths. To this was given the designation *continental rise*. The ensemble of shelf, slope, and rise came to be known as the "continental margin." All these terms have, since 1945, become more or less well known to the laity.

For the scientist a change in profile marked off the continental shelf. This appears at different depths, perhaps 20 to 550 meters, with an average of 133 meters.[1]

The Truman administration preferred to define the shelf according to its maximum depth ("isobath"), rather than by the borders suggested by marine science. The proclamation used an isobath of 100 fathoms, an arbitrary geologic line which, however, was *practically* significant, that is, in terms of accessibility and, of course, *future* accessibility. According to Senator Pell three years later, there was still no exploitation at a depth greater than 30 meters.[2] Since then, forecasts of accessibility have indicated far greater depths.

It should be noted that delimitation by isobath was generally accepted (but with the use of the metric system, so that a depth of 200 meters, for example, took the place of a 100-fathom measure, that is, 183 meters).

In a communiqué accompanying President Truman's proclamation, it was explained that the decision taken by the American government "would

[1] According to the eminent marine geologist, K.O. Emery of Woods Hole. Many of my observations have been borrowed from Emery's numerous studies.

[2] Hearings of the United States Senate Commission on Commerce, September-November 1969, p. 130.

render possible an orderly development of an underwater area of 750,000 square miles." This referred to the isobath of 100 fathoms; the change to a depth of 200 meters meant an increase to 845,000 square miles.[3] The margin of error in the estimations was probably substantially greater than the difference made by changing the reference isobath.

The 1945 figure was nearly two million square kilometers; the 1969 figure exceeded two million. This means that the underwater area over which the United States asserted jurisdiction is greater than the surface of the ten states of the European Common Market.

The Truman proclamation was a break with tradition. It occasioned widespread repercussions, the character—or rather, the characters—of which ought to be understood. These are two important subjects that are not dealt with in this article except for noting them summarily, in order to give more space to a discussion of the motives of the Truman administration in initiating an action that would lead to the overthrow of the *ancien regime* of the sea. Through discussion and analysis of these motives, we get into the *economics* of the ocean.

The Break with Tradition

I trust I will be pardoned for setting down a number of truisms: the sea does not lend itself to human habitation, but on the other hand, it does allow expeditious passage. Men can behave on the sea only as nomads. They cannot be sedentary beings.

On its surface the sea possesses little or nothing equivalent to those accidents of terrain that have served for centuries to mark off the domains of sovereignty or terrestrial dominion, and we cannot easily erect markers to delimit private preserves or properties. Because of this natural difference, the sea has not known the political divisions and private subdivisions that are characteristic of men's activities on land. It has not been subject to the complex and highly differentiated *institutional* evolution of the land.

In connection with the nomad-sedentary polarity, we know that terrestrial nomads have played a double role with regard to sedentary humans, the one beneficial to commerce, the other that of robbers, pillagers, and the like. Something analogous can be said of the role of sea nomads with respect to terrestrial sedentaries. But on the earth, the inimical role of nomads has usually predominated over the commercial, and social progress has been achieved by suppressing the nomads. Even when sea nomads were guilty

[3]These figures were given respectively by Russell Train and Senator Pell during the Senate hearings mentioned in footnote 2, pp. 104 and 122.

of numerous attacks, accompanied by much cruelty and destruction, the *positive* side of their activity grew in importance and even became *decisively* important in the development of civilization. To judge matters in purely terrestrial terms, it can be said that the sea has remained in a prehistoric condition. Nonetheless, it is on, or in connection with, the sea that the forms of modern life have developed. For example, it was in the world's seaports that a blending of products and populations has often been achieved. (See, for example, the description of Antwerp by Luigi Guiccardini, 1572.) In these ports, there were many social innovations, and creative imagination was excited.[4] It was in connection with such places that the first industrial production—the construction of naval vessels—began.[5] Plato's works contain the well-known description of the shipyards of the Piraeus. In these ports *collective* commercial enterprise originated, as well as the concepts of insurance and double-entry bookkeeping.

At the beginning of his well-known codification of Maritime Laws[6] the jurist Pardessus said: "If civil laws be intimately connected with the nature of Government, its *mores* and national habits, the same cannot be said of the laws of maritime commerce. Produced in *every* locality by like needs, they derive from this fact a *universal* character corresponding to what Cicero well said of Natural Law: *'non opinione sed natura jure constitutum'*. Since they concern the *universe* in which navigators form a single family, so to speak, their spirit cannot change with national boundaries." I shall not stop to consider whether it is the similarity of needs or the absence of boundaries that brought about the uniformity Pardessus praised, but will be content to remark that the absence of boundaries endured for a long time because there was no particular point at which there was sufficient interest in changing this condition.

There was interest in the rights of access to those regions where terrestrial wealth could be extracted. It was this interest which caused conflict to break out between the Portuguese, who discovered the route to the East Indies, and the Dutch, who could not tolerate being excluded. (This particular dispute has remained a classical one because of the attention paid to it by Grotius.)

The interests of national commerce were finally reconciled with freedom of navigation by terrestrial customs arrangements. Moreover, it is conceivable that acceptance of the principle of nonintervention, with regard

[4]It is certainly because ports were the locus of marvellous stories that Thomas More used this setting for the account of his Utopia, using the discourse of a fictitious Portuguese navigator (1518).

[5]Galileo situated his dialogues *(Discorsi)* in the naval dockyard of Venice. In them, he wrote of the "Two New Sciences Relating to Mechanics and Motion" (Leyden, 1638).

[6]Pardessus, *Collection des Lois Maritimes,* T.1, Paris, 1828.

to naval vessels, encouraged *political* control of the territories that were sources of riches. In all historical periods, the principal economic interest in the sea has arisen from the *terrestrial riches* to which control of the sea lanes gave access. If the original concentrations of capital had to do with the sea, it was with the sea as a route to the riches of the earth. And though, in all ages, fishing in the sea has been practiced, it has remained until quite recently an activity more artisanal than industrial. In the legends of all countries the fisherman is represented as being poverty-stricken,[7] the commercial navigator *(viator)* and his sedentary associate *(stans)* as rich. When Grotius argues for the freedom of the seas, he is taking the position of large commercial enterprise.[8] In his *Mare Clausum,* Selden responded by defending the point of view of a national fisherman.

Countries relatively advanced in navigation were only minimally interested in protecting their local fisheries from foreigners. But they were always interested in opening navigation routes to foreign riches. So it was scarcely surprising that the concept of "open seas" came to prevail over that of "restricted" seas. Also, the doctrine established became one of open seas for *everyone.* The national state reserved for itself only a narrow strip of three miles from its coastline, a strip that was designated the "territorial sea."[9]

Did the United States break with this centuries-old order of things by its proclamation in 1945? Perhaps it did not wish specifically to do so, but intention is one thing and result another.

Repercussions of the Proclamation, or the Vindication of Selden

To go into the details of national reactions would be to digress from our subject, but let us keep in mind three aspects of these reactions:

[7]The poor fisherman extracting treasure from the sea figures in all the legends of the world. It is characteristic that the fisherfolk who played an important role in the War of Independence of the United Provinces called themselves "sea beggars."

[8]We know that the attention Grotius gave to matters of the sea had its source in the mandate given him by the West Indies Company in order to justify the violent capture of a Portuguese galleon in the Straits of Malacca by one of its captains, Heemskirk. It was with this in mind that he wrote his *De Jure Praedae* in 1604. His famous *Mare liberum, seu de jure quod Batavis competit ad Indica Commercia* (1609) was taken from the 12th chapter of this great pleading (which was not published until 1868).

[9]We have to go back to 1576 to find a more ambitious statement. Chapter 10 of the first book of Jean Bodin's *Six Livres de la Republique* briefly enunciates—after having stated that the coastal marshes and salt works can be private property: "But the rights of the sea belong only to a sovereign prince, who may impose charges out to 30 leagues from his territory, if there is no other sovereign prince to impede him from doing so . . ." (30 marine leagues are equal to 90 marine miles).

First, there was no protest.

Second, there occurred a "generalization" of Washington's claims by every country possessing a marine littoral and a continental shelf adjacent to this littoral. This principle was the object of an international agreement signed at Geneva in 1958 under the auspices of the United Nations. This agreement, concerning the continental shelf, can hardly be said to have influenced world opinion, an opinion which was not conscious of the fact that the states having designs on the sea had divided up submerged "territories" among themselves in this manner. These territories, according to the conventional definition of the continental shelf, included a total area of 27 million kilometers, that is to say, an area greater than the surface of North America (21½ million) or of the Soviet Union (22,400,000) and equal to that of Asia (the Soviet Union excluded). Moreover, the language of the agreement made the delimitation of the continental shelf nonlimitative, since the following was written into the first article of the agreement: "The term "continental shelf" is used as referring (a) to the seabed and subsoil of the submarine areas adjacent to the coast, but outside the area of the territorial sea, to a depth of 200 meters or, beyond that limit, to where the depth of the superjacent waters admits of the exploitation of the natural resources of the said areas. . . ."[10]

It appears by now that the expression "continental shelf," originally borrowed from the geologists, was so far from its primary scientific meaning as to denote everything that technological progress allows.

Third, Washington's initiative called forth even more comprehensive claims. On October 11, 1946, the government at Buenos Aires seized the initiative by decreeing that the "sovereignty" (a term avoided in the Truman proclamation) of the Republic of Argentina extended not only over its continental shelf, but also over the waters covering it, described as the "epi-continental sea." The second article did indeed stipulate that the use of the epi-continental sea for navigation would not be affected. But *fishing* rights were clearly affected, and it is for this reason that I have used the expression "Selden's vindication."

Possibly the American decision in 1945 did not infringe on the international law that was operative up to that time, especially since it had to do with an entity which had never been the object of consideration, namely, the resources of the marine soil and subsoil. On the other hand, the Argentine decision undeniably impinged on the former regime of the oceans. There was flat opposition, which brought definite consequences. Would

[10]See the commentary of René-Jean Dupuy, in *La Souveraineté au XXe siecle,* R.J. Dupuy, ed., Paris: Armand Colin, 1971.

Buenos Aires ever have thought of the annexation of the epi-continental sea if there had been no Truman proclamation? The Argentinians, in a decree embracing something avoided by the Americans, were searching for a concrete technical equivalent.

In Buenos Aires and elsewhere, the question was probably seen as this: The United States is extending its political power to the marine resources, which their technical arm will enable them to attain; so, for we who do not possess an equal technological capacity, are there not other marine riches that we might lay hold of? Why should we not extend *our* political power to them?

Here I introduce the term *marine content*, which is alien to juridical and scientific language but which comes naturally to the mind of an economist, to contrast the use of the sea as an *infrastructure* of transportation with the *extraction of its contents*, living or nonliving. If there is a historical reason for distinguishing between the new activity of submarine mining and the ancient activities of navigation and fishing, there is an analogous reason for lumping the activities dealing with marine content.

It was this analogy that caused the Latin Americans to lay claim on the riches contained *in* the epi-continental sea, as well as on those of its surface and bottom. The United States had "flown" the flag on the ocean bottoms; others had advanced theirs up to the surface.

It soon began to appear illogical to countries preoccupied with fishing rights to trace marine borders under their control with reference to the continental shelf or to some conventional definition of it. It was also inconvenient for those Latin American nations which bordered on the Pacific and which, consequently, had negligible expanses of continental shelf—judged from the geological, or conventional, point of view—to a depth of 200 meters. This situation produced the Declaration of Chile (June 25, 1947), announcing that the Chilean government was "extending protection and control" over a maritime zone extending 200 miles from its coastline. On August 18, 1952, the Declaration of Santiago followed, by which Chile, Ecuador, and Peru proclaimed exclusive sovereignty and jurisdiction over a maritime zone of a flat 200 miles, including the "subjacent" soil and subsoil.

The national claims that Washington had enunciated with respect to its continental shelf had not only been generalized, they had been transformed. A chain reaction at the international level had appeared, dislocating what had long been international space.

Matters might have taken a different turn. This was a time when the United Nations was beginning; it was one in which the United States enjoyed international prestige as no other country in modern times had; it was one that saw an American administration on the point of manifesting an unheard-of international conscience in its policies with respect not only to a devastated Europe but to the underdeveloped countries. Would its policies have been followed internationally if it had taken some initiative in modernizing the international regime? Could this administration have taken into account the new technical possibilities of exploitation of the deep seas, as well as working for the prudent management of the living resources of the seas? A great opportunity was missed—or more accurately, it was not perceived. Something very different was done, and we must find out why.

Motives in the Truman Proclamation

I do not know of any study by American political scientists of the decisions that led to the proclamation in September 1945 and am therefore reduced to conjecture. Here it seems appropriate to first eliminate the motives that are unlikely to have ever existed. Was it really urgent that American interests constitute a "game preserve"? Where were foreign interests armed with sufficient technologies and sufficient financial means even to appear to possess the ability to intrude into such a preserve? If the concept of a "game preserve" became a general one, might it not be disadvantageous to American interests, that is, to a technologically advanced country? Could any profitable reserving of two million square kilometers be worth more than the restriction of 25 million square kilometers? Have we before us an example of *protectionism* on the part of a country in an area in which it was technically superior? Did Great Britain offer an example of protectionism with regard to textile products at the beginning of the 19th century? A quick examination leads us to dismiss a protectionist motive.[11]

We *can* be fairly certain that the U.S. proclamation was instigated by the Department of the Interior, which argued, on one hand, that future supplies of hydrocarbons in the United States called for exploitation of the sea beyond the limits of the territorial waters (the traditional three miles), and, on the other, that large expenditures for research would not be taken

[11]Moreover, we can be sure that Washington foresaw and admitted the generalization of the claim it advanced. This can be found in the justification of the proclamation as first announced: first, there is a world need for new sources of petroleum and other materials; second, technological progress makes possible the exploitation of such resources in the subsoil of the continental slope, now or in the near future; and third, there exists a need for some recognized jurisdiction for the conservation and prudent exploitation of these resources. It is certain that Washington had communicated its intention, at least to the Mexican government, which was going to make an identical declaration the following month. The American government did not fear being imitated; it hoped to be. What displeased it was the transformation of this claim by the example of Argentina; and it was against this that diplomatic protestations were made.

on by American business if it did not obtain exclusive rights to explore and subsequently to exploit a given area of the sea. To obtain such concessions, however, it would be necessary to have an authority possessing powers to grant them. This step would be that the federal government would claim jurisdiction.

A second consideration was: Any petroleum produced beyond the borders of the U.S. could be brought into the American market only on the condition that it be accompanied by importation certificates, that is, be subject to quotas as well as entry duties. Exclusion of petroleum extracted beyond territorial waters from these inconveniences would be needed in order to extend federal jurisdiction.

It is fairly certain that both of these considerations were urged by the Interior Department in connection with the 1945 proclamation, since identical considerations were more recently advanced by the same agency, in order that federal jurisdiction not be limited to the 200-meter depth, but be extended to the continental slope and even to the continental rise, that is, to the entire continental margin.

Another consideration, different from the industrial preoccupations of the Interior Department, was added, probably in 1945. In the United States, the territorial waters within the standard limit of three miles were under the jurisdiction of the states bordering them and therefore of their respective state governments. Without federal intervention, the state governments might have secured the right of granting concessions beyond the limits of the jurisdiction, but the proclamation deprived them of this possibility by reserving this right to the federal government. What has been said about states' rights explains the expression, "outer continental shelf" that recurs again and again in federal documents. What is beyond territorial waters is under federal authority. In light of this consideration, the Truman proclamation assumes the aspect of a *precedent* for international authority. The proclamation restrains the states within their historical jurisdictions in order to subordinate to a common authority whatever might occur beyond them in the future.

The American Fear of Running Short

One might ask, why did the American government move so precipitously to encourage research on and exploitation of the high seas? It was obviously not for whatever financial gains exploitation would bring to the U.S. treasury. The royalties received in 1971 by the federal government for exploitation of petroleum and gas on the outer continental shelf amounted to a mere $346 million, of which $330 million came from the Gulf of Mexico and $16 million from California.[12] What appeared to have spurred the federal government was a psychological phenomenon that recurs time and again in the United States—anxiety about *future* supplies of petroleum.

The combination of the objective fact of prodigious wealth in natural resources, on one hand, and a highly subjective attitude related to the fear of shortages in these same resources, on the other, is a curious American trait in the eyes of Europeans. We witnessed an outbreak of this susceptibility at the time of the Korean War, in the panic buying of 1950. On the heels of this, President Truman ordered a study of the future availability of raw materials (up to 1975), a study that became famous as the Paley Report.[13]

This episode was only one extraordinary manifestation of an always latent, but easily aroused, anxiety. To advance a psychological hypothesis, I risk little in asserting that the very foundation of American culture is an amalgam of pietism and pragmatism. It is more than possible that the large-scale wastage of the Creator's gifts that characterizes American civilization inspires vague sentiments of guilt and anxiety about the rising level of expectations.

This same consciousness has recently erupted in a passionate concern for the environment. But whatever the moral foundation may be, American opinion has obviously been subjected frequently to periods of anxiety over natural resources, especially petroleum. This is easily understood, for just as the English model of growth involved coal and steam transportation, the American model was founded on petroleum and the means of transportation associated with it.

Ever since 1919, anxiety about future supplies of petroleum had been expressed over and over again. For example, a director of the Bureau of Mines averred that domestic fields could never suffice to meet national demands.[14] The director of the Geological Survey agreed: "Americans will either have to depend on foreign supplies, or consume less, or perhaps both."[15]

A member of the same bureau carried this alarmism further: "We should expect, unless consumption is slowed, to find ourselves dependent on foreign petroleum deposits to the tune of 150 to 200 million barrels a year—perhaps even by 1925. . . . Add to this the probability that in five years, perhaps even in three, production will have begun to lag because of exhaustion of reserves."[16]

[12] *Petroleum Press Service,* March 1972, p. iii (of the French edition).
[13] *Resources for Freedom,* Washington Supt. of Doc., June 1952, 5 vol.
[14] Van Manning, in *National Petroleum News,* October 20, 1919. In 1919 U.S. production comprised 64.3 percent of world production, but that only took care of national consumption.
[15] George Otis Smith, *National Petroleum News,* May 5, 1920.
[16] David White, "The Petroleum Resources of the World," in *The Annals,* May 1920.

Concerning the first statement, it might be said that the level of imports predicted was not reached until more than 30 years after the prediction. As for the second, American production (about 443 million barrels in 1920) had surpassed 1.7 billion in 1945. (Including off-shore production, it was 3.5 billion in 1971.)

These warnings coincided with a change of attitude on the part of American petroleum companies. Founded in a society that seemed to abound in deposits, why were they not, first of all, concerned with insuring their reserves? It is typical that Standard Oil (founded in 1870, 11 years after the discovery of petroleum in the United States) began as a corporation for refining and distribution, leaving research and extraction to private individuals, much in the manner of European milk companies today. On the other hand, west European corporations (especially in Holland and England) had to go prospecting to discover and exploit *outside* the nonproductive areas of western Europe. As a result, they acquired concessions all over the globe, which later inspired American firms to do likewise. The dismemberment of the Ottoman Empire offered an opportunity of penetrating a highly attractive area. Expert opinion ought not only to have interested American firms, but to have encouraged the federal government to back up American claims vis-à-vis European firms that had been there first but which were scarcely hospitable to newcomers.

A comparison of 1920 (the year marking the take-off point of American enterprise in the petroleum basins of the Eastern hemisphere) and 1945 (the year of the take-off point in underwater exploitation) comes to mind. These two temporal points of departure appeared in their own time as necessary for the maintenance of the positions of American firms. The country that had made the principal contribution to making petroleum the vital fluid of industrial society could scarcely be expected to envisage any prospect of finding itself the first to be deprived of it. Yet this was conceivable in the future. The relation between *proved* reserves and current production is doubtless much too sensitive an indicator, for only a few years of slowdown in exploration are necessary for estimates to become worthless.[17] (This actually happened during the Second World War.) After 1945 the stimulation of exploration reestablished the normal relation of 12½ to 1. In studying this situation *after* recovery, it is possible to discern the sources of the Americans' anxiety.

By 1948 the United States was responsible for 58 percent of world production, whereas their own proved reserves amounted to not less than 36 percent of the proved reserves of the world. However, this proportion

[17]By which is implied both the discovery of new sources and raising (former) estimates of known sources through further exploration.

of the proved reserves greatly exaggerated the Americans' real share of world resources. The main point was that exploration in the United States was far more elaborate than anywhere else; proved reserves therefore represented a much larger proportion of actual unexploited resources than they did elsewhere.

One expert, Louis G. Weeks, whose reputation was to grow, has illuminated the situation. According to his geological estimates of world petroleum stocks, the original share of the United States came to only 18 percent of the total.[18] From this it followed that the U.S. share in presumed reserves must be very much smaller, perhaps as low as 10 percent.

Thus, light shed on the disproportion between geological stocks on American territory and the tempo of its exploitation obviously justified the attitude of American companies toward other regions where, according to Weeks, 400 billion barrels of presumably exploitable resources remained to be discovered[19] and also toward the continental shelves of the world, for which Weeks tentatively gave a similar figure.[20]

Orientation toward other regions of the world succeeded so well that by 1970, the five major American firms were extracting less than 26 percent of total production from North America (the United States and Canada);

[18]According to Weeks' estimation, the initial endowment of the earth was 610 billion barrels, of which 110 belonged to the U.S. The *proportion* is the interesting thing: quantitatively better estimates were made by Weeks, thanks to the progress of exploration. The figures for 1948 quoted here are found in the Paley Report, T.2, p. 166.

[19]The estimate of the resources remaining to be discovered is necessarily hazardous, since it is founded on a rough estimate of the initial geological stock. From this presumed initial value, one deducts the historical sum of what has already been extracted to the date of the statement, and the condition of the proved reserves at that date. The sum constitutes the presumed, and not the proved, resources. The known parts of the calculation are represented by the sum of the extractions which were made and the proved reserves, but the estimates of the initial stock progress with time and study. Thus in 1928, the estimate of the initial stock of the U.S. was on the order of 39 billion barrels; 20 years later, it was 110 billion.

[20]Today, the estimates of 1948 appear much too small. At the World Congress on Petroleum, held in Moscow in 1971, Weeks presented a study entitled "Marine Geology and Petroleum Resources," according to which the potential resources in hydrocarbons are:

	Billions of Barrels in Petroleum Equivalent		
Class of Source	Offshore	Ground	Total
Petroleum liquids	790	1,500	2,290
Petroleum gases	400	800	1,200
Secondary recovery of petroleum	360	1,000	1,360
Heavy petroleum sands	200	700	900
Total:	1,750	4,000	5,750

Petroleum Press Service, September 1971, French ed. p. 338.

60 percent of their total was derived from the Eastern hemisphere.[21]

It is impressive to contrast the progress of world production with that of the United States. Taking 1948 as a base, the index of American production in 1971 was 187 and world production 525; that is, the former had not even doubled, whereas the latter had increased more than fivefold.[22]

However, more interesting here is the orientation toward *offshore* production. In the available statistics, production is distributed according to country, with no distinction made between production on land and under the sea. The absence of this distinction in national statistics is based not only on law but on natural fact. Drilling under the sea has consisted primarily of following the course of known terrestrial deposits into the sea. Most exploiters were reluctant to advance into deep waters, given the technical difficulties that had to be surmounted. So when Humble Oil secured a lease for the exploitation of sectors lying between 300 and 1,800 feet deep in the Santa Barbara Channel (February 1968), the record depth of wells exploited was 140 feet[23] and therefore well within the limit of 100 fathoms (600 feet) assigned to the continental shelf by the 1945 proclamation. Technology advanced, however, with great speed. This rapid advance is illustrated by the fact that the first offshore drilling rig was set up in 1949; 20 years later, there were 199.[24] Technologically the effort was enormous. Even though it is clear that results remain to be seen, petroleum presently coming from underwater exploitation already comprises a substantial portion of world production. It may even be true that it constitutes one-fifth of total production.[25] If this estimate is valid, underwater production already equals the total world production of 1948.

[21] As appears in the following table from data collected by the First National City Bank:

Firms	U.S.A. & Canada	The rest of the Western hemisphere	Eastern hemisphere	Total
	(production in thousands of barrels daily)			
Standard (N.J.)	1,116	1,455	2,094	4,665
Gulf	746	201	2,110	3,057
Texaco	905	258	1,824	2,987
Standard (Cal.)	537	68	1,799	2,404
Mobil	481	104	988	1,573
total:	3,785	2,086	8,815	14,686

[22] Even more striking was the reduction of the share of proved reserves of the U.S. in the total of the world proved reserves: the proportion fell to 6.6 percent at the end of 1969. One can surmise that the change of orientation toward exploration contributed to the drop.

[23] *Ocean Industry,* January 1971, p. 23.

[24] *Ocean Industry,* September 1970.

[25] *Petroleum Press News,* September 1971, reporting a statement by Weeks in Moscow.

Petroleum and the Sea

I do not believe I have been too much preoccupied with petroleum, for the whole process of overthrowing the older ocean regime began with the Truman proclamation, and the American decision was certainly made with petroleum problems uppermost in mind. The principal changes in the use of the seas during the last 27 years have been tied in with the problems of petroleum. For example, navigation is today, as in all past times, by far the most important use of the sea for the global economy. During the period considered, we have witnessed the replacement of coal by petroleum as the principal energy source for navigation. We have observed the enormous development of the use of petroleum in maritime transportation. It represents not only the major portion of the mass transported (1.3 billion tons out of a total of 2.5 billion), but, calculated in terms of ton miles, it comprises 62 percent.[26] Calculated in this manner, transportation of petroleum has almost quadrupled, compared, say, to the total transportation of cereals, coal, and ferrous minerals. More than half the tonnage of petroleum transported by sea goes to western Europe. Crude oil constitutes more than two-thirds of all cargoes arriving in Europe by sea. The immense importance of petroleum in marine traffic clearly reflects the position it holds in our industrial civilization, which, beginning as a civilization of coal, quickly became a civilization of petroleum, or rather, of hydrocarbons, since the close chemical relative of petroleum, natural gas, is coming into ever wider use. Safe methods of volume reduction (by liquefaction) were the necessary condition for it to become, in turn, an object for important marine traffic.[27]

Hydrocarbons have become one of the foundations of economic life, not only as sources of energy,[28] but as a raw material from which the chemist is able to synthesize a great variety of materials. The ancient alchemists merely proposed to create *known* materials; today's chemists actually create new materials which possess the *desired properties.*

Even more rapid than the growth of hydrocarbons for the production of energy is the growth of their more complicated functions. In 1969 some

[26]According to an analysis by the Norwegian firm, Fernley and Egers (1971), in *Petroleum Press News,* March 1972. For confirmation, OECD: *Maritime Transport,* Paris, 1971. The 62 percent figure mentioned breaks down as follows: raw petroleum, 55 percent and petroleum products, 7 percent.

[27]This innovation is of French origin. It allowed the transportation of liquefied natural gas (GNL) by ad hoc vessels called *méthaniers,* from Algeria to the United Kingdom, beginning in 1964 and to the north of France, beginning in 1965.

[28]In the U.S. in 1957, coal was still the principal source of energy: 44 percent of the total, 33 percent for petroleum and already 14 percent for natural gas. In 1970 petroleum comprised 44 percent, but the share of natural gas had grown even more, more than 33 percent.

51 million tons of primary organic products were extracted from them, of which two-fifths were used to produce plastics. The volume of organic products derived from hydrocarbons is rising from 13 million tons in 1960 to an estimated 165 million tons in 1980. More to the point, for Europe, according to these estimates, it will rise in two decades (1960–80) from 2.3 million to 60 million tons.

As for plastics, the principal outlet for petrochemical products, production grew from one million tons in 1948 to 20 million today, and it is estimated that it will reach 90 million by 1980.

"Taking volume of production as the base, the total production of plastics surpasses that of nonferrous metals; only wood, cement, and steel are produced in greater volume than plastics.[29]

The Maritime Problems of Petroleum

Since petroleum today is vital to the international economic system, it is understandable that the problems it poses are also international, problems such as those of its transportation in international spaces (seas interposed between national habitats). Such transportation is by tankers, the dimensions of which have grown enormously since the Second World War. The largest tanker 30 years ago had a capacity of 16,000 tons; in 1971 there were tankers in service with capacities of 230,000 tons, and tankers designed to hold 500,000 tons are under construction.*

Basic concepts, which are limited by their terrestrial origin, must change. On sea, the transportational infrastructure is a "gift of nature" and does not naturally impose limits on vehicle size; on land, however, infrastructure must be planned. The legendary quarrel of Oedipus with his father, Laertes, broke out over the use of ruts and tracks for chariot traffic. We know the historical importance of the construction of the Roman roads and how crucial it was for European civilization when their maintenance was abandoned after the fall of the Western Roman Empire. We know that civilization then was confined to coastal zones and towns accessible by river. Land transportation only became important once again as a function of governmental investment in road construction. Then came the railroad era. It is significant that the first line was constructed in accordance with the proposal of Stephenson to bypass the ship canal dug by Lord Bridgewater.

Land vehicles have never been able to sustain traffic without planned

---

[29]The "world" production given here does not include the communist countries. *Petroleum Press News*, March 1970 (French ed.), p. 89.

*Tankers of nearly 500,000 tons deadweight are already in operation, and tankers of 750,000 tons deadweight are now under construction. (Ed.)

and costly infrastructures. Since these infrastructures determined where one could take such vehicles, relatively small size and carrying capacity limited the dimensions of the vehicles and the loads they could carry. Little such limitation was necessary on the sea, where shippers can increase dimensions and cargo whenever it appears economical for them to do so. According to a study done three years ago, the cost per ton of transport is found to diminish by more than three-fourths in passing from tankers of 20,000 tons (dwt.) to tankers of the 230,000-ton class.[30] This economy of private costs of the shipper admittedly does not take into account the vast public expenditures to make seaports usable by oceangoing giants. In the absence of international agreement, port authorities are forced to assume these expenditures as best they can.[31]

The rapid growth of maritime traffic creates congestion in the straits, which sometimes leads to collisions. The Straits of Dover (in which traffic has grown to perhaps 700 vessels every 24 hours[32]) was the scene of 40 collisions in four years, including a number of sinkings which made navigation even more dangerous, since the wreckage was not usually cleared from the sea floor. Due to their increasing size, tankers aggravate such congestion and increase the risk of collision. Moreover, because of their content, the rupture of hulls can cause serious pollution.

Giant tankers are subject to accident outside the straits. The *Torrey Canyon* episode made a profound impression on European opinion. Arriving from the Persian Gulf, the *Torrey Canyon* was bound for Milford Haven and did not enter the channel at the widest point. It foolishly hugged the Scilly Islands at a speed of 17 knots and ran aground on a reef 15 miles from the westernmost point of England. The shock collapsed 6 of the 18 reservoirs, which contained 117,000 tons of Kuwait crude oil. Since the hull was left to the action of the waves, all that was not pumped out of the reservoirs (which had in the beginning remained intact, or almost so) was spilled into the sea. For the effects on marine biology, see the study by J.E. Smith.[33]

One aspect, however, is worth mentioning. The *Torrey Canyon* was flying the Liberian flag and its commander had worked without interruption for 365 days. "Six months of uninterrupted tanker service are common; for, given the daily operational cost of £15,000, large tankers have to be in

[30]Cf. Requier-Desjardins, L'evolution des transports maritimes et l'environnement socio-economique. Memoire de Prospective Sociale de l'Université de Paris, I.

[31]The instructive example of a large international firm might be cited. The firm erected its own terminal, which was adequate for handling vessels in the 230,000-ton class; they took care to distribute their cargo in much smaller units at this terminal.

[32]See the editorial in the *Guardian,* January 13, 1970, following a chain of accidents which resulted after the sinking of the cargo ship *Brandenburg.*

[33]Smith, *Torrey Canyon Pollution and Marine Life: A Report by the Plymouth Laboratory of the Marine Biological Association of the United Kingdom,* Cambridge University Press, 1970.

service from 350 to 355 days a year with less than 24-hour intervals for charging and discharging," wrote a commander of the British Navy in an article with the provocative title: "Can We Delay the Next Tanker Disaster?"[34] The article appeared after a series of major accidents had occurred, most of them involving vessels flying the Liberian flag. This provoked violent denunciations from the president of the British Union of Merchant Sailors, concerning vessels flying a flag of convenience, which allows shipowners to work officers and crew in a manner both harmful to them and dangerous to others.

Liberia has the largest fleet in the world today, yet the population of this country scarcely exceeds one million. The degree of Liberian economic development is revealed by the fact that, according to the most recent information, the country has fewer than 5,000 telephones. This farcical situation would defy the fantasies of the most imaginative authors; it is, indeed, almost a satire. It should be noted that the rapid development of the Liberian fleet has been accompanied by a decline of the American. This would represent a felicitous transfusion of money from the rich to the poor were the affair not a mere legal fiction.[35] All this would be very convenient for private interests, who wish to escape American taxation and regulation, were it not that its consequences are so grave (particularly considering the number of accidents that befall the Liberian fleet).

The gross insufficiency of *any* regime of freedom of the seas, in which shipowners are subject to such obligations as are prescribed by the country under whose flag the vessel navigates, is clear; the necessity for controlled international regulations become equally clear. It is necessary to emphasize (with Ranken) to what degree the organization of maritime transport lags behind that of aerial transport in nearly every respect. This lag is not surprising. The use of the medium of the air is a recent phenomenon which appeared rapidly in technically advanced countries. It called forth a vast amount of attention, and it was only natural that rational regulations would be enacted. On the other hand, use of the marine medium is ancient. Since established customs tend to correspond to long-existing conditions, it becomes difficult to replace antiquated regulations with rational rules that correspond to changed conditions. The difficulty is compounded by the fact that a far wider degree of consent is needed.

That petroleum plays a major role in maritime transportation and must therefore play a major role in maritime pollution was revealed to the world by the *Torrey Canyon* incident. Accidents are a massive and obvious source of pollution, but dumping into the sea was an unobserved source until very

[34]M.B.F. Ranken, in *Ocean Industry,* June 1971.
[35]One of the effects of this transfer of flags is to render the American balance of payments more and more negative in the area of maritime transportation.

recently, when the nations involved, with some success, were able to reduce the practice of dumping at sea.

Accidents and dumping, taken together, have probably contributed less to pollution than hydrocarbon use on land, the end products of which reach the oceans by the winds and rivers, since synthetic compounds fabricated by the hydrocarbon industry are much more poisonous than the hydrocarbons themselves. For everything dumped into the sea by runoff from terrestrial sources (a veritable *cloaca maxima*), defense of the seas calls for the same kind of regulation that is observed on land. This is clearly a part of national sovereignty and comes under the competence of the Conference on the Environment. It is probably sufficient that such rules be adopted by those countries that are large per capita consumers of hydrocarbons. It would be premature to raise obstacles to the development of countries which remain small consumers, and their natural refusal to cooperate cannot be allowed to create valid excuses for others. But it would scarcely be unreasonable to require that drilling in the sea, an operation so likely to result in pollution, be made to obey universal safety regulations. I say "scarcely unreasonable," since they are in every case the operations of the same kind of technologists who are nearly always employees of international firms.

The Distribution of Submarine Basins

In terms of the wealth of the sea, hydrocarbons have already, in commercial value, outstripped the value of the production of the fishing industry, a lopsided tendency which seems certain to grow. Other raw materials extracted from the seas are, at least for the time being, of relatively little importance.[36]

It is generally admitted that further progress in world consumption of petroleum will cause increased demand on marine sources. The progress of technology permits the extraction of petroleum from ever-greater depths, hence each state, assuming that it has a coastline, will be interested in extending its jurisdiction as far out to sea as possible.[37]

We may ask why this apparent similarity of interests is illusory. Is it

[36]According to a recent estimate, the value of all such materials extracted represented only 1/12th of that of hydrocarbons. It must be noted, moreover, that of this 1/12th, chemical products from seawater (including water itself) comprise more than three quarters. The use of seawater does not pose any problems of delimitation. Data from the Dow Chemical Co. (1969), quoted by John Flipse, *Undersea Technology*, January 1970, p. 45.

[37]The most extreme thesis in this respect is that national jurisdiction would embrace not only the continental shelf, but also the continental slope and rise; in sum, all of the continental margin. This would be true to the extent that the neighboring country is far off; when it is close by, jurisdiction would extend to the median line.

because different countries are unequally situated with regard to personnel and technology? Is it due to the difference of interests between the "advanced" and the "developing" countries? It is hard to understand why the state of technology in a given country would make such a difference. The most advanced techniques are (and will be) applied in the epi-continental seas of the least advanced countries of the world, as well as those of the most advanced countries, with arrangements made through concessions with firms on land. Also, given the large role played by petroleum royalties in the budgets of countries with weak economies, it would appear that they have an even greater interest in extending their control over underwater deposits than do the advanced countries.

The dividing line of *national interest* does not pass between the "advanced" and the "underdeveloped" countries; rather, it passes between those countries whose epi-continental sea seems promising and those for whom it does not.

If we take into consideration the volume of petroleum exploitation on the territories of the Third World, we see how little their location coincides with any concentration of population. In fact, petroleum royalties come mostly from desert areas. In 1970, for example, $5.5 billion royalties were paid out in the Eastern hemisphere among states whose total population was slightly less than 50 million—that is, a small fraction of that of the Third World. From this total (if we subtract Iran, with 28 million inhabitants, and Iraq, with 10 million), there remain less than 12 million inhabitants in states which together received $3.9 billion. (Saudi Arabia, with eight million inhabitants, $1.2 billion in royalties; Libya, with two million inhabitants, $1.3 billion in royalties; and, finally, Kuwait, Abu Zabi, Qatar, Bahrain, Oman and Dubay, taken together, with 1.2 million inhabitants, and $1.4 billion.[38]) Thus a disproportionately large share of royalties goes to a small fraction of the population of the Third World. This distribution of royalties is extremely unequal, quite simply as a result of natural endowments exceedingly unevenly distributed.

There is little reason to believe that the distribution of hydrocarbons in marine subsoils is less unevenly distributed.[39] There is even good reason to think that this unevenness will reinforce rather than correct the inequality already existing on land. The process of "diagenesis," the generative force in the creation of petroleum deposits, took place over millions of years, during which the earth-sea boundaries fluctuated widely. So it isn't surprising that the Mexican and Persian Gulfs, both of which possess great re-

---

[38] *Petroleum Press Service,* September 1971 (French ed.), p. 327.
[39] According to L.G. Weeks, "In the underwater zone extending to a 300-metre depth, only 4% would be rich in petroleum."

sources in petroleum in their emerged parts, are rich in their submerged parts.

Bearing in mind that prediction is made on the basis of present knowledge, it can be said that the countries already producing onshore petroleum can look forward to the exploitation of their epi-continental seas and therefore will be interested in seeing that the limits of national jurisdiction be pushed out as far as possible. This interest is heightened to the degree that national economies are weaker and, consequently, that their budgets are more dependent on royalties.

In the case of the other countries of the Third World, for which neither past production nor the prospect of future exploration gives promise of underwater riches, do their interests lie in gambling by allying themselves with those claiming expansion of jurisdiction, or do they lie rather in sharing royalties collected by an international organization? Let us go further: if gain by expansion is chancy, it is nevertheless preferable to nothing, however slight the possibilities may be. On the other hand, sharing in internationally collected royalties will be zero if the sum of these royalties are zero. This sum is bound to be zero if resource exploitation is under the jurisdiction of the coastal state as far out as the resources can be exploited, as is provided by the Geneva Treaty of 1958. The result is the same if the elasticity of the boundary is replaced by an enlargement of the concept of shelf, so as to include the slope or the rise.[40]

Even if the limit of national jurisdiction is fixed at the 200-meter depth, and if all extraction beyond this point is regulated by, and royalties paid to, the international community rather than to the coastal state, the sum of these will remain too small for a long period to make any important contribution to international distribution.[41] On the other hand, they could be the means of *collective* enrichment. The question is: Is collective enrichment more urgent than progress in food production?

[40]If the continental shelf zone comprises 28 million square kilometers, and that of the continental rise, about 19 million square kilometers, the total margin covers about 15 percent of the total surface of the earth as a whole, 21 percent of ocean space, and is equal to 50 percent of dry land. According to the estimate of Menard and Smith, "Hyposometry of ocean basin provinces," *Journal of Geophysical Research,* vol. 1971 (1966) pp. 4305–25. Quoted by K. O. Emery in *Continental Margins of the World,* reprint, Woods Hole Oceanographic Institute, 1970.

[41]Let us suppose the royalties to be $1 per barrel—a rate which is already being surpassed for the payments to the countries of OPEC—but, in order to encourage the enterprise to go beyond the 200-meter depth, one would have to be content with a lower rate. I leave to the reader the task of confronting the billions of barrels with the billions of inhabitants.

Primacies in Energy-Producing Matter

It is characteristic of modern society that marine space assumes new attrac-
tiveness as a source of energy-producing matter for the very good reason
that modern society stands in marked contrast to all preceding societies, in
being based on the consumption of energy-producing materials. In all an-
terior societies, action was produced by the expenditure of living energy,
human or animal.[42] The great divide in the history of man is to be found
at the point at which he began to use physical instead of physiological
power. Our frame of reference was so closely tied to animal power that we
still measure the work done by combustion engines in units of horsepower.

Industrial civilization was launched by "inputs" of coal; ever since, it
has relied more and more on hydrocarbons. (Nuclear energy has so far
played only a minor role.) The demand for energy-producing materials
seems insatiable. This demand is destined not only to expand in the developed countries but also in the underdeveloped ones. Energy-producing
matter furnished by nonliving forms of life is, in this respect, the basis of
our *material* civilization, and just here, lies the contrast with all preceding
civilizations, as well as to primitive society. In the former, as in the latter,
work was done by living species, human and animal, nourished by inputs
of animate matter. In this sense, they were *biological* civilizations. What
remains biological in our society is we ourselves, plus those inputs necessary
for us to continue to live. We look for these inputs from living species, not
from inorganic matter. We are fundamentally the supreme parasites on a
vegetable base which *sometimes* feeds us directly, but more often through
intermediate animals.

In order to merely exist, we require a quantitatively smaller input than
that required for our civilization. According to a recent study, the material
civilization of the United States requires a per capita input of energetic
matter equivalent to 80 times the biological input necessary for the bare
sustenance of an individual.

If there were merely small quantitative differences in our needs, the
problem of an adequate food supply for an expanding population could be
easily solved; for world consumption of energy materials is about 12 times
the nutritional input needed to feed the population. Moreover, the progress-
ing production of energy-producing materials is considerably greater than
that of the population. However, there is a qualitative difference. We know
how to feed ourselves only with living species. For long epochs, the human
race was merely able to take them wherever they could be found and

---

[42]Energy from the wind, which is irregular, is, it seems to me, the only other source that
can be mentioned as important before the use of combustible fossils.

without having to be concerned about their reproduction. The result was that our ancestors were in a perpetual race with famine. Societies that existed by hunting and gathering were small, and extensive space was necessary for the survival of even small groups. After the Neolithic, man developed agriculture and stock-breeding, both of them qualitatively and endlessly improved on.

It seems strange that this improvement was not extended to the greater part of the surface of the globe, that is the seas, which cover 71 percent of it. In this respect, man has remained at the level of the hunting and gathering civilizations. It is, therefore, not surprising that most of the earth's surface furnishes, in tonnage, a mere 2 percent of man's food supply.[43]

This is a shocking state of affairs, given the lack of nourishment (especially that due to lack of protein) of a large part of the world's population and given, too, the concern frequently expressed about the *future*. We may well ask if it is not an inescapable conclusion that the contribution of the seas to human nutrition must become a major preoccupation of the international community.

Sea-Hunting

Since food production from marine spaces proceeds by way of hunting, this logically entails foreseeable results. Production is small even in those regions containing the greatest number of fish. The North Sea is exceptional, in that it yields five tons per square kilometer.[44] This amounts to a high yield, compared with other zones, but even this figure means only 50 kilograms per hectare (2 1/2 acres).

In sea-hunting, the best-equipped hunters are advantageously situated. And the most mobile are in a favorable position to invade the least exploited zones to the detriment of those who have been using them, provided that reserved areas are not involved. "Technological progress often puts the most highly developed countries in a superior position, being able to dispatch their highly mechanized fleets far from their home bases. This, in turn, is liable to exhaust the resources near those very countries in which lack of protein is well attested."[45]

[43]In order of importance, in terms of tonnage, vegetables make up 4/5ths of our food, animals 1/5th, with marine animals making up 1/10th of this 1/5th. However, it should be noted at the same time that marine animals furnish 1/10th of the animal proteins needed and, in addition, are much easier to assimilate than vegetable proteins.

[44]R. Letaconnoux, assistant director of the Institut Scientifique et des Techniques des Pêches Maritimes, in CNEXO, *Colloque International sur l'Exploitation des Oceans,* Bordeaux, March 1971, Theme II, vol. I.

[45]P. Adam, Chief of the Division of Fisheries, OECD.

26   THE TIDES OF CHANGE

The Soviet Union's fleet is the main example of this invasion. It alone possesses 49 percent of the world's fishing vessels of more than 100 gross tons each. Soviet supremacy is easily explained by the fact that fishing activity was traditionally artisanal. When the transition was made from artisanal forms to "enterprise," this particular sphere of human activity did not greatly interest large established capital. Thus it is in countries where small private enterprise was abolished that the technologies of large-scale enterprise were first introduced.[46]

Most of us are familiar with the inevitable results—an increase in the volume of catch accompanied by a gradual depletion of the supply of fish. Fisheries volume doubles each decade but only by including a growing proportion (recently as much as 37 percent) of humanly nonconsumable catches, which are turned into "fish meal." This "trash" catch is thus available for consumption, but one might ask: *whose* consumption? The answer is that since such meal is not readily acceptable to humans, it is consumed mainly by chickens and pigs.[47]

I cannot go into detail here about the high-level discussion presently going on among experts concerned with the "end limit" to fishery resources. I note only that it is not surprising that experts arrive at very different results because they envisage different total volumes of very different composition. In any case, the discussion relates to the "biological pyramid" of Schaefer, in accordance with which all forms of oceanic life rely on a base of phytoplankton, the "bed" of minute, stationary, or actually mobile, vegetable matter, which is capable of photosynthesis. (It is an excellent moral that all forms of life rely on the humblest.) These phytoplankton nourish a whole hierarchy of small animals—the zooplankton and certain herbivorous fish. The next higher level of fish are nourished by them, which, in turn, are nourished at a higher level, and so on. Gross "living volume" decreases from level to level by between 80 to 90 percent. Man, the supreme parasite, is nourished at, and by, the highest level. It goes without saying that the total volume to be obtained in this way depends on a more or less marked descent to productive lower levels.[48]

[46]One might add another motivation: the country is poor in coastlines.
[47]Lowering the cost of producing chickens by more than one-half in 20 years is due, to a great extent, to the use of fish meal. Chapman, *Planning and Development in the Oceans,* p. 23.
[48]For a clear statement of this, see J. A. Gulland, ed., *The Fish Resources of the Ocean,* FAO, 1970, pp. 307–19. One finds Schaefer's pyramid, which is quantified according to the following method: Schaefer assumes the annual fixation of carbon by the phytoplankton to be 19 billion tons; he accords the latter a tenfold living weight of 190 billion tons, from which, level by level, the living weight of each successive level is deduced through the application of a coefficient of ecological efficiency, on the basis of three hypotheses: an efficiency of 10, 15, or 20 percent, and the efficiency is probably not the same for the different changes in level.

But, however they make their calculations, experts are unanimous in agreeing that species are ultimately exhaustible through overexploitation, which prevents adequate reproduction. This concern was apparently never felt in past centuries. For example, Vattel remarked in 1758:

> It is manifest that the exploitation of the open sea, in navigation and fishing, is harmless and *inexhaustible;* he who navigates or fishes in the open seas disturbs no one, and the sea, in these two respects, can supply the needs of all men. But, even so, Nature does not give any man or men a right to expropriate for themselves resources whose use is innocent, inexhaustible and sufficient for all. . . . [49]

I have emphasized Vattel's adjective "inexhaustible" because it can have two very different meanings. When the sea is an infrastructure for transportation, it is not, in this respect, exhaustible by the use made of it.[50] But we have to do with an entirely different matter when our concern is with exploitation of its *contents,* for any prey is exhaustible through bad management.

Let us continue a moment with Vattel. Drawing from the notion of *inexhaustible* the conclusion that "to undertake to make oneself the sole master and to exclude all others, constitutes the will without reason to deprive them of the benefits of Nature," he states by way of contrast: "Since the Earth is no longer able to supply of itself all necessary or useful things without cultivation to an extremely multiplied Human Species, it becomes convenient to introduce property rights, so that every person can apply himself with greater success to cultivating his fair share. . . ." This is the reasoning of Latin American countries when they undertook to assert jurisdiction over their epi-continental sea with regard to fishing. History had united the two ancient uses of the sea—navigation and fishing—and the "nature of things" reunited them, that is, pitted living content against material content. If sovereign states appropriate the material content of their continental shelves, there is no reason why they could not appropriate the living content of the epi-continental sea (and it is well known that the epi-continental seas are zones dense in marine fauna).

One might well think that the argument justifying the appropriation of epi-continental seas is stronger than the arguments for continental shelves. If living, as well as material, resources are vulnerable to exhaustion,

---

[49]M. de Vattel, *Le Droit des Gens ou Principes de la Loi Naturelle Appliqués a la conduite et aux affaires des Nations et des souverains,* London, 1758, p. 243, T.I.
[50]It is subject to congestion in the straits, but that is another matter.

living resources may be maintained and even improved through adequate care. This prospect of resource maintenance *and* improvement is indeed a proper justification of the right to exclude anyone who would disturb efficient and beneficent administration. On the other hand, we do not today have the confidence of 18th-century authors as to the automatic nature of the blessings of private enterprise. Granted that natural exhaustible riches should not be abandoned to pillage by irresponsible parties, we are not one whit assured that, once an "allottee" has been found, he will administer these resources in the long-term interest of mankind. Only a very short time has elapsed since we even began to recognize *at all* that wise administration of natural resources of our planet is a major problem.

"Poor" Countries and Fishing

It is understandable that poor countries would prefer to reserve to themselves the living riches in proximity to their coasts. Included in this "wealth," fishing is important to their economy for three reasons: (1) from a nutritional point of view, that is, as a means of nourishing their populations; (2) from an economic point of view, for exportation (Peru being the best example); and (3) from a social point of view, as affording the possibility of employment.

From the point of view of employment, it is necessary, I think, to set aside the traditional concepts of orthodox economists. According to them, it is better for the fish to be caught by foreigners *if* these foreigners bring to bear more efficient methods of production. But better for whom? Certainly not for the fishermen of some coastal country who will lose the occupation that gives them their livelihood or who, at the very least, will find such occupation much less profitable. Is it better for the proper use of the labor force of the coastal country in question? Almost certainly not, since such a country lacks the necessary capital for the creation of jobs and, moreover, cannot more productively employ unemployed fishermen. It can, of course, *buy* the fish caught by others. But then, will such purchases be reasonably inexpensive? And, if so, inexpensive in what sense? Imports are inexpensive or expensive according to the "counterparts" one can furnish. It is precisely the problem of furnishing counterparts—acceptable exportations—that causes monumental difficulties for the underdeveloped countries.

It was reasonable for industrial England in the 19th century to allow most of its agricultural activity to disappear—first, because there was at that time a lively demand for British products abroad, and second, because there was a congestion of capital seeking to employ manual labor at home. Finally, this occurred because the manual labor transferred from agriculture to industry could supply a greater amount of foodstuffs through imports paid for by exports. But such conditions are the very opposite of what is found in the case of a poor country, which is bound to protect its fisheries and fishermen. This is the reason that impelled Ambassador Arvid Pardo to include Article 54 in his Ocean Space Draft Treaty: "The coastal state can reserve the exploitation of the living and nonliving resources of its national ocean space to its nationals."[51]But if a country can have a negative interest in excluding others, one can also have a positive interest in developing the sources of its goods.

Here is a contrast between living and nonliving resources. Activity brought to bear on nonliving resources can only be by way of extraction—simple in principle but immensely difficult in execution, calling for the emplacement of sophisticated techniques and costly equipment. So a country that reserves its continental shelf to itself is obliged to manage its exploitation by way of granting concessions to enterprises possessing the necessary means. In the case of the poorer countries, this can only mean to foreign enterprise. The national state comes into the picture merely by being the granting agency for permits for exploration, concessions, *and* by taxation and reception of royalties.

The activity of extracting living resources can indeed be exercised by small local enterprise, but in that case, it must be kept in mind that extraction is not the only activity. Fortunately, marine populations can be developed through appropriate measures. (This was already the case 2,000 years ago for oysters, and, with the Japanese, for shrimp.) Moreover, such measures can be extended to numerous other species, depending on the support given to research and development in this field.[52] These maricultural activities are particularly promising for poor countries, since most operational expense essentially goes for manual labor. Therefore, the most useful contribution to be made in the area is adequate technology. (It should also be said that, as far as the techniques in question can be extended to nomadic species, they will probably prove to be beneficial to all coastal countries.)

Fascinating perspectives are offered by the "St. Croix experiment." Water drawn from a depth of 830 meters was sucked up to the surface and was found to be charged with nitrates and phosphates; that is, it carried fertilizers that enriched the phytoplankton, thereby making it capable of maintaining a denser fauna.[53]This means that the phenomenon of the Hum-

[51]In this draft treaty, the national ocean space (I would prefer the term *national marine space*) is defined according to the formula advanced by the Latin American states—a belt of 200 marine miles.

[52] See the work of the White Fish Authority in Great Britain on sand-dabs, turbots, sole, and the black coalfish: CNEXO, Theme II, vol. I.

[53]O. A. Roels et al., "Nutrient-rich water: the most abundant resource of the deep sea, in CNEXO, *Colloque International sur l'Exploitation des Océans,* Theme IV, vol. I.

boldt current (which produces the prodigious fecundity of the anchovies in Peruvian catches) was artificially reproduced. The authors of this experiment have publicized the value it represents for countries with steep continental shelves.

Lack of competence prohibits any further account by me of the prospects of mariculture. But it is unnecessary to possess much particular knowledge to sense that, of all the ocean research, the most vital is concerned with increasing its nutritional contribution. The only other research that rivals it in importance for the human species is concerned with the influence of the seas on climate. Unfortunately, neither the former nor the latter is at present very high on the scale of research-expenditure of the advanced countries.

Physical Residues—Moral Residues

And this leads us naturally to the problem of an international authority of the oceans, whatever its legal makeup is going to be. It would have a geographic domain, and it would have tasks to perform.

How will its geographic domain be defined? To put it quite crudely: as the residue of national claims. We have seen how the extent of these claims has been broadening. It is difficult to imagine an international agreement except on the basis of the most comprehensive and extensive national claims (ocean floor as well as superjacent waters; 200 miles, as in the Pardo proposal). Under these circumstances, the international authority will still retain a vast domain; but the revenues to be taken from this domain are an entirely different matter.

The revenues one naturally thinks of are those to be derived from the material resources of international ocean space. The first that come to mind are the hydrocarbons. But here we are faced not only with the problem of their accessibility in very deep waters (a problem which, in time, may be solved by technical progress) but with the question of their existence on the abyssal plains of the oceans. I say, "abyssal plains," given the present trend toward the extension of national jurisdiction, which potentially includes the possibility of engulfing the continental slopes and even the rises; the whole continental margin—way beyond the limits of the shelf itself.

Now, according to most geologists, it is highly unlikely that deposits of hydrocarbons exist outside the continental margins. The reason is clear. Essentially, hydrocarbon basins are cemeteries of living forms—liquid or gaseous collections of the debris of life. Logically, therefore, they should be found only in those areas where living forms existed for long periods in some density. It seems, however, that ever since the beginning of life, or at any rate, for a very long time, density has been a function of the vicinity near land. Even though the borders of continents have changed greatly in time, these changes have not affected the abyssal plains.

This opinion of the scholarly world, which I unfortunately must present here in a most summary way, is not conducive to encouraging enterprises to undertake expenditures for exploration which may have little chance of being profitable.

The revenues of the international authority from the exploitation of hydrocarbon resources depend, therefore, on the manner in which the limits of national jurisdiction are defined. Even supposing that these national jurisdictions leave a substantial portion of the continental margins to the authority, this authority would still have to persuade enterprises to look much further from shore for what they could find much closer, that is, to undertake more hazardous research and more difficult exploitation. In this, the authority could only succeed by offering much more favorable financial conditions; that is, concessions would have to be free and royalties small.

On the other hand, the abyssal plains abound in metals which can be scooped up from its surface. This is because the abyssal plain is part of the earth's crust, which is itself abundant in metals. But is it less costly to harvest ore-bearing nodules from the seabed surface at great sea depths than to mine metal which is buried, even at lesser depths, on the land? This is doubtful; if one wished larger royalties, he would discourage mining from the seabed.

But here is a consideration that is foreign to the calculations of business enterprise as it is constituted today: mining activities on the land are destructive of the environment and of people's habitats.

As early as 1920 Pigou deplored the fact that damage done to the landscape by mining was not accounted for in the usual calculations of national revenue.[54] In the summer of 1971, popular opinion in Great Britain rose against the government's encouragement of mining research in the national parks of the British Isles. The British government had voted a credit of 90 million pounds in support of the research of some 30 mining companies, of which the Rio Tinto is the most important. The Lake District, whose beauty is celebrated and much enjoyed by tourists, was to be prospected.

Two thoughts come to mind. First, it would be better to extract metals from the seabed, and second, the government must subsidize this type of research. Would it not be better, then, to subsidize it a little more in order to reorient it toward the seabed? It would be an excellent thing for the

[54]A.C. Pigou, *The Economics of Welfare,* London, 1920.

environment, but it would not be profitable to the international authority, since it would cost a great deal.

Here we come to the core of the contrast between two different concepts of an international authority for the oceans. According to one concept, its geographic domain would be a source of revenue which it could then redistribute in favor of the underdeveloped nations. This concept holds only if national jurisdiction is limited to the three-mile territorial sea. The international authority cannot play this role if its geographic domain is a residue whose material promise is small and far off.

Another concept of the authority is offered by *Pacem in Maribus.* If national claims leave the authority with a physically insufficient residue, they still leave it with an immense, diversified, and capital residue on the moral level.

The authority would have to deal with all those issues which do not respond to private interests and to the short-term interests of enterprises or governments, in addition to long-term considerations on a planetary scale —more specifically, the various functions of ocean space and its uses by mankind. Some of these are as yet little understood by the public, such as the impact of the oceans on the earth's climate or their function as a recipient of waste disposal *(cloaca maxima).* Other uses are traditional (transportation and navigation). Still others have only recently begun to preoccupy public opinion (mining and recreation). On the basis of a full analysis of all of these functions, concrete proposals must be made for the improvement of services. If the resources are available, technical assistance must be given to the poorer countries, to enable them to profit from the services.

I am afraid it would be illusory to think an international institution could be vested with much real power. Its intellectual and moral power, instead, could be very great and therefore efficient. The very idea of an international authority responds to a vague but powerful feeling abroad today: *let us take care of this planet, for we will find no other one; let us use its resources with wisdom and equity.* Is not the best response to this sort of feeling the creation of an institution which would seek all the needed improvements in the uses of this the largest part of the globe?

CHAPTER 2

An Ocean Development Tax

JOHN EATWELL, JOHN LLEWELLYN, AND ROGER TARLING

This essay attempts to illustrate the economic and, in part, political problems surrounding the general issue of international cost-sharing in the establishment of an Ocean Regime. We will focus particularly on the proposed Ocean Development Tax (ODT) as a means of determining the distribution of international burdens. A central assumption of the analysis is that the nation-state will be the point of revenue collection and that the Ocean Regime will have no control over the way the nation-state chooses to divide the tax burden among its citizens.

The objective of the ODT is seen as the raising of a given amount of money to finance the Ocean Regime, *not* as a general tax which yields a variable volume of finance which is then distributed to various oceanic projects. A major weakness of the ODT proposal to date, especially in terms of the search for an international agreement, has been the inability to spell out exactly what the benefits of an Ocean Regime might be and how they would be distributed. An open-ended tax commitment would only make the problem worse.

We shall consider the economic criteria that underlie the conception of an ODT and by which it should be judged, as well as the operational structure of an ODT, in particular, the type of information required for decisions to be made on the form which the ODT will eventually assume.

*This is the theoretical portion of a longer report prepared for Pacem in Maribus II. The entire report was introduced as an official UN document for consideration by the Committee on the Peaceful Uses of the Sea-Bed and Ocean Floor Beyond the Limits of National Jurisdiction.

It must be kept in mind throughout that a proper fiscal evaluation of the ODT requires the tax to be viewed as only part of the total financial package of an Ocean Regime.

In Part I the relationship between tax base and tax rate is considered. It is argued that the problem of the tax rate determination is of secondary importance compared to the problem of definition of the tax base. In Part II the vexing problem of tax incidence is aired, and the problems implicit in defining the state as the taxable unit are discussed. These problems also play a role in Part IV which debunks the idea that the ODT can in itself contribute to efficient resource utilization. In Part III we attempt to establish the criteria by which a particular form of the ODT might be considered "equitable" and relate these criteria to traditional UN usage.

Tax Rates and Tax Base

Discussion of the economic implications of an ODT should carefully differentiate between the analysis of the construction and enumeration of the tax base and the formulation of tax-rate policy. The tax base defines not only the breadth of activities to be taxed but should also provide the link between the volume of revenue and changes in the volume or intensity of the activity that is taxed. Furthermore, examination of the relationship between the economic environment of the elements of the tax base and variations in the tax rates defines the *real* incidence of fiscal activity and the consequent influence of fiscal activity on economic behavior.

On the other hand, given the tax base and the appropriate knowledge of incidence, variation of the absolute and relative levels of tax rates enables the fiscal authority to pursue particular economic goals.

We argue here that the major empirical problem in the establishment of an ODT is the formation of an agreed-upon tax base and the provision of a mechanism whereby the tax base may be appropriately adapted through time. Tax rate determination does not involve the same type of empirical problems, but rather raises social and political issues which would be the basic concern of the international agreement establishing the ODT.

The Tax Base

The revenue (R) yielded by a particular fiscal policy is defined simply as the tax base (B) multiplied by the tax rates (T). The tax base need not be expressed as a single magnitude, B and T may be n dimensional column vectors, the components of which measure different elements of the tax base perhaps in different units, and the revenue the scalar sum:

$$B \ T = \epsilon'_i \qquad B_i T_i = R, \qquad i = 1 \ldots n.$$

For example one component of B, B_j may be measured in physical terms, as in the case of street frontage for urban taxes or gallons in the case of motor fuel taxation; the corresponding tax rate, T_j, being expressed in money units per physical unit (for example, cents per gallon). Or element B_k may be expressed as a value, such as the value of income in the case of income tax, and the corresponding tax rate, T_k, as a simple proportion (for example, 30 percent) or as a proportion that is a function of the size of B_k, as in the case of a progressive income tax.

The tax base need not merely differentiate between commodities; it may also differentiate between modalities of tax collection. In this case, B may become a matrix, each component of which B_{ij}, measures the amount of commodity *i* in location *j*, and so on. The tax rate can then also be varied by commodity and locality, although the complexity introduced by greater disaggregation of the tax base may be a disincentive not compensated by the consequent increase in precision.

When a tax system is as potentially complex as the ODT, in which a series of heterogeneous activities are to be taxed, a tax base expressed as a single magnitude in a particular or single value is undoubtedly attractive. Not only does a simple value system apparently ensure comparability between different components of the tax base, but it is also deceptively easy to manipulate, as for example in the case of an all-embracing 1% tax. If an unambiguous measure of the value of the output of ocean space could be found, and this was demonstrated to be the foundation of a legitimate and equitable tax system, considerations of convenience might well lead to its adoption.

But there is no a priori reason why a simple value base should be such a foundation. Every element of the tax base should be measured in a manner which ensures that the levied tax influences the intended *economic* dimension. For example, suppose a tax were to be levied in the United States on motor vehicle production in order to finance research and development into anti-pollution engines and to discourage pollution by motor vehicles. The imposition of a simple quantity-based tax based on the size of engines—say 20 per 1,000 c.c.—might be both appropriate and straightforward. It would be unnecessary to distinguish between Ford Pintos and Cadillacs, except on the basis of their engine size, or to distinguish between models which were more expensive because they were fitted with electric windows and those which were not, because the value of the vehicle would be irrelevant to the economic problem under consideration. Similarly, diverse vehicles such as combine-harvesters, road graders, and speedboats would all be caught in the tax net and all would contribute to the elimination of the pollution they cause. No relevant complication is introduced by the fact that there would be considerable variation in the final price of the different products in which similar engines are incorporated.

Thus the problem of constructing a tax base involves a definition of the theoretically correct economic base and then the design of an empirical system which minimizes the inevitable compromises necessary in the adaption of reality to the theoretical ideal. We have, therefore, investigated the relationship between some simple tax bases and the economic objectives of the ODT. In particular, we have conducted a detailed investigation of the tax base appropriate in the case of fishing and have demonstrated that the enumeration of the value of world catch (even if this were a simple task) would provide a tax base that is economically *inappropriate* for a fiscal system with the objectives of the ODT. Similar exercises have been conducted with respect to ocean transport, and in both cases suitable bases have been devised on the assumption that the tax should reflect as accurately as possible the utilization of ocean space.

The second characteristic of the tax base is that it should be comprehensive. All activities that involve the economic exploitation of the ocean space should be included in the tax base of the ODT. A list of activities is provided in the *Note sur une Taxe de Developpement Oceanique* by the Centre National pour l'Exploitation des Oceans. The list includes: maritime transport, naval construction, fishing, offshore oil drilling (and other minerals), tourism and recreation, and also mentions scientific research, cable-laying, and pollution. Others have suggested ocean prospecting and military uses too.

It is apparent that some activities such as military use and probably pollution present insuperable difficulties. Nation-states display a natural reluctance to reveal military information, and since the only reliable estimation of the cost of pollution is the cost of preventing it, estimation depends more on international agreement on limitation of pollution than on the machinery of the ODT. If such an agreement placed the onus for preventing contamination on the nation-state from which it emanates, the cost of prevention would automatically be allocated to the appropriate source.

It is difficult to understand the rationale for the inclusion of naval construction in the tax base, except as a device for "catching" otherwise elusive maritime interests, for the ODT has been advanced primarily as a tax on ocean *utilization,* and construction is not necessarily directly linked to use. Some of the other categories are also debatable, but it is clear that any list should include maritime transport, fishing, oil, and minerals. All activities in these four categories should be enumerated in the tax base—including such activities as "subsistence fishing"—up to the point where the size of the observation does not warrant the cost of data collection. The base will then serve not only as the foundation of the fiscal system but will also provide the statistical information required for any rational ocean policy. If it is then decided that the taxation of, say, subsistence fishing is inequitable, the subsistence fishing elements in the tax base should be taxed at a zero rate. Without comprehensive information, the manipulation of tax rates in the pursuit of social or economically desirable policies will be inhibited.

There appears to be no *economic* rationale for the limitation of the ODT to ocean space beyond the limits of national jurisdiction. Indeed, the potential economic distortions implicit in such a limitation would be a strong argument against the imposition of the tax as it is presently conceived.

Thus the tax base should be economically meaningful and comprehensive. The data base required for such a construction of the tax base does not at present exist for all categories of ocean utilization, but we have been able to provide a sufficient quantity of illustrative material to examine the economic implications of an ODT system.

Tax Rates

The ODT has customarily been proposed as a 1% tax on the value of "all revenues derived from the sea."[1] As we have intimated in our discussion of the characteristics of the tax base, a simple system of this sort, although attractive, may be inappropriate. If the tax base is differentiated, then the tax rate system may have to be differentiated too. In fact, the ability to differentiate the tax system—by for instance making the tax levied on a particular country a function of the Gross Domestic Product (GDP) per capita, or the proportion of ocean produce in GDP—would be a positive benefit.

The tax rate system, as opposed to the tax base, would thus become the focus of international debate. It may be thought that the complexity of a differentiated system would delay negotiation, but it should be recognized that a 1% value-based system with no discriminatory elements would never be agreed upon because of the excessive burden that would fall on particular nations. Although once the need for differentiation is recognized, one would hope that the form of the agreed-upon schedule would be strongly biased in favor of simplicity. By separating the issues of tax rates and tax base, the potential for fruitful discussion is probably increased.

It should be apparent from the above discussion that the major empirical problem in the development of an ODT at the present time is the lack

[1]Cf. The statement by the Representative of Canada to the Enlarged U.N. Committee on the Peaceful Uses of the Seabed and the Ocean Floor beyond the Limits of National Jurisdiction, May 24, 1971.

of a tax base that can be agreed on, and an examination of the economic criteria on which such a base should be constructed. It is not within the scope of this essay to construct a complete tax base; it is our task to delineate the economic characteristics of such a base and to illustrate some of the economic and statistical problems implicit in its construction.

Incidence

Although fiscal policies are often proposed, debated, and even implemented using the naive assumption that legal incidence is equivalent to real incidence, all know that this is probably incorrect. The question of real incidence is so complex, however, that no noncontroversial solution to the problem has been proposed.

Legal incidence is defined as the legal point on which a tax falls; for example, a corporation tax has legal incidence on corporate profits. Real incidence, on the other hand, is defined as the point from which the real resources implicit in the tax payment are extracted. In other words, real incidence is on the individual, corporation, or state that suffers a reduction in real income as a result of the imposition of the tax. For instance, if a corporation tax of 10% were levied on company A, and company A raised its prices by 10% and suffered no fall in sales, while the legal incidence is on company A, the real incidence falls on the purchasers of the products of company A. But the circumstances that govern the ability of company A to pass on the tax are complex.

In the case of the ODT, the problems of real incidence are equally complex, but some attempt must be made to trace the real effects, since the reaction of economic units to the imposition of the tax will depend more on real effects than on legal incidence.

The Role of State

It has already been agreed in the ODT discussions that the point of legal incidence of the ODT will be the nation-state. In the first stage, payment of the tax will imply a fall in national income of the paying state to the extent that payments are used, directly or indirectly, to extract real resources from the state. For most countries the fall in national income will be equal to 100% of the tax payment, although in the case of some reserve currencies, the fall in national income may be zero. (Problems of exchange rates are discussed below.)

The ultimate incidence of the tax, then, depends on the policy of the state. There is, of course, no reason that the state should pass on the tax at all; the national tax system is a device of national economic management, not necessarily of resource "extraction." If the state should choose to tax oceanic activity of its own nationals, then the ultimate real incidence will depend on the strategies adopted by the states. For example, suppose the U.S. decides to impose all the ODT on the offshore oil companies. Then all the tax would probably be absorbed by the companies, unable to raise prices due to competition from other oil sources. On the other hand, a tax placed on Liberia's tanker fleet would, at least in part, be passed on to the purchasers of tanker capacity; thus the ultimate incidence would fall *outside* Liberia.

Since we cannot predict the reaction of nation-states to the ODT, and it is probably unrealistic to expect states to establish the expensive machinery required for the imposition of the ODT on all the oceanic activities which define their tax liability, any evaluation of ultimate real incidence is impossible. We have thus fallen back on the legal location of the ODT in these discussions.

Exchange Rates

If all countries were to pay the ODT in domestic currency expendible only on domestic production, problems of exchange rate changes, nonconvertible currencies, and variable price levels would be eliminated. Since this is unlikely to be the case, the "burden" on any particular country will be influenced by exchange-rate variation and domestic inflation. This will *a fortiori* be the case if the tax base is valued at "standard prices" in terms of a single currency, say U.S. dollars. It should, in particular, be noted, that exchange rates do not in any precise way represent the relative purchasing power of different currencies. Indeed, Gilbert and Kravis (10) find that the official exchange rates may misrepresent "real" income by one quarter or more. Thus one cannot expect the ODT financial burden to accurately reflect the distribution of real welfare effects between countries.

Pricing problems are mitigated to the degree that many ocean products such as oil and tanker capacity are traded on world markets and thus possess a "world price," usually fixed in a given currency. To the extent that this is not the case, as it certainly is not in the case of fish, no valid, precise formula can compare the real welfare effects of ODT contributions between different states. But as Schelling has pointed out:

If we drop the idea of a formula, and think rather of the development of "criteria," or even more loosely of "relevant considerations" for the negotiation of country shares, many of the theoretical problems discussed earlier become, if not "soluble," at least resolvable. While a formula has to be simple and precise, "considerations" can be numerous and less well-defined; and principles can gradually be forged to which exceptions can be made for the cases to which the principles are least applicable. (21)

The problem of nonconvertible currencies remains. The only solution to this problem is an institutional one. Countries with nonconvertible currencies must be given the opportunity to contribute directly to the ocean regime at an agreed-upon rate per unit of tax base.

Problems in the Calculation of Real Incidence

The extent to which a tax imposed on a producer can be passed on to the consumer depends on the extent to which the consumer, forced by a higher price, switches his demand to some other product or to increased savings. This notion is made explicit in the concept of "elasticity of demand," which is the proportionate change in quantity that results from a stated proportionate change in its price, all other phenomena (in particular, real incomes) remaining constant. The elasticity of demand can in principle be estimated from observations of different prices and quantities at various times. The limiting cases are usually taken to be the values 0 and infinity. When the elasticity is zero (meaning there is no change in the quantity demanded when the price is changed), the *whole* of the tax will be passed on. When the elasticity is infinite, even an infinitesimally small amount of the tax passed on will cause demand to drop to zero, so that if the product is to be sold, it will have to be sold at the pretax price. This, in turn, means that the tax will have to be borne by the producer who may experience a fall in total profit or may reduce his total sales or both.

Considering a region as a closed entity (that is, disregarding for the moment the consequences of interregional trade), it follows that the impact of an ocean development tax would depend largely on the price elasticity of demand of the regional consumers. If the price elasticity of demand for fish were high, as is likely to be the case in a country with a high per-capita income, a large switch away from fish in favor of other forms of protein would be expected. In poorer countries a large part of the tax on fish would in all probability be borne by the consumer.

But perhaps an even more important point is how the existence of interregional trade would cause the initial legal tax burden ultimately to be allocated between countries. If a region is exporting a product for which the price elasticity of demand is low, it will pass the greater part of the tax on to the importing region. For example, in the case of petroleum, where, as the recent OPEC negotiations have shown, the price elasticity is low, a tax

on ocean tanker services would almost certainly be passed on to the importing country. Fish exports, however, might be expected to be considerably
price-elastic so that major exporters such as Norway would be unable to
pass on anything like the full value of the tax to their export markets.

The ultimate regional and interregional resolution of the tax incidence
is therefore difficult to assess with certainty. Nevertheless, approximate
answers can be obtained given a certain amount of basic data. In the first
place, it is *essential* to know the magnitude of trade flows in both directions
for each broad ocean activity. For a regional assessment it is strictly necessary to have data only on interregional flows, but this has to be aggregated
from country data, so that, given the basic data, a full country study could
be performed. Second, it is necessary to estimate price elasticities. These
could, in the first instance, be assumed, and compared later with estimates
calculated from true series data.

It is essential, therefore, that extra data be obtained if the crucial
question of ultimate tax incidence is to be resolved. To that end, a question-
naire, which is required to provide the basic data for the calculation of the
ODT tax base, has been carefully designed so that over time the data so
collected would permit calculation of both the interregional flows as well
as provide basic data for the calculation of elasticities.

Equity

Problems of fiscal equity are customarily considered under the broad criteria of "ability to pay" or "benefit." "Ability to pay" fiscal systems are
organized in such a way that an individual contributor pays an amount
determined by his ability to pay, defined in some general way. An example
is the progressive income tax. Under an ability-to-pay scheme, the amount
an individual contributor pays is not linked to the amount of benefit he
receives from the institution to which he subscribes. "Benefit" systems, on
the other hand, are based on the proposition that contributors should pay
for the benefits they receive without regard to their individual circumstances. This may be the case, for instance, in certain statutory insurance
schemes.

The arguments for the ocean-levy schemes advanced to date (18) (22)
have been couched in quasi-"benefit" terminology modified by some ability-
to-pay provisos for developing countries. Broadly, nations are expected to
contribute to the ODT to the extent that they benefit from economic exploitation of ocean space. But this approach contains an important ambiguity.
The benefit derived from the exploitation of ocean space is not the benefit
of services financed by the ODT. The ODT is not levied in proportion to

the amount of benefit accruing as a result of the operations of the Ocean Regime. To resolve this ambiguity it might be claimed that the benefits of the operations of the Ocean Regime accrue in proportion to a given state's utilization of ocean space, but although some benefit may accrue to all, it would be difficult to sustain an argument for strict (or even approximate) proportionality.

A simple ability-to-pay criterion designed, say, as a levy on all member states in proportion to the national incomes measured in some agreed-upon manner does not, however, seem to be entirely appropriate for financing an Ocean Regime, since the Ocean Regime is directly linked to an activity in which states participate to significantly different degrees.

At the time of its formation, the UN delegated to a Contribution Committee the task of finding a fair system for sharing costs among member countries. The Committee was instructed to follow the principle of "capacity to pay," and the suggestion was made to it that national income would be the "fairest guide" to follow. The formula eventually suggested by the Committee was based not only on national income but was progressive, " . . . in the case of countries with low per capita income only a portion of the total national income will be taken into account for assessment purposes, while in the case of countries with high per capita income all or practically all of national income would be considered." (25) This was, in fact, a continuation of the general approach of the League of Nations. (21, p. 3)

Thus international agencies which provide "general" services have been financed on an ability-to-pay basis. Specialized agencies providing "general" services—UNESCO, UNCTAD, etc.—have also developed financial arrangements within an ability-to-pay framework, although this has been overlain by the particular interest which some states have taken in particular organizations, the Danish interest in UNESCO, for example.

Only those organizations that provide very specific services, such as IMCO and IATA, are linked in any way to a "benefit" criterion, and even in this case the linkage of tax payment to specific benefit is rather loose.

What has appeared remarkable in our survey of international cost-sharing practices has been how very ad hoc many of the financing arrangements are. An extreme example is that of the original League of Nations Covenant, whereby costs would be divided in proportion to the members' contributions to the Universal Postal Union. Such ad hoc arrangements suggest an unwillingness on the part of nation-states to commit themselves to any set of principles that might return to embarrass them on a future occasion.

In the context of the history of international cost-sharing arrangements, the ODT can only be judged revolutionary, in that it attempts to clearly define a set of criteria under which contributions to the Ocean Regime will be made. This may add to the difficulty of gaining acceptance for the scheme. Nonetheless, the very ambiguity of the "benefit" criterion of the scheme may aid in its eventual acceptance. If the tax base were formulated in the comprehensive manner suggested in this essay and accepted as a fait accompli, then negotiation of tax rates would appear a more attractive negotiating proposition, even if, as Schelling suggests, "the search for an equitable formula is likely to be a gentlemanly guise for bargaining." (21)

One must, however, pose the question whether the cost of organizing an ODT is really worth the eventual revenue. In our view it is worthwhile *only* if the ODT tax base is viewed as a device for fixing contributions which are then revised periodically. An ongoing tax system, in which the tax is levied on a continuously varying tax base (as a standard national income tax system), would be excessively complex and costly (as national income tax systems show). If, however, the ODT were used as a means of determining *fixed* contributions at specific intervals, it would be a more practicable proposition. Furthermore, the process of negotiation would provide a great incentive for member states to assist in the formation of an accurate data base, since the inability to attest to one's own utilization of ocean space might weaken bargaining positions. The ODT tax base would therefore provide the basic material for an international cost-sharing scheme and provide the information without which an international Ocean Regime could not operate effectively.

Efficiency

It has been suggested that the ODT may in itself contribute toward a more efficient and rational management of ocean space.* There may appear to be some theoretical justification for this viewpoint. Any simple programming solution of the problem of maximization of a given objective function in the face of the constraint of scarce resources has as its counterpart a set of weights which may be interpreted as the prices implicit in an optimal allocation of resources. Thus the utilization of scarce ocean space at zero cost implies a misallocation of resources. Intertemporal extensions of the same theory provide dynamic pricing rules for utilization of scarce resources through time. (This is the approach of O. Burt and R. Cummings [2], H.S. Gordon [11], R.L. Gordon [12], and J. Quirk and V. Smith [20]. A slightly different approach, based explicitly on the concept of dynamic

*Cf. the remarks of Ambassador Castañeda of Mexico, in Borgese (1, pp. 23–24).

forward markets, is found in M. Posner [19].)

Although the problem of the technological optimization of scarce resource utilization is unambiguous, the extrapolation of the programming counterpart to the marketplace, implied by the interpretation of dual weights as prices, is less convincing. The approach implies not only perfect markets at the present time but also perfect future markets and perfect knowledge of future technology. Such an approach to a very real problem has no obvious operational value. Even in a static sense, the presumption that the "free" supply of scarce ocean resources will lead to a general misutilization of world resources, taken as a whole, has as its prerequisite the existence of perfect resource markets. Since perfect markets do not exist, there is no obvious reason for preferring any one price system to another. No particular price system has any more meaning in terms of welfare maximization than another.

Furthermore, the corollary that follows from these arguments—that the international exploitation of exhaustible resources may be controlled by manipulation of the price system—is equally invalid. Such a manipulation would require not only an inconceivable amount of information flowing to the fiscal body but also a degree of sensitivity that is impossible in terms of the operational constraints imposed on an international organization. This approach at an international level is also surely utopian in terms of the degree of submissiveness it assumes on behalf of nation states.

In fact, the form of utilization of ocean resources falls into three classes:

1. Use of the ocean which does not exhaust *any* of its qualities; for example, the use of the sea by shipping in noncongested areas.

2. The use of ocean resources which, although exhaustible, may, if exploited correctly, be preserved indefinitely; the fish population is a clear example.

3. The extraction of resources that cannot be replaced.

In a purely theoretical model category, number 1 would be charged at zero, while numbers 2 and 3 would be charged at prices dependent on the appropriate intertemporal optimization exercise. Although we may be somewhat scathing as to the operational significance of such exercises, they do alert us to the problems of the divergence of private and social objectives in resource utilization. If "society" wishes to preserve the stocks of resources in category 2 and limit the rate of exhaustion of resources in category 3, it must find some way of restraining "private" activity (it should be remembered that in a world context, "social" applies to the global community and "private" may apply to a state as well as to private companies). In our view, the only way to exercise such restraint is by international agreement fixed in quantitative terms. The ODT is too crude an instrument to be of any direct value. Its role is to finance an organization that can develop the requisite procedures for optimal control of resource utilization.

Even if the ODT were likely to be an effective instrument in the control of resource utilization, we would not recommend its use for this purpose. Our position is based on Tinbergen's well-known proposition, that an effective fiscal system should contain at least the same number of instrumental variables as it has targets. (23) If the number of instrumental variables is less than the number of targets, it is not possible to pursue all targets simultaneously. A corollary of this proposition is that any one instrument should not be used to pursue more than one target simultaneously. The ODT could not be used effectively to raise a particular volume of revenue *and* to act as an interventionist device in ocean-product markets. It is easy to imagine circumstances in which these two rules would be incompatible.

Therefore, in general, we reject any arguments concerning the relative effects of the imposition of the ODT on the efficient allocation of resources or concerning the usefulness of the ODT as an instrumental variable in the control of resource exploitation. It should be noted that this argument works both ways, although we cannot envisage the ODT itself contributing to efficient resource utilization, we cannot envisage it disturbing resource utilization in any significant way either. An exception to this might be that of shipping. The use of the sea by ships does not imply the exhaustion of the ability of the sea to carry other ships. The economic cost to the world community is therefore zero. Thus, except insofar as the Ocean Regime facilitates the movement of shipping, the ODT may cause a distortion in the utilization of transportation resources between sea and, say, air. This might be particularly important in passenger transportation.

To a certain extent, therefore, ocean transportation is qualitatively different from other forms of oceanic activity. The justification for its inclusion in the tax base can only be the belief that the Ocean Regime will yield substantial benefits to shipping as well as other ocean activities.

In conclusion, it must be noted that since the point of tax collection is the nation-state, and we can have no general presumption that the states will pursue any specific fiscal policy with respect to their own oceanic activities, we cannot assume that the tax will influence resource utilization in any given direction. Under the circumstances, international agreement on quantitative controls is more probable than any internationally agreed-upon operational system of financial control.

Summary

The arguments we have made may be summarized as follows:

The tax base is conceptually distinct from tax rates and is the major empirical problem in the path of the establishment of an ODT.

The tax base may be in the form of a variety of magnitudes, but it should be both comprehensive and economically meaningful.

Tax rate variation, not manipulation of the tax base, should be the basis of tax exemption.

The problem of real incidence is practically insuperable, particularly in view of the differing policies of the states toward oceanic activities; thus we must fall back on legal incidence as the basis for discussion.

International monetary considerations can distort even the legal basis of incidence. No precise formula should be expected to emerge from negotiations, but the ODT tax base will provide the empirical underpinning of such negotiations.

The revolutionary nature of the ODT proposal will undoubtedly cause it difficulty in the world forum, but the linkage of the tax to ocean utilization is a persuasive concept, particularly if modified by ability-to-pay considerations.

The ODT should be regarded as a device for fixing national burdens in an international cost-sharing system, not as a genuine ongoing tax system. It would, however, be subject to periodic revision.

The ODT has no direct role to play in facilitating the optimal utilization of ocean resources.

We noted the qualitative difference between shipping and other forms of ocean utilization.

Bibliography

Borgese, E.M., *Report and Comments* (on Pacem in Maribus II), Malta, 1971.

Burt, O.R. and R.G. Cummings. Production and Investment in Natural Resource Industries, *A.E.R.*, 1970.

Committee on Resources and Man, National Academy of Sciences—National Research Council, *"Resources and Man"*, W.H. Freeman & Co., San Francisco.

Department of Statistics, Wellington, *New Zealand Official Yearbook 1969*, Wellington, New Zealand, 1969.

Eatwell, John, On the Proposed Reform of Corporation Tax, *Bulletin of the*

Oxford Institute of Economics and Statistics, Nov. 1971.

F.A.O. *Technical Conversion Factors for Agricultural Commodities,* F.A.O. Rome, 1960.

F.A.O. *Yearbook of Fishery Statistics: Fishery Commodities 1970, Vol. 31.* F.A.O. Rome 1971.

F.A.O. *Yearbook of Fishery Statistics, Vol. 30—Catches and Landings 1970,* F.A.O. Rome 1971.

F.A.O. *Production Yearbook Vol. 24. 1970,* F.A.O. Rome 1971.

Gilbert, M., and I. Kravis. *An International Comparison of National Products and the Purchasing Power of Currencies,* O.E.C.D. Paris, 1954.

Gordon, H.S., The Economic Theory of a Common Property Resource: The Fishery, *J.P.E.,* 1954.

Gordon, R.L., A Reinterpretation of the Pure Theory of Exhaustion, *J.P.E.* 1967.

Hotelling, H., The Economics of Exhaustible Resources, *J.P.E.* 1931.

Josling, T.E.; B. Davey; A. McFarquhar, A.C. Hannah, and D. Hamway. *"Burdens and Benefits of Farm-support Policies"* Trade Policy Research Center, 1972.

O.E.C.D., *Main Economic Indicators,* O.E.C.D., Paris.

O.E.C.D., *Agricultural Statistics, 1955–68,* O.E.C.D., Paris, 1969.

O.E.C.D., *Food Consumption Statistics, 1960–68,* O.E.C.D., Paris, 1970.

Pacem in Maribus II, *Working Papers on the Ocean Development Tax,* Malta, 1971.

Posner, M.V., The Rate of Depletion of Gas Fields, *E.J.,* Supplement 1972.

Quirk, J., and V. Smith. Dynamic Economic Models of Fishing in A. Scott ed. *Proceedings of the H.R. MacMillan Fisheries Economics Symposium,* Vancouver, 1969.

Schelling, Thomas C., *International Cost-Sharing Arrangements,* Essays in International Finance, No. 24. Princeton University, 1955.

S.I.P.R.I., *Towards a Better Use of the Ocean,* Alinquist & Wiksell, Stockholm, 1969.

Tinbergen, J., *Economic Policy—Principles and Design,* North Holland, Amsterdam, 1967.

Turvey, R., Optimisation in Fishery Regulation, *A.E.R.,* 1964.

U.N. General Assembly, *U.N. General Assembly document A/80,* U.N. 1946.

U.N. *Yearbook of National Accounts 1969, Vol. 1: Individual Country Data,* U.N. New York, 1970.

U.N. *Monthly Bulletin of Statistics,* New York, 1970.

U.N. *Statistical Yearbook,* U.N. New York.

CHAPTER 3

Mater Omnium: Automated Energy and Material Wealth from the Sea

IRVING KAPLAN

An analysis of alternatives in the production of energy and a design for the application of nuclear fusion, automation, and industrial integration to the nonpolluting production of the material needs of the post-industrial world. A discussion of the sociopolitical implications.

Commercial automation is available today, which can perform any function required in industry except the creation of new ideas. In the mid-1960s the development of integrated circuitry (microelectronics), a method of manufacturing electronic circuits in very small monolithic chips of silicon or metal oxides, was brought to fruition. This great development brought a number of extremely important benefits. The circuits were about a thousand times smaller than anything previously manufactured commercially; they were extremely reliable and could be expected to last some 150,000 years if no catastrophic event destroyed them; they used very little electricity; and they were thousands of times less expensive to produce than the previous generation of transistorized circuitry. Early microelectronic computers such as the IBM 360 were one to five thousand times less expensive to produce than the previous generation of computers, and the cost reductions grow as the development of automation continues. Thus in recent years there has been a tremendous growth of automation in the United States. If a product is not easily automatable, it can usually be redesigned or replaced by another product which either performs the same function or makes that function obsolete. At present, about 75 percent of the United States "labor force" is no longer working productively, being either unemployed or on welfare, attending college or some other type of post high-school education, working in education, in the armed forces, in the greatly expanded civil service and police forces, in the recreation industry, or in one or another of the "corps" (Peace Corps, Teacher Corps, Neighborhood Youth Corps, Vista, etc.). This huge segment of what was once a productive population cannot technically be said to be unemployed. Rather, it is negatively employed, the United States having created new "industries" which consume the products of automated industry and which consume the time of the individuals "working" within them. At the present rate of technological progress, the obsolescence of human labor in technological nations such as the United States will occur well before 1980.[1] This is the first revolution of our lifetime, and the consequences for the human personality and institutions will be immense.

Automation is the revolution that is removing man from the world of work in the traditional sense of the word, yet an equally important revolution is now imminent. This is the revolution in energy which is to be born with the end of the fossil fuel age and the advent of new energy sources and technologies. There are a number of such technologies and resources. I believe that nuclear fusion energy will prove to be the most effective, a belief that is supported by the following considerations:

1. Whatever reserves of oil and coal we have in the earth can best be utilized as chemicals rather than as fuel. Even the relatively pure carbon in anthracite coal is valuable as a source of complex organic chemicals such as rayon and nylon. The complex molecules found in oil are even more valuable as sources of plastics, fibers, drugs, and foods. The urgent need for these materials (for example, the "miracle" fibers for cordage and textiles, rigid foamed plastics for structures, etc.) and the growing population provide a chemical market for all of the world's oil and coal which depends only on the will and creativity of the industries concerned.

2. The extraction of fissionable materials is exceedingly costly when compared with the extraction of deuterium. It involves mining operations which are often ecologically harmful, dangerous to the miner, and unsightly, whereas deuterium is extracted from water with simple ease and high efficiency.

3. Fission presents a constant danger of catastrophic events despite ingenious safety engineering. The disposal of the radioactive ashes from fission reactors is a problem that has not yet been solved and which could become as costly as the extraction of fissionables. These ashes remain radioactive for thousands of years. The fast-breeder reactors required to produce

[1]Kaplan, I.E., *The Projected Effect of Automation on Future Navy Personnel Requirements, Part II, Implications for the Navy's Environment, The Nation,* SRM 67–3. August 1966, U.S. Naval Personnel Research Activity, San Diego, Ca.; Kaplan, I.E., "The Imminent Revolution in Cybernation," in *Committed Spending, A Route to Economic Security,* ed. R. Theobald, New York: Doubleday, 1968.

energy for today's world population will be capable of producing 10 to 100,000 atomic warheads per year, dispersed over the entire world. These reactors will introduce the lasting danger of catastrophic accident, radiation leakage, sabotage, or destruction by war or insurrection. Each incident may kill millions of people and make large areas uninhabitable for hundreds or thousands of years.

4. Generation of electricity from solar energy is limited to sunny regions and requires much surface area. Even with large storage capacity, such systems may not be able to cope with long periods of cloudiness. Large areas of solar conversion devices will redistribute the heat balance of local, and possibly large, regions.

5. Satellite solar converters will have to be extremely large, will be very costly, will sacrifice energy in transmission to earth by attenuation in airborne dust and water and even to the air itself, will be dangerous if the powerful microwave beams fall on life or property, and will be eroded or even catastrophically damaged by meteorites, requiring expensive repair.

6. Windmills will be as subject to climatic aberrations as land-based solar energy converters. The investment in these structures will have to be very large and they will require much surface, whether on land or sea.

7. Tidal energy converters will also require much investment and surface area, although they would be more reliable than any of the other methods mentioned above.

8. Harnessing the thermal gradients of the ocean can provide man with all of his energy needs, yet the operating efficiency will be only 2 or 3 percent. Thus, the size of such an enterprise will be great, requiring a larger investment than any of the other means discussed here.

9. Geothermal energy is easy to tap in many areas and is universally available with deep drilling. However, the earth's mantle and crust are found to be good insulators so that the heat, which is produced at a steady rate from the fissionable materials, will not flow fast enough to replace local "cool spots" created by mining the heat. Earthquakes may thus be caused by the resulting contractions and by the displacement of subsurface waters.

10. Fusion energy will be reliable and independent of all conditions except major catastrophes. As will be explained later, fusion plants can be constructed by a method which will make them very inexpensive. They produce few toxic substances or radioactive ashes, the radioactivity that is involved in the reaction is transient, containable, and productive via conversion to energy. Should any event cause disruption of the thermonuclear reaction, it simply collapses without explosion, and should a catastrophic event (such as bombing or earthquake) open the reactor structure, there will be only a small release of radioactive tritium gas. Materials can be selected for the structure which will make residual radioactivity minimal. Fusion reactors will be about a million times safer than fission reactors.

11. Fusion will be the most flexible source of energy, being suitable for ships and spacecraft, as well as for stationary power plants of huge capacity.

12. The amount of deuterium fuel required will be so small that the electrical requirements of the United States can be derived from a kitchen tap. The biochemical role of deuterium is not known, but the addition of a neutron to the hydrogen nucleus (producing deuterium) does not alter the chemical characteristics of the atom, changing only its mass. Deuterium would not, then, seem to have an ecological significance other than that of the more numerous isotope of the element, hydrogen.

Solar, wind, geothermal, tidal, and thermal gradient methods of energy production all represent passive, or "gentle," ways of converting the most available forces in nature. Is this the wisest direction for man to take? If we are soon to be visited by a cold period or ice age, it will become more difficult to convert natural energy for man's needs. What is more, man will be robbing the environment to concentrate energy for himself. A cold period would require that man give up many of his activities and resources and recede both in his geographic territories and in his ambitions. Passive energy may find itself unable to cope with other critical situations (droughts, storms, floods) and would create a major restraint on human progress.

On the other hand, the fusion of light atoms gives man the most powerful and plentiful source of energy presently known. It is a source which, if used with trained discretion, can enable him to ward off the major catastrophies of nature—to build a habitat resistant to a glacial period, to overcome drought and flood, and possibly even to change the orbit of the earth or migrate to a new place in the galaxy in the distant future.

Those working in fusion forecast that fusion reactors will be operating commercially in 10 or 15 years. My own forecasting experience has shown that the predictions of scientists and technicians are systematically conservative. Thus I have taken it upon myself to predict commercial fusion reactors in eight or ten years. Little public thought has been given as to the ways in which fusion will be used. This article is an attempt to outline one way in which our new technologies may be combined with fusion energy to draw both energy and materials from the sea and from man's waste, this via the integration of several industrial functions which have been traditionally considered as separate domains.

Some Basic Aspects of Nuclear Fusion

Nuclear fission divides heavy atoms such as uranium and plutonium into lighter elements such as lead and helium and releases energy in the form of neutrons, protons, lighter radiations, and thermal energy. Nuclear fusion, on the other hand, fuses together light atoms such as deuterium, tritium, helium 3, and lithium into other elements or isotopes which are usually heavier than the elements which entered the reaction (often a heavier element can be transmuted into lighter elements; for example, a lithium 6 and a deuterium can combine to produce a helium 3, a helium 4, a proton, and much thermal energy). If the fusion reaction begins with two atoms of deuterium, elements and isotopes are produced which are themselves fusionable and enter into a chain of fusion reactions. Thus helium 3 and tritium, first-step products of deuterium + deuterium fusion, recombine with deuterium to produce helium 4, the stable gas. A plasma of virgin deuterium, then, becomes a mixed plasma of reacting elements. One of these elements, tritium, is radioactive. However, since tritium (with a half life of 11.3 years) is only a transitory phase of the deuterium-helium[3] reaction and will be present in only small quantities at any given time, the danger from leakage to the environment will be relatively small.

Fusion is very considerate of the environment. It produces no radioactive wastes. The reactor structure can be built of metals which will have a short radioactive life (measured in days). There is no possibility of explosion. If it is part of an industrial complex, the fusion reactor will create only a negligible amount of thermal "pollution" and will produce energy and fuels which can be transported to provide pollutionless power for many uses. This will encourage the saving of fossil chemicals for use in materials rather than spending these chemicals inappropriately as fuels. The prospect that fusion reaction could provide all of the planet's energy requirements in a practically pollutionless manner (except for the inevitable thermal pollution created by the user, which may even turn out to be beneficial), at relatively very low cost, and the present existence in science of a strong optimism about the success of fusion, make it mandatory that the development and use of this energy source be expedited.

Yet the industrial nations invest only a small amount of research and development in fusion and its applications ($29 million for 1971 in the U.S., whereas Skylab, for instance, cost $2.7 billion). The heavy investment in the existing fossil fuel industry, in the machinery which uses fossil fuels, and in fission reactor development is the immediate reason for the lack of interest in the development of fusion. However, the environmental crisis, on one hand (there is important evidence that the earth's cooling trend over the last 2,000 to 6,000 years, is accelerating very quickly; and the pollution problem), and, on the other, the great material benefits fusion can bring to a suffering world make it imperative that such a powerful and inexhaustible source of energy be developed to its utmost application, and soon.

Since containment of the fusion reaction (the last major problem remaining) has not yet been demonstrated, and the cost of building a reactor will depend significantly on the costs of containment and/or laser systems, the cost of a fusion reactor can only be roughly estimated as ranging from the equivalent cost to one-third less than the cost of a fission reactor of the same output. Deuterium is, for all practical purposes, in infinite supply. The reserves presently in the ocean will last between 2.7 and 45 billion years depending on the size and needs of the population.[2]

The deuterium can be very cheaply extracted from water by an automated process, each gallon producing deuterium equivalent to 300 gallons of gasoline in energy. Little or no storage will be required and the extraction will cost only an infinitesimally small percentage of the electrical output of the reactor. Thus the main costs will be the initial cost of the reactor and the initial cost of the distribution system, to which the cost of maintenance, depreciation, and replacement, plus interest on capital, must, of course, be added.

Fusion researchers have predicted commercial use of magnetically contained fusion in 10 or 15 years (although newer estimates, originating at policy-making levels, have increased this estimate to 30 years). This could be shortened to 8 to 10 years by according priority support to an organized program of concurrent scientific research and engineering toward an integrated industrial complex.[3] However, a newer approach to fusion energy is now being pursued. This is laser fusion, whereby a frozen pellet of fuel will be ignited to fusion reaction by lasers. In the U.S., Dr. Keith Brueckner of KMS Fusion, Inc. has predicted scientific proof of feasibility for this method in the immediate future.

Energy Requirements of the World Population

The requirements for energy in different regions vary in accord with factors such as climate, cultural practices, beliefs and values, population, physical geography, and religion. On the other hand, some anthropological studies show that when the industrial culture comes in contact with nontechnological cultures, the latter accept the technology, life styles, beliefs, and values of the former. Man's need for security, greater efficiency, stimulation, and comfort leads him to accept the innovations of industrial culture. Thus I am assuming that all peoples will want energy and, arbitrarily, for lack of another simple criterion, that they will want the same

[2]Information on fuel resources is taken from Gough, W.C., and Eastland, B.J., "The Prospects of Fusion Power," *Scientific American*, February 1971.
[3]Discussion with Dr. Richard F. Post, Lawrence Livermore Laboratory.

amount of energy per capita as is enjoyed in the United States.[4]

The *Annual Report* of the U.S. Federal Power Commission for 1971 states that the total U.S. production of electricity for the year ending November 1971 was 1,718 billion kilowatt hours (kwh). Based on the U.S. population of 210 million, the per capita consumption was slightly over 8,000 kwh per year. This per capita figure can be used as a world goal indicative of a much higher material quality of life, but it is patently misleading as a measure of energy requirements when we consider that automotive vehicles, factories, mines, railroads, ships, farms, and aircraft use much energy in the form of fossil fuels rather than electricity, that environmental considerations will not allow the expanded use of these fuels as a large part of the energy economy, and that the expanded use of these fuels will only deplete them faster. Fusion energy, or fission energy, as electricity, direct heat, or stored as hydrogen or sodium, will soon have to replace the fossilized carbon chemicals for all energy purposes as the fast-growing organic chemistry industries require greater amounts of this large group of carbon-based molecules.

Based on this reasoning, it is more logical to determine the total amount of fossil-derived energy produced for all purposes (including electricity) in the United States, convert these sources to electrical terms, and use the total per capita figure as our world goal. Thus we find that the *total* amount of energy produced from anthracite coal, bituminous coal and lignite, crude petroleum, and natural gas in the United States during 1971 was equal to 18,250 billion kwh (hydroelectric and nuclear fission energy and the energy derived from industrial explosives totaled slightly over 323 billion additional kwh, but we will not count this, as these sources are not likely to be replaced by fusion in the near future). Based on this expended energy, the per capita consumption was 86,904 kwh, over 10 times the energy produced as electricity alone.

Rounding off our per capita world energy goal to 87,000 kilowatt hours per year, we can use it both minimally and maximally to determine the range of energy requirements during the next 30 years of population growth. The present population is about 3.7 billion. Since the immediate industrialization of the world is impossible, we will assume that world industrialization will be possible at about the time the population reaches 4 billion, an optimistic assumption. Such a population will require 348

---

[4]There are many electrical uses and conveniences which are not yet commonly used in the United States. The acceptance and use of new electrical technology will increase the per capita electrical consumption in the U.S. Nevertheless, electrical distribution and utilization in the U.S. leaves much room for efficiency. New techniques and materials (e.g., electroluminescence, superconducters, more efficient electromechanical machinery, etc.) will tend to reduce the per capita consumption of energy if it is the will of industry to do so.

trillion kwh of energy per year if we are to fulfill our goal of 87,000 kwh per year per individual. The fusion reactors required to produce such a quantity of energy will have a power capacity of 41 billion kilowatts. The costing of this energy is considered in the section on economics.

Some Considerations of Environment and Alternative Energy Sources

Those who are persuaded that human growth must be limited soon will be concerned with the encroachment of the required amount of fusion energy on the environment. Given any stable population, this amount of energy, powering the kind of integrated factory system described below, will be theoretically able to support this population at any reasonable level of wealth merely by recycling all waste. Thus all chemical pollution can be eliminated. Even the use of land for manufacturing and agriculture will be minimized by the integrated factory. The thermal pollution produced by the integrated factory can be shown to be well within the limits of toleration by the following considerations: the earth receives 13×10^{23} calories of radiant energy from the sun annually, of which 46 percent, or 5.98×10^{23} calories reach the earth's surface.[5] Converted to kilowatt hours, the solar energy reaching the surface is equal to $69,499 \times 10^{16}$ kwh annually. At the 1971 rate of total energy production in the United States, a world population of 4 billion would require the equivalent of .00005 percent (348 trillion kwh) of the solar energy reaching the earth's surface annually. This is a small proportion, and even a theoretical population of a hundred billion would release a tolerable amount of thermal "pollution" to the environment (.00125 percent of the annual solar flux).

The Multifarious Problem

A shortage of fresh water will make itself felt in the populated regions of the earth within a few decades. Fresh water, as a biological imperative, appears to be mankind's greatest potential problem. Nevertheless, other important problems also require attention; it appears that all of them may be subject to alleviation or solution through an integrated approach.

In addition to a worldwide water shortage, we are faced with a strong trend toward a colder climate. Some geologists and climatologists have predicted either a Little Ice Age such as occurred in the latter parts of the

[5] *Encyclopaedia Britannica,* 1968, vol. 15, p. 281.

16th and 17th centuries (causing famine), or a major ice age lasting many millenia.[6] A major ice age is thousands of years overdue if we accept the geological evidence for warm and cold periods, each lasting about 10,000 years. Such a climatic change would occur within a hundred years, would lower the temperature of the whole earth, and would cause thick glaciers extending down, perhaps, to the 35th latitude. Agriculture would be restricted to the relatively small land masses of the middle latitudes. (The cooling climate would counteract the impending water shortage, certainly within 20 years.) Other problems of great importance are the unreliability of weather, even during a warm age, and the constant impact of this factor on human life support; the growing awareness of wealth among the poor of this world and the exploding need for energy and materials in this vast majority of the population; and the variety of pollutions produced by the immature and inefficient modes of contemporary industry.

The method of attacking problems in science, industry, and government has evolved strongly in the direction of specialization. This is all well and good, except for the fact that each discipline offers solutions from its own orientation. We are left with a chaos of solutions, a great many of which fall into conflict with other solutions. This increases the overall problem rather than reducing it. The industries and institutions created by such solutions, if not operating at a significant degree of cross-purpose, are inherently inefficient because they usually produce waste material or energy which cannot economically be used by other processes. It can be argued that an integrated (efficient) life-support system will bring an area of sterility into the culture and will further circumscribe man's freedom by limiting his diversity. It can be argued from psychology, however, that material wealth will increase man's freedom and creativity. Much research remains in the areas of projected needs of the world's regions before a design for an integrated world production capability for fresh water, minerals, and energy production and distribution can be attempted. Political and cultural considerations may prove to be as important as those of material need, and flexibility must be the structural rule as oncoming technological innovation seeks to integrate with the original design.

Mineral Resources and Requirements

The substance of greatest concern to life on earth is fresh water. In many areas of the United States, agriculture and urban population concentrations

<hr>

[6] Hays, J.D., "The Ice Age Cometh," *Saturday Review of the Sciences*, vol. 1, no.3 (April 1973).

have long ago depleted their local water supplies. In agricultural areas, wells have often lowered the water table by hundreds of feet, whereas the large metropolitan areas must divert water from rivers and will soon run out of wilderness areas which they are now using as watersheds. As these sources are depleted, the pollution of remaining sources of water is accomplished through sewage, industrial waste, mining concentration, and the intrusion of seawater as fresh water is pumped from groundwater systems. The study prepared by the Food and Agriculture Organization of the United Nations for the U.N. Conference on the Environment in June 1972 reports that a severe shortage of water can occur over the world within a few decades. This report states that the desalinization of seawater is too expensive as a solution to the freshwater crisis. A number of conservation policies and plans are proposed which are in the tradition of efficient management of existing resources. One of the most innovative of these plans is proposed by the Greek regional planner Constantinos A. Doxiadis. This would seek to concentrate 19 billion people on about five per cent of the earth's habitable surface. Forty-five percent of the surface would become the earth's agricultural area, with a population of two billion. Half the land surface would serve as a natural watershed and would be virtually uninhabited.

This plan is drastic in its treatment of people and in its restriction of freedom. Perhaps too much emphasis is placed on the economic cost of desalinating salt water as against the human costs. The cost of producing fresh water from the oceans can be reduced by the concomitant extraction of elements which are separated from the water, by the materials and manufactured wealth produced from these elements in the industrial complex, and by the food which can be grown hydroponically (algae or vegetables) within the industrial complex and horticulturally on farmland which is integrated into the complex so as to derive the most benefit from the water, chemicals, electricity, and the low-grade heat produced.

The production of basic products such as electricity, fresh water, chemicals, and thermal energy by nuclear fusion would possibly be economically feasible each in its own right. The integrated and interdependent production of basic products and of the second order of manufactured goods will make this system extremely feasible in the sense of conserving investment, labor, and ongoing costs.

All of the earth's resources are bound by the chemical law of conservation of matter. So long as nuclear processes do not alter the atomic structure of our chemicals, the earth's wealth will remain intact and will be subject to recycling. Thus the oceans can be viewed as a huge sink from which chemicals can be taken and in which they will be replaced by natural processes of recycling. It is easy to see how fresh water is returned to the sea in sewage, runoff, and seepage through the continental sedimentation.

This process is also largely responsible for the original mineralization of the oceans and for the future recycling of many of the minerals to be extracted. Contemporary theory holds that the crust of the earth is mainly basalt, a rock which does not have a rich variety or quantity of industrially significant minerals. The continents (high granitic features of the crust) contain the variety of minerals that have been most accessible to man. Thus the minerals in the oceans are basically those which belong to the ocean floor or have been dissolved from these deposits, as well as minerals which have been washed or leached from the exposed portions of the continents and which are either deposited on the ocean bottoms or are in suspension or solution. Thus a very large reserve of minerals, including highly soluble minerals, remains on the ocean bottoms. Should nuclear fusion be used to extract minerals from the ocean solution, these minerals would be replenished to the solution from the sediments on the bottom or directly from the continental runoff. The main problem is the distribution of chemicals in the ocean solution. While there are 49.5 million tons of sodium and 6.4 million tons of magnesium per cubic mile of ocean solution, there are only 47 tons each of iron, aluminum, molybdenum, and zinc; 14 tons each of copper, tin, uranium, and arsenic; nine tons each of nickel, vanadium, and manganese; five tons of titanium (a metal of increasing importance which may be difficult to replace with other metals or alloys); two tons each of antimony, cobalt, caesium, and cerium; and half a ton or less of the important metals tungsten, cadmium, lead, mercury, and bismuth. Lithium, which may be necessary to the fusion process, is found in the ocean solution at 800 tons per cubic mile. On the other hand, the ocean solution contains 89.5 million tons of highly corrosive and toxic chlorine per cubic mile. Other active elements, sodium (49.5 million tons), calcium (1.9 million tons), potassium (1.8 million tons), bromine (306,000 tons), fluorine (6,100 tons), and iodine (280 tons) are present in considerable quantities (see Table 3.1). Some of the active elements are of special interest because they represent auxiliary sources of energy which may be used in portable power plants or for transportation. Thus what appears to be a surplus of dangerous chlorine and sodium may be recombined to provide useful energy, and the resultant salt recycled into the sea.

Sodium, as we have seen above, is the most abundant metal in the ocean solution. Although its structural qualities are insufficient to make sodium a serious competitor with magnesium, for instance, its electrical conductivity ranks third among the metals (by cross-section, sodium is a poorer conductor than copper by a factor of 2.5, a better conductor than iron by a factor of 3.23, and better than steel by a factor of 4.62). Protected from oxidation by a coating, sodium can provide the least expensive means of distributing the electrical energy generated by fusion.

TABLE 3.1

CONCENTRATION AND AMOUNTS OF 60 OF THE ELEMENTS IN SEAWATER

Elements	Concentration (mg/l)	Amount of element in seawater (tons/mile³)	Total amount in the oceans (tons)	Amount of element extracted to produce the world's requirement of fresh water for 1 year (tons/year)		Percent of world requirements for industrially important elements to be extracted as a by-product of fresh water in 1 year
				(4 billion pop. 2717.43 miles³)	(7 billion pop. 4755.51 miles³)	
Chlorine	19,000.0	89.5×10^6	29.3×10^{15}	$212,808.5 \times 10^6$	$425,617.3 \times 10^6$	inexhaustible
Sodium	10,500.0	49.5×10^6	16.3×10^{15}	$134,411.9 \times 10^6$	$235,397.3 \times 10^6$	inexhaustible
Magnesium	1,350.0	6.4×10^6	2.1×10^{15}	$17,378.5 \times 10^6$	$30,435.2 \times 10^6$	895,664.0
Sulphur	885.0	4.2×10^6	1.4×10^{15}	$11,404.6 \times 10^6$	$19,973.1 \times 10^6$	5,472.0
Calcium	400.0	1.9×10^6	0.6×10^{15}	$5,159.3 \times 10^6$	$9,035.5 \times 10^6$	inexhaustible
Potassium	380.0	1.8×10^6	0.6×10^{15}	$4,887.7 \times 10^6$	$8,559.9 \times 10^6$	inexhaustible
Bromine	65.0	306,000.0	0.1×10^{15}	830,909,493	1,455,183,000.0	
Carbon	28.0	132,000.0	0.04×10^{15}	358,431,546	627,726,000.0	
Strontium	8.0	38,000.0	$12,000.0 \times 10^9$	103,184,839	180,709,000.0	
Boron	4.6	23,000.0	$7,100.0 \times 10^9$	62,453,981.5	109,376,500.0	
Silicon	3.0	14,000.0	$4,700.0 \times 10^9$	38,015,467.0	66,577,000.0	
Fluorine	1.3	6,100.0	$2,000.0 \times 10^9$	16,563,882.1	29,008,550.0	
Argon	0.6	2,800.0	930.0×10^9	7,603,093.4	13,315,400.0	
Nitrogen	0.5	2,400.0	780.0×10^9	6,516,937.2	11,413,200.0	
Lithium	0.17	800.0	260.0×10^9	2,172,312.4	3,804,400.0	
Rubidium	0.12	570.0	190.0×10^9	1,547,772.59	2,710,635.0	
Phosphorus	0.07	330.0	110.0×10^9	896,078.87	1,569,315.0	
Iodine	0.06	280.0	93.0×10^9	760,309.34	1,331,540.0	
Barium	0.03	140.0	47.0×10^9	380,154.67	665,770.0	
Indium	0.02	94.0	31.0×10^9	255,244.99	447,014.0	
Zinc	0.01	47.0	16.0×10^9	127,623.35	223,508.5	0.684
Iron	0.01	47.0	16.0×10^9	127,623.35	223,508.5	.007
Aluminum	0.01	47.0	16.0×10^9	127,623.35	223,508.5	0.14
Molybdenum	0.01	47.0	16.0×10^9	127,623.35	223,508.5	17.2
Selenium	0.004	19.0	6.0×10^9	51,592.42	90,354.5	
Tin	0.003	14.0	5.0×10^9	38,015.467	66,577.0	2.38
Copper	0.003	14.0	5.0×10^9	38,015.467	66,577.0	1.1
Arsenic	0.003	14.0	5.0×10^9	38,015.467	66,577.0	
Uranium	0.003	14.0	5.0×10^9	38,015.467	66,577.0	
Nickel	0.002	9.0	3.0×10^9	24,438.516	42,799.5	
Vanadium	0.002	9.0	3.0×10^9	24,438.516	42,799.5	.8
Manganese	0.002	9.0	3.0×10^9	24,438.516	42,799.5	22.58
Titanium	0.001	5.0	1.5×10^9	13,576.952	23,777.5	
Antimony	0.0005	2.0	0.8×10^9	5,430.781	9,511.0	
Cobalt	0.0005	2.0	0.8×10^9	5,430.781	9,511.0	

The oceans contain an inexhaustible supply of hydrogen and oxygen, which could be used to power the conventional internal combustion engine. They are actually better suited for this purpose than are the petroleum distillates, both from engineering and environmental considerations. Thus the active chemicals may be viewed as stored energy which can be utilized for a diversity of purposes. Fusion can make this energy available. If sufficient energy is available, in-solution mining of minerals appears to hold great mechanical and political advantages over ocean-floor mining.

It is true that the proportions of the chemicals provided by the ocean solution do not match the proportions in which man presently consumes these chemicals. Thus in the steel age we find that in-solution mining will yield over one and a third million tons of magnesium for every ton of iron. At first glance, it appears that the oceans will not provide the materials required by the steel age without a tremendous investment of energy and extraction equipment. On second thought, however, it seems more likely that the steel age will give way to an age of magnesium and plastics, and that magnesium alloys or plastics can perform most of the functions of steel more efficiently and effectively. Presently important chemicals such as tungsten, chromium, titanium, nickel, vanadium, and manganese occur at proportions of only a half ton or less to nine tons of metal per cubic mile of water. Nevertheless, integration and the low cost of energy will be such as to make the extraction of these metals "economical." It is not important to belabor the proportions of materials available in seawater anyway, as long as these materials remain available from recycling "waste" via the fusion flame, conventional mining operations, and as seabed deposits (for example, the red clay, 200 meters thick on the ocean bottoms, contains easily available iron, manganese, silicon and other metals; and the silicous and calcarious oozes, also plentiful and easily available, can yield much carbon and an excess of silicon and calcium). The extraction of minerals might be considered as a mere by-product of the processing of seawater. The amount of seawater to be processed possibly should be determined at first by the amount of fresh water required for life, comfort, recreation, and esthetic needs.

To determine the amount of water required by the world population, let us first consider the water requirements of the United States. The United States is used as a model because this highly industrialized and agricultural country is also lavish in its use of water by the individual. More water is processed through the distribution system of the United States than is distributed in any other industrially developed area of the world, and more water is consumed per capita. Thus in 1960, 270,000 mgd (million gallons of water per day) entered the distribution system, with 68,000 mgd actually consumed by evaporation and leakage. Assuming that the same rate of loss will continue, it was estimated that 559,000 mgd would be required in 1980 and 888,000 mgd would be required by the year 2000.[7] From these figures, it is calculated that the 1970 requirement for water of a population of 206,000,000 was at the rate of 414,500 mgd, or 2,012 gallons (269 cubic feet) per individual each day (this comes to a United States total of 137 cubic miles of water for the year). In 1970 each person used 98,252 cubic feet of water for the year. Let us round this figure off to 100,000 ft^3 per capita per year and use it as a consumption goal for the world population. With rising efficiencies of water distribution methods and by using existing water sources, withdrawals of a 100,000 cubic feet per capita of fusion distilled water per year should provide the world population with a theoretical surplus of water, which could irrigate large areas of desert and provide much water recreation to inland areas.

For the amount of fresh water we are discussing, a world population of four to seven billion will also extract a large bonus in minerals. The first four columns of Table 3.1 are reproduced from a table found in J. L. Mero's book, *The Mineral Resources of the Sea.*[8] The original source of the data is E. D. Goldberg's "The Oceans as a Chemical System," in *The Seas, Ideas and Observations on Progress in the Study of the Seas.*[9] Goldberg cautions that the table has deficiencies, in that many of the values given are for a single set of analyses of surface water and that it is not safe to assume that this proportion is representative of the average ocean concentration. For our purpose, however, the table is admirable. The fifth column lists the amounts of each of 60 elements available in the salts separated from the fresh water required in one year, both by the four billion population and the projected seven billion population. The sixth column lists the yearly percentage of world requirements provided by column five (for any size of population). Again, since the United States is a great and inefficient consumer of materials, the world requirements derived from the per capita consumption of the United States in 1970 represent a generous calculation.[10] The formula for world requirements implies that the U.S. consumption rate is a goal for the rest of the world. It is admitted that this is an arbitrary goal and that there are sources of inaccuracy. Will tropical countries require as much lead, for instance, even for a high quality of life? To what degree will efficient usage and recycling contribute toward meeting the require-

[7]Piper, A.M., *Has the United States Enough Water?*, Washington, D.C.: U.S. Government Printing Office, 1965.
[8]New York: Elsevier, 1965.
[9]Vol. 2, ed. M. N. Hill, E. D. Goldberg, C.O'D. Iselin, and W. H. Munk, New York: Wiley, 1963.
[10]*Statistical Abstract of the United States, 1971,* United States Department of Commerce, Bureau of the Census—Minerals, Washington, D.C.:U.S. Government Printing Office, 1971.

ments in the future (ecological concern is forcing a greater effort in the area)? How will fast-changing technology affect material requirements? These questions can and should be studied; the human resources, however, were not available for this article. Thus the simplified method for arriving at the figures in column six of Table 3.1 is:

$$\frac{X \text{ (tons required by a pop. of 7 billion}}{} = \frac{U. \ S. \ consumption. \quad \bullet \quad 7 \ billion}{206,000,000 \ (1970 \ U.S. \ pop.)}$$

number in fifth column • 100 = % world requirements produced as a by-product of fresh water in one year

If the world's main supply of fresh water were to come from the oceans, a number of the by-products that are separable from sea salt via the energy of the fusion torch are immediately seen to be of great industrial significance.[11] Beginning from the top of Table 3.1, the amount of salt produced in a year would be far beyond the world's needs, either as the salt or as the elements. The large surplus of the active elements chlorine and sodium could be useful in providing energy for portable power plants or for transportation. In situations where it is desirable—in rocketry or welding, for instance—the structural and fuel characteristics of sodium can be combined into very efficient mechanisms. Also extremely useful as a nonpolluting energy source is liquefied hydrogen, which can be extracted in huge amounts from fresh water (rather than as a by-product).

The present use of elements in industry is governed by the availability, as well as by the discovery, of valuable properties in the elements. The huge increase in the world's supplies of magnesium, sulphur, calcium, potassium, bromine, carbon, strontium, and boron, and the sizeable increase in supplies of fluorine, argon, nitrogen, lithium rubidium, phosphorous, and iodine all promise the creation of new industries and a higher quality of life. Perhaps the most important and dramatic increase will be that of the availability of magnesium. Magnesium is adaptable to all ways of forming and, in architecture for instance, can easily be formed into integral shapes to provide structural, membranous, conducting (fluids, air conditioning, electricity), insulating, and decorative functions in a unified manner. The characteristics of magnesium make it adaptable to skyscrapers, bridges, aircraft, and even the working parts of machinery (magnesium alloys are used in rocker arms, push rods, pistons, heads, and blocks of high-performance engines). Where hardness is required for wear purposes, hard metals are alloyed, inserted, or plated on. The structural and mechanical properties of magnesium alloys (essentially strength and lightness) are so favorable that the decline of the

[11]The fusion torch concept was proposed by Bernard J. Eastlund and William Gough in "The Fusion Torch: Closing the Cycle from Use to Reuse," Division of Research, U.S. Atomic Energy Commission, May 15, 1969.

iron age and the swift beginning of the magnesium age are predictable as soon as the deuterium-fueled ocean regime energy and materials factory becomes a fact. Thus the projected yearly production of 30,435.2 million tons of magnesium for a world population of seven billion is over six times the 4,771.4 million tons of structural and mechanical metals (steel, aluminum, magnesium) projected for the same population from the 1970 United States production statistics. The huge surplus of magnesium will thus find new applications such as are now being fulfilled by plastics, wood, plaster, and masonry.

Toward the end of Table 3.1 are the less soluble elements. Except for chromium, lead, and mercury, these elements are rare on land as well as in the ocean solution. Thus, a large use having developed for lead, which is in fair supply, the ocean solution will yield only .001 percent of the projected requirements. Gold is scarce regardless of the source, and the tonnage which will be yielded each year as a by-product of fresh water will be 1.14 percent of the established world requirement. The in-solution yield of metals such as gallium, scandium, and niobium may allow expanded uses when a small but reliable source such as we are talking about is developed.

Carbon and organic chemicals are also plentiful in the oceans—not only in solution, but in suspension as particulate matter and as algae, plankton, and microbes. Thus the 132,000 tons of dissolved carbon in each cubic mile is only a small part of the substantial resource. Low-temperature distillation, centrifuging, and other techniques will be able to extract a large variety of organic compounds, including high-grade proteins, in significant amounts. Again, extraction at the rate of 4,756 cubic miles per year will not affect the 330-million-cubic-miles ocean ecology appreciably (.0014 percent).

In addition to the necessary reliable source of fresh water required by a large world population if it is to avoid the permanent drought that is predicted (if an ice age does not make itself felt first), the ocean solution yields about 166 million tons of solids for each cubic mile of water, and these chemicals are either already valuable or potentially valuable. Assuming that all of the solids taken from the ocean will be used by industry (a generous assumption, since most of the vast amount of sodium chloride will probably be put back in the ocean), man will be borrowing approximately 789,413 million tons of minerals from the ocean per year for a doubled population. This amount is indeed small, since the oceans have some 5×10^{16} tons of mineral matter in solution, about 1 percent of the minerals currently involved in the sedimentary cycle. The amount of dissolved minerals transported to the oceans via rivers, streams, and ground water is about 250×10^{14}g (250 microgeograms) per year.[12] (A microgeogram is equivalent to .5 km^3 or .3 mile^3 in volume, or over 25×10^9 tons

[12]Garrels, R.M., and MacKenzie, F.T., *Evolution of Sedimentary Rocks,* New York: Norton, 1971, pp. 98, 103.

of mineral material.) The 789,413 tons of chemicals borrowed from the ocean yearly amounts to less than four thousandths of a percent of the amount of chemicals transported annually to the ocean. Thus we need not fear that man's needs will alter the balance of the ocean solution except in transient and local ways. Whereas man's efforts at dry-land mining can deface the surface of the land and cause further erosion and ecological change, he will not be able to affect the ecology of the oceans or the geology of the planet to any noticeable degree through in-solution mining.

The Ocean Regime Energy, Fresh Water, Materials, and Transportation Factory (the Integrated Factory)

An integrated factory that is automated, constructed to resist breakdowns, powered by free and inexhaustible fuel, able to extract its own raw materials from the ocean and from the total waste of the civilization which it serves, and is capable of producing the complete array of industrial output with which we are now familiar is also capable of reproducing itself—theoretically at no cost except for transportation of the new factory to its site and its assembly there. This factory is well within the capacity of present-day technology and awaits only its source of power, the fusion reactor.

We must think of more than just energy production. Integration of automated industrial processes will, in turn, create new fusion reactors at little cost, and the costs of the fusion reactors which have been calculated in Table 3.2 can be virtually wiped out, regardless of the size of the population for which we are building. Integration and automation, to the degree that we create an organism which can reproduce itself from the stuff which it extracts from its environment, is technologically feasible today.

If man processes only that amount of seawater required for fresh water, it appears that metals such as manganese, which are currently important as alloying metals, will not be produced in sufficient quantities unless the magnesium and plastic age decreases the requirement for them. One alternative, to meet the possible need, is to process more seawater than is required for the world's freshwater supply. Another alternative is to use the energy produced by the fusion reactor, possibly in the form of hydrogen or sodium and chlorine, to mine the ocean bottoms. The first alternative can be realized via simple automation and virtually costless energy, despite the huge amount of water that must be processed for the extraction of these specific metals. The second alternative requires exploration, complex machinery to operate at depths below the 12,000 feet which are anticipated, portable power plants, and vessels to transport the mineral to land, where it must be processed further. It will take a closer examination than I am

TABLE 3.2

COST OF FUSION REACTORS TO THE WORLD UNDER VARIABLES
OF POPULATION AND MODE OF ENERGY USE

	Population of 4 Billion	Population of 7 Billion
At the rate of 1971 electrical production in the U.S. (8000 kwh per capita/year)	$767.5 billion ($511.2 billion)*	$1.3 trillion ($865 billion)*
At the rate of 1971 production of all major forms of energy in the U.S. (87,000 kwh per capita/year)	$8.2 trillion ($5.6 trillion)*	$14.35 trillion ($9.6 trillion)*

*According to Dr. Richard F. Post's cost estimate.

presently capable of to make a concrete decision between the two alternatives. It may be more efficient in effort and resources to process mind-boggling amounts of ocean solution by using equally fantastic amounts of very cheap automated energy. It is quite probable, also, that technology can adjust itself to do without large amounts of those metals which are extremely dilute in the ocean solution.

The Industrial Process.

The integrated factory (Figure 3.1) is tentatively seen as follows. Sea water will be pumped through the fusion reactor and brought to superheated temperatures as a coolant. The superheated water will then be piped to the freshwater condenser and mineral concentrator for conversion into fresh water and mineral concentrate (sea salt). If a greater output of either water or mineral concentrate is required, additional sea water will be processed through the use of surplus electricity where possible (via membrane osmosis, electrolysis, or distillation). The fresh water will be used in two ways: first, by direct distribution to the consumer, and second, for on-site hydroponic application. It seems probable (made mandatory either by the projected population growth, the predicted freshwater shortage, or the predicted little, or major, ice age) that hydroponic food production will be required because of its highly efficient use of water, chemicals, and space and the ability to force faster growth through the control of conditions.

Fresh water will be rechemicalized to hydroponic specifications. This water will then be used for applications such as the continuous-function

algae plant and forced-growth vegetable and fruit factories. As the hydroponic capacities grow and the need for basic foods is fulfilled, increasing
production will be in the area of the more luxurious foods. The food
products can be processed and packaged on the site. As the conditions of
climate and population become stringent, the growth of meat animals will
become less efficient and the production of meat substitutes from sources
such as factory-grown soy beans, algae, and fungi will increase. Other
important sources of food will be the direct extraction of food chemicals
from the seawater intake and the direct chemical synthesis of foods.

Sidney Holt has brought to my attention a proposed method for producing high-protein food, which appears to be feasible. The idea grew out
of work by John D. Isaacs of the Scripps Institution of Oceanography.
Low-grade heat from a reactor is piped into a small area of the ocean. The
release of warm water creates an upwelling volume of water, which has the
boundary qualities of a vortex. The stirred-up nutrients and energy in this
volume of water produce algae and therefore zooplankton and the fish
which feed on these organisms. This creates a marine food farm which is
harvested by pumping and filtering high-protein soup as intake for the
plant. A secondary benefit is the higher saturation of chemicals in the warm
waters of the upwelling and the fact that the current of warm water constantly sweeps over and dissolves, or suspends, the minerals of sites which
could be selected for their deposits of manganese or other chemicals.

The chemical concentrate can be separated into the required elements,
compounds, and mixtures by various processes. The primary source of
elemental atoms will most likely be the process of fractional distillation,
using the high heats supplied by Eastlund and Gough's fusion torch. Electricity and lower heats can be used for the separation of chemicals via
chemical reactions, crystallization, polymer resin processes, and electrolysis. The injection of impurities into the hot plasma of the reactor will
produce photons capable of producing hydrogen from water at very low
cost. The chemical concentrate from seawater is notably low in a number
of important elements such as iron; thus, although the magnesium, sodium,
sulfur, and carbon compounds taken from seawater will go a long way
toward replacing iron and other materials in many of their functions, the
fusion reactor can recycle all of man's waste into many of those chemicals
which are scarce in seawater. Much of this waste will have to be transported
from the sites of use. However, by the very fact of the integration of
production processes, many chemicals which today are released as waste
will be recycled on the site.

The materials and energy required by industry will be present together
at one site. Nothing will be more efficient than to combine these via automated and integrated processes into the manufactured consumer goods on

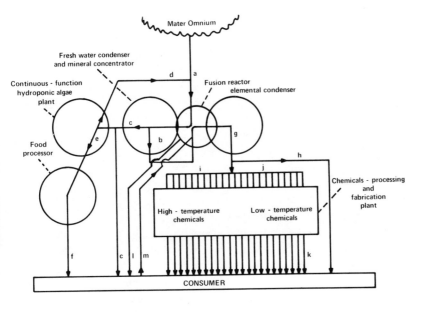

Mater Omnium

Fresh water condenser
and mineral concentrator

Continuous - function
hydroponic algae
plant

Food
processor

Fusion reactor
elemental condenser

d   a

c

e   b   g

h

i   j

Chemicals - processing
and
fabrication
plant

High - temperature
chemicals

Low - temperature
chemicals

f   c l m   k

CONSUMER

a   Seawater, used as reactor coolant, then condensed into
    fresh water and mineral concentrate.
b   Mineral concentrate is atomized in fusion flame, then
    fractionally condensed in elemental condenser.
c   Fresh water to consumer and to continuous - function
    hydroponic algae plant, where it is mineralized for
    hydroponic use.
d   Used hydroponic water is cycled back into seawater supply.
e   Algae to food processor.
f   Processed and semi-processed foods to consumer.
g   Elemental chemicals to consumer or further processing.
h   Elemental chemicals to consumer.
i   High - temperature elemental chemicals to high - temperature
    processing and fabrication.
j   Low - temperature elemental chemicals to low - temperature
    processing.
k   Processed and fabricated materials to consumer or further
    processing.
l   Electricity to consumer.
m   Used materials from consumer to fusion flame for recycling.

Fig. 3.1   Simplified model of an ocean regime energy and materials factory

67

the same site. This portion of the integrated factory (the Chemicals Processing and Fabrication Plant, Figure 3.1) is represented in Figure 3.2 and shows the interlocking of industrial processes and the means of recycling waste within the complex.

The integrated factory must transport electricity and quite possibly, other forms of energy such as hydrogen or sodium; fresh water; bulk chemicals such as salt, fertilizers, food concentrates, and plastics; foods; and manufactured consumer products. These must go from the integrated factory to the consumer, and transportation must be provided for the recycling of the consumer's waste back to the factory. All of these products must follow a common direction in order to reach their destination; it is also probable that the direction of the individual's travels through his region will coincide. The logical expansion of the integrated factory will therefore be a transportation network for electricity, fluids in large volume, bulk, and people. Again, it seems only logical to design an integrated system for this purpose. Such a system will include a bus bar for the more efficient distribution of electricity, large diameter pipe for fresh water, and a monorail (or similar structure) train system for human and bulk transportation. In regions with cold climates it may be more effective for the factory to produce massive amounts of hydrogen which can be piped to various centers of the region in liquefied form. Burning this hydrogen will provide energy (heat and electricity) and water (the combustion product) for the population. In cold climates the waste heat from hydrogen combustion plants or engines may have positive values. The use of the hydrogen system could make conduits for electricity and water unnecessary.

Creation of a World System of Integrated Factories.

How does a system of integrated factories come into being? Two basic requirements must be met before such a system can enter the planning and building phases. The first of these is a high level of confidence in the achievement of a feasible fusion reaction. At present, this confidence is very high. The conservative estimate of scientists working in the field is that magnetically contained fusion will be proven feasible between 1975 and 1980, and laser-induced fusion may prove scientifically feasible even sooner.

The second requirement is the organization of sufficient resources to build one all-purpose or multi-purpose integrated factory. Such a factory will be so automated and programmed as to replicate itself, and each of its offspring will be similarly capable. Thus the resources of the organization need be large enough only to plan and build one integrated factory and to plan and redesign subsequent factories so as to make them most suitable for the regions in which they will be operating.

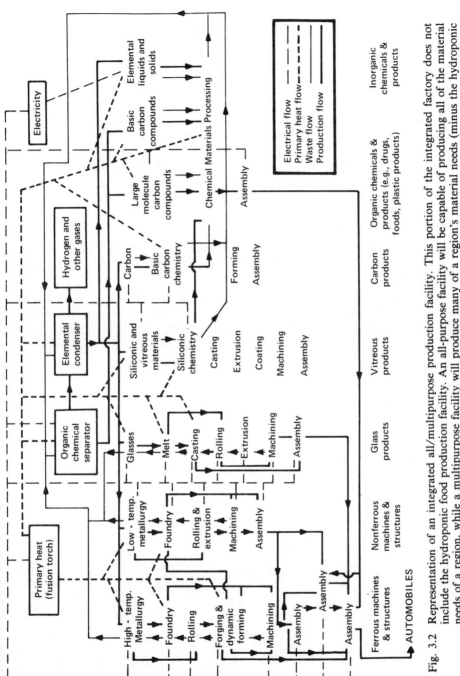

Fig. 3.2 Representation of an integrated all/multipurpose production facility. This portion of the integrated factory does not include the hydroponic food production facility. An all-purpose facility will be capable of producing all of the material needs of a region, while a multipurpose facility will produce many of a region's material needs (minus the hydroponic foods but including synthetic foods). The processes shown are for a single product, an automobile.

69

Unfortunately the industrial world has a vested interest in existing production facilities, research effort, and tradition. At the present time, the investment in fast-breeder fission reactors is so great that the sponsors of fission technology are wedded to it despite the enormous danger inherent in it. This situation makes the major industrial powers uninterested in a world organization for the integrated factory. Such an organization must therefore be formed by the developing nations. Although individually, each nation of the developing world would have to sustain an extremely heavy burden on its resources if such an attempt should be made to develop and build an integrated factory, an organization of several developing nations could afford the resources for one replicating factory with only a moderate investment on the part of each. However, should the industrial powers decide that the threat of either a little ice age or a major one, or the threat of a worldwide drought, are sufficient to overcome the concern for existing investment, their membership in an organization for the integrated factory would greatly increase the speed with which this type of factory could be distributed over the world.

If fusion became operational in the near future and if there existed a world organization for the development and construction of the integrated factory, planning and design could begin immediately. The design of the reactor and of the integrated factory could, in fact, be accomplished concomitantly with the remaining work in fusion by completing and using existing nuclear and industrial technology and by starting research on regional needs; best factory sites; hydroponic, synthetic, and ocean grown foods; and distribution-transportation networks. Since most of the technological knowledge and design already exists, a small group of nuclear engineers and a group of 200 engineers working on the industrial processes and their integration should be able to develop and build the first self-replicating factory in a relatively short time. An effort begun in 1974 should reach experimental completion about 1979–81. If the factories are fully automated and programmed for self-replication, a schedule of factory installations, at the rate of one replication per factory per year, could be a geometric progression, as follows:

1979	1 factory
1980	2 factories
1981	4 "
1982	8 "
1983	16 "
1990	2,048 factories

The number of factories required cannot be calculated until more is known about the production and distribution efficiency of large versus small factories, population distributions, cultural and climatically determined needs, and physical geography. Large factories should be able to replicate themselves at the same rate as smaller factories and may be more desirable, because a greater production capacity would be built in a shorter time. On the other hand, if available resources are limited, smaller factories may be called for during the early phases of construction, and the development of a high level of world productivity will be delayed.

Another problem is that of skilled workers for assembling the factories. Where labor is available at lesser cost, it may be more economical in time and money to rely on labor rather than on automatic building devices. If such is the case, a geometrically expanding skilled labor force will be required. This labor can be recruited from the regions in which the factories are being built, but each new crew can best receive its training on the sites of previous factory construction. Thus each construction site may also be a training site.

Economics of the Project

It has been estimated that a nuclear fusion plant will cost about the same as a nuclear fission plant of the same capacity. This figure is much too high, however, for a number of reasons. To begin with, it is based on the cost of a fission reactor, which is one of a few and is unique in much of its design and construction. Had a hundred such reactors been built to the same plans and by factory methods, the cost of each would probably be considerably lower than, for example, that of the San Onofre reactor. What is more, the research and development costs which were calculated into the cost of the San Onofre plant have not been spread over any plants; but the prototype and the chargeable research and development cost may have been as high as 20 percent of the total. Another factor in cost reduction will be that a greater density of the population will increase the efficiency of electrical distribution and use. A doubled population will probably increase population densities (due to man's communal needs) and will thus require a smaller per capita investment in fusion reactors. Last but not least, the integration of industrial machinery and processes with each other and with the fusion reactor will make the integrated factory much more efficient than the present energy-industry-distribution system and thereby require a greatly reduced total investment.

Nevertheless, we calculated the capital cost shown in Table 3.2 the expensive way—from the cost of a single one-of-a-kind fission-powered generating plant. If no attempt was made to include the money-saving considerations in the calculations of Table 3.2, it is because technology has brought us to the point where a multi-purpose automated and integrated factory complex powered by the inexhaustible energy of fusion would be capable of reproducing itself from the materials contained in the ocean solution and in man's waste (or from low-grade ores such as the red clay of the ocean bottoms). On this basis, the total cost of building the first of a chain of moderately-sized self-replicating units operating on a 500,000-kw-capacity reactor would be $1 billion to $2 billion ($100 million for the reactor). Once operating, the first factory could earn the investment back merely by reproducing itself. As each new factory is put into operation, the profit on the original investment will increase by the amount of the investment, and ultimately to the point whereby this profit, reinvested as productive machinery, will be equal to hundreds or thousands of times the original investment.

Since a major feature of each complex is the interrelatedness of processes, contributing not only to low building and operating costs but to the conservation of land, energy, materials, and human labor within this automated and self-maintaining complex, the ecological benefits will be great; and once the complex is operating, the production processes should be virtually free. It may be worthwhile, however, to look at the cost of fusion energy in its own right, apart from its possible integration into new-process resource management.

My rule of thumb for estimating the cost of a fusion reactor is to assume the same cost as for fission reactors. This is a high estimate, since Dr. Richard Post of the Lawrence Radiation Laboratory estimates that the cost of fusion plants will be one-third lower than the cost of fission plants if the highly efficient and less expensive direct-conversion method, which he has devised for the conversion of the ionized plasma to direct current, is used instead of conventional generating machinery. Nevertheless, we will adhere to the more conservative cost estimate, so as to allow for unforeseen contingencies. Thus, since the San Onofre fission plant in southern California, with a capacity of 450,000 kw, cost $90 million to complete in 1967, we can use the figure of $200 per kw capacity as the construction cost of fusion reactors (since the route of economic inflation is not very predictable, it will do little good to correct this figure for inflation). At the $200 per kw rate, the fusion reactors needed to produce the energy requirement for four billion people will cost $8.2 trillion. For the seven billion population expected by the end of the century, the cost will be $14.35 trillion (if we calculate from the 8,000 kwh per year per individual, based on United States electrical production in 1971, the cost of fusion reactors for four billion people [3,837,673,000-kw capacity] would be $767.5 billion and the cost for seven billion people [6,715,927,750-kw capacity] would be $1.3 trillion).

Table 3.2 compares the costs of fusion energy plants for the world under alternative assumptions of a four billion population, a seven billion population, the 1971 electrical production of the United States as a per capita consumption rate for the world, and the 1971 United States production of *all* types of energy as a per capita use rate for the world.

The cost of electrical plants for a population of four billion at the 1971 rate of electrical production in the United States would be $767.5 billion ($511.2 billion according to Dr. Post—upper left of Table 3.2). Despite the fact that this alternative presents the minimal manner in which we can bring electrical energy equivalent to that of the U.S. to the world, it is between 385 and 767 times the cost of the first self-replicating integrated factory (reactor included). If we were to spend the money instead on a few integrated factories, we would come out far ahead in a few years.

The energy expended, other than electrical, would be 10 times that of the electrical energy if we use the U.S. in 1971 as a model (Table 3.2). This would be ecologically disastrous. The efficiency of the industry served by electricity will be much less if this industry is not integrated. Losses will be due to electrical line loss, chemical and thermal waste, excessive transportation of materials within the production processes (as at present), and either labor costs or increased difficulties in the design of automation.

The ecological benefits will be minimal if we use the 1971 production of electricity in the U.S. as a model, but very beneficial if we eliminate fossil fuel (both direct energy and as converted to electrical energy) and fission-generated energy, since many pollutants, including much thermal pollution, will be eliminated. In comparison, the ecological benefits will be maximized by the integrated factory, since the factory will be a consumer of all waste, will free much land from industrial and agricultural use, and will produce the least thermal pollution.

In economic terms, the cost-benefit analysis for the alternatives presented in Table 3.2 is as follows: If we were to charge the consumer at the rate of two cents per kwh, the 32 trillion kwh per year required by a population of four billion at the 8,000-kwh-per-capita rate would bring a gross return of $640 billion per year. Since the fuel is free and the plant would be highly automated, we can allow a generous 20 percent of this return for maintenance and another 10 percent for expansion (at the U.S. rate). This leaves approximately $448 billion per year to amortize the $767.5 billion investment. At this rate, amortization would take a bit over 20 months. Since the same ratio of electrical energy to population holds for a population of seven billion, amortization for this population will require the same amount of time.

Using the model derived from the 1971 production of all major forms of energy in the U.S., we find that the 348 trillion kwh required by a four billion population would bring a return of $6,960 billion per year on the $8.2 trillion investment. At this rate, amortization would take a bit over 14 months, the same time being required by a population of seven billion.

This discussion does not include the costs of energy distribution because these initial costs are complex and varied. Costs will depend on the capacity of existing distribution systems, population growth rates and densities, climate, geography, and the technology available at the time of construction (for example, multi-purpose distribution systems, sodium versus superconductors, and so on). This system can be built by the integrated factory. Neither does the cost discussion include interest. This is under the assumption that funds for energy development would be provided in the form of "soft loans" by an organization such as the World Bank. Efficiency of construction and distribution will require regional design on the basis of world physical geography and population densities. The benefits are seen either as the provision and distribution of electricity to the world at the same rate that it is presently consumed in the United States (Table 3.2) or as the replacement of *all* forms of energy with electricity, this at the same rate of production as the combined energy production in the United States. Either of these alternatives is easily amortized under present concepts of economics and will produce energy at very low per capita costs.

Despite the fact that a cost-benefit analysis of the integrated factory is not feasible here, it is obvious that the integrated factory will benefit from free fuel, the integration of structure and process, the efficient use of all temperatures of heat with little waste, the recycling of its own material waste, and the curtailment of much transportation of materials in process. The economic benefits of the integrated factory should thus be much greater than those derived from today's industry. These benefits may be so great in economic terms that it might be feasible to replace existing industry with integrated factories as fast as they could be built. If we consider the financial benefits derived from the fresh water and chemicals produced by fusion energy, the economic feasibility of integration is dramatic.

The cost of equipment for distilling fresh water and, in a sense, for the fractional distillation of the ocean's chemicals is unknown except that much of this equipment will be integrated with the reactor itself, thus saving much of the investment. Examining the financial returns on the fresh water produced, we find that a cubic mile of fresh water will be worth over $294.3 million at the sales rate of $.20 per hundred cubic feet (California communities sell water at about $.30 per hundred cubic feet). The requirement of a population of four billion for one year would thus have a market value of $.8 trillion. A year's production of magnesium would be worth over $12.2 trillion at the 1969 rate of $700 per ton. The gold extracted in one year would be worth over $63.3 million at the 1970 rate of $36.39 per fine ounce.

A year's production of chlorine, sodium, sulphur, calcium, potassium, vanadium, and silver would be worth over $571 billion dollars at 1969 rates. Thus, if a trillion dollars (a high estimate) is invested in reactors and extraction equipment for water and the other chemicals, the investment would be repaid over ten times in the first year alone.

The inaccuracies of the type of cost-benefit analysis presented above are major. For instance, I base all benefits and costs on 1967–70. In those years chemicals such as magnesium were scarce and expensive. Extraction of water and chemicals from the ocean solution as I have presented it would quickly drive the prices of these commodities down in a free economy, and amortization would take longer. What I am saying, of course, is that the solution of the problem of scarcity will trigger some fundamental changes in our concepts of economics. The benefits of a trillion-dollar investment in fusion reactors and extraction equipment is beyond calculation and imagination if we think in terms of human well-being.

PART II

ARMS CONTROL
AND OCEAN
SURVEILLANCE

The following articles were part of a study project sponsored jointly by the International Ocean Institute and the International Peace Academy and directed by General Indar Rikhye, in preparation for Pacem in Maribus III, 1972.

The project clarified a number of basic points. First, there can be no doubt that the oceans are beginning to play a decisive role in the strategies, both offensive and defensive, of the major powers. Strategic weapons systems, now vulnerable on land, are being moved into the protective opaqueness of the oceans. The consequences of this shift have not yet been fully measured. Pollution and the danger of accidental release of radioactive material and other poisons into the oceans are increasing with the rate of military movement in the oceans. Detection systems, pumping megawatts of acoustic energy into the oceans and relying on the use of the entire ocean space, including the seabed, make the ocean "ring like a bell," as Dr. Hirdman points out. What effect this may have on the delicate systems of communication of various marine animal species—chemical and acoustic communications systems on which their social organization and survival depend—is at present not known.

Second, while military uses often *comp ete* and *conflict* with peaceful uses of ocean space, they are also intimately and inseparably linked with each other. Military and civil scientific research are thus linked. Civil scientific research inevitably has a military spinoff, and vice versa. The internationalization of much of peaceful and civil ocean research, which is inevitable if freedom of research is to survive to any degree, will have an impact on military research and its traditional secrecy. Since many of the technologies and institutional arrangements needed for pollution-monitoring and control are the same as those required for arms control—as is pointed out by Craven—pollution controls will have a considerable arms control effect. This is a theme that ran through all contributions to the project. Elizabeth Young has coined the term "passive disarmament" for this development.

Third, existing "active" disarmament and arms control agreements in the oceans, including the Treaty Prohibiting the Emplacement of Nuclear Weapons and Other Weapons of Mass Destruction on the Sea-Bed, are totally inadequate, and it is not likely that more effective agreements for "active" disarmament will be forthcoming in the foreseeable future. Progress toward "passive disarmament," as a by-product of multi-purpose scientific surveillance of the oceans is more likely or, to some degree, inevitable.

Fourth, inspection powers, while internationally agreed on, will probably be "delegated" for some time to come to nation states for implementation. An international military surveillance force, as described by Bjørn Egge and anticipated, in a more general form, in U.S. Senator Clayborne Pell's prophetic Senate Resolution 33 of 1967, seems far remote in the future.

Dr. Sven Hirdman was for many years deputy director of the Stockholm International Peace Research Institute. He is now counselor to the Swedish Embassy in Peking. Dr. John Craven has been the designer of the U.S. Navy's Poseidon system. He is now Dean of Marine Studies at the University of Hawaii. Elizabeth Young is a British expert and free-lance writer on arms control and disarmament and the author of *Farewell to Arms Control*. Colonel Egge is on the staff of the Norwegian Ministry for Foreign Affairs. He has been an advisor to the Secretary General on peace-keeping in the United Nations and a member of the International Peace Academy.

CHAPTER 4

Prospects for Arms Control in the Ocean

SVEN HIRDMAN

I. Introduction

The purpose of this article is to discuss the possibilities for arms control in the ocean. The emphasis is on the undersea environment—the seabed and the deep ocean waters; surface developments are dealt with more summarily. The information presented is drawn from open sources only. For evident reasons, more is known about developments in the United States than in the Soviet Union, and so the discussion is largely centered on US affairs. However, this is mainly for illustrative purposes; while the United States at present is a leader in military undersea technology, other great powers, in particular the Soviet Union, may in time catch up with the United States, partly or wholly.

Over the last 10 years the vast undersea space has been subject to increasing militarization. New technology is pushing the research frontiers forward, allowing military systems to penetrate deeper into the ocean. This applies both to traditional submarine systems and to new military uses such as fixed submarine detection systems and manned underwater stations. This development in undersea technology is accelerated by changes in the strategic competition among the great powers. A significant factor is the increasing vulnerability of land-based military systems caused by advances in surveillance techniques and missile accuracy and the use of multiple warhead missiles. The result is a gradual shift of the main arms race from land-based systems to submarine-based systems which can make full use of the protection afforded by the undersea environment.[1]

There have been efforts to control the militarization of the ocean, but so far without much success. After negotiations which started in 1968, a treaty prohibiting the emplacement of nuclear weapons and other weapons of mass destruction on the seabed and ocean floor and in the subsoil thereof was adopted at the end of 1971. It went into force only on May 18, 1972. By outlawing only nuclear weapons systems fixed on the seabed, for which there is very little military interest anyhow, this treaty fails to influence the main arms race in the ocean. Further, the United Nations has been concerned with reserving the seabed for exclusively peaceful purposes and with constructing a new international regime for the oceans. However, the definition of "peaceful purposes" remains a moot point.

In looking at the oceans from an arms control point of view, it is important to treat the whole undersea environment as an entity. In particular, military uses of the seabed cannot in most cases be isolated from submarine warfare in the waters above the seabed. Indeed, there are direct links between military installations on the seabed, antisubmarine warfare, ballistic missile submarine systems, and the strategic balance between the United States and the Soviet Union. If these relationships are not understood and realistically evaluated, there is a risk that any arms control measures contemplated will fail in their purpose while the arms race goes on unabated in other directions.

This article is divided into three main sections. The first deals with present and future military uses of the deep ocean; the second analyzes the sea-bed "denuclearization" treaty,[2] while the third discusses possible future arms control measures in the ocean. In the short space available, it is impossible to make a complete survey of all existing military uses of the deep ocean or of the negotiations on the Sea-Bed Treaty. Reference is therefore made to the chapter, "The Militarization of the Deep Ocean: the Sea-Bed Treaty," in the *SIPRI Yearbook of World Armaments and Disarmament 1969/70,*[3] to the study, "Arms Control in Hydrospace: Legal Aspects," by E.D. Brown,[4] and to the sources quoted in these two standard works.

[1] The point is discussed more fully in the *SIPRI Yearbook of World Armaments and Disarmament 1969/70* (Stockholm, 1970), pp. 93–101. See also *World Armaments and Disarmament, SIPRI Yearbook 1972* (Stockholm, 1972) for an assessment of the present strategic situation.

[2] The prohibition of chemical and biological mass destruction weapons implicit in the Sea-Bed Treaty is only theoretical as far as actual sea-bed installations are concerned.

[3] Pp. 92–184.

[4] Woodrow Wilson International Center for Scholars, Washington, Oceans Series 301, June 1971.

II. Military Uses of the Deep Ocean

The deep ocean is exposed to a variety of military uses, all of which have a bearing on possible arms control measures in the ocean. The most important uses from an arms control point of view are summarized below. For more detailed information about deployed and planned oceanic weapons systems, reference is made to the *SIPRI Yearbook 1969/70.*[5]

Deployment of Ballistic Missile Submarines

For both the United States and the Soviet Union, the oceans have a central importance as deployment areas for ballistic missile submarines of the Polaris or Poseidon types. Hiding in the deep ocean, practically invulnerable to attack because of the characteristics of the undersea environment, these submarines constitute the most reliable second-strike forces of the United States and the Soviet Union.

The United States is converting 31 of its 41 Polaris submarines to Poseidon submarines equipped with MIRVed missiles. Each Poseidon will have 16 missiles with probably 10 independently targetable warheads each, implying that by about 1975 the US will have about 5,440 nuclear warheads deployed on board ballistic missile submarines. (The remaining 10 Polaris submarines will have 16 missiles with 3 warheads each.)

No present development in antisubmarine warfare seems to threaten the invulnerability of the Polaris/Poseidon submarines. According to the most recent US government statements, their invulnerability is assured at least until the late 1970s. However, as a hedge against unforeseen future developments in undersea warfare, work has already started on a replacement force for the Polaris/Poseidon submarines—the Undersea Longrange Missile System (ULMS). The ULMS concept provides for the basing of ICBMs on new, large, quiet, deep-diving submarines whose deployment area will be at least 10 times as large as that of the Polaris submarines. About 30 ULMS submarines, recently baptized Tridents, are planned at a cost of about $1 billion each (that is about $30 billion for 30 Tridents, against $13 billion for 41 Polaris). Funding for ULMS is increasing rapidly: from $10 million in 1969-70, $44 million in 1970-71, and $140 million in 1971-72 to $940 million in 1972-73 (requested). According to current plans, construction will start in 1974-75, with the first Trident becoming operational in 1978. ULMS is planned for a long lifetime—from 1980 to 2000. The formal decision to go ahead with the construction of ULMS was long left contingent on the outcome of the SALT talks. However, the sharply

[5]Pp. 106–54.

increased funding for the system, and past experience with similar processes, indicated that the US government's decision was predetermined. This was confirmed by the SALT agreements concluded in Moscow on May 26, 1972, and the Administration is now soliciting Congressional agreement to the full development of ULMS.[6]

The Soviet Union is generally lagging behind the United States in the development of ballistic missile submarines. At the beginning of 1972, the Soviet Union had 25 "Y-class" submarines, equivalent to the early versions of the US Polaris. The rate of construction is high, probably 8 to 10 a year. According to US Secretary of Defense Laird, the Soviet Union may have built 42 Y-class submarines by the end of 1973. (These figures were confirmed by the 1972 SALT agreements.) These submarines and their missiles are generally regarded as inferior to the US Polaris and Poseidon systems in numerous aspects. Recently a new, longer-range Soviet SLBM has been reported, the SS-NX-8 or "Sawfly," with a range equivalent to that of the Polaris A-3 missile (about 2,500 miles); it is believed that it has or will have multiple warheads (MRV but not MIRV).

According to the SALT agreements concluded in Moscow on May 26, 1972, the United States and the Soviet Union have agreed to limit submarine-launched ballistic missile launchers (SLBMs) and modern ballistic missile submarines to the numbers operational and under construction on the date of signature of the agreements. The limits specified are: for the United States, 710 SLBMs and 44 modern ballistic missile submarines, and for the Soviet Union, 950 SLBMs and 62 modern ballistic missile submarines. Both for the United States and the Soviet Union the limits set are higher than the number of SLBMs and submarines actually operational at present. Further, modernization and replacement of ballistic missile launchers is expressly permitted. What is even more important is that there are no limitations on the number of warheads carried by the SLBMs.

Thus, the US ULMS/Trident ballistic missile submarine system is in no way limited by the SALT agreements, since the total number of submarines planned is well below 44—in fact, the 31 Tridents planned may carry up to 22 launchers each and still be below the limit on SLBMs agreed upon at SALT—and there are no restrictions on the number of multiple warheads which these missiles may carry.[7]

In addition to the United States and the Soviet Union, the United

---

[6]There is also a proposal to develop an upgraded Poseidon force—consisting of longer-range missiles (5,500 miles) in existing Poseidon submarines—to serve either as an interim force before the ULMS is fully developed or possibly as an alternative to the ULMS, if that system should not be developed as planned.

[7]For an analysis of the SALT agreements, see *SIPRI Research Report nos. 5 and 6, Strategic Arms Limitation, Parts I and II* (Stockholm: September 1972).

Kingdom has four operational ballistic missile submarines and France is building five. Should more nations go nuclear, it is conceivable that they may also try to develop ballistic missile submarines because of the strategic advantages presented by such systems.

Nuclear Attack Submarines

For operations in the undersea environment, nuclear-powered systems have significant advantages not only for ballistic missile submarines but for attack submarines with ASW and antisurface ship functions. Indeed, both the United States and the Soviet Union are pressing ahead with construction of nuclear-powered attack submarines. With, at present, more than 50 nuclear attack submarines operational and 18 of the new advanced SSN-688 submarines under construction or to be funded (at a cost of about $150 million each), the US Navy is moving close to an all-nuclear submarine force. Further, a development option is maintained for an advanced high-performance nuclear attack submarine, which will incorporate electromagnetic drive for very quiet operations but which may cost several hundred million dollars per submarine.

The Soviet Union has some 300 nuclear attack submarines operational. The Soviet building rate is about seven a year, compared to six for the United States. At present Britain is the only country other than the United States and the Soviet Union that has nuclear attack submarines. Five British SSNs were planned for 1972. France, Italy, and China may build such submarines in the near future.

Antisubmarine Warfare

Antisubmarine warfare (ASW) involves the use of a variety of weapons systems and sensors deployed on surface ships, submarines, aircraft, helicopters, satellites, buoys, and on the seabed, which are used against the strategic ballistic missile submarines and attack submarines of the other side. ASW relies heavily on oceanography and other sciences, but so far developments in submarine warfare are outpacing those in antisubmarine warfare. For a technical survey of ASW, reference is again made to the *SIPRI Yearbook 1969/70.*[8] Only those developments that are of major significance for the following discussion of arms control measures will be noted here.

All three main ASW tactics—barrier control, ocean surveillance, and submarine trailing—have substantial shortcomings. In narrow oceanic areas such as the pass between Scotland and Iceland, guarding the entrance

[8]Pp. 106–22.

into the Atlantic, fixed detection sytems and antisubmarine submarines may observe the passage of enemy submarines, but once the submarines have passed the barrier they are, in most situations, lost to control; that is, neither trailing with another submarine nor the use of airborne sensors gives much hope of locating the enemy submarine when it dives into the deep ocean. At most, one or two submarines may be found in this way, but not a whole submarine force which has escaped interception (for example, before the outbreak of hostilities) at the barrier.

The seabed and ocean floor have been used for nearly 20 years for deployment of acoustic submarine detection systems (sonars). Since they can be installed at fixed positions, bottom sonars are much more efficient than other sonars for accurately measuring the distance to a target submarine. Because of the need to use very long base lines to receive the long sound waves necessary for submarine detection, bottom sonars are as a rule installed in widely separated pairs—at a greater distance from each other than is possible with shipborne sonars.

The United States has led this development, and there are several types of passive and active detection systems deployed on the sea floor along the US East and West coasts and in various barrier zones guarding the exit of Soviet submarines into the deep-ocean areas.[9] During the last few years significant research advances have been made in active acoustic detection systems, relying on the pumping of megawatts of acoustic energy into the ocean so as to make a whole ocean basin "ring like a bell" and thereby betray the presence of submarines.[10] For this, giant transducers are required which are now shipborne but in the near future may be installed on continental shelves and in other shallow areas. For sound discrimination purposes there is, further, a requirement for receiving networks of advanced electronic equipment. These may include structures on the seabed and particularly on sea mounts.[11] Experimental use is also being made of the "deep sound channel"—which occurs at a depth of about 1,000 meters in the Atlantic and Pacific—for very long-range submarine detection.

The newest acoustic detection systems are integrated systems that rely on the use of the whole ocean space, including the seabed. The United States, for instance, is reported to be considering the design and construction of the largest undersea acoustic system ever conceived—the Suspended

[9]The systems are code-named CAESAR, COLOSSUS, BARRIER and BRONCO. See *SIPRI Yearbook 1969/70*, pp. 148ff.

[10] See the paper by Dr. V. C. Anderson, "Ocean Technology", in *Impact of New Technologies on the Arms Race*, ed. B. T. Feld et al., Pugwash Monograph: MIT Press, 1971, pp. 201–16.

[11]The US, United Kingdom, and France, in cooperation, have installed three acoustic detection towers at depths of 400, 600, and 800 meters on sea mounts off the island of Santa Maria in the Azores (*Le Monde*, February 12, 1972).

Array System—a project that will cost around $1 billion and involve under-water structures, acoustic transducers, and electronic systems on an extremely large scale.[12]

Advances are also being made in oceanwide surveillance from the surface and from the air through the use of sonobuoys and shipborne and airborne (including spaceborne) sensors. The main problem here is that the electromagnetic and magnetic anomaly detection (MAD) sensors used in airborne systems have a very limited penetration capacity in seawater and therefore are reliable only for near-surface detection of submarines. However, airborne sensors can cooperate with acoustic sensors on buoys and ships and in this way achieve greater detection ranges. The vastness of the oceans and the evasive capacity of a modern nuclear submarine still make detection an extremely difficult, if not hopeless, task.

Among the several weapons used against submarines, mention should be made of torpedoes, mines, missiles, and depth charges. These means of attack may have either conventional or nuclear warheads. The US has developed a torpedo mine, CAPTOR, which is an M-46 torpedo encapsulated in a mine launched from aircraft, surface ships, or submarines. Because it can be launched in advance and then wait for the appearance of an enemy submarine, CAPTOR may have a particular application as a barrier control weapon.[13] While the deployment of mines outside territorial waters is forbidden in peacetime under the laws of war, mines may be deployed quickly and in great numbers at the outbreak of hostilities.

One particular development in surface naval ships which may influence the future of submarine and antisubmarine warfare is the development of large air-cushion vehicles—captured air bubble (CAB) or surface effect vehicle (SEV)—capable of riding at speeds of 50 to 100 knots over the oceans. Because of their speed, these vehicles may be able to outstrip both submarines and torpedoes. Plans have been made to develop CABs of several thousand tons which could serve as small ASW aircraft carriers. The US Navy is now developing air-cushion vehicles as a priority project. Technology is also making possible the development of large, stable platforms which may serve as floating airfields and improve the prospects for ocean surveillance and control.

New Undersea Technology

New developments in undersea technology are gradually allowing man to penetrate deeper into the oceans. In the military field two developments are

[12] *Undersea Technology,* December 1971, p. 9.
[13] Cf. the article, "Study May Settle Controversy on Need to Match Soviet Subs," in *Washington Post,* November 26, 1971.

of particular significance—the construction of manned underwater stations and the development of deep-diving submersibles. These and other new developments rely on new ocean technology, including pressure hulls of new materials, underwater power systems, new buoyancy materials, underwater construction techniques such as reentry into the seabed, saturation-diving techniques, and underwater communications. The demand for this new technology has come not only from the military exploitation of the oceans but also from the civil sector, in particular from offshore oil exploitation.

During the last 10 years several experiments with manned underwater laboratories have been carried out at continental shelf depths, involving the use of "saturated" divers who have stayed undersea up to one month at a stretch.[14] The United States, France, and the Soviet Union have led in this field. Operating from these so-called sealabs, "saturated" divers may perform repair work and various construction tasks on submarine detection systems.

Beyond continental shelf depths one-atmosphere shelters must be provided if man is to be able to stay under the ocean. Through its Deep Ocean Technology program, the US Navy has been engaged in developing construction techniques for such manned stations, which eventually may be deployed at any depth in the ocean. The main interest has been in constructing a manned underwater station (MUS) for use at a depth of 2,000 meters, for instance on a sea mount. But concepts have also been developed for stations to be installed at depths of 4,000 meters and 7,000 meters, which would include the greater part of the deep-ocean floor. Currently an experimental concrete station, project Seacon, is being built by the US Navy at shallow depths off the coast of California.[15] The final project may incorporate a nuclear reactor for the supply of power. Manned underwater stations may be installed not only on the seabed, using metals, glass, and concrete construction, but they may also be built into the subsoil using advanced drilling techniques and lock-out facilities. The concept for such subsoil stations, which may be difficult to detect and destroy, is called Rocksite. Eventually, Rocksites may be installed on underwater ridges or isolated sea mounts for the purpose of deep-ocean surveillance and submarine support.

However, interest in military manned underwater stations has diminished somewhat recently, at least in the United States. Part of the reason may be temporary budgetary restraint, but there is also a growing realization that unmanned systems may be preferable to fixed manned installations for operational, cost, and human security reasons.

[14]Cf. the list of such experiments in the *SIPRI Yearbook 1969/70*, p. 144.
[15]*Undersea Technology*, August 1971, p. 13.

Many different types of advanced, deep-diving submersibles have been developed for military, industrial, and scientific purposes. The most advanced types in operation include free-swimming submersibles able to perform work with outside manipulators at depths below 2,000 meters, that is, considerably below the maximum collapse depths of existing submarines. The US Navy has developed a deep submergence rescue vehicle (DSRV), one of whose functions is to rescue disabled submarine crews. In order to do this, it has been provided with a lock-out facility which allows it to mate with a submarine—and, possibly, also with future, manned underwater stations. The DSRVs, of which two have been constructed so far, can go to a depth of 1,700 meters, are able to ride piggyback on a mother submarine and are air-transportable. Because of these and other characteristics, they are likely to permit a significant extension of continuous, submerged submarine operations. Another advanced US undersea vehicle is the nuclear research and engineering submersible, NR-1, the first nuclear-powered submersible. The NR-1, which became operational in 1969 and probably has a depth capability of at least 1,000 meters, is, among other things, equipped with external wheels for riding on the ocean floor. Other submersibles are being developed, both in the United States and Japan, for operations down to 7,000 meters.

In summary, the following conclusions may be drawn about the impact of new undersea technologies on the militarization of the deep ocean. Full military use of the continental shelf is already possible with advanced diving techniques. Life support may be provided by sealab-type stations, and vehicles, machines, and tools have been adapted for work at continental-shelf depths and deeper. Military activities on continental-shelf depths are likely to include installation and repair of submarine-detection systems, mine warfare, operations of attack divers, and in the future, possibly, service and support of submarine systems.

Beyond continental-shelf depths, advanced submersibles, in particular of the DSRV type, permit an extension of the operations of existing nuclear submarines. Unmanned work systems already exist for carrying out work on the deep-ocean floor. Before the end of this decade experimental one-atmosphere manned stations may be installed at depths of about 2,000 meters probably on underwater ridges and isolated sea mounts. The future military functions of these stations would be primarily ASW operations. Toward the end of the century, technology may allow the deployment of underwater stations to depths of 7,000 meters.

The fact that a combination of military, economic, and scientific motives lies behind this technological drive into the deep ocean may make it well-nigh irresistible. The direct military applications which can now be discerned may not even be the most important. The military are taking a new environment in possession for functions which may be defined later when mankind has adapted itself to work and life under the ocean on a grand scale.

III. The Sea-Bed Treaty

The only arms control agreement that applies to the deep ocean is the "Treaty on the Prohibition of the Emplacement of Nuclear Weapons and other Weapons of Mass Destruction on the Seabed and the Ocean Floor and in the Subsoil thereof," which is a very limited measure indeed. This Sea-Bed Treaty was negotiated at the Geneva Disarmament Conference in 1968-70, opened for signature in February 1971, and went into force on May 18, 1972 after the required number of 22 countries, including the United States, the Soviet Union, and the United Kingdom, had completed their ratification procedures.

The principal obligation of the treaty is the undertaking of the parties not to emplant or emplace nuclear weapons or other weapons of mass destruction on the seabed and ocean floor and in the subsoil thereof beyond the outer limit of a coastal seabed zone of 12 miles. The prohibition also extends to the emplantment or emplacement of structures, launching installations, or any other facilities specifically designed for storing, testing, or using such weapons.

The Sea-Bed Treaty was based primarily on a US proposal to outlaw the fixed installation of weapons of mass destruction from the seabed outside a three-mile coastal zone. A Soviet proposal to outlaw all military installations on the seabed was not successful. However, the treaty contains an article obligating the parties to continue negotiations in good faith concerning further measures in the field of disarmament for the prevention of an arms race on the seabed.

The military significance of the Sea-Bed Treaty must be regarded as very low. In its present form the treaty essentially bans only fixed nuclear missile installations from the seabed. While such weapons systems were once under consideration, for instance in the United States, any plans were soon abandoned for good military, technical, and economic reasons *before* the seabed became a disarmament issue. From a military point of view, the deployment of nuclear missiles on board mobile carriers, for example, ballistic missile submarines, is much preferable in order to use to the full the ocean's advantages for protection—essential to any credible second-strike force. The point may be illustrated by a quote from a 1969 statement by a former Assistant Secretary of the US Navy:

Senator Pell: Do you have any concern about moving in terms of prohibiting mobile weapons systems from operating on the sea-bed?

Dr. Morse: No, I do not really—otherwise I think we may end up banning things that do not have any military use and certainly we can get widespread agreement on that. One has to remember that the great advantage of deploying a weapons system at sea is mobility, and that if one bans only fixed nuclear weapons systems at sea he may well be banning something that doesn't have any value anyway. Consider the Polaris, if the Polaris fleet were anchored at fixed points it certainly would not represent the threat that it does today.[16]

While the treaty prohibits the deployment of moored nuclear mines and mobile nuclear carriers which can only move in contact with the seabed, neither of which presents much military interest, it does not prohibit the temporary stationing of nuclear missile submarines on the seabed. The installation of nonmass-destruction applications of nuclear power, such as nuclear power reactors supporting military underwater stations, is not prohibited.

Thus the Sea-Bed Treaty amounts to the banning of something which does not exist and which, even in the absence of the treaty, was not likely to develop. Indeed, the treaty is not likely to limit the military uses of the ocean floor, even less of the deep ocean. It does not in any way restrict the operations of ballistic missile submarines nor does it prohibit manned military underwater stations and ASW detection systems. Since it permits the placement on the seabed of facilities servicing free-swimming nuclear weapon systems, the treaty will be no obstacle to the development of a nuclear arms race in the whole of the sea environment.

This point may be reinforced by a quote from another official US statement, keeping in mind that the United States by far leads all other nations in the military exploitation of the deep ocean and the seabed. During the hearings on the US ratification of the treaty in January 1972, the representative of the US Defense Department said the following about fulfilling the obligation not to install nuclear weapons on the seabed beyond the 12-mile zone:

---

[16] *Activities of Nations in Ocean Space,* Hearings before the Subcommittee on Ocean Space of the Committee on Foreign Relations, US Senate, 91st Congress, 1st session, July 1969, p. 45.

We can, without difficulty, undertake this obligation. We have no plans for doing what the treaty would forbid. To be very explicit on that, the United States has no plans for placing weapons for mass destruction on the seabed. We are not aware of any plans on the part of others to do so. We thus see the treaty as preventive rather than proscriptive, as protection for the future rather than a limitation on the present.

However, the Defense spokesman also said:

The Joint Chiefs of Staff have authorized me to state: "The Joint Chiefs of Staff interpose no objection to the ratification of the Seabed Arms Control Treaty. They reiterate their concern, however, that any additional constraints on military use of the seabeds beyond the prohibitions contained in the treaty would bear a potential for grave harm to United States national security interests."[17]

The original Soviet position on demilitarization of the seabed was that there should be a general prohibition of the use of the seabed for military purposes. Although the Soviet Union in 1970 compromised with the United States on a ban of fixed installations of weapons of mass destruction only, it has since then, both in the CCD and the UN seabed committee, advocated further demilitarization of the seabed. However, at the same time the Soviet Union has expressed sympathy for a Swedish and a Mexican proposal that a future general prohibition of military installations on the seabed should not include activities of a purely defensive character, such as means of communication, navigation, and tracking submarines, or not of a directly military character, such as the use of military personnel for peaceful purposes.[18]

With regard to the positions of the nonnuclear-weapon states to the seabed demilitarization issue, two points may be noted. First, there was a Canadian proposal to prohibit not only weapons of mass destruction but also all other weapons, military activities, undersea bases or fortifications from which military action could be undertaken against the territory, territorial sea or air space of another state, including but not limited to: shore bombardment weapons or systems; devices capable of disrupting communications, air, and maritime navigation and other peaceful pursuits; devices

---

[17] *Seabed Arms Control Treaty*, Hearings before the Committee on Foreign Relations, US Senate, 92nd Congress, 2nd session, January 1972, p. 10.

[18] See the statement by the Soviet representative to the CCD on 24 August 1971. Disarmament Conference document CCD/PV. 532.

to counter, disrupt, neutralize, or render ineffective any defensive instruments of another state—that is, detection, surveillance, defensive fire control, and so on; installations from which manned incursions could be mounted against another state; and chemical or other means of destroying or denying the seabed resources of another state.

Second, several nonnuclear-weapon states, including Canada and India, indicated strong preference for a ban on all foreign military installations on their continental shelves. The reasons advanced included protection of national security and noninterference with the coastal states' right of exploitation of the natural resources on their own continental shelf.

To sum up: the basic weakness of the Sea-Bed Treaty is that it is directed only toward one part of the undersea environment, the seabed, which from a military and arms control point of view cannot be separated from the movements in the waters above the seabed. Undersea warfare and antisubmarine warfare make use of the whole of the sea environment. The use of ballistic missile submarines and other naval vessels relates the oceans directly to the strategic balance between the great powers. Because of the influence of these factors, it was possible only to reach agreement on a militarily insignificant measure—the "denuclearization" of the seabed. This is not to deny that the Sea-Bed Treaty may have other—political and psychological—advantages. These may include confidence-building between the United States and the Soviet Union, some general agreement on the need for international verification, and increased concern about the military uses of the oceans, leading to more relevant measures in the future. The last issue will be discussed in the next section.

IV. Prospects for Arms Control in the Ocean

Limitations on present and future military uses of the deep ocean may come about, if at all, in three main ways: *(a)* through the direct influence of changes in weapons technology; *(b)* through the voluntary restraint of the great powers in order to preserve their existing strategic deterrent forces; and *(c)* through the negotiation of international arms control treaties. Each of these alternatives will be examined in turn.

The Impact of Technology

With regard to the influence of present military technology, the point has already been made that existing military uses of the seabed are part and parcel of submarine warfare. In particular, devices for detecting submarines have for years been installed in many seabed areas. Indeed, installations on the seabed have, so far, offered many technical and economic advantages compared to the use of shipborne and airborne systems and the use of buoys —floating or moored—for detection purposes. However, the use of stable surface and mid-water sonobuoys may, in the future, lessen the technological dependence on fixed bottom installations for submarine detection purposes to some extent, although bottom sonar installations will remain more difficult to discover.

New mid-water mooring techniques may in a similar way influence the deployment of mines in the deep ocean—although it should be recalled that the laying of mine fields outside territorial waters is forbidden in peacetime.

These new developments may possibly diminish some present military uses of the seabed by allowing some activities that are now carried out on the seabed to be carried out in mid-water. The significance of any such changes is hard to judge.

In a longer-term perspective, the use of fast air-cushion surface naval vessels and of giant nuclear-powered freight aircraft may alter the nature of submarine warfare because: *(a)* the air-cushion vehicles may outstrip the submarines and their torpedoes and *(b)* the giant nuclear freight aircraft may lessen the dependence on surface ships for transporting vital supplies in times of war.[19]

Other and probably much stronger trends work, however, in the opposite direction—toward increasing militarization of the deep ocean. The main one relates to the need for protecting strategic deterrent forces. Because of its special properties, the ocean will be a much more secure place for such forces than any other environment. Even if the ocean were to become completely transparent to sound in the future—if not for other reasons then for cost reasons an extremely remote possibility—the decisive advantages will still remain on the side of the deep-diving and quiet nuclear submarine, not on the side of antisubmarine warfare.

The Impact of Strategy

The SALT agreements concluded in Moscow in no way alter the fact that nuclear ballistic missile submarines will remain the main strategic second-strike weapons systems of the United States and the Soviet Union for the foreseeable future. So far nothing seems to threaten the survivability of ballistic missile submarines as a deterrent force. However, as a hedge against unknown future developments in ASW, some proposals have been made to limit the use of sonars in the oceans and to declare certain areas

[19]See the paper by Dr. D. G. Brennan, "A Note on Bridging the Differing Soviet and American Objectivities of Sea-Bed Demilitarization", in *Proceedings of the Symposium on the International Regime of the Sea-Bed* (Rome, 1970), pp. 513–17.

of the oceans out of bounds to one or the other of these two powers. Such proposals have, for instance, been made by a Pugwash symposium:

> 1. Prohibition of a system of sonar arrays in the oceans. Such a provision would both assure that an ocean-wide ASW system based on sonar would never be deployed and alleviate the fears about the vulnerability of seabased forces. Because the deployment of such a system would involve a vast logistical undertaking, which could not be done in a clandestine manner, this provision could be easily monitored.
>
> 2. Designation of large areas of the ocean where one or the other of the superpowers would agree not to place any of its military systems but which would be available to the other. Such an agreement would eliminate the concern about hunter-killer submarines. Furthermore, if these areas were adjacent to the coastlines of each nation, the fear of a large massing of submarines off the coast for a pre-emptive attack would disappear.
>
> These two provisions would allow each country to have a high degree of confidence in the continuing reliability of its seabased deterrents. This confidence could then permit agreement on the limitation of landbased systems.[20]

The point has also been made that since both the United States and the Soviet Union have agreed not to defend themselves against land-based missiles by building large ABM systems, it does not make sense for them to defend themselves against submarine-launched missiles by means of ASW. In this view, bottom detection systems against ballistic missile submarines should have low priority.[21]

The main complication with regard to such proposals is, of course, that ASW has a dual function: it is directed not only against ballistic missile submarines but also against antiship, or attack, submarines. As long as there are no changes in the threat presented by attack submarines, nations will probably find it difficult to agree on limits on ASW.[22] Due to such interdependence of military systems, the difficulties in removing any one of them completely and the support and pressure from the military services for new

---

[20] *Impact of New Technologies on the Arms Race,* p. 368.

[21] Brennan, "Note on Bridging."

[22] However, some experts are now coming to the conclusion that it is technically possible to differentiate between strategic ASW and tactical ASW, which might make it possible to achieve a prohibition of some forms of ASW threatening the stability of the submarine-based nuclear deterrent forces of the US and the USSR. Cf. the article, "Anti-submarine Warfare and National Security" by Dr. Richard L. Garwin, in *Scientific American,* vol. 227, no. 1 (July 1972), p. 14.

advanced systems, the use of the oceans by submarines and other undersea military systems is more likely to increase than to diminish in the future.

In 1971 Sri Lanka launched a proposal for demilitarizing the Indian Ocean. While it is probably true that the Indian Ocean is the least militarized of the main oceans, it is a vital naval transit area, where the interests of the great powers, including the United States, the Soviet Union, and China, intersect. Despite this, reductions in the military activities in the Indian Ocean should be feasible, and one can clearly see the interest of the coastal nations of the area in such measures.

Pursuing the Sea-Bed Treaty

Pressure is already building up for continued international negotiations on further demilitarization of the seabed in accordance with the obligation contained in the Sea-Bed Treaty. The Soviet Union and several nonaligned nations have put forward proposals in this direction.

The main pressure will probably be for widening the scope of the prohibition contained in the Sea-Bed Treaty, that is, to prohibit more weapons systems than merely fixed mass-destruction weapons. Canada has already presented a list of conceivable conventional weapons systems which, in its view, should be banned from the seabed. Since there does not seem to be much military interest in developing such or similar weapons, an agreement to this effect may be achieved, but again it would for this reason have little significance. An agreement may eventually be reached on prohibiting all military systems on the seabed with the exception of means of communication, navigation, and detection, and of scientific installations, as already proposed by some nations. Even such an agreement would, however, probably not have much impact on the military uses of the deep ocean, the main thrust in the development of military technology being concentrated on mobile systems and their supporting infrastructure.

Another set of issues relates to the military uses of the continental shelves. Here the international political development seems to favor the interests of the coastal states in the over-all uses of the shelf. Therefore, coastal states may eventually be able to obtain an international agreement banning all foreign military installations which without their consent have been deployed on their shelves or within a similar predetermined limit.

However, there is likely to be much more military opposition to further demilitarization of the seabed than was the case with the seabed denuclearization treaty, as evidenced, for instance, by the statement of the US military. This implies that any future negotiation may be lengthy and, again, result in insignificant measures.

Verification of Oceanic Arms Control Agreements

Verification is never the main problem with regard to arms control agreements. The main problem is whether nations are willing to undertake the obligations imposed by an arms control agreement. With regard to verification of oceanic arms control agreements, the following points may be made:

1. Through existing national means of surveillance—including aircraft, reconnaissance satellites, and naval vessels—the number and types of the naval vessels of the other side may be easily verified. It may be harder, but not impossible, to determine their complement of weapons.

2. The same and other means of surveillance permit the detection of the installation of large military systems on the seabed, because the installation cannot take place without substantial surface activities.

3. While the location of surface vessels at any given time can be determined with relative ease, the location of submarines in underwater transit is much more difficult, particularly when the submarines have been deployed in the open ocean outside natural barrier areas.

4. The location of on-bottom military systems after they have been installed is very difficult, particularly with regard to small devices such as submarine detection systems and to in-bottom structures. If the approximate location is known, it may be possible to find such installations by using active acoustic detection and other means. Under most circumstances it should be less difficult to detect fixed installations than mobile systems.

Interaction of Civil and Military Interests

Civil and military interests in the deep ocean interact in several ways. The point has already been made that much the same technology is used for both military and civil purposes, including the commercial exploitation of the resources of the oceans and the seabed. The scientific exploration of ocean space has both military and civil aspects, particularly in a longer time perspective.

The fact that many seabed installations such as navigation and detection facilities may serve both military and civil needs is likely to make it more difficult, if practicable at all, to reach agreement on the removal from the seabed of all installations that may have military value. The United Nations has already unanimously adopted the principle that the seabed and ocean floor outside national jurisdictions should be reserved for exclusively peaceful purposes. However, there are conflicting national views as to how this principle should be implemented:

(a) Some nonaligned nations have taken the view that it means prohibiting all military activities, including all activities by military personnel, on the seabed.

(b) The Soviet Union, among others, interprets the principle as prohibiting all military activities for offensive purposes but not, for instance, the use of military means of communications or the use of military personnel for scientific purposes.

(c) The United States considers that the test of whether an activity is "peaceful" is whether it is consistent with the UN charter and other obligations of international law. Since in the US view the term "peaceful purposes" does not preclude military activities generally, specific limitations of certain military activities will require the negotiation of a detailed arms control agreement. Military activities not precluded by such agreements would, in the US view, continue to be conducted in accordance with the principle of freedom of the high seas and exclusively for peaceful purposes.[23]

Whenever an international regime is set up for regulating the economic exploitation of the seabed, there are likely to be problems involving military interests. The international machinery will presumably allocate licenses for the exploration or exploitation of specific seabed areas. What will happen if one nation, purposely or not, asks for the license of an area where another nation happens to have placed secret military installations?

Military interests have a substantive impact on the current international efforts to negotiate a new legal framework for the oceans, including the limits of the territorial seas. A special, thorny civil-military issue is the right of passage through straits connecting international waters. An extension of the present average three-mile limit to an average of 12 miles would mean that about 116 present international straits would come within the territorial waters of coastal nations. This would mean that naval vessels would have only the right of innocent passage through these straits, many of which are strategically important. It is interesting to note in this connection that, as one of its major points for the Law of the Sea negotiations, the United States has demanded that the right of innocent passage through straits be replaced with the concept of "free transit," implying *(a)* that

[23] Statement by the US representative to the United Nations Ad Hoc Committee on the Seabed, 23 August 1968.

submarines may pass through in submerged state, and *(b)* an unconditional right of overflight for aircraft.[24]

V. Conclusions

In summary, the following conclusions may be offered:

1. Because of the impact of changes in technology and strategy, the oceans are likely to be of even more military interest in the future than now.

2. The US and the USSR have, in their own interest, already agreed on some quantitative limits of numbers of ballistic missile submarines. In the future they may also bilaterally or in the context of the CCD negotiations agree on some measures reducing the destabilizing effect of ASW on ballistic missile submarines, provided they can solve the difficulties caused by the involvement of ASW with other forms of naval warfare. Even if the US and the USSR kept their numbers of ballistic missile submarines down, the total numbers of such submarines might go up in the future because of the military policies of other countries.

3. It may be possible to reach international agreement on prohibiting the deployment of conventional offensive weapons systems on the seabed, but this may not be very significant since, with the exception of mines, no such weapon seems to have been developed.

4. Coastal states are likely to press for the exclusion of all foreign military installations from their continental shelves.

5. The military-scientific exploration of the deep ocean and the seabed will continue as a very strong trend. One way to lessen suspicion about the offensive purpose of such exploration may be to internationalize as much as possible of this research; that is, nations engaged in undersea exploration should to the greatest possible extent invite other nations to participate in their activi-

---

[24] The Straits of Malacca and of Singapore present an interesting case. Not long ago, the governments of Malaysia and Indonesia declared their intention to extend their territorial waters to 12 miles, which would mean that the narrowest passages of the straits would no longer be international water. Such action would affect the interests of many nations, including the United States, the Soviet Union, and Japan. China has recently supported the Malaysian and Indonesian policy and maligned the intentions of the Soviet Union and Japan regarding these straits.

ties.[25] A valid example may be the installation of manned underwater stations at great depths.

6. The new legal framework to be negotiated for the oceans at the upcoming Law of the Sea Conference may introduce certain modifications to present military uses of the seabed, the territorial waters, and international straits. However, these modifications are not likely to be very substantial in view of the strong factors working in the opposite direction.

7. Any measures beyond this, such as limiting the traditional forms of naval warfare, including the deployment of surface ships and attack submarines, will probably have to be taken up in the context of general and complete disarmament in a different political atmosphere than at present.

---

[25]See the suggestions made by the Soviet scientist I. E. Mikhaltsev in the paper "Technical Means for the Investigation and Exploitation of the Ocean" in *Impact of New Technologies on the Arms Race,* pp. 219–20.

CHAPTER 5

A Legal Regime for Arms Control and Pollution Control in the Oceans

JOHN P. CRAVEN

Quite independent negotiations for legal regimes in the ocean have been in process, on the one hand for purposes of arms control and on the other for purposes of pollution control. In the first instance, the United Nations Disarmament Conference has been one forum for international draft treaties, and the SALT (Strategic Arms Limitation Talks) have provided a significant bilateral mechanism for collateral agreements on arms in the ocean. Draft treaties and agreements for pollution control have been the responsibility of the Intergovernmental Maritime Consultive Organization of the United Nations. The separate nature of these proposals and negotiations suggests the possibility of conflicting regimes or of lost opportunities for cooperative agreement. It is therefore of legitimate concern to question the possible conflict between the two regimes, the interaction between these two quite different inhibitions in the use of the ocean and whether a common regime can be developed. To answer these questions we must first examine the generic nature of the two functions, the problems that are shared in common and the problems that are peculiar to each.

At first glance, there are pronounced similarities. The major elements of each legal regime will be:

1. The definition of the prohibited behavior.
2. The mechanisms for determining that a violation has occurred.

3. The mechanisms for unequivocally identifying the offending party.

4. The machinery for redress as a result of the violation.

5. The means for resolution of disputes.

The Prohibited Behavior

For both regimes the definition of the prohibited behavior will be difficult to frame in operational definitions which will, if followed, avoid the prospective harm and at the same time permit legitimate commercial and military use of the oceans. Such definitions will be particularly difficult with respect to pollution. This may be seen from the very difficulty of identifying pollution. To a first order, any substance that is introduced into the ocean which is different in chemical, thermal, or biological characteristics from the receiving waters is a pollutant. For example, the Environmental Protection Agency of the United States has to date identified some 85 potentially dangerous ocean-polluting substances. These include materials such as hydrogen peroxide, which degrades rapidly into water and oxygen, chlorine, which reacts rapidly to form common chloride salts, various biodegradable oils, and other materials which would have only a temporal or local effect. The measure of harm or benefit to the receiving waters by the introduction of such substances into the ocean is a highly subjective and goal-oriented decision on the part of world societies.

In such assessment there are unavoidable trade-offs between:

Human economic activity versus short-term biological damage

Short-term and immediate threats to human health versus long-term integrative damage to life and health or reduction in longevity

Benefits to human life, health, and economic well-being at the expense of life and health of lower trophic forms of life

Political, psychological, and esthetic factors, as against economic and ecological factors.

Familiar examples are found in each category:

Sea-borne transit of oil versus the potential for oil spills

Diagnostic and therapeutic use of radiation (x-ray, sunbathing) versus increased risk of cancer or genetic damage

The use of DDT and other insecticides for improved crops, as against damage to birds and other wildlife

The disposal of nerve gas and other military chemicals at sea versus the less safe but more politically acceptable land-based disposal.

The last example is of particular importance in considering the measure of harm from a pollutant. The characteristic feature of nerve gas, for example, is that it must be highly reactive to be effective and must exist in fairly concentrated form. Indeed, in dilute form, nerve gas formulations have been and are employed for medical purposes. The damage to the environment by the release of large quantities of this material in the deep ocean is demonstrably local and temporal and probably below the threshold of biological assessment. But the psychological and political attitudes toward such disposal are very strong. Indeed, many readers of this article will find themselves reacting strongly and negatively with respect to such apparently sanguine statements with respect to ocean disposal of nerve gases. As a consequence, it is a fact of international political opinion that such disposal ought to be prohibited.

For this reason, it is highly probable that some substances will be identified as ocean pollutants even when their discharge has no measurable effects. For those pollutants having a measurable effect, different nations will have different criteria for assessing the harm and, as a result, the quantity of pollutants which is regarded as damaging. It is already clear that some economically less well-developed nations are willing to pay a pollution penalty during the development process which more affluent nations will not tolerate.

Four characteristics of pollution have varying degrees of difficulty in harm identification. The pollution may be acute or chronic and persistent, and it may be either point source or diffuse. In the first category are the dramatic spills of oil or pollutants which result in immediate and identifiable harm. Such phenomena as oil on the beach, red tides, fishkills, Miyamoto disease (acute mercury poisoning) are readily observable and usually identifiable as a result of a single source or event. International consensus on the levels that will produce acute pollution should be easily obtained.

On the other hand, for chronic or persistent pollution such as the buildup of heavy metals or pesticides in the food chain or the diffusion of long-lived radioisotopes in the ocean, it will be difficult to identify the magnitude of the harm and even more difficult to identify the contribution of any incremental source. If the pollutant is a point source in the ocean (surface or submerged discharge), then the nature of ocean diffusion and transport is such that the effect will be highly local. This is particularly true for discharges in the deep ocean. If the discharge does not enter into the food chain, the effect of point source discharge is more confining, and it would be difficult to have any significant effect on the broad ocean as a result of discharge. Assessment of point source pollution may be accomplished on a municipal or regional basis and on such basis should be amenable to international agreement. Unfortunately, the majority of broad-ocean pollution comes from airborne sources. Thus, radioactive fallout, DDT, PCB, and other broad-ocean pollutants originate as aerosols or attachments to particulate materials. The assessment of the source and the relative contribution of each source to the pollution harm will be difficult.

As vexing as is the problem of assessment of the harm associated with various pollutants, it is not nearly as difficult as assessment of the threat to international peace and security posed by various magnitudes and types of sea-based arms deployment. It is still an unresolved international issue as to whether peace is best preserved by a demilitarized ocean or by an armed but arms-controlled ocean. The current possessors of nuclear weapons have for the most part adopted a common notion of security through deterrence. This notion suggests that the existence of a nontargetable retaliatory force is a requisite for peace between two nuclear powers of opposing ideologies or goal structures. It has also been suggested that stability is further assured if the strategic systems possessed by each side are incapable of delivering surprise attacks; from a technical standpoint such are best deployed at sea. Ballistic missile submarines of limited range are the most clearly feasible weapon systems of this type.

This particular concept of sea-based strategic deterrence which appears to have been adopted in whole or in part by the governments of France, Britain, the USSR, and the US, is not compatible with the notion of a denuclearized ocean. It is thus now generally recognized that the Treaty to Prohibit Emplacement of Weapons of Mass Destruction on the Seabed and Ocean Floor is more symbolic than substantive. This is particularly true since it is as easy, or easier, to design systems that float above the ocean floor as it is to design systems fixed to the ocean floor.

The question of strategic disarmament in the ocean is thus inextricably tied to the question of world strategic disarmament, with a high probability that land disarmament will precede disarmament in the oceans as a basis of stability. The hoped-for limitation on strategic weapons in the ocean must then be one of control and more specifically assurance that such weapons cannot and will not be used preemptively.

There are similar dilemmas with respect to tactical, sea-based weapon systems. There is hardly a coastal nation that does not maintain at the least a patrol and defensive naval capability. The conversion of such capability into an aggressive capability is, to a large extent, a problem of quality, quantity, and deployment. As in the case of strategic weapons, the only hoped-for control on the immediate horizon is one of determining deployments, assessment of such deployments as defensive, and mechanisms to limit and prevent surprise tactical attacks.

In addition to deployment constraints, other constraints on sea-based weapon systems can include prohibitions against the use of biological or chemical weapons and limitations on yield, accuracy, and range of the deployed weapon systems. (It should be noted that the further constraint of quantity or any combination of parameters which result in de facto disarmament will probably not be acceptable to nations which determine their sea-based tactical requirements according to their own concepts of an adequate defense.)

The Mechanisms for Determining that a Violation Has Occurred

With the exception of a few previously mentioned ocean pollutants which are politically unacceptable but otherwise nonmeasurable, it is practically a tautology that an ocean pollutant is defined by the fact that it or its effect can be measured.

Certainly, in the long run, nations of the world will not, or cannot, be concerned with discharges into the ocean environment which cannot be measured in the acute phase or as an integrated chronic effect. It is for this reason that detection of ocean pollution will be a reasonably straight-forward task. The acute cases are obvious; but even the more elusive substances such as DDT, radioisotopes, and mercury and heavy metals are now measurable by modern techniques in parts per trillion. *The central problem of pollution control is not the determination of its existence but the determination of the source and the parties responsible for its dissemination.*

This problem is very different from that associated with arms control. Weapons-system designers have been conditioned for the past century by the concept of a free and unrestricted ocean. Their systems have been designed to be undetectable even when confronted by an aggressive antagonist who is permitted to operate in close proximity to the deployed fleets. The quintessence of this art is embodied in the modern submarine. Designers of all nations having submarine fleets, nuclear or conventional, have concentrated on designs which are acoustically quiet, which do not emit pollutants or other measurable effluents, which have a self-contained or nearly self-contained ecological system, and which attempt to blend in every way with their ocean environment. The ability to detect systems deployed in violation of arms control agreements of the type now under consideration is in fact beyond the present and foreseeable state-of-the-art.

On the other hand, the number of nations that have the present technological capability and capital resources required for clandestine design construction and deployment of weapons systems of military significance is extremely limited (probably not more than five). *The control problem of arms control enforcement is not the identification of the violator but the mere determination that a violation has in fact occurred.*

Mechanisms for Unequivocally Identifying the Offending Party

The marked difference between the two functions (that of policing pollution agreements and that of policing arms control agreements) is such that quite different systems will develop unless and until the hopelessness of currently proposed solutions becomes evident.

In the monitoring of pollution, numerous suggestions have been made to aid in the problem of source identification. At the most permissive level, each nation that is threatened by oceanic pollution will be required to maintain its own surveillance network to monitor every ship or installation which has a potential for pollution, to detect the pollutant very shortly after its discharge, to be ready to prove on the basis of oceanographic, meteorological, and navigational information that the ocean pollutant did in fact emanate from the indicated ship or platform.

Considering the enormous number of ships which such surveillance would entail, the distance over which pollutants travel, the increasing liability which is assigned to offending ships or installations, the heightened motivation for nonreporting of accidents, etc., such a technique is certain to be frustrated by the cost of the surveillance measures and by the avoidance tactics taken by offending parties. Except for acute cases involving wrecks or groundings such as the *Torrey Canyon,* many pollution incidents will go unapprehended.

At the next most permissive level, proposals have been made that ships' fuels and liquid cargoes be "tagged" by chemical or isotopic means. This technique would make it mandatory to introduce chemical or nuclear additives to each liquid so that it could be identified as to source in the event of a pollution spill. Although an adequate number of "signatures" would be available by the technique, a number of problems are involved which may make such a procedure difficult to enforce. For example, refueling at sea or transference of fuel from one ship to another is a common occurrence. Such transfer process would require eradication of the tag of the transferor and the addition of the tag of the transferee. This would be difficult in the case of chemical tags and virtually impossible in the case of nuclear tags. The alternative would be the maintenance of detailed logs in order to identify the last clear possessor of a pollutant having multiple tags.

At the most restrictive level of surveillance is the requirement of onboard inspection. At the present the Canadian legislation establishing a

100-mile zone in the Arctic for pollution protection is the extant legislation which moves the furthest in this regard. This legislation requires that all vessels carry certain pollution-control equipment, that they show evidence of financial responsibility, that vessels submit to boarding and inspection, that vessels be prohibited from navigation within prescribed safety control zones, and are prohibited from all navigation during certain seasons.

In the total spectrum from voluntary reporting to onboard inspection, it is my view that at the present time onboard inspection by an independent or international inspectorate represents the only technically feasible means for early identification and reporting of a pollution incident and the un-equivocal tracing of the pollutant from the source to the locale in which the harm is threatened or occurs.

In the arms control parallel, two types of arms control situations can be envisaged—prohibition of certain classes of armaments and locales of deployment and restrictions on deployment of restricted systems. In the former category are the restrictions of the previously cited Sea-Bed Treaty outlawing emplacement of weapons of mass destruction on the seabed, and in the second category is the international prohibition on "Q" boats (that is, the requirement that warships be clearly identifiable as such). The "detection of violations" problem associated with the first of such restrictions is that truly enormous "mine-like" weapons deployed on the seabed and activated only on command are virtually undetectable in any foreseeable state-of-the-art except during the period of initial deployment. If detection of a violation of this type is to occur, it must be the result of intelligence or observation during construction or by detection, challenge and inspection upon first deployment. Such detection cannot take place unless surveillance systems are deployed in close proximity to ports of egress. In addition, the right to inspect both merchant and military shipping which are suspect must be permitted if the surveillance system is to be effective. From a technical standpoint, such a system is most easily accomplished if inspectors are permitted on merchant ships and war ships. Such inspectors would be able to communicate unambiguously to the surveillance systems the legality of the transiting ship. This would reduce the investigation activity to one of intercept and investigation of unidentified transitors.

It has been demonstrated that arms control systems of the second type (permitted systems deployed under restrictions which limit their offensive or preemptive potential) are technically feasible for both strategic and tactical systems. The effectiveness of such schemes has also been shown to require some form of onboard inspection. *It is therefore my conclusion that for very different reasons, pollution control systems and arms control systems are not yet technically feasible without onboard inspection by a neutral, international or even an antagonistic inspectorate.*

The Machinery for Redress and the Means for Resolution of Disputes

In light of this conclusion, we may now examine the evolving nature of proposed international pollution treaties and proposed international arms control in the sea. To date, in the field of pollution, this has consisted of modifications to existing conventions (International Convention for the Prevention of Pollution of the Sea by Oil, 1954, as amended) and new conventions (International Convention Relating to Intervention on the High Seas in Cases of Oil Pollution Casualties, International Convention on Civil Liability for Oil Pollution Damage, Draft Convention for the Regulation of Transportation for Ocean Dumping).

The international community is in fact in a process of ferment seeking to estimate and determine reasonable standards for ocean dumping and ocean discharge. The thrust of these conventions is that of establishing standards, liabilities, and measures to limit liability. Quite obviously, these conventions will be useful in the case of acute pollution where a casualty has occurred, and acts of salvage and pollution containment are in simultaneous process. In such instances, it will probably be in the best interest of all parties to submit to Admiralty Jurisdiction for resolution of respective liabilities. On the other hand, the proposed conventions are relatively weak with respect to chronic pollution or noncatastrophic accidents. Only relatively ineffective measures for detection, such as the maintenance of oil record books on a tank-to-tank basis are provided by present conventions. Jurisdiction for enforcement is limited to the flag state for violations in international waters and is concurrent with the jurisdiction of the coastal state in national waters. As in most international treaties and conventions, the conventions may be abrogated or denounced by the states parties to the conventions upon notice. Presuming that international standards can be set and presuming currently proposed treaties and conventions are ratified, it appears that the detection and control of chronic pollution and noncatastrophic accidents will remain an international problem.

In the field of arms control, even the benefit of technical standards established by appropriate commissions or organizations is not available. Mechanisms for separating technical standards from basic treaty provisions are not yet well established, and only a limited number of treaties and declarations of principles relating to arms control are now in existence (1958 Convention on the High Seas, Treaty to Prohibit Emplacement of Weapons of Mass Destruction on Seabeds, UN General Assembly Declaration of Principles Governing the Seabed beyond National Jurisdiction, etc.). Results of bilateral negotiations with respect to the SALT talks are as yet unknown and the only other inhibition on sea-based arms are those inherent in the Non-Proliferation Treaty or other conventions of worldwide scope.

Under the present direction of treaty and agreement, it is difficult to see any effective arms control measures in the near future.

Overshadowing all of these considerations is the yet to be determined width of the territorial sea and the limits of the continental shelf. Since pollution control may be regarded as a defensive measure on the part of a coastal state, the widest possible territorial sea will provide such state the greatest means for protection and enforcement; but since arms control may be regarded as a defensive measure on the part of the world community vis-à-vis the deploying or coastal state, then the narrowest possible territorial sea is required to permit surveillance and control. The same statement may be made with respect to the width of the continental shelf, with the further note that surveillance systems tend to consist of static sensor arrays mounted on the seabed, that the continental shelf jurisdiction is frequently wider than the territorial sea, and that as a result arms control surveillance measures would be inhibited or precluded in the instance of a narrow territorial sea and a wide continental shelf.

In assessing the competing influences, two questions arise—how wide a territorial sea would be required to assure the coastal state protection for pollution control, and how narrow a territorial sea and continental shelf is required to insure effective arms control? To the first question, the Canadian regulations suggest that 100 miles is a minimum and the International Convention for the Prevention of Pollution suggests that 50 miles is an appropriate minimum. From a technical standpoint, the limit is indeterminate, depending on pollution standards and magnitude of the accident. Even so, it appears that the order of magnitude of at least 100 miles is required to minimize the probability that a spill in international waters does not have a significant effect on the coast. The answer to the second question is in turn dependent on the nature of the shelf. If a coastal state has a wide, shallow barrier reef or shelf, then egress to the broad ocean must be made through narrow and monitorable passages at a significant distance from shore. If the coastal state is adjacent to deep water, then the full coastline is available for clandestine transit. For some nations, therefore, nothing less than the 40-foot depth contour would qualify as a sufficiently narrow territorial sea for the purposes of arms control.

We may therefore conclude that the present direction of developing treaties on arms control and pollution will not simultaneously satisfy the requirements of each. *It is therefore the single thesis of this article that simultaneous solution can only be accomplished through international onboard inspection of all commercial and military ships which will transit or are capable of transiting in international waters.* The cost of such a system is equivalent to a first order of that of an additional crew member for each ship. This price will be small in comparison with any other conceivable surveillance or control scheme. Under proper safeguards with respect to communication with the inspectors and techniques for safeguarding their independence in reporting, legal regimes for pollution and arms control can be developed which will not inhibit the use of the seas for commercial purposes or the use of the seas for legitimate military defense.

CHAPTER 6

Arms Control in the Oceans: Active and Passive

ELIZABETH YOUNG

Arms Control and Enforcing the Law

In his *The Leviathan,* Thomas Hobbes wrote: "Covenants, without the Sword, are but words, and of no strength to secure a man at all. . . . If there be no Power erected, or not great enough for our security, every man will, and may lawfully, rely on his own strength and art, for caution against all other men." This is the situation that will develop in the more economically appetizing parts of the oceans unless the rule of law is soon established. Because the rule of law depends on the ultimate sanction of legitimate force, we cannot be seeking totally to disarm ocean space, but rather to convert the role of armed force from that of offensive tool of national purpose into that of legitimate backing for the policing arrangements of whatever ocean regime, cooperative or centralized, regional or universalist, we manage to set up. The speed at which armed force at sea can be converted from weapon to police truncheon depends on the conjunction and interaction of a number of developing situations: the evolution and extension of universal law and regulation for ocean space; the progress of general arms control and disarmament; the rate and manner in which the various ocean industries (including, of course, the fishing industry) develop; and the kind of protection and control they turn out to require from national governments and from the international regime.

The scale of this protection and control should not be underestimated. For instance, the United Kingdom now has submarine frontiers on the continental shelf, with a number of (fortunately friendly) states: Norway, Denmark, West Germany, Holland, Belgium, France, and Ireland. (The U.K. also has a variety of other air and sea frontiers—air defense, oil and other forms of pollution, traffic monitoring, fishing zones, possibly sonic boom zones—within all of which the government has certain duties.) The vulnerability to attack of the offshore hydrocarbons industry, its rigs, pipelines, and mammoth tankers is only now beginning to penetrate the official mind. The lifeblood fuel, oil, is at even greater risk on the shelf of the North Sea than it is in the sea lanes off South Africa.

Implicit in every form of lease is an undertaking on the part of the lessor to guarantee the lessee's "quiet enjoyment" of whatever is being leased to him. As far as Her Majesty's oil company lessees in the North Sea are concerned, this presumably means protection of their property against attack, whether criminal or military. All other parties going about their rightful business are entitled to this protection as well. But how it is to be provided and maintained is not clear.

Active and Passive Disarmament

The international presence: passive disarmament and arms control

Disarmament and arms control, as they are related to the sea, may be considered under two heads—active and passive. *Passive* disarmament and arms control take place whenever nonmilitary activities are carried on in such a way as to preclude or discourage military activities, particularly, of course, by disturbing or preventing the secrecy in which they are normally carried on. Thus any seaward extension of national limits restricts—at least, psychologically, at the most, physically—the freedom of others to use those waters for military purposes. International activity can, of course, have the same effect. So far it has been the unconsidered by-product of the activities in question, but this could and perhaps should be changing.

The activities of the various existing and planned United Nations bodies and of an ocean regime's own organization are bound to result in a considerable international presence in ocean space (provided, of course, that the regime is more than the mere licensing body desired by the advocates of laissez-faire). This presence, of itself, would have an arms control effect proportionate to its scale and to the range of its activities; at some point, it will be necessary to consider how this effect can be enlarged and enhanced. In practice, disarmament and arms control measures are effective to the extent that they are verifiable and that they allow in the minds of interested parties a quality of certainty superior to that provided by their own armed forces and by military alliances and alignments. Consequently, any international inspectorate, research exercise, or monitoring body is part of a de facto international verification system. In setting them up, the arms control significance of the information they are to acquire should be kept in view and eventually concerted. If the Conference of the Committee on Disarmament (CCD) in Geneva takes over, as it should, the task of monitoring the observation of existing arms control agreements, the body set up to do this would be the natural recipient and organizer of this information. This is probably a long-term development. Neither military superpower will like the prospect of international verification, but given that the military implications of any new regulations or law for the sea will be carefully weighed by governments, it is only right that the arms control implications should also be considered.

The reader may notice that no mention is being made of international police forces or armed peacekeeping forces. As the Russians say, this is not accidental. There is virtually no chance of such a force, with any real authority, being agreed on in the General Assembly in the foreseeable future. Observation forces with the right to report violations, joint constabularies deriving limited local authority directly from national governments—these seem the maximum plausible until regional or international bodies acquire a great deal more real power than they now have. If the United Nations Conference on the Law of the Sea does pass into the law the idea of the Exclusive Economic Zone (EEZ) and/or the patrimonial sea, and if powerful regional regimes are set up along the cooperative "matrimonial" lines suggested for the Caribbean or for the seas off East Africa (and desirable in the North Sea), regional armed constabularies are likely to develop. But in no sense will they be an international constabulary writ small; but rather, national constabularies writ large.

The international presence: formal agreements.

Active disarmament and arms control occur when military activity is forbidden or limited by formal international agreement. As far as the sea and seabed are concerned, the sum of such agreements to date amounts only to the relevant provisions of the Partial Test Ban,[1] the sea-bed treaty,[2] and

[1]Treaty Banning Nuclear Weapons Tests in the Atmosphere, in Outer Space and Under Water, August 5, 1963.

[2]Treaty on the Prohibition of Emplacement of Nuclear Weapons and Other Weapons of Mass Destruction on the Sea-Bed and the Ocean Floor and the Subsoil Thereof. Opened for signature on February 11, 1971; came into effect on May 18, 1972.

the Strategic Arms Limitation Interim Agreement and Protocol on Offensive Weapons.[3] There is also a small bilateral agreement between the U.S. and the U.S.S.R. on "the prevention of incidents at sea"[4] (which, in fact, could usefully be made multilateral, as the Russian naval commander-in-chief has suggested).

The Antarctic Treaty, which went into effect in June 1961, did not affect the rights of states "with regard to the high seas within" the relevant area (south of 60°) and neither continental shelf nor seabed is mentioned.

The Partial Test Ban did little, if anything, to control or limit the development of weapons for use at sea (it probably did prevent some pollution by radioactivity).

The Sea-bed Treaty which refers to the whole area beyond a 12-mile coastal margin, was confirmatory rather than preventive. There is no reason to suppose that nuclear weapons installations fixed to the international seabed would ever be militarily more attractive than mobile submarine vehicles. It is, and is likely to remain, more difficult and more expensive to build a fixed habitable installation on the seabed than to build a vehicle that can be introduced from elsewhere. A fixed installation is easier for an enemy to locate, either during its construction or subsequently, than one which is even only somewhat mobile; and governments are unlikely to wish to leave nuclear weapons unattended. The treaty includes no machinery for the international control of its own enforcement, beyond a system of "rights to consult" culminating, in the event of "violations being found," in an appeal to the Security Council, where all five nuclear powers hold a veto. As a coastal state has the right under the *Convention on the Continental Shelf* to erect structures on the seabed and to declare 500-meter safety zones around them up to the surface of the water, evidence of a coastal state's own violation of the treaty would probably be difficult to obtain. There was discussion about establishing a right of entry to structures so as to verify that they did not contain nuclear or other mass-destruction weapons, but as coastal states wish to maintain defensive equipment on their own shelf approaches and as scientific research is, in any case, legitimately conducted on the shelf only with the permission of the coastal state, the idea collapsed. However, the Soviet Union seems to hold that states already enjoy the freedom to erect platforms, "fixed installations," etc., under their own exclusive jurisdiction, anywhere outside another state's territorial waters, for the purpose of conducting scientific research. The situation is in need of clarification.

[3]Interim Agreement between the U.S. and the U.S.S.R. on certain measures with respect to the limitation of strategic offensive arms. May 27, 1972.

[4]U.S.-U.S.S.R. Accord on Incidents at Sea. May 25, 1972.

The Russian-American Strategic Arms Limitation Interim Agreement, agreed on in May 1972, limits, among other strategic systems, the numbers of missile-launching nuclear submarines and of nuclear submarine-based ballistic missile launchers. It allows the substitution of a number of such missile launchers for an equivalent number of land-based launchers dismantled. It does not control numbers of nonballistic nuclear missiles (e.g., cruise missiles) nor include existing numbers of ballistic missiles launched by other than nuclear submarines (though it does cover their replacement). The grand total of missile-launching nuclear submarines permitted is 44 for the U.S. and 62 for the U.S.S.R. and of launchers, 710 for the U.S. and 950 for the U.S.S.R. (Overall totals, including fixed land-based launchers but taking no notice of multiple reentry vehicles or of mobile land-based launchers, which are not limited either, come to 1,710 for the U.S. and 2,424 for the U.S.S.R.)

The situation today, as far as strategic weapons based at sea goes, is that, roughly speaking, the two major nuclear powers have, or shortly will have, equal numbers of Polaris-type submarines. Both are pursuing the development of deeper-diving submarines and longer range submarine-launched missiles. At the moment, Russian submarine-launched missiles do not have as many warheads as the newest American missiles, but their overall megatonnage may well be superior. More targets are within short range of the open sea in the U.S. than in the U.S.S.R. and the Soviet Union has a substantial number of older types of submarines capable of launching short- and medium-range missiles (some submerged and some from the surface) armed with strategically (rather than "tactically") significant warheads. It has been traditional, in the highly respected International Institute of Strategic Studies (IISS) and Stockholm International Peace Research Institute (SIPRI) strategic missile counts, to omit these latter classes of missile-launching submarines, but as the ranges of their missiles are understood to be of one to several hundred miles and given the initial range of the submarines, these weapons systems could well also be deemed strategic. So could nuclear-bomber-bearing American aircraft carriers, and presumably also the aircraft carriers the Soviet Union has recently begun to build.

Formal and informal proposals for international agreement

This, then, is the limit of agreement. During the last few days of the SALT negotiations, the Soviet Union declared that it proposed to deem British and French missile-launching submarines limited by the bilateral SALT agreement, a unilateral assertion twice made and twice rejected by the United States. There have been some other ideas: total nonmilitarization of the oceans is still discussed at Geneva (and it has been put forward by the Soviet Union). However, it is unnegotiable, because it would be at once important and unverifiable (the nonemplacement of nuclear or other weapons of mass destruction is also unverifiable, but the activity banned seemed implausible enough at the time for military logic alone to vouch for the treaty's provisions being implemented).

In 1964 there was a Russian proposal to ban nuclear missile-launching submarines from the Indian Ocean and another in 1968 for maritime nuclear-free zones. In 1971 Mr. Brezhnev suggested discussions about distant-water fleets, a topic which would raise problems of definition and identification. For instance, would trawlers with electronic gear be included in the discussion? These problems could be as difficult as those of verification of the nonnuclear, nonmilitarized condition of any part of ocean space or floor.

In 1972 the United States announced that it had approached the Soviet government to discuss the possibility of their agreeing to limit their respective military presences in the Indian Ocean and the Persian Gulf. Further news has not emerged. Some weeks earlier, in December 1971, the Twenty-Sixth General Assembly had adopted a *Declaration of the Indian Ocean as a Zone of Peace* (Resolution 2832 XXVI) by a vote of 61–0, with 55 abstentions. The resolution was repeated in 1972. Each time, the abstentions have included most members of NATO and the Warsaw Pact. Each time Japan has voted in favor, and Australia and China voted in favor in 1972. An ad hoc committee has been set up to carry out studies.

The difficulties are, probably conclusively, against a general treaty for the demilitarization or for the denuclearization of the Indian Ocean. Even without shore bases, great power naval units increasingly can be serviced and supplied at sea. Nuclear submarines on station are, of course, entirely independent, and it was particularly the possibility of their deployment by the US in the Indian Ocean that suddenly, in the last few years, gave that previously confrontation-free area strategic significance. This possibility became important for the Soviet Union when the range of Polaris missiles became such that they could reach the Soviet Union from the northwestern Indian Ocean. With the earlier types of Polaris missiles, they could not. The point was that the United States was not known to be deploying Polaris III or Poseidon-launching submarines there, but that they could. Whether American-Russian discussions of "military restraint" in the Indian Ocean and elsewhere could succeed would depend on what kind of restraint the United States has in mind and on whether either side is willing to by-pass the nuclear issue and be satisfied with what would be unverifiable declarations about nuclear submarines. Easier to agree to would be a limit on the number and types of naval units operating in particular seas, a ban on bases, or facilities for reconnaissance and antisubmarine aircraft, and so on; such things would be verifiable. It could, moreover, much like the Treaty of Tlateloco, which made Latin America a nuclear-free zone, be negotiated and substantially put into effect by the Indian Ocean coastal states alone.

(In 1972 Oman was the only Indian Ocean state not to vote in favor of the Indian Ocean resolution.) Such a treaty would not be complete, because the Indian Ocean contains a few residual French and British island colonies and territories and, of course, Mozambique. (Lacking desert island bases, the Soviet Union has established several semi-permanent bases in the Indian Ocean in the form of mooring buoy-berthing stations.)

The present Indian Ocean resolution is misconceived to the extent that all manifestations of great power rivalry cannot be locally eliminated— unlike, for instance, in the Mediterranean and perhaps the Baltic, which bottlenecked as they are by narrow straits, local determination could theoretically clear of extraneous warships. Those manifestations, which can be eliminated or reduced on local initiative, are, in fact, those which most intrude, directly or indirectly, in the political and military activities of local states. This the presence of nuclear submarines in the deep ocean does not do. The location of such submarines at any given time is not known. Their overall number is known in the case of the US through the ordinary disclosure of government policies and statistics. In the case of the Soviet Union, again through publications of the American government, the figures are derived from satellite observation of construction yards, submarine pens, and so on. This lopsided state of affairs seems likely to continue, and verification of any "elimination" or of a reduction in the numbers of nuclear submarines agreed on in the SALT context, will not be done at their place of deployment—at sea.

Indeed, it is the "invisibility" of submarines at sea and the near invulnerability this confers that makes them the least provocative and therefore the least unsatisfactory of all the strategic weapons systems. They are in no danger, as are fixed land-based missiles, of being taken out in a first strike, so there is no motive for launching them in expectation of attack. This makes it likely that they would be the last strategic system of all to be dismantled in the best conceivable disarmament process—agreed to only in SALT.

Of course, there is a theoretical threat to their invulnerability. A breakthrough may yet come in antisubmarine warfare (ASW). As Admiral Sir Peter Gretton has put it, without sonar, hunting for submarines used to be like hunting for a needle in a haystack; with sonar, it became like looking for a knitting needle in a haystack. There are indeed modern improvements, but by and large, it seems likely that they will continue to favor the quarry rather than the hunter. Satellite observation is unable to do much to alter this. It is physics, not technique, that determine how far you can see through water. The next generation of missile-launching submarines will, anyway, be deeper-diving than present ones and their missiles very much longer-range, which will make the haystack bigger. It is sometimes suggested that a moratorium on ASW capabilities and research would help strategic stability. But once again, although declarations might be exchanged, verification would be impossible. Moreover, it would be hard to argue that states should not have the right to establish whatever antisubmarine surveillance and detection systems they can on the seaward approaches to their territory, if only to discourage enemy submarines from coming near enough to be used in a first strike.

The National Presence

For the present, there is no great prospect of much more "active" arms control or disarmament, relating to ocean space and floor, being achieved by international agreement. There is no great prospect, either, of anything much in the way of armed international constabularies beyond regional ones set up to service regional agreements. However, some of the rights and duties the Caracas conference is likely to recognize and allocate may well have an arms control effect, by way of various diminutions to the freedom of the high seas, coupled with continuing extension of national jurisdictions, of their enforcement, and of the use of national forces for the enforcement of international jurisdiction.

Under particular threat at Caracas are the freedom to fish, the freedom to emplace military equipment on the seabed (if, indeed, it exists), the freedom to conduct research, the freedom of navigation (including that of submerged submarines) through international straits and in the various zones of exclusive jurisdiction that may be set up, and the freedom to set up platforms and artificial islands in or under the high seas. The most immediately poignant of these for the great naval powers appears to be the issue of international straits. For their submarines to be required to travel through all international straits on the surface would be a major blow, particularly to the Soviet Union. A uniform legitimization of 12 miles for the breadth of territorial waters would wholly territorialize 116 commercially much-used straits, among others, the Straits of Dover, Gibraltar, Malacca (between Malaysia and Indonesia), Hormuz (the entrance to the Persian Gulf), Bab el Mandeb (the entrance to the Red Sea), the Robeson Channel (between Canada and Greenland), and the Bering Straits (between Alaska and Siberia). Various archipelago states—the Philippines and Indonesia—would become watertight. Straits already wholly within territorial waters include the sound between Denmark and Sweden (the entrance to the Baltic) and the Dardanelles (the exit to the Black Sea), for which a special regime already exists. The Suez and Panama Canals do not qualify as straits, nor would a canal through the Kra peninsula in Thailand, but it is worth noting that there was a call, if only halfhearted, for the "neutralization" of such canals at the meeting of the Security Council held recently in Panama.

The argument before the conference about straits is this: at one extreme the Soviet Union has put forward (July 25, 1972) draft articles "on straits used for international navigation," which would entitle all vessels (including warships and submerged submarines) in transit through such straits "to enjoy the same freedom of navigation . . . as they have on the high seas," even when the straits lie "within the territorial waters of one or more coastal states." It would be incumbent on vessels not to conduct military exercises of any kind, not to cause pollution and to observe international rules (that is, IMCO-recommended rules) about traffic separation. The flag states, as opposed to the offending vessel, would be liable for any damage, and the coastal state would not "be entitled to . . . require ships in transit to stop or to communicate information of any kind." This is in line with current Russian policy. In negotiating the seabed treaty, the Soviet Union was particularly concerned about excluding from its provisions any coastal states' right of veto over verification operations within the limits of its continental shelf, lest "the coastal states should come to consider themselves empowered to exercise control over the activity of any vessel or any submarine close to their continental shelf."[5] The view seems to omit consideration of such developments as 100 mph surface-effect vehicles or underwater transporters, which are already under development. The US had earlier produced a draft milder than the Russian, but also to the general effect that in international straits there should be freedom of navigation just as in the high seas. A new principle, "free transit," was proposed. The opposite view, held by the developing countries' group of 77 in the committee, is that this would "introduce discrimination between states possessing straits and those not possessing them." As the Tanzanian delegate put it, "a submarine which would have to navigate on the surface in the waters of a state without a strait . . . could navigate under the surface of the waters of a neighboring state which did possess a strait." (August 4, 1972, Subcommittee II). Moreover, states ought not to have to join IMCO in order to regulate traffic which might well endanger their interests. The Chinese delegate (China is one of the 77) pointed out with relish the discrepancies between Soviet practice within its own territorial waters and what it was recommending for others: warships require prior authorization to sail in Russian territorial waters (and it is not always given), submarines must remain on the surface at all times, all vessels must comply with the pre-

[5]Y. Tomitin, "Keeping the Sea-bed Out of the Arms Race," *International Affairs,* January 1970, p. 45.

scribed "navigation, radio-telegraph . . . sanitary . . . and other regulations," and foreign vessels violating any of these "shall be liable to arrest." The Soviet Union sometimes claims that all of its own vessels, being state-owned, are by definition immune from arrest.[6]

Both the Soviet Union and the United States showed considerable alarm at the prospect of the group of 77 getting their way. The US delegation "appealed to the fundamental sense of fairness for all delegations, and asked only for treatment equal to that accorded to every other nation" (August 3, 1972). Many delegates must have heaved a sigh of relief that a superpower was at last feeling what they had felt so often.

In practice, things are beginning to move in the direction desired by the 77. Malaysia, Indonesia, and Singapore, whose territorial waters include the Straits of Malacca (through which 90 percent of Japan's oil and most of Europe's Far Eastern trade is carried) in 1971 declared their intention jointly to control the constantly increasing traffic. A survey done in cooperation with Japan discovered 37 shallows which could endanger the movement of giant tankers and other large vessels. Naval vessels are already required to inform the appropriate coastal state of their intention to pass through the strait.

The Shah of Iran is now said to be considering a 50-mile territorial zone, as well as establishing, with Oman, a pollution-control post at the Strait of Hormuz, at which all vessels proceeding into the Persian Gulf would be inspected. Oil pollution is one grave danger in the Persian Gulf; subversion is another. No doubt, the delivery of illicit arms could be prevented at the same time as oil pollution.

The Swedish government, which, together with Denmark, controls the entrance to the Baltic, has for some years been discussing with the Soviet Union the possibility of making the Baltic a "sea of peace." The Swedes wish to interpret this as meaning the exclusion of warships, while the Soviet Union interprets it as meaning the exclusion of all warships except those belonging to the coastal states—a position which might eventually have a bearing on demilitarization proposals for the Mediterranean (the Soviet Union would like to be considered a Mediterranean state).

International Enforcement

All of these unilateral declarations of enlarged jurisdiction, the governments concerned are prepared to defend with force, in theory, and sometimes in

[6]S. Gureyev, "Immunity of State Sea-going Commercial Vessels," *International Affairs,* January 1972, p. 77.

practice. If international jurisdiction is declared in any form by the Caracas conference, it, too, will have to be enforceable, and the means of enforcement will have to be made available to the regime. This problem, while fundamental, is seldom considered either in Great Britain or the international community.

The agenda for the Caracas conference does not specifically provide for its discussion; yet if a regime is unable to call on policing and enforcement facilities, it will be worth little more than the paper it is written on. The present system for enforcement at sea of internationally-approved regulations (concerning, for instance, the discharge of oil or traffic-separation schemes) is quite inadequate. The only more-or-less international policing system in existence is that implicit in the workings of the international insurance market, where a bad record or bad equipment is penalized by the effective levying of fines in the form of heavier premiums. Otherwise, of the three elements of policing—the right of entry (or boarding) and inspection, the right of seizure and arrest, and the right of penal jurisdiction—the first is sometimes operated mutually among participants in fishing agreements, while the second and third remain almost exclusively in the hands of the flag government. As such ("hands" including those of "flag of convenience" states, whose convenience lies precisely in their low "social" and safety standards and in their inadequate powers of enforcement), the present system effectively relaxes the law for the benefit of self-selected evaders of the law.

CHAPTER 7

An International Multipurpose Surveillance System

BJØRN EGGE

Introduction

One of the problems connected with a potential agreement on an international regime of the ocean space and floor is that of surveillance of this space and the verification of compliance with established rules. The "Treaty to Prohibit Emplacement of Weapons of Mass Destruction on the Seabed and Ocean Floor" signed February 11, 1971 by 63 nations prohibits emplacement of nuclear weapons on the seabed. Verification of compliance or noncompliance with the treaty may entail unforeseen difficulties. The international political climate is characterized by a general lack of mutual confidence among states and groups of states. The state-of-the-art regarding technological detection equipment may also present obstacles to arms control in ocean space.

However, the necessity for introducing other control functions has recently come to the fore. These functions comprise environment control against pollution of the seas and control of activities which threaten the conservation of living resources in the seas.

These new control functions, combined with other activities to the general advantage of mankind such as oceanographic research and high seas search-and-rescue operations, indicate the need for an international institution to control such activities in the future. These activities have one thing in common: they all need a centralized, land-based management machinery and a sea- and airborne operational element to provide platforms or equipment carriers for the various kinds of detection and verification functions under international command and control. These platforms could be used in common for all control functions, including arms control.

On the basis of this general thesis, this article discusses briefly the precedents and preconditions for the establishment of an operational, international surveillance machinery. The article does not pretend to be an exhaustive systematic analysis of all aspects of the issue area of ocean surveillance on a cost-benefit basis. Its main purpose is to suggest a practicable *institutional structure* for a worldwide international system of multipurpose surveillance for the ocean space and floor, if the establishment of such an organization should prove necessary.

In order to make clear the preconditions for a potential future organization, it is necessary to give some background information and to state the basic set of assumptions underlying the thinking. The focus is on what *can* be done from a technical point of view and what ought to be done from an ecological and international security point of view, more than what is possible politically. Within the international global system, this article gives priority to the operational surveillance and control functions as precursor to a more elaborate international law enforcement system.

The functions it seems necessary to cover are, first, the relatively noncontroversial pollution control and sea-life conservation control, in addition to sea safety and rescue functions. At a later stage the operational machinery could take on some of the more controversial functions inside the arms control spectrum. This might initially be done only in selected areas until the machinery is tested.

In this article, only surveillance and reporting functions will be discussed. Enforcement and administration of sanctions will not be considered.

An international surveillance system should comprise whatever parts of ocean space will be left when national sovereignty limits have finally been decided, which depends on agreements yet to be made. The international machinery could also, on request, perform control functions inside areas under national jurisdiction in cases where host nations are incapable of carrying out the functions by their own means.

The suggested machinery will operate within the framework of the UN system. It can be adjusted to perform operational functions in the field for a number of UN agencies that do not possess this capability today. The aspect of organizational link-up should be left for later discussion. Many relationships are changing in the international community. A final decision as to the detailed organizational structure of a surveillance organization and its relationship to other institutions can be taken only with due regard to other international institutions existing at the time. This article will outline only suggestions for a structure based on ideas held at the present time, given the existing conditions in the international community. Therefore, the suggestions made should be regarded as a basis for discussion and not as a final proposal.

The political obstacles to the establishment of an international surveillance system are so many and so strong that it seems hardly worthwhile to even discuss the matter. However, the international political climate is constantly changing. There seems to be a justification for international institution-building whenever member nations see their own advantage in supporting it. The common interest in fighting marine pollution and the preservation of the living natural resources of the sea may prove to be of such importance that national self-interest may be mobilized. In addition, continuation of the arms race on the seabed may eventually prompt support for a surveillance organization. On the other hand, arguments for the paramount importance of preserving secrecy at sea for the sea-based strategic nuclear deterrent seem to militate against a too-elaborate international surveillance system.

As long as a surveillance organization of moderate size and means is assigned strictly monitoring and reporting tasks and does not get involved in direct administration of sanctions, the degree of controversiality can be held at a tolerable level. This would reflect national attitudes toward United Nations peace-keeping functions, where the unarmed observer missions seem to evoke far less criticism than the force level operations with a built-in enforcement capability.

Political hesitation, however, remains the main obstacle to the establishment of a surveillance organization. The moment political agreement is reached, the financial aspects can be cleared and the technological capability acquired to do the job.

The financial obstacles to establishment of a surveillance organization are a function of political attitudes. If the organization could be financed from the revenues obtained from industrial activity in international waters, as suggested in some proposals, it would obviously help to eliminate some of the financial worries.

The operating costs of the organization will depend largely on the scope and specific tasks assigned it. The higher the level of detection in the arms control field required, the greater the costs will be. The costs will also increase with a greater area to be inspected, and they will be influenced by the type of inspection chosen.

The problem of air and surface surveillance of the high seas seems to have been solved technologically, but underwater surveillance techniques seem not to have reached a level of confidence which can give adequate assurance of detection. The present depth limit of practical seabed construction is approximately 200 meters. The prognosis for the coming decade is that this limit will reach approximately 500 meters. Problems will arise for an international surveillance organization without access to ASW (antisubmarine warfare) technology to cope with detection and surveillance tasks at such depths. Technological breakthroughs may, however, occur and facilitate the task. Until this comes about, underwater surveillance on behalf of an international organization is faced with large obstacles.

Precedents of Inspection and Control of Activities at Sea

General

The idea of inspection and control of activities at sea is not new. Some of these functions are being performed today on national, regional, and international levels. Other writers have gone into this issue in detail and it is therefore not considered appropriate to do so in the context of this paper.[1]

The National Level

The most elaborate inspection systems at sea at the national level will be found in the fishing industry. The purpose of the inspection is protection against intrusion of foreign elements in national waters and ensuring the observance of fishing laws and regulations. Outside the nationally declared fishing limits, the task of the national inspectorate is to protect the rights of its own fishing fleet.

The British Fishery Patrol Squadron, supported by the Royal Navy, is well known. In the US the Coast Guard performs the functions of inspection and law enforcement. In Norway the Royal Navy is charged with inspection and protection. Similar institutions exist in most coastal nations.

As exploitation of oil on the continental shelf becomes more customary, policing of national codes grows more substantial. New in the field, the Norwegian government, among others, took great care to establish detailed rules for personnel safety and measures to prevent oil pollution.[2]

---

[1]For the factual information here I am especially indebted to Robin and Frances Murray for their excellent essay, "An Examination of the Existing Constabularies and Inspectorates Concerning Themselves with the Sea and the Seabed," *In Quiet Enjoyment, Pacem in Maribus Papers,* Vol. I, Malta: Royal University of Malta Press, 1971, pp. 173–233.

[2]See Government of Norway, *Regulations Relating to Safe Practice, etc., in Exploration for and Exploitation of Petroleum Resources of the Seabed and its Subsoil.* Royal Decree of August 25, 1967 (English translation, UN A/Ac 135/1/Add. 1, March 12, 1968).

The Regional Level

At the regional level the North East Atlantic Fisheries Commission can serve as an example of inspection rights which extend to ships of other nationalities rather than the flag state of a ship. The contracting states have inspectors from their own national fishery protection service on board their own ships at sea. These inspectors have the right to inspect any fishing vessel of any of the contracting states. The inspection covers net and fish sizes, and the right of inspection varies with the nationality of the inspector, since no common rights were agreed upon. The inspectors will only report violations of agreed-upon rules and regulations. Seizure and penal jurisdiction remain in the hands of the flag state.

Another example of a regional agreement containing an operative policing clause is the International Pacific Salmon Fisheries Convention. This is an agreement between Canada and the United States to coordinate programs for the conservation of Fraser River sockeye and pink salmon stocks. The Convention provides for "cooperative" seizure and arrest. The two contracting parties each have a specified area within which they are responsible for patrolling and seizing vessels from either country. The area includes their own territorial waters plus a portion of the high seas covered by the Convention. Once arrested, the vessel in question is to be delivered to the nearest point to the place of seizure in the country to which the vessel belongs.

The Japanese-Soviet Fishery Treaty for the Northwest Pacific specified an international control system which included the right to board and inspect vessels of the other party on the high seas. This "cooperative" inspection has since been considerably developed. In 1965 the parties agreed informally on the supervision of the Japanese salmon fishery in a specific part of the Convention area by Soviet inspectors carried on board Japanese patrol vessels. The following year a further informal agreement permitted Soviet officials to be present at Japanese fishing bases in Hokkaido in order to inspect the counting of fish catches. This Convention also provides for cooperative seizure, which is a rare phenomenon in international practice. However, jurisdiction remains with the flag states. Cooperative jurisdiction in this field is still unknown in the international community.

An example of regional patrolling and surveillance of the high seas for reasons of safety is the International Ice Patrol (IIP). The IIP is operated by the US Coast Guard in the heavily traveled shipping lanes of the North Atlantic. This is done on behalf of interested nations in order to provide day-to-day warnings of dangerous conditions during the iceberg season.

Not a single life has been lost due to icebergs since the patrol was established shortly after the *Titanic* disaster in 1912.[3]

The International Level

There is no known, truly international, policing of national vessels or of phenomena in international waters. The closest one can come to the principle in this respect may be the International Whaling Commission (IWC) scheme for international observers, adopted in 1963 but so far not implemented. This scheme envisaged the appointment of inspectors to factory ships of the contracting parties. The international inspectors would be paid by and be responsible to the IWC. A working group met in 1967 to consider possible implementation of the plan, but there are as yet no concrete results of the negotiations.

Regarding oil pollution at sea, the 1954 International Convention for the Prevention of Pollution of the Sea by Oil, as amended in 1962, provides the basis for laws concerning this issue on the high seas. The practical usefulness of the provisions, however, are limited by the lack of effective operational inspection and enforcement means. National elements such as ships and aircraft provide certain information, but this has generally not been sufficient as a basis on which to mount successful prosecution.

Disposal of radioactive waste on the high seas is one area where international law has given instructions, perhaps with somewhat greater degree of compliance. Article 25 of the Geneva Convention on the High Seas requires states to prevent pollution resulting from radioactive waste disposal and instructs them to cooperate with international organizations in doing so. In May 1966 the IAEA (International Atomic Energy Agency) convened a panel of experts to discuss research and experience in radioactive waste disposal, and in 1967 five countries cooperated in an experimental operation to dump 10,893 tons of waste under international supervision in the eastern Atlantic, about 450 kilometers from the nearest land. A similar operation was carried out in 1969 with officials from the waste-disposing countries, escorted by officers from West Germany, Ireland, Japan, and Portugal.

Lessons for the Future

Examination of the precedents in surveillance of activities at sea suggests a requirement for an international monitoring effort in the fields of live-resource preservation and control of maritime pollution by oil and

[3]U.S. Department of Transportation, *Facts and Functions.* Washington, D.C.: U.S. Government Printing Office, 5000–0049, January 1971, p. 8.

hazardous waste. When potential arms control verification is added to this list, there seems to be justification for the establishment of an international surveillance organization for the ocean space and floor with an operational capability.

Basic Principles for the Establishment of an International Surveillance Organization

Before a detailed suggestion for an organizational structure of an international surveillance system is presented, it is necessary to state certain basic principles for the establishment of such an organization. It is important to keep these principles in mind if the final organization is to fit into the political, economic, and technological realities prevailing in the international community. The principles are intended as general guidelines for the organizational process only and should not be regarded as hard and fast rules.

As a general principle, it is suggested that an international surveillance organization for the ocean space and floor be connected with the United Nations system of international institutions. An International Ocean Space Surveillance Agency (IOSSA), could for instance, be made a subsidiary organ of the International Ocean Space Institutions (IOSI), proposed in the Maltese Draft Treaty.

If this blueprint is adopted as a general framework, the IOSSA could be made responsible to the Assembly of the IOSI. The IOSSA could be the operational arm of the IOSI secretariat. Article 155 (d) assigns inspection functions to the secretariat, which could appropriately be carried out by the IOSSA in the field. In Article 155(j), the secretariat is given the task of maintaining a register of the disposal of radioactive wastes in the international sea. This function could be performed by the Ocean Space Documentation Section of the IOSSA HQ Staff.

The IOSSA would have liaison with the three major subsidiary organs of the IOSI through the secretariat for execution of necessary tasks in the field:

Ocean Management and Development Commission
Scientific and Technological Commission
Legal Commission.

Under the functions and powers of the Scientific and Technological Commission is listed, among other things: "The Commission shall establish standards with regard to contamination of the marine environment by pollutants and shall establish a system of monitoring of the oceans for pollution." It seems logical to assign the operative part of this paragraph to the IOSSA.

The Council may also give specific instructions for execution in the field which could be channeled through the secretariat of the IOSI. Article 142 of the suggested Ocean Space Treaty gives the Council authority to "investigate any situation or any action by states which might gravely impair the natural state of ocean space or might endanger the ecological or territorial integrity of the international sea or which might be seriously prejudicial to the maintenance of law and order in ocean space." This function would naturally fall under the purview of the IOSSA.

When the entire IOSI system is established and the suggested International Maritime Court is operative, the IOSSA could refer reports on violations to the secretariat, which, again through appropriate channels, would submit claims to the IMC.

For the purpose of this article, to illustrate the requirement for and to demonstrate the practical and organizational aspects of the operational elements of an ocean regime, the Maltese proposal is suggested as a model framework. In Figure 7.1 it is shown how the IOSSA might be connected with the IOSI system. Figures 7.2 and 7.3 show the suggested IOSSA organizational diagrams. The IOSSA idea could, however, be adjusted without difficulty to the French, UK and US models if the international community so desired. It should be a general principle in the establishment of an international surveillance organization that emphasis be put on the operational capability and on flexibility in organizational relationships.

Another basic principle to guide the establishment of a surveillance organization should be the broad scope of the functions the organization would cover. Once the organization has operational units at its disposal, it will be capable of taking on a number of different kinds of assignments.

For reasons of economy of resources, a multipurpose organization will be an advantage. It is therefore suggested that the organization be given tasks in the fields of maritime pollution control and ocean living resource preservation and at a later stage verification of arms control agreements.

Another important principle for institution-building in the international field should be the controlled, flexible, and gradual growth of the organization. It is suggested that a start be made by coordinating existing national activities within the field of interest and accumulating of data as to requirements for international control and the possible acceptability of such control.

As the functional area is canvassed by existing offices, the gradual expansion into independent activity can take place by incremental additions, not by a sudden build-up of a large, autonomous organization.

Emphasis should be placed on cooperation with existing national and

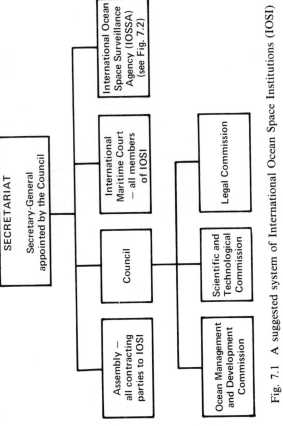

Fig. 7.1 A suggested system of International Ocean Space Institutions (IOSI)

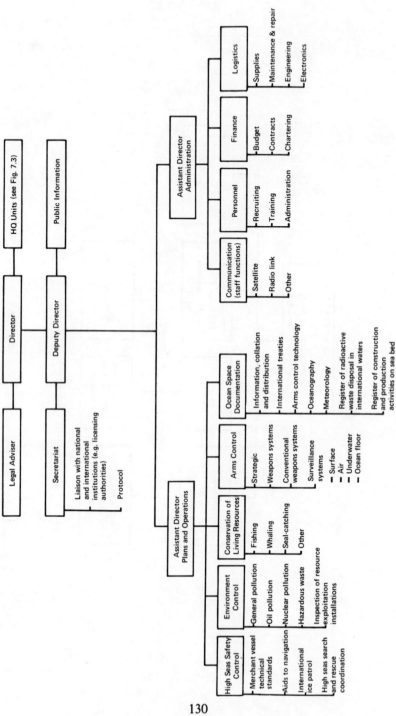

Fig. 7.2 A suggested International Ocean Space Surveillance Agency (IOSSA)

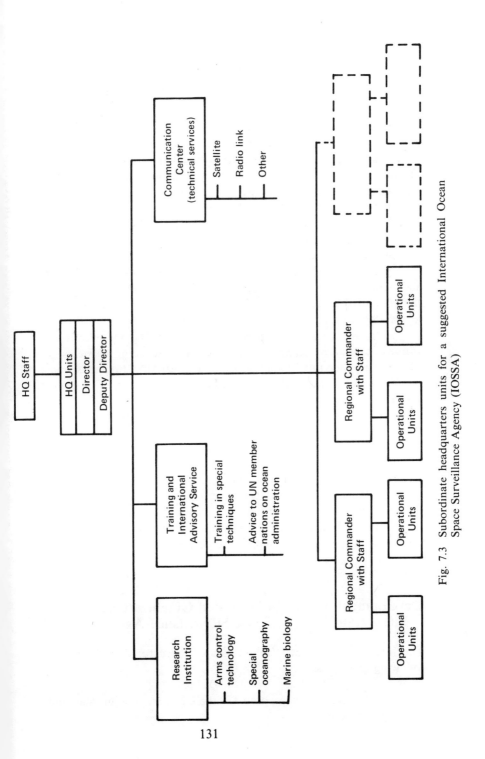

Fig. 7.3 Subordinate headquarters units for a suggested International Ocean Space Surveillance Agency (IOSSA)

131

international bodies. Only when vital requirements cannot be met through other operational organs, should steps be taken to develop such capability within the suggested surveillance organization. Extreme caution should be shown from the very beginning that the international organization concentrate on monitoring, surveillance, and verification in order to establish facts in accordance with the directives of the political guiding bodies. Enforcement or administration of sanctions should be assigned only to the operational elements at a later stage when complete consensus expressed in unanimity of votes in the appropriate political organs can be achieved.

An example of an action that would require full consensus is the right of hot pursuit of a vessel that has been caught *in flagrante* in serious violation of an international agreement. Dr. Pardo has detailed provisions for such occasions in Articles 25 and 147 of the Maltese Draft Proposal. The principle of hot pursuit is recognized in international law.

A full-fledged international system of surveillance of the ocean space and floor covering the entire globe would be prohibitively costly. It is therefore mandatory to conserve resources such as ships, aircraft, technological detection equipment, and manpower.

There are several examples of expense limiting the effectiveness of various inspection systems, particularly their seagoing elements. Every effort should therefore be made to avoid duplication of functions among all the UN organs concerned with surveillance and between the international and national agencies with interests in the same field.

One important financial source of support for an international surveillance organization such as the suggested IOSSA would be revenues from the international licensing system for industrial and other economic activities in international waters. This has been proposed by the Canadians, by Dr. Pardo and is also mentioned in the US proposal. The French proposal advances the idea of levying taxes on companies holding exploitation licences in the areas allocated to them. The British working paper suggests that the international agreement should provide for the payment of international royalties and for licensing fees respecting operations conducted under the regime.

Development Toward a Suggested Organizational Structure: International Ocean Space Surveillance Agency (IOSSA)

The Surveillance Agency (IOSSA) should be structured on the basis of the following principles:

—It shall be incorporated in the UN system of international organizations.

—It will be built up gradually according to actual requirements and consensus among UN member states.

—It will be financed partly or wholly from revenues arising
from resource exploitation.

—The best available technology will be used in securing
operational success of the machinery.

—The suggested final structure of IOSSA, as shown in Figures 7.2 and 7.3, represents an advanced stage of the implementation of the Agency which will be reached only through a gradual, evolutionary development over a considerable period of
time.

—The functions to be performed by the IOSSA are to be
decided by competent UN organs through accepted procedures.
This also goes for the degree of control and authority to be exercised by the Agency within each functional area.

—The geographical area to be covered by the operational
units in the field are to be decided by competent UN bodies in
recognition of international rules and regulations. The rules for
the delimitation of the area where IOSSA's operational elements
will operate will be governed by the international law of the sea
and seabed in power at the time of operation.

The present state of affairs in matters of ocean control is characterized
by a comparatively lively activity on the national level, some regional
activity, and intense discussions without comparable institutionalized machinery on the international level. From this stage, a progressive, time-
phased development could be followed toward a full-fledged operational
machinery some time in the future. Five phases of a potential development
will be discussed below. The three phases of implementation of the staff and
operational elements of the international machinery are subdivided into
three functional aspects: the central staff function, the regional staff function, and the operational functions in the field. It is considered essential that
these three groups of functions be kept apart for analytical and practical
organizational purposes.

First Phase: Coordination of Present National Activities

In this phase the existing staff element or the UN Secretariat dealing
with the ocean space and floor could be reinforced. An inventory of existing
national and international activities regarding the issue area could be
worked out. If overlapping functions were identified, there could be efforts
to coordinate them.

If the UN Secretariat felt that there were areas that were neglected in research, requests for assistance could be made to member states capable of undertaking additional functions.

In the areas of pollution control and embryonic arms control, the UN Secretariat could issue requests to national institutions for surveillance and reporting of violations of international agreements and give guidance for operational approaches. Reports could be evaluated at the UN office and action in the form of submission of reports to flag states and/or public exposure of facts could be taken.

Second Phase: Organizational Planning

Based on experience from the first phase, a planning group could be established. Parallel with the activities of the Secretariat, it could prepare a blueprint for a separate, specialized agency under the auspices of the United Nations. The planning group could be commissioned to produce a detailed and flexible plan for an institution which could undertake all the practical and other functions necessitated by the development of international law regarding the ocean space and floor, which would include:

> Delimitation of ocean and sea areas and suggestions for international responsibilities under each area according to existing international law
> Surveillance of the high seas
> Some oceanographic and meteorological research functions of practical international interest
> Verification of compliance with arms control agreements
> Reporting of national industrial activity on the seabed and of incidents and irregularities
> Suggestions for dealing with violations through procedures leading to legal proceedings.

Third Phase: Implementation of the International Machinery— IOSSA

Central staff functions. This phase would include the appointment of a director and a nucleus central staff for the international machinery. During this phase the limited staff could be given the opportunity to prepare for its activities and should consequently not be given executive, operational tasks.

The following staff elements could be given skeleton staffing:

Director
  deputy director

        legal adviser
        public information
    Plans and Operations
        environment control (pollution, etc.)
        high seas safety
        conservation of living resources of the ocean
    Liaison with international organizations
    Personnel and Budget

Regional Staff Functions. During the third phase no regional headquarters should be established. However, the Central Staff could investigate the requirements for a regional machinery and explore the possibilities for later establishment of subordinate elements. In the meantime, working relationships between the central machinery of the IOSSA and national operational agencies should be established through bilateral, legally binding treaties to the effect of supporting the surveillance capabilities of the IOSSA.

Operational Functions in the Field. During the third phase the central headquarters should develop a network of bilateral agreements between the UN and member states to the effect that national seagoing units and airplanes overflying the oceans should report suspected violations of the different international treaties to be controlled.

Fourth Phase: Expansion of the International Machinery—IOSSA

Central staff functions. The skeleton control staff could in this phase be further developed. Experience as to the operational exigencies of control functions will have been gathered. Based on this experience, an embryonic arms control element could be added to the operational staff. Its initial function would be to establish a data bank of all available information on arms control techniques pertaining to the ocean space and floor. Based on this information, negotiations could be carried on with member states possessing the necessary aircraft and seagoing vessels and detection devices to secure their cooperation in arms control verification.

In the fourth phase efforts could be made to establish the right of hearings in the suggested International Maritime Court, provided it was established and prepared to function in this capacity.

An inventory of all licenses issued for industrial activity in international ocean space should be kept in the documentation section of the central headquarters.

Regional Staff Functions. In the fourth phase it would be advantageous to develop a regional network by establishing small staffs in a few areas when activity at sea indicates that this is necessary. These staffs should serve only as intermediate links between the central headquarters and the national institutions. They would also be the contact points for the international observers introduced in this phase, as explained below.

Operational functions in the field. During the fourth phase the IOSSA could work toward introduction of international observers on board national vessels and aircraft. The observers would enjoy international status and immunity. They would be placed on board commercial craft initially, but negotiations could be carried on to extend the arrangements to include naval vessels and aircraft for arms control purposes.

Fifth Phase: Finalization of the International Machinery—IOSSA

Central Staff Functions. The central staff could in this phase be expanded to full size. A suggestion for a possible organizational structure for a fully developed central staff capable of meeting the essential requirements is shown in Figure 7.2. The necessary support functions, the headquarters units as shown in Figure 7.3, could also be established in this phase.

The suggested organizational structure will probably stand a chance of full implementation only in the distant future. A change in the present international climate with a higher degree of mutual confidence is required. The concept of supreme national sovereignty is still too deeply ingrained to envisage a turn toward full compliance with international law. International law enforcement and administration of international sanctions are therefore not considered feasible in the foreseeable future.

In clear-cut cases with irrefutable evidence, however, the right of hot pursuit and arrest may be possible. In addition, the right of indictment by the suggested International Maritime Court (when it becomes operational) may be within the realm of possibility.

The suggested headquarters units to support the field activities, as shown in Figure 7.3, are necessary if the system is to function effectively.

Regional Staff Functions. In the fifth phase regional operational headquarters could be established. At this time, the requirement for a few internationally controlled (chartered or owned) ships and aircraft may have become so clear that the funds would be made available for their acquisition. The direct operational control of the sea and air units would be the responsibility of the regional headquarters.

Operational functions in the field. In this last phase of the development of an international machinery for the surveillance of the ocean space and floor, operational units under international control seem to be a logical consequence.

It is hardly a realistic goal to envisage a great number of ships and aircraft for this purpose.* National surveillance systems will probably continue to be present in coastal waters and parts of the international ocean space. It might be more realistic to project a small number of international seagoing and airborne units to perform the tasks not covered by national institutions. Particularly as platforms for more sophisticated sensors and other detection equipment become available, it seems to be important to have independent units under direct international control.

Size and Scope of the Suggested International Ocean Space Surveillance Agency

The general trends and pace in the development of international cooperation alone indicate the magnitude of the eventual IOSSA. This development is dependent on a multitude of unpredictable variables. If sound organizational principles are applied and expansion is kept strictly to the fields where national agencies are unwilling to engage themselves or are incapable of doing so, the IOSSA could be limited in size and scope. Accurate cost and manpower requirements for a fully developed international organization can be estimated only when operational tasks are given and detailed planning figures are available.

Most national agencies with functions similar to those falling under IOSSA are integrated into the naval service, as in the USSR or they are split up among several agencies as in the United Kingdom. The best openly available basis for comparison is the United States Coast Guard. Even this organization has a variety of functions to perform which would not be applicable internationally. In addition, the USCG has the advantage of using the worldwide base facilities of the US Navy or Air Force, which is difficult to evaluate in terms of direct expense.

In spite of these reservations, the USCG may serve as a useful model, as Senator Claiborne Pell has pointed out.**

The US Coast Guard comprises 4,479 officers, 1,338 warrant officers, 32,202 enlisted men (aggregate 38,120), plus 1,047 cadets at the Coast Guard Academy (fiscal year 1972).† The 1970 budget was $584 million. The

---

*Regarding potential low-cost purchase of ships in the "moth-ball" fleet, see UN Document A/C 2/271, 17 November 1971: *Report of the Economic and Social Council;* letter dated 16 November 1971 from the Permanent Representative of Malta to the UN addressed to the Secretary-General, p. 31.

**Pell, with Harold Leland Goodwin, *Challenge of the Seven Seas,* New York: William Morrow & Co., 1966, pp. 238–41.

†*Jane's Fighting Ships, 1971–72.* London: Sampson, Low Marston & Co., 1971, p. 574.

organization deployed 307 floating units and a total of 168 aircraft, including 104 helicopters.*

The USCG currently has the following mission:

- To enforce or assist in the enforcement of applicable federal laws on the high seas and waters subject to the jurisdiction of the United States.
- To administer all federal laws regarding safety of life and property on the high seas and on waters subject to the jurisdiction of the United States, except those laws specifically entrusted to other federal agencies.
- To develop, establish, maintain, operate, and conduct aids to maritime navigation, ocean stations, icebreaking activities, oceanographic research, and rescue facilities.
- To maintain a state of readiness to function as a specialized service in the Navy when so directed by the President.**
- For the fiscal year 1970 the distribution of the financial means was as follows:
- 65 percent related to multipurpose search, rescue, navigational aids, port security, and law enforcement activities.
- 15 percent related to oceanography, meteorology, icebreaking and other marine sciences;
- 15 percent related to military activities;
  5 percent related to merchant marine inspection and safety.†

The geographical area of operation of the USCG is minute compared to the area that would eventually be covered by IOSSA. On the other hand, many functions performed by the USCG would not need to be performed by IOSSA. A formidable and well-organized institution such as the USCG would probably be capable of performing many functions on behalf of IOSSA at a relatively low cost in terms of additional operational units and direct financial expense.

The USCG is mentioned here only for comparison, in order to give a general idea of the size and cost of an operational system. The IOSSA will be different in many respects from the USCG. Assigned functions, staff structure, operating procedures, and actual seagoing and airborne units would be modeled on international requirements as distinct from national tasks.

*Armed Forces Report, 1971. Department of Defense publication, Office of the Director of Information, Secretary of the Air Force, Washington, D.C.: U.S. Government Printing Office, 1971: 0–417–731.
**Janes Fighting Ships, p. 574.
†Ibid.

The exact structure of such an organization is impossible to predict. Time, events, and unquestionable requirements will be the determining factors in the development. The organizational structure shown in Figures 7.2 and 7.3 should be regarded only as a potential solution to the institutional problem.

Concluding Notes

This article may easily be disregarded as being produced for a world that does not exist. I would tend to agree with this. Nevertheless, the requirements have been stated, the facts have been assembled, and the ideas presented in the hope that they can serve as an illustration. It is written in the hope that decision-makers and practitioners in the field can make use of separate elements of the article as the need may arise.

The problem of controlling the seas exists and grows, rather than decreases, in size and scope. The logical consequence would be for some action to be taken sooner or later.

PART III

THE DEVELOPMENT OF THE MEDITERRANEAN

The International Ocean Institute's Mediterranean studies have been continuous since 1971. This is due not only to Malta's location at the center of the Mediterranean Sea, but also to the fact that action in the region seemed indeed most urgent. With advancing urbanization and industrialization of the coastlines (especially on the northern shores), with the discovery of oil, increasing tanker traffic, and the swelling of tourism, pollution was assuming alarming proportions —all this in a sea whose peculiar circulation pattern and hydrological conditions render it particularly vulnerable. The Mediterranean is a sick sea. Unless rather drastic steps are taken in the near future, it may become a dead sea.

The Mediterranean is also a uniquely beautiful sea, a gem in whose perfection nature and history have collaborated. It is the common heritage of some of the world's greatest and oldest civilizations. Not only the peoples around its shores, but mankind as a whole has a vital interest in its salvation. Yet cooperation to this end is stifled by political antagonisms which often erupt in wars, by differences in economic systems, and by the opposing interests of the developed nations on the northern shores and the developing nations in the south.

In a way, the Mediterranean is a world ocean in a nutshell. Solutions to its problems might provide models for the solutions needed for the world ocean as a whole.

During the first phase (1971) the International Ocean Institute focused its attention on what seemed to be the most urgent problem—the pollution of the Mediterranean. The first and last chapters in Part III are concerned with that phase. Focusing on Mediterranean pollution led to two clear conclusions. First, it is futile to deal with pollution alone. Pollution is a symptom or a syndrome. To combat it, you have to strike at the causes, and these lie in human activities, not just in the oceans, but on land as well. Second, the Mediterranean is part of the world ocean, and many of its problems transcend the boundaries of the Mediterranean. This is true especially of shipping, as it is true for military activities which, alas, have made of the Mediterranean one of the worst concentrations of armed (partially atomic) forces in the world.

The "Mediterranean Council to Combat Pollution" which is proposed at the end of Part III, thus should be considered with a twofold caveat: if it is to be effective at all, its competences must be reformulated so that it can deal with *development* and *resource management* rather than with pollution alone; and it must be conceived as an integral part of the world ocean system, considering the interrelatedness of the ocean *problematique*.

There are, however, a number of underlying assumptions which remain valid also in the enlarged context. First, pollution cannot be controlled by a *code*. Pollution control is a *service* that must be performed by an *institution* which, at present, does not exist. Second, the problems of pollution must be tackled *integrally*, not piecemeal. It is inadequate to deal with pollution by ships alone, when the bulk of pollution is river- and atmosphere-borne. Third, the problems of pollution—which are the problems of ocean management—are such as to require new modes of cooperation and joint decision-making between politics, industry, and science. They require a new *science policy*, and

142

new instruments for the making of science policy. Fourth, any oceanic organization or institution, assuring a sharing of benefits from a rational management of the common heritage of mankind, must also be in a position to impose a fair sharing of burdens. There must be fiscal provisions assuring the effective and independent functioning of the institution. Contributions based on the *uses* of ocean space and resources and modified by a GNP factor so that rich nations pay more than poor nations, seem to be the best solution.

The second phase of the International Ocean Institute's Mediterranean studies, aided by a grant from the Ford Foundation and supported by the United Nations Development Programme, dealt with all uses of ocean space and resources in the Mediterranean and their interaction. This should eventually lead to *interactance models,* which can be computerized. Such models would indicate where one use of the ocean interferes with, and detracts from, the profitability of another use. They would help in setting priorities and identifying research needs and managerial requirements. The studies on fishery, tourism, and the military uses of the Mediterranean are samples of this second phase of our project. We are now entering a third phase, which will be "operational" and will begin with experiments in improving the fisheries of the area and a study of the systemic implications of such attempts.

Lord Ritchie-Calder is a Senior Fellow at the Center for the Study of Democratic Institutions. Dr. Holt was United Nations senior regional scientific adviser in Malta and is now director of the International Ocean Institute. Dr. Gonen is professor of geography at the University of Jerusalem. General Badurina is councillor to the Ministry of Foreign Affairs of Yugoslavia, and Elisabeth Mann Borgese is a Senior Fellow at the Center for the Study of Democratic Institutions.

CHAPTER 8

The Pollution of the Mediterranean

LORD RITCHIE-CALDER

Thus you make a model of the Mediterranean Sea. . . . In this model let the rivers be commensurate with the size and outlines of the sea. Then by experimental observations of the streams of water, you will learn what they carry away of things covered and not covered by water. And you will let the waters of the Nile, Don, and Po and other rivers of that size flow into the sea, which will have its outlet through the straits of Gibraltar. . . . In this way you will soon see whence the water currents take objects and where they deposit them.

Leonardo Da Vinci
c. 1500 A.D.

Without reducing it to Leonardo's scale, the Mediterranean in its natural proportion of 1/140th of the area of the oceans provides a model for our present-day studies of hydrospace. Apart from its physical characteristics, its history encompasses those human activities which gave us the substance of civilization and which, in their modern excesses, blight that civilization with pollution.

Geographically the Mediterranean is an interior sea connecting with the Atlantic through the straits of Gibraltar with the Black Sea through the Dardanelles and with the Red Sea through the man-made Suez Canal. Those narrow passages limit the exchange of water between the seas. The maximum east-west extent from Gibraltar to the Gulf of Iskenderun is more than 2,300 miles and the north-south extent between the coasts of Yugoslavia and Libya is nearly 850 miles. Its area (including the Sea of Marmara but not, as Leonardo did, the Black Sea) is approximately 970,000 square miles.

Shifting Continents

Geologically the Mediterranean lies in the jaws of an intercontinental system, the study of which is now revealing some of the most exciting evidence of continental drift by which the land mass broke up and the continents drifted apart. The Mediterranean is a model situation since it can be physically studied by onshore stations around it and by survey ships of many nations upon it. With a combination of modern methods, seismic, gravimetric, palaeomagnetic, sonar soundings, core-drillings and paleo-ecological techniques which can identify the conditions prevailing in the geological epochs, the earth scientists are now assembling a convincing picture.

This recalls the vast crustal movements within the unitary land mass which compressed the sediments of the primeval ocean into the mountain-building system. The corresponding folds produced the troughs, and the flooding of them created the major basins of an inland sea. (With no more evidence than the marine fossils of the Tuscan plains, Leonardo, 470 years ago, wrote: "And the peaks of the Apennines stood up in the sea in the form of islands surrounded by salt water. Nor did Africa as yet behind its Atlas mountains reveal the earth of its great plains naked to the sky. . . . And above the plains of Italy where flocks of birds are flying today fishes were once moving in large shoals.")

Then in the process of continental drift, the "jaws" opened. On the hinge of the Middle East, the Eurasian and African continents moved apart, creating the Adriatic Sea between Italy and Yugoslavia, shattering the southeastern ranges between Greece and Asia Minor and thus forming the Aegean and opening the connection between the Mediterranean and the Black Sea, parting the straits at Gibraltar.

The evidence is that the "jaws" are closing again at a rate of about one centimeter a year. As the African and Eurasian plates meet, the African plate slides under the European, so that the structure of the sea-bed in places consists of two continental layers, one superimposed on the other. This underthrust accounts for the lateral system of earthquakes in Italy and the Balkans. It also accounts for the seismic activity in Turkey and Iran, in the hinge of the jaw. With those crustal movements and its live volcanoes, the Mediterranean is a laboratory for studying the contemporary geological process.

Moreover, the marine terraces appearing above and below sea level and encircling the Mediterranean record the variations in the sea level during the glacial advances and the interglacial periods. The discovery of unusual deposits of minerals and of interesting evaporites in the cores secured on the *Glomar Challenger* 1970 survey, suggest that at one time the Mediterranean basin dried up under extreme conditions of evaporation.

This complex geology is of great scientific interest, but commercial curiosity has also been aroused and there has been intensive prospecting for oil. In February 1971 Spain's state petroleum company, CAMPSA, working with Shell, confirmed that the first offshore oil strike had been made at a depth of 1,800 meters, near Benicarlo. Preliminary estimates indicate that the oil deposit might be worth $1.4 billion. More wells are to be sunk in the vicinity.

Moving Waters

The narrow straits of the Mediterranean have dictated its hydrography. It is practically two seas, with its distinct eastern and western basins. Each is subdivided into secondary basins, and the whole system accentuates the prevailing problems of pollution.

The surface waters of the Atlantic enter the Mediterranean through the narrows at Gibraltar. These Atlantic waters are the main source of nutrient regeneration of the waters of the Mediterranean and maintain the physical-chemical equilibrium of the sea. The other main sources of replenishment are the Ebro, the Rhone, and the Po in the west. The others, for example, the Arno and the Tiber, have their watersheds so close to the sea as to be hydrologically gutters of local consequence but hydrographically insignificant. (Locally, in terms of flooding or pollution, they cannot be dismissed.) In the east (in spite of Leonardo who thought the Black Sea was fed by the Danube, the Don, the Dnieper, and by a presumptive underground tributary from the Caspian as a reservoir of the Mediterranean), the Black Sea complex has little or no influence on the system. The Vardar, from the Balkans into the Aegean, has a minimal influence. The man-made Suez has an insignificant effect. The Nile, in spite of its volume as the conduit from equatorial Africa, makes no decisive contribution to the hydrographic balance sheet.

The salinity of the Mediterranean is one of the highest that exists (lesser only than that of the northern Red Sea). The surface salinity increases from west to east, from 36.2% to 39.2%. In this, the eastern rivers have some effect: the levantine salinity as far north as Mt. Carmel is reduced from 39% to 36% during the August-September floods of the Nile, and the discharge of the Vardar reduces the salinity by about 2% in the Gulf of Salonika. This salinity factor is due to heavy loss of water by evaporation, particularly in the south and east where the rainfall is lowest.

This raises the perennial question: Why doesn't the Mediterranean overflow its banks? Apart from the rivers flowing in, there is the influx of surface water from the Atlantic. This generates the principal current of the southwest of the Mediterranean, which follows the coast of north Africa eastward. The Alboran Basin, between Spain and Morocco, acts as a submarine reservoir for the inflowing Atlantic surface waters, and most of its water down to 200 meters comes from this influx, which also forms the main mass of water on the continental shelf of Algeria. The current generated by the incoming Atlantic divides, just off Sicily. One branch carries on eastward, while the other travels up the west coast of Sardinia and across the Tyrrhenian and Ligurian Seas to reach the Provençal Basin. During the winter the surface water of the Riviera is chilled by cold winds and, growing denser as it cools, sinks to mix with the bottom waters. This factor is of interest not only to physical oceanographers but is of importance in the transport and destination of dangerous pollutants.

At the eastern end of the Mediterranean the saltier water is formed during the winter between Rhodes, Crete, and Cyprus.

What emerges from the study of the diverse parts of the Mediterranean is that the principal currents circulate in a counter-clockwise direction, impelled in the first instance by a thrust of the Atlantic surface waters along the African coast.

There is, however, another phenomenon which explains the riddle as to why the Mediterranean does not overflow. Under the incoming waters of the Atlantic, at the Straits of Gibraltar, there is a deep outgoing current of denser, saltier, colder water moving into the outer ocean. (This outgoing deep current enabled German and Italian submarines, with their engines cut off, to drift silently past the detection devices of the Gibraltar base.) It has now been calculated that 31,600 cubic kilometers of water enter the Mediterranean from the Atlantic and 30,000 cubic kilometers go out. A similar, but very much smaller, split-level exchange takes place with the Black Sea through the Bosphorus—so small that it is like a spot of ink diffusing in a village pond. The water inventory, including river supplies and precipitation, is balanced by evaporation.

Three "Lungs"

The Mediterranean has three "lungs": Provençal Basin, Upper Adriatic, and the Aegean. This respiratory system is critical to the entire Mediterranean.

What keeps a sea alive and sustains life in it is the oxygen content of the water. That oxygen is acquired by interaction with the atmosphere. In the surface layers where photosynthesis occurs, by which plants and organisms convert the sun's rays into biological systems, this oxygen is essential to the biological process, but it is also released into the water by that process. The supply of oxygen to the deep waters involves a mechanism by which the oxygenated surface waters, by cooling, become denser and sink. This cooling takes place where cold continental air masses flow over the water. The chill winds spill down from the Alps into the Provençal Basin and on the other side of Italy into the northern Adriatic and in the case of the Aegean from the mountains of Turkey. The waters thus transferred to depth off the southern coast of France go into circulation in the western Mediterranean. Those from the Adriatic pass over the sill of the straits of Otranto and travel eastward. The Aegean waters circulate in the Levant.

The main causes of depletion of oxygen in the "living" waters are the excessively high temperatures prevailing in the summer, the degree of un-compensated biological activity in the photosynthetic zone, and the decompostition of organic materials in the sea-bed. Because the Mediterranean is an enclosed sea, anything which affects the "lungs" affects the whole system.

Arthur R. Miller of Woods Hole Oceanographic Institute, an oceanographer with long experience of the Mediterranean, reckons that there is a complete turnover of Mediterranean water every 80 years. The north Atlantic is feeding on the surface water poor in nutrients but carrying oxygen, and in the reverse direction, through the lips of Gibraltar, the Mediterranean is thrusting the denser, saltier water in a long tongue which stretches far across the Atlantic. Over the decades, in the vertical and latitudinal circulation, the waters will be transfused. But what will man have done to the waters in the fourscore years?

The system is precarious. Nutrients are scarce and the sea is poor in the production of primary organisms which nourish the higher organisms, including the food fish for human consumption. Elements that could sustain marine life are inaccessible in the basins at depths below 300 to 400 meters, where complete disintegration of organic matter occurs, accentuating the oxygen depletion. In those respects the eastern Mediterranean is worse off than the western, having only about a quarter of the nutrient elements and even less oxygen.

It can be said that these natural anomalies have existed through eons (indeed, the evidence of the dredgings and corings and the paleo-ecological studies have proved this) and that the *Mare Nostrum* of the Romans helped to sustain civilizations before and after them. That is true, but the ecological balance has always been precarious, more so than the Baltic, another practically-enclosed sea but with more hydrographic stimulation from the outer seas, less so than in the Black Sea. The situation in the Baltic has now reached such a serious crisis that oceanographers and governments are on panic-stations alert. The Black Sea below 200 meters is stagnant with no deep-sea life and all-pervading hydrogen sulfide, the product of organic decay.

The Mediterranean is like an invalid whose prognosis is "You only have so long to live unless. . . ." The "unless" offers a reprieve from the death sentence, but it means the reversing of present trends, providing care and treatment, and the stopping of pollution.

The Impact of Man

Man has been tampering with his environment ever since he became *homo sapiens;* that was the precondition of his survival. Of all the creatures, he was the least likely to survive. He was naked to the elements and to his enemies. He had neither fang nor claw, fur nor feather, scale nor carapace. He could neither outwrestle nor outrun his natural predators, but could outreach them with clubs or spears and slings. He made fleshing tools to strip them of their pelts to clothe his nakedness. He mastered fire, which terrified all other creatures, and used it to heat his caves and cook his food. To that extent he has modified his environment, because, with clothes and heat, he could overcome his climatic restraints and could migrate over the face of the earth.

When he became a tiller of the soil and a domesticator of animals, he could settle. He became the craftsman, the miner, the city-builder. He enclosed himself in his man-made environment and lived with his own pollution. If his filth became excessive or he defiled the waters, he was beset by pestilences. If, in effect, he threw his wastes into his neighbor's backyard, he would contract from his neighbor the contagion which he generated. He had to regulate his excesses by sanitary ordinances.

Civilizations grew in the Nile Valley and the Delta and along the Tigris and Euphrates and then along the littoral and on the islands of the Mediterranean—Egypt, Crete, Greece, Carthage, Rome. And the sea must have seemed amply big enough to take all the sewage and all the residues. The first mineral pollutants of the Mediterranean can be dated from the copper workings of Cyprus, the iron workings of Asia Minor, and the tin workings of the Phoenicians. Mercury has been found in Egyptian tombs of 1500 B.C. and was mined in Spain, Italy, and along the Adriatic. The Cloaca Maxima of ancient Rome carried the sewage to the Tiber and the Tiber carried it to the sea. The canals and lagoons of Venice for centuries have received human waste.

The Rivers

Natural debris is waterborne into the Mediterranean by four great river systems—the Nile, Rhone, Po, and Ebro. The Nile is 6,720 kilometers long and its basin covers a tenth of the area of the African continent. On the modern political map, it traverses Uganda, Kenya, Rwanda and Burundi, the Congo Republic, the Sudan, Ethiopia, and Egypt. From the equatorial lakes of Victoria and Albert, the White Nile has cut its way northward, carving great gorges and demolishing mountains on a scale that modern mechanical machinery has not achieved. So, too, has the Blue Nile tumbling out of Ethiopia and its large tributaries, the Sobat and the Atbara. This hydraulic mining has carried along the river-course, minerals of every description and has carved out a sewer for the natural organic wastes of the rain forests and the swamps. It has been said that "the Nile made Egypt"; indeed, its silt, organic manure, and waters provided the arable land and irrigation for the fertile valley of the Lower Nile in an area where the precipitation is too low to sustain crops. It cut the gateway through Nubia through which ancestral man, a tool-making animal, migrated northward from his East African origins to spread his species and techniques around the world.

One of his earliest ventures into environmental control was the water management of the Nile itself, culminating in our times in the High Aswan Dam, which has turned the Nubian Valley into a lake 800 kilometers long, to control floods, store water for systematic irrigation, and generate electricity. A quarter of the capacity of the dam is earmarked as a silt trap, and in order to replace the natural soil nutrients which will be trapped with the silt, the hydroelectricity will produce artificial fertilizers. This drastic intervention will have unforeseeable effects in modifying the environment. Its consequences for the Mediterranean cannot be properly appraised without far more research, hydrographic, chemical, and biological. Although, relative to its size, the Nile seems to make a disproportionately small contribution to the total water inventory of the Mediterranean, the floodwaters of the Nile have spread as a fresh-water surface layer as far north as Mount Carmel. The delta has aggregated as a silt trap and has acted like a series of baffles to reduce the momentum of the river, now further checked by dams and barrages along its course. Nevertheless, an agricultural regime intensified in the Valley with artificial fertilizers, pesticides, and herbicides cannot but contain the hazards which are all too familiar.

Another big river is the Rhone, 808 kilometers long, originating in the Swiss canton of Valais, flowing through Lake Geneva across France between the Alps and the Central Plateau. Forty kilometers from the Mediterranean, it divides into two branches, the Grand Rhone and the Petit Rhone.

Between them they enclose the delta region of the Camargue. The drainage system of the Rhone and its tributaries is linked by canals with the basins of the Loire, Seine, Rhine, and Moselle. The river system has been "managed" by dams and barrages which, by hydroelectric generation, have increased the industrial capacity and population of the region.

The Ebro, 880 kilometers long, drains a catchment area about one-sixth the area of Spain. The Ebro collects 222 tributaries, the largest of which have been used for hydroelectric power and water storage systems for irrigation. It spreads itself through a large delta onto the continental shelf which extends to and beyond the Balearic Islands before it descends to the Algero-Provençal basin.

The river Po rises on the borders of France and Piedmont and travels 680 kilometers to the Adriatic. On its way, it receives 26 tributaries and drains Lakes Como, Maggiore, Iseo, and Garda. Within its catchment area of 27,000 square miles it includes the city complexes of Pavia, Milan, Mantua, and Modena. It has always been a "problem river." Even in pre-Roman times, dikes were built to restrain its inundations. Over the centuries a great deal of money and engineering ingenuity has gone into the prevention of flood disasters which have periodically occurred in spite of, or because of, the embankments. Silt deposits have raised the riverbed, so that the embankment also had to be raised; thus abreast of Ferrara, it has become an aqueduct on the level of the housetops. Nevertheless, the surplus of silt is such that the Po is extending its delta into the Adriatic about 60 meters a year.

The Winds

The Mediterranean is an outsize dustpan. It collects the airborne contaminants, both natural and man-made, from the three continents around it. There is no such thing as a "Mediterranean climate." It has several climates, ranging from the desert system of North Africa to the high-precipitation system of the mountains of Europe and Asia Minor. It is both marine and continental. Its recumbent geographical position, stretched out from west to east, makes it part of the westerly weather system with its passage of cyclones and their associated frontal precipitation, but it is also on the edge of the Asian monsoon system.

The relatively warm waters of the Mediterranean form a large area of low pressures with several centers, and cold air is drawn in from the adjacent land masses. In summer, however, the waters remain relatively cooler than the surrounding land, so that the regional high pressure coincides with the subtropical high. Precipitation decreases from north to south and from west to east. The annual precipitation can range from 450 centimeters of rain near the Dalmatian coast to 2 centimeters in the Sahara.

The great diversity of land and water conditions give rise to peculiar and complex wind systems. Among them are the sirocco, originating in the hot desert regions of Africa and blowing toward the northern shores; the etesian winds of the monsoon system which in the eastern Mediterranean are steady, dry northwesterly and northerlies; the bora of Yugoslavia and the mistral of southern France, and others resulting from the cold dry air moving down from the mountains to the sea.

Thus the meteorology of the Mediterranean, fraught with so much importance in the atmospheric transport of pollutants and contaminants, is something which calls for a great deal of research and understanding. Over a long period of time the winds have shifted vast quantities of desert dust and volcanic ash from Etna, Vesuvius, Stromboli, and other active cones and are now circulating large quantities of man-made mischief which are deposited in this ecologically vulnerable basin.

The Burden of Residues

For millions of years the Mediterranean, like the oceans in general, has been receiving substances which we consider pollutants: radioactive nuclides as the result of cosmic ray bombardment from outer space and the erosion of rocks containing radioactive elements; the erupted products of volcanoes and chemical-rich effluvia from seismic vents; mercury, lead, and other metals and hydrocarbons such as those found in oil, coming from natural submarine seepage, due to earthquake ruptures and from the natural decay of marine plant and animal life; the accumulated effects of hydraulic mining —the natural erosion by rivers and by coastal waves; and the wind-transported particles from the continental hinterlands.

The difference between now and millions of years ago is that human activities, multiplied by the numbers, needs, and ingenuity of an enormously increased population, are adding to the concentrations of such materials and particularly of such man-contrived materials as chlorinated hydrocarbons and radioactive materials, which did not exist in nature and with which the marine ecology cannot cope. Such activities, divorced from nature, are doubling the natural concentrations of marine chemicals and introducing new chemicals in concentrations approaching those of the naturally occurring chemicals. For example, the oceans are most important in maintaining the carbon-balance in the biosphere. Millions of years ago, the sun encouraged the growth of the primeval forests, which became coal and the organic growth in the seas which became oil. The hydrocarbons, converted in the geological pressure cooker, were locked away—reserves of carbon withdrawn from circulation. In the industrial era those reserves have been drawn upon in increasing amounts, to be released into the atmosphere by the chimney stacks and exhaust pipes of modern engineering. During the past century the combustion of those fossil fuels has released more than 360 thousand million tons of carbon into the atmosphere in excess of the natural amounts. This continues at a rate of 6,000 million tons-plus a year. The concentration of carbon in the air we breathe has increased by approximately 13 percent above the balance of a century ago.

The ocean contains about 130 million tons of carbon dioxide, about 50 times as much as the air. The oceans exchange about 200 thousand million tons of carbon dioxide with the atmosphere. When the atmospheric concentrations rise, the oceans absorb some of the surplus, and when they fall, the oceanic reservoir tends to replenish the air. The organic life of the sea, using the light rays of the sun, converts the carbon dioxide to its processes of growth, but the plants also exhale carbon dioxide. This is a delicate mechanism with which man is tampering.

The Web of Life

Marine life is a fine web of interrelated food chains, all of which depend on the chemical constituents of the sea. Diversity of species is essential to the stability of the ecological system. Crucial to the entire food chain is the phytoplankton, which is responsible for 90 percent of the oxygen of the earth. The phytoplankton provides the "pastures" for the rising scale of sea creatures. Their function and profusion depend on the surface layers to the depths penetrated by the sun's rays, which are indispensable to photosynthesis.

The ecological balance of the complex chain of life can be upset in a variety of ways. Some pollutants simply poison the animals and plants with which they come in contact. Others make such demands on the oxygen dissolved in the seawater that other living things competing for that oxygen suffocate for lack of it. Some pollutants encourage excessive growth of a single species of plant or animal so that it prevails over others. Other pollutants are concentrated in species which have an affinity for them, without deleterious effects to themselves, but pass them on up the chain in increasing dosages until they become dangerous or lethal to another species, including humans.

An example of direct poisoning was the consequences of the spilling into the Rhine of 200 pounds of endosulfan, which killed over 100 tons of fish.

An example of the second is that of oil: apart from the killing of sea birds, etc., the natural decomposition of an oil slick involves its oxidation by the action of bacteria (and those might even increase the nutrients available in the food web), but the process depletes the dissolved oxygen supply on which marine life depends. One liter of oil would deplete 400,000 liters of seawater of its oxygen.

An example of the third is eutrophication arising from both domestic and industrial discharges, which provide an excess of nutrients such as nitrates in fertilizers or phosphates in detergents. This produces a "bloom," a rapid growth of responsive marine species, usually phytoplankton, which multiply at the expense of other species. This is familiar in the coarse, slimy blue algae associated with the outfalls of untreated sewage or the "red tides" of the Florida coast, or the different-colored tides off the coasts of Sri Lanka, Brazil, and Spain. Obnoxious smells are usually associated with such blooms, which in their proliferation kill other forms of life; when they die, the blooms cause the deoxygenation of the water and the production of a sea-desert.

An example of the fourth is the now-familiar story of DDT, which can directly kill insects by paralysis. One of its virtues in the prevention of insect-borne diseases is its persistence, lasting decades. It has been estimated that about 1,000 million pounds of DDT have already been introduced into the biosphere; what with the wind-borne aerosols of spraying and the run-off from agricultural activities and its long life, most of that has ended, or will end up in the oceans. DDT, like other chlorinated hydrocarbons, is not readily metabolized but is stored in fat. Even when it is metabolized (changed by physiological chemistry in the body itself) the end result is another form of chlorinated hydrocarbon. Thus DDT (and the other chlorinated hydrocarbons) accumulates in marine life and is concentrated in increasing proportions in the food chain. Oysters have been found to amplify small concentrations of DDT 70,000 times in one month. DDT has been found in penguins in the Antarctic, where DDT has never been used, thousands of miles from any sprayed areas.

Deliberate Disposal

Another method of pollution—and "method" is the proper term because it is deliberate—is the transporting of wastes into international waters by vessels. This is done in two ways: dispersed waste and containerized waste. The first includes dredging spoils, industrial wastes, garbage and trash, discarded machinery, and sewage sludge. (There have been proposals for using discarded automobiles and automobile tires to create artificial shoals of repair reefs.) This dumping has been indiscriminate and largely ignored until something had to be done about tankers getting rid of their oil residues in the open seas.

The second consists of putting wastes in containers in the hope that they will be kept secure for long periods. This concern is with wastes whose dispersion is recognized as dangerous. Hopefully, the containers, whether concrete or metal, will remain intact, but concrete crumbles and metals corrode in seawater, and the nature of the contents is likely to help the process. This has been the method of disposal of surplus explosives, radioactive trash, chemical weapons such as lethal gases, and too-hot-to-handle industrial wastes.

This situation has existed for a very long time—including the disposal of the massive, lethal surpluses of two world wars—and the amounts and locations are not known because governments have regarded their inventories of military wastes, like their stockpiles of military weapons, as deep, dark secrets. They do not disclose what they dump nor where they dump it. There is no international registry of disposals and, more likely, individual governments are no longer aware of what they did with all of it. In terms of millions of tons of lethal materials, the ocean bed is like a minefield of which the charts have been mislaid. This is true of the Mediterranean.

Occasionally, the facts surface. The discovery in recent years that the level of arsenic in the Baltic was abnormal led to the disclosure that 7,000 tons of arsenic had been dumped in concrete containers almost 40 years ago. That, properly dispensed, would be enough to kill three times the world's population. Danish fishermen, operating off the Swedish coast, have been badly burned by fish contaminated by German mustard gas dumped by the Allies after World War II.

Nations do not know what other nations are doing in this haphazard business of drowning dangerous substances, and there is, even now, no adequate international machinery for dealing with it, even when it becomes known. In August 1970 it became public knowledge that the United States military proposed to dispose of a stockpile of defective warheads filled with powerful nerve gas. They were leaking and could not be dismantled, so they were placed, complete with their detonators, in concrete "coffins." They could not be disposed of, as apparently happened in the past, off the coast of New Jersey, because it had been discovered that fish are inquisitive and come in shoals to investigate unfamiliar objects. If the "coffins" had been leaking ("diffusing" was official euphemism), the fish might have been affected and the poison might have got into the food chain of American fisheries. So the "coffins" were put in the hulk of a cast-off ship which was sunk in the Atlantic deeps. The Bahamas government, whose country was nearer the risk site than the United States, protested ineffectively through diplomatic channels.

The Mediterranean, like the wider oceans, is unprotected from this kind of dumping and has already had more than its fair share. In this context, "containers" can be read to include "ships of war." During two world wars the Mediterranean was a naval battleground, and millions of tons of warships and supply ships were sunk with all they contained, including live ammunition and chemical weapons, tanks and bunkers full of oil. (During World War II, 415 Allied ships, totalling 1,740,250 tons, were sunk in the Mediterranean. Estimates of Axis losses bring the figure to 3,000,000 tons, approximately.) It is likely that, as has been suspected in the North Sea, unidentifiable oil slicks may be due to the breaking up of wartime-sunk ships. And for "oil," read other things as well.

Today the Mediterranean is patrolled by the navies of the two super-powers, the US and the USSR. According to an article by former Chairman of the US Joint Chiefs of Staff, Admiral Arthur W. Radford the US navy there deploys 43 surface vessels, two aircraft carriers, and six to eight submarines. The Soviet fleet consists of 60 surface vessels, no aircraft carriers, and 10 to 12 submarines. All of these are nuclear-armed and some may be nuclear-powered. Apart from a "shooting-match," those ships on continual maneuvers are a pollution hazard.

That accidents can happen was demonstrated by the aviation incident at Palomares on the coast of Spain. A B-52 and a KC-135 refuelling tanker collided in midair near Palomares on January 17, 1966. The bomber crashed and four unarmed hydrogen bombs separated from the aircraft. One landed intact in a dry riverbed. The second and third bombs released radioactive material in the middle of a populated area. The fourth was retrieved from the ocean three months later. Contaminated soil was loaded into 4,810 steel drums and shipped to the U.S. to be buried at the Atomic Energy Commission's "nuclear burial ground" at Savannah River, South Carolina, under 10 feet of earth.

One redeeming feature of this unfortunate affair was that the US authorities accepted full responsibility. For obvious military reasons they had to recover every scrap of the nuclear components, but they also undertook to decontaminate and rehabilitate the area and compensate the inhabitants for the effects on their livelihoods. If the same applied to offending industries and if they had to scrape up, ship, and bury their pollutants and garbage in their own backyards, they would apply more stringent precautions.

Wasted Wealth

The trouble with industrialists (and with their customers demanding cheap products) is that they ignore the wealth they are wasting. The product is regarded as an end in itself, something to be made profitably or sold cheaply. The residues are the rejects and in fumes and effluents become pollution. What they are recklessly discarding, however, may be useful in other ways and with proper management could be valuable by-products.

Italy, now wrestling with the burden of industrial pollution, provides a salutary example. Throughout the millenia, the volcanic vents at Lardarello near Pisa had been breathing out natural pollution in the form of hot gases. In one of the world's earliest and most effective efforts at harnessing geothermal energy (the heat of the earth's crust), enough electricity is being generated (384 m.w.) to supply the equivalent of the power needed to run the Italian railways, but at the same time, economic chemicals are being recovered from the gases.

Single-cell protein, which could be used to supplement the diet of protein-deficient millions, can be produced by the action of certain types of bacteria in breaking up oil residues which, as "waste," is an affliction.

Since the Industrial Revolution, thousands of millions of tons of incompletely-burned coal have been spewed out of chimneys as soot to blacken our cities and cumulatively to upset the carbon balance in the atmosphere. But coal, as the great dye-stuff and drug industries have shown in their balance sheets, is one of our richest sources of chemicals. From the flue-dust of chimneys is now being recovered the rare element germanium, the basis of the modern transistor industry.

Eutrophication, which gives rise to destructive and disfiguring growths of unwanted plants and organisms, is mismanaged enrichment. Whether it be domestic sewage spilling into the rivers or onto the beaches or industrial effluents being discharged in seaward pipes or dumped from barges, it is nutrient in the wrong place. Domestic sewage can be treated to make it safe and processed to make it profitable. Industry could find other uses. For instance, when the British scientists in 1940 canvassed the Americans to determine whether penicillin could be mass-produced, the answer lay in cornsteep liquor, an embarrassing waste product of starch-making. This castaway nutrient was admirable for growing the mold *penicillin,* from which penicillin is obtained and lending itself to deep culture and the technology which put antibiotics on a mass-production footing.

Many of the residues or rejects that are now menacing the Mediterranean could, from being dangerous liabilities, become assets. They could be recycled, but better still, they could be part of the cycle from the start, if they were considered in the cost-benefit studies of any new product of industrial development.

In principle, antipollution legislation restraining manufacturers from discharging untreated wastes should make them think again about their residues, but in practice, big corporations are disposed rather to switch to countries where the regulations are less stringent. Since the war, Mediterranean countries seeking capital investment and new industries have lent themselves to this practice with apparent economic benefit but at excessive social cost in terms of the quality of life of their own peoples, the ravaging of their touristic coasts, and still unmeasured consequences to the Mediterranean ecosystem.

Domestic Pollution

The capacity of the sea to deal with organic wastes depends on the oxygen used by bacteria to convert organic material to inorganic substances. This has been expressed as BOD_5, which means the biological oxygen demand during five days. To that has to be related the amount of phosphorus. The burden of pollution from Italian population and industries can be grasped from the following data which relates to averages of years 1967-71:

DATA ON POLLUTION OF THE MEDITERRANEAN,
BY ITALIAN COASTAL POPULATION AND INDUSTRY IN 1967*
(Figures provided by Professor Marchetti, Institute of Zoology, Milan University, April 1971)
(Coast of Italy includes Sicily & Sardinia)

NLength of the coast, km	7,170
Number of municipalities	664
Population living along the coasts	16,161,426
Number of factories	138,829
Chemical factories	1,589
Number of days spent by tourists in coastal resorts in one year	47,224,713
Number of passengers landing from ships and embarking in ships	17,295,241
BOD** produced by population and tourists in tons per year	292,000
BOD** produced by population and tourists in tons per km of coast per year	407
Metabolic pollution produced by coastal population and tourists—calculated on tons per year of:	
Phosphorus	16,206

*No significant change in 1971
** Biological oxygen demand

Nitrogen	64,897
Discharge of detergents along the coast	109,755
Total BOD** (total pollutional load) produced by population + tourists + factories in tons per year	874,905

This gives a picture of domestic pollution around the coasts of the Mediterranean where, with few exceptions, sewage, without treatment or without adequate treatment, goes directly into the sea and is the principal source of pollution.

But the picture looks worse when it is localized; for instance, the littoral from Barcelona to Genoa, a stretch of 2,000 miles, has a population of 11,000,000 permanent residents. In the north Adriatic sector, from Venice to Trieste, with 810,000 inhabitants, pollution has already passed the danger point.

In the already critical areas the resident populations in increasing and new industrial projects are attracting more workers and themselves adding to the quota of pollution. There are also the holiday coasts, with millions of tourists contributing to the BOD_5 and phosphorus.

Nor do the estimates take into account the effects of the rivers, which act as sewers for the hinterland populations and defile the coasts. The Po brings down the domestic pollution corresponding to a permanent population of 4,440,000 inhabitants; the Arno drains the wastes of 3,200,000, and the Tiber of 4,800,000.

Industrial Pollution

Consideration of industrial pollution that enters the Mediterranean ecosystem cannot be confined to effluents, the unwanted residues or rejects which are drained waterwise into the sea. In the complex meteorology of the enclosed sea, atmospheric currents ensure that fumes, dusts, and aerosols will finish up in the sea. One has also to include, even at geographical distance, tips, slag heaps, and even buried waste from which toxic substances can be leached out and through the river systems reach the sea. It must include transport and pipelines and seaward drilling for oil. It must also include the products of manufacture. For example, the Lombardy farmers who complain of the detergents and the industrial solvents, which from the Po get into their irrigation water to the detriment of their soil and their crops, must also recognize that, as customers of the manufacturers, they are passing on excess fertilizers, herbicides, and pesticides to the Adriatic.

One must also take into account the nature of industrial practices. For instance, mercury, the clinical effects of which are a matter of human concern, has long been extensively (and innocently) used in papermaking as a fungicide to destroy organisms that interfere with the manufacturing process. It has also been used in the making of caustic soda which is used in pulping and bleaching newsprint. Furthermore, woodpulp is an avid absorber and concentrator of mercury from the vast volumes of water used in papermaking. It is possible to forbid, as Canada, Sweden, and other countries have done, the use of mercurious fungicides and to do something about the bleaches, so that the risks in the effluent are constrained. But it also turns out that when paper is finally burned, mercury is released in the smoke. If it is not to get into fish, which have a strong affinity for mercury, there must be check and double check. Liquors from pulp industries can be toxic and can taint the flesh of fish. Furthermore, the chemicals can interfere with the assimilation process of phytoplankton. The oxygen content of the sea, into which pulpmaking effluents spill, may also be impaired, since sulphite liquors may contain half the content of the wood that was pulped. The breakdown of this amounts to between 200 to 500 kilograms BOD_5 per ton of pulp.

There are many pulpmills impinging on the Mediterranean basin: in Spain, at Barcelona, Valencia, and Motril; in Italy, on the Murano Lagoon in the north Adriatic; in Yugoslavia; in Algeria, at Annaba, Algiers, and Mostaganem; in Greece, in Salonika; and in Turkey at Izmit on the Sea of Marmara.

When farming was a closed-circuit operation, when the soil provided the food and the animals returned the waste *in situ* as manure to produce more food, it would not have been considered a source of industrial pollution, certainly not of the sea. Today, it is a significant factor, not only in terms of artificial fertilizers in washouts and runoffs, but of animal wastes which are disposed of in river drainage which finishes up as eutrophication in the estuaries and shore areas. This is a function of increased population, the feeding of which requires a magnified animal population. Free-run food animals which once nourished the soil have given place to intensive, and even factory, farming with sewage waste going into the drains. Slaughter-houses and manufacture of feeding stuffs involve waste disposal. In the United States, the volume of animal waste has been estimated at 10 times the volume of human waste. *(Marine Pollution Problems and Remedies,* UNITAR Research Report No. 4). The proportion may not be as high in the Mediterranean region, but the food industries of Spain, France, Italy, Yugoslavia, Greece, Turkey, Israel, and Algeria make a significant contribution, which was not recognized until the nature of eutrophication was examined.

The FAO experts, for the Conference on the Pollution of the Seas, identified the sources of industrial chemical wastes around the Mediterranean:

Spain: Iron-smelting (Sagunto); metallurgy (Barcelona); industrial textiles (Barcelona); tanneries (Barcelona); pulpmills and feeding stuffs (Barcelona, Tarragona, Castelon, Alicante, and Cartagena).

France: Chemical works, feeding stuffs, pesticides, detergents (Marseilles); docks and dockyards (La Seyne, La Ciotat, Marseilles, Port de Douc, Sête); metal industries (Marseilles); cement works (Fos). The main industrial activity, present or projected, is in the coastal region between Sête and Toulon. The principal pollutants are metallic (chrome, nickel, zinc, lead, and bromide), pesticides, fungicides, detergents, colorings, phenols, acids, sulphur products, polyesters, alcohols, and glycols.

Italy: Pyrite mining (southwest Sardinia); alkalis and pyrites (mouth of Arno); metallurgy, cement-making, feeding stuffs (Gulf of Naples); metallurgy (Gulf of Taranto); marble-sawing (Bari); pulp-making (Murano); all kinds of industries at Porto Ravenna, Spezia, and Genova. At Venice, 76 varied industrial establishments dump their wastes into the lagoon.

Yugoslavia: Pulp-making, ports and docks, iron works, aluminium works (with serious pollution from the bauxite); cement-works, plastic manufactures, industrial chemicals, and textiles.

Algeria: Industrial chemicals, feeding stuffs, detergents, pesticides (Skikda, Annaba, Algiers, Oran); papermaking (Annaba, Algiers, Mostaganem); iron-smelting, metallurgy, and mining of ores (Skikda, Annaba, Oran, Ghazaouet); plastic manufacture (Skikda and Algiers); acid-accumulators (Mostaganem); tanneries (Oran).

Greece: Papermaking, metallurgy (Salonika); tanneries (Salonika, Volos, Athens); plastic manufacture; rubber manufacture, industrial chemicals, textiles, feeding stuffs, tobacco, ports and docks (Athens and Piraeus).

Turkey: Papermaking, feeding stuffs, pesticides (Izmit); oil products, ports and docks (Istanbul).

Israel: Petrochemicals, industrial chemicals, detergents, feeding stuffs, tobacco (Haifa).

Oil Pollution

In spite of the closure of the Suez Canal, the oil traffic in the Mediterranean has not diminished. The supertankers may be making the long haul around the continent of Africa with oil from the Persian Gulf, but the oil ferries within the Mediterranean itself have increased because of changed circumstances. One is the development of the oilfields of Algeria and Libya, involving not only the shipment of well-oil but of liquefied natural gas. Another is the development of inter-European pipelines, so that Italy is now providing the throughput for the markets of South Germany, Austria, and

Switzerland by a trans-Alpine "oil-grid." The oil is transferred from the tankers to the pipeline terminal at Trieste. The other pipeline terminal for the trans-European system is at Fos near Marseilles. These pipelines are serviced by tankers which fill up from supply lines from the Middle Eastern oilfields with their terminals in Syria and Lebanon. Israel now has a pipeline from Eilat at the head of the Gulf of Aqaba to Askalon on the Mediterranean. The Egyptians, since the closing of the canal, have constructed a pipeline from the Red Sea to the Mediterranean. In the eastern Mediterranean there are five refineries and eleven loading points corresponding to the terminals of pipelines. There are two main pipeline terminals in Libya at Marsa el Harega and Tripoli and a main terminal at Arzew in Algeria.

Another aspect of oil activity around the Mediterranean is the development of oil refineries in the littoral countries themselves. Italy, for example, has the capacity to refine nearly twice as much oil as it needs for its own purposes, and the demand for export petroleum is growing. This vigorous expansion, so important to the postwar economy of Italy, has awkward implications. It is estimated that by 1975 it will be handling over 150 million tons, as Ing. Raffaele Girotti, Vice-President of ENI (Ente Nationale Idrocarburi), the Italian state petroleum corporation, said to the International Conference on Oil Pollution of the Sea (7–9 Oct. 1968 at Rome). These figures highlight the urgency of the problem of port capacity, which so far has only been partially appreciated and solved. Less has been done to improve existing facilities and new ports of the traditional type, whereas more has been done in constructing jetties and sea-lines. These last facilities, accommodating the larger tankers, have sprung up in increasing numbers along the coast, but although they are less costly, they are also less secure in rough weather and involve the risk of pollution.

Those offshore installations, man-made islands, are not only used for the mooring and pumping out of tankers, but are being developed as sites for refineries. Since oil has been discovered on the continental shelf, they will be supplemented by offshore drilling rigs like the one which triggered the oil spill in the Santa Barbara Channel off California. The outlook (in both senses of the word) for the holiday coasts of Italy is not appealing.

The practice of discharging tank washings from oil ships has been going on in the Mediterranean for a long time. Well-intentioned shipmasters carrying oil wastes back in ballast for disposal at base through the Suez Canal, when it was still open, found that it was regarded as cargo and subject to dues. The result was that they got rid of it in the eastern Mediterranean. Other ships dumped elsewhere because it was convenient. In a report published in 168 *Science* 245 (10 April 1970), Michael H. Horn, John

M. Teal, and Richard H. Backus described how on a Mediterranean survey cruise for the Woods Hole Oceanographic Institution, tarry lumps were found in at least 75 percent of the tows made by neuston nets on the surface of the sea. Since, by the nature of the hydrographic peculiarities of the Mediterranean, those tarry lumps become accumulative, much of it ends up on the littoral beaches, damaging the recreational facilities. It would seem that the Mediterranean, within its enclosed system, has received more than its fair share of the million tons a year of oil discarded by world shipping.

Damaged Lungs

The Provençal Basin and the northern Adriatic, together with the Aegean, are the "lungs" of the Mediterranean.

As has been shown in the discussion of the oceanography of the Mediterranean, the Provençal Basin is responsible for the "respiration" of the western Mediterranean, and the Adriatic for the "respiration" of the eastern Mediterranean.

Let me recapitulate: oxygen, which keeps a body of water from becoming stagnant and sustains marine life in it, is acquired by interaction between the atmosphere and the surface waters. In the upper layers, to a depth limited by the penetration of the radiant energy of the sun, which the phytoplankton use to convert sea nutrients into the biological systems that are the start of the food chain for all marine life and eventually for humans, the process of photosynthesis releases oxygen into the water. The supply of oxygen to deeper waters and to lower circulation depends on a mechanism by which the oxygenated surface waters, by cooling, become denser and sink. The cold air from the continental system, spilling over the Alps into the Provençal Basin and into the Adriatic, provides this mechanism and puts the oxygen into circulation and also provides currents which transport other substances, including persistent pollutants.

Anything that impairs this mechanism or aggravates the pollution can alter the character of this enclosed sea, both in terms of hydrodynamics and the ecosystem. This could happen in two ways, by counteracting the cooling process and by inhibiting the photosynthesis. Man's activities could do both.

Because in those areas, the lobes of the "lungs," the pollution has become a visible affront and a public health hazard, more detailed research on the extent and effects of pollution has been carried out than in any other part of the Mediterranean. The findings are grim.

In the upper Adriatic, from Trieste to Ravenna, over 400 experimental stations were established in a study on which Professor L. Majori reported to the International Conference on Oil Pollution of the Sea. They tested for microbial presence, for BOD_5, and for detergents. They set standards: very pure; little polluted; moderately polluted; polluted; and very polluted. Professor Majori reported that the hygienic situation of the stretches of the sea under observation had "already been notably compromised." Almost all of the seacoast from Trieste to Monfalcone was classified as "polluted." From Grado to Lignano the values of detergents were particularly high and the Lagoon of Marano had "the characteristics of a partially purified sewer." Slightly better conditions (but still qualifying as "polluted") were found from Bibione to Jesolo and from Venice Lido to Chioggia. An extremely grave situation existed at the mouth of Porto Ravenna. The BOD_5 was excessive and the oxygen was reduced to 10–30 percent saturation. The reason was undoubtedly the fact that almost all the liquid refuse from the adjoining urban and industrial areas and from the hinterland was discharged into the sea without any corrective treatment. The Port of Trieste area itself was graded "very polluted" on all counts, including dangerous intestinal germs. The Bay of Muggia was intensively examined in connection with the siting of the trans-Alpine pipeline terminal. The BOD_5 figures were bad and the prospects of oxide reduction (to dispose of surface oil) poor. The microbial situation was also bad; all fish had disappeared. Some places were less bad than others, but since the worst were so seriously affected, that is no commendation.

One interesting observation arose from the Adriatic studies: the peculiar role of synthetic detergents, which were all-pervasive. The normal process of reoxygenation of the water is prevented because of the particular construction of the molecule of detergent in the interaction water—air, with the formation of a more of less uninterrupted film.

The region of Marseilles is comparable to Trieste, as part of a large conglomeration of ports and industries and a big population pouring domestic waste into the sewers which debouch into the sea, untreated. The bacterial load in the water is beyond safety limits, and the marine sediments are impregnated with intestinal germs 100 meters from shore. The dissolved oxygen in the waters of the port is depleted, and when there is no wind stirring, there is an absence of oxygen in depth. Once again, there is a burden of detergents in the Bay of Marseilles. There is a selection of pesticides and an overcast of oil. The flora and fauna have suffered with a general diminution in the number of species and the aggrandizement of some others.

The Sick Sea

The "lungs" are unhealthy. We can diagnose the complaint, which demands more drastic treatment and legal measures more draconian than the authorities have so far employed or concerted with their neighbors, in this transnational problem. The short-term prognosis is obvious: things will get worse because the effects will be multiplied and magnified by the increase in industrial activity without adequate services to deal with the wastes or restraints commensurate with the problem. The health of millions will be in danger. Recreational beaches will be tarred and ordured. The sea will be out of bounds for bathers. The trees will go on dying along the coasts, suffocated or poisoned by the polluted sea winds. The quality of life will be diminished.

The long-term prognosis depends on a great deal more interdisciplinary, international research because only then will we know how far the Mediterranean Sea has been impaired and how we can repair the damage. We still want to know, like Leonardo, "where water currents take objects and where they deposit them"—especially if they are foul pollutants, likely to poison the living waters and the living things in them.

CHAPTER 9

Mediterranean and Black Sea Fisheries

S.H. HOLT

The countries with coasts on the Mediterranean and/or Black Seas ("Mediterranean and Black Sea Countries"—MBS, in the tables) produce annually about 16 percent of the world catch of marine fish, and they consume about 18 percent of this catch. Those with coasts on the Mediterranean ("Mediterranean Sea Countries"—MS) produce about 6 percent and consume 9 percent (1969 and 1970 data).[1] Their production as a percentage of their consumption is 89 and 59 percent, respectively; the rest is imported into the region—about 1.2 million metric tons for the region as a whole, and 2.2 million tons for Mediterranean countries (the USSR is a major net *exporting* country). Of the total catch by Mediterranean and Black Seas countries, only 10 percent is taken within the region; the equivalent figure is 20 percent if we consider the catch in the Mediterranean itself by the Mediterranean countries. The rest is taken by them elsewhere, mainly in the Atlantic Ocean. These countries clearly have a collective interest, both in the state of the living marine resources of the region and in the maintenance of external fishery resources, whether or not they themselves exploit them.

The total annual catch of fish and shellfish from the Mediterranean and Black Seas was, from 1938 to 1955, at the level of about 700,000 tons. It

[1] "Fish Resources of the Ocean," prepared for the Indicative World Plan (IWP) of FAO, compiled and edited by J.A. Gulland and published in revised version by Fishing News Books, London. This brings together the basic information up to 1969. The reader is referred to this, while here I add some more recent statistics. I am indebted to colleagues in the FAO Department of Fisheries and particularly to Messrs. Gertenbach, Robinson, and Troadec for leading me to pertinent statistical information.

166

then grew somewhat and has stayed since 1965 at around one million tons. It is now less than 2 percent of the world fish catch. This percentage has been gradually declining, because catches in most other regions have been increasing steadily, some rapidly.[2]

Over the eight-year period, 1965–71, world marine fishery production increased at an average rate of 4.3 percent per year. The Mediterranean and Black Sea countries collectively did considerably better than this—6 percent—but that includes the USSR, whose fisheries expanded vastly during this period. The Mediterranean countries' catches grew more slowly than the world average—little more than 2 percent annually, despite the considerable growth of the Spanish fisheries, which alone account for 46 percent of the 1970 catch by those countries. The world figure for the period is also much influenced by the USSR catch. The world growth rate, excluding the USSR, was only 3.5 percent. This is also the rate of growth achieved by those Mediterranean countries with coasts *only* on the Mediterranean or Black Seas. Even so, Table 9.1 shows that most of their increase came from *outside* the Mediterranean. The growth rate of catches *within* the basin does not exceed 2 percent in any grouping.

The increase in world catches is now leveling off. FAO has estimated that the potential yield from the Mediterranean and Black Seas could be about 1.5 million tons, and this ultimately would be just over 1 percent of the sustainable world ocean yield (excluding whales).[3] Part of the supposed 50 percent increase from the Mediterranean would come from stocks presently "underfished," the rest by the more rational exploitation of stocks which are now "overfished."

The bulk of the Mediterranean catches are of small shoaling pelagic species, particularly anchovy, as well as sardine. The demersal catches are rather low absolutely and in comparison with other regions; "basses, etc." are fairly important, and unsorted and unidentified fishes form a large statistical category. Bluefin tuna and bonito are important, as are shellfish. There is a considerable potential for shellfish culture, particularly molluscs.

By contrast with some other important fishery regions, a high proportion of the Mediterranean fish catch is for direct human consumption almost entirely within the region. Only in Morocco does a large proportion

[2]1.8 percent of the *marine* fish catch in 1971; 1.7 percent in 1969 (lowest year); 2.2 percent in 1964, the first year of published FAO statistics broken down by marine areas. It may be noted that the surface area of the Mediterranean and Black Seas is 0.9 percent of the world ocean surface; and their continental shelves comprise 1.7 percent of the world total shelf area (0–200m); 3 percent of the area less than 1.000m.

[3]Since the FAO estimates of global potential were published, the world catch has leveled off sooner than anticipated. We are perhaps already nearer the maximum than was thought in 1970. The Mediterranean catch might in the future be a relatively more important part— say, 2 to 3 percent.

TABLE 9.1

MEAN ANNUAL FISH CATCHES AND PERCENT ANNUAL INCREASES, 1964–71, AND FISH CONSUMPTION, 1969–70

m + f = marine + freshwater	Production tonnes × 10⁻⁶		$\frac{m}{m+f}$ (%)	Fraction of World production (%)		Annual rate of increase in production (%)		Consumption World Prod. (%)	Production Consumption (%)
	m + f	m		m + f	m	m + f	m	m + f	m + f
World	61.0	52.9	(87±1)	(100)	(100)	(3.8)	(4.3)	(100)	(100)
World excluding USSR	55.0	47.7	(87)	(90)	(90)	(4.1)	(3.5)		
MBS countries – Total	9.3	8.4	(89±1)	(15.2)	(15.9)		(6.0)	(18)	(90)
– within MBS	—	1.0		—	(1.9)		(1.4)		
MS countries – Total	3.3	3.1	(96±1)	(5.4)	(5.9)		(2.0)	(9)	(60)
– within MS	—	0.6		—	(1.1)		(1.7)		
MBS* countries – Total		0.72			(1.4)		(5.6)		
– within MBS		0.58			(1.1)		(1.9)		
MS* countries – Total		0.65			(1.2)		(3.5)		
– within MS		0.44			(0.8)		(1.8)		

MBS countries—having Mediterranean and/or Black Sea Coasts
MS countries—having Mediterranean coasts (including Turkey)
MBS* countries—having coasts *only* on Mediterranean and/or Black Sea
MS* countries—having coasts *only* on the Mediterranean (but including Turkey)

Percentages in parentheses
MBS* countries take 56% of the total catch in MBS
MS* countries take 71% of the total catch in MS

Total catch by MBS* countries / MBS countries = 9%
Total catch by MS * / MS countries = 21%

of a Mediterranean nation's catch go for reduction, and that is mostly taken in the Atlantic.

These facts give the clue to a more significant evaluation of the Mediterranean fisheries. On the basis of *value* of landed catch, they contribute now (1969 data) not 2 percent but 6 percent of the world marine fish supply.[4] Among the 15 marine areas by which FAO compiles fishery statistics, the Mediterranean and Black Seas in the period 1968–70 ranked 12th by weight of catch but fourth by value. The value exceeded that of the catches from several important fishing regions, among them the southeast Pacific (including the Peruvian anchovetta fishery prior to its collapse), the eastern tropical Pacific (including the important tuna fisheries there), and the northwestern Atlantic. When all the world fish stocks are fully exploited, the Mediterranean will probably rank 14th by weight of sustainable yield, but ninth by value, and continue to contribute 6 percent or more of the world total potential value of nearly $18,000 million (at 1970 prices).

The tendency to dismiss the Mediterranean as an impoverished, insignificant fishing area must therefore be challenged. In addition, being to a considerable extent artisanal, or small-scale industrial, the Mediterranean fisheries employ rather large numbers of people. The economic and social significance of the fisheries within the region should not be obscured by the newer and profitable interests of tourism and oil. Indeed, the uses of this part of ocean space are not all in conflict; the futures of both tourism and fisheries depend greatly on the growing state of pollution being brought under control.

Looking at the geography of the fisheries and, in particular, at the location of the fishing countries, one notes, first, that all the catches from the Mediterranean and Black Seas are taken by countries coastal to the region and that catches are reported to FAO by all those countries except Gibraltar, Monaco, and Albania. We next need to break down further the statistics, to distinguish Black Sea (including the Sea of Asov) catches from those in the Mediterranean proper. With the exception of Turkey, catches in the Mediterranean by countries bordering on the Black Sea, and vice versa, are negligible. Turkish statistics separate Black Sea, Sea of Marmara, Aegean and "Mediterranean" regions. I have made a detailed analysis of these for the years 1967–69 and made appropriate adjustments to the total catch figures for earlier and later years. Although at the time of writing, FAO statistics cover the years up to 1971, figures for several important countries for 1971 and 1970 are only estimates; 1969 is therefore a convenient recent reference year. In Table 9.2 the catches in the Sea of Marmara (which average 24 percent of the catch by Turkey and 3 to 4 percent of the

[4]Estimated as 8.6×10^9 sus. landed value in 1969.

TABLE 9.2

MEDITERRANEAN AND BLACK SEA CATCHES—TONNES $\times 10^3$

Catch in —	1964	1965	1966	1967	1968	1969	1970	1971	Mean 1964–71 catches	%
MBS	959	991	1031	1115.6	1030.6	944.4	1068	1048	1023.4	(100)
— Black Sea	328	358	401	455.1	381.0	259.7	385	350	364.6	(36)
— Sea of Marmara	32	31	27	36.6	29.5	46.1	24	26	31.5	(3)
— MS	600	601	603	623.9	621.1	638.6	659	672	627.3	(61)

total harvest by all countries from the region) are shown separately. The Mediterranean catch ranges from 56 to 68 percent of the total (mean = 61 percent), with no clear trend during the period 1964–71. The pattern of variations is, however, different in the two basins: the Mediterranean catches have been increasing slowly but steadily, while Black Sea catches have fluctuated.

For the Mediterranean proper, a significant further breakdown is according to the catches by countries on the "European" side and on the "African" side. In 1969, 541,000 tons (85 percent) were taken by countries on the north shore; 88,000 tons (14 percent) by those on the south shore; 7,000 (10 percent) tons by the Levant countries of Israel, Lebanon, and Syria; and 2,500 tons (0.4 percent) by the independent islands of Malta and Cyprus. There are no trends in this distribution during the period. In fact, whichever way we break down the statistics, the picture is one of stable distributions (see Table 9.3). The catches by the north-shore countries—led by Italy, which takes over half of the 541,000 tons, and Spain, which takes another 20 percent of it—are not, however, all taken from the northern side of the Mediterranean. This fact is behind the bilateral negotiations and arrangements on fishing between the bigger fishing powers of Europe and the North African states.

The geographic breakdown corresponds largely to the distinction between developed and developing countries. The five more developed countries—France, Spain, Italy, Greece, and Israel—took 79 percent of the Mediterranean catch in 1969, that is, four times as much as the developing group. Again, there is no trend during the period. Likewise, the catches of the EEC countries are disproportionately high.

Apart from the connection with the Black Sea, catches in the Mediterranean are significantly affected by two "outside" ocean influences—in the west by the penetration of Atlantic water and in the east by the intrusion of Indo-Pacific species via the Suez Canal. Although the biological productivity of the Mediterranean is still not well measured, it seems agreed that the eastern basin is not so well endowed as the western basin and the Adriatic; this difference is also reflected in the catches by countries grouped on an east-west basis. From 82 to 87 percent come from the western subarea bounded by Albania and Libya and 13 to 18 percent from the eastern subarea bounded by Greece and Egypt. The eastern area is roughly equal in area to the Black Sea and half that of the western subarea so defined. The catch from it, per square kilometer, is thus one-third to one-half that from either of the other two subareas. A drop in the eastern subarea between 1965 and 1966 is due to a halving of the catches by Egypt, which have not since recovered. Finally, as is noted later, the grouping of the catches from the eastern half of the western subarea "central zone" by Italy, Libya, Malta,

TABLE 9.3

GEOGRAPHY OF MEDITERRANEAN (MS) CATCHES—TONNES×10³ AND (%)

	1969		Population early 1970		1969 MS catch per capita (kg.)
	Catch in MS	(%)	× 10⁻³	(%)	
Total	638.6	(100)	289.0	(100)	2.2
by North-shore countries	540.7	(85)	205.6	(71)	2.6
by South-shore countries	88.4	(14)	70.6	(24)	1.3
by Levant countries	7.0	(1)	11.9	(4)	0.6
by independent islands	2.5	(0.4)	0.9	(0.3)	2.8
by "developed" countries	504.4	(79)	149.8	(52)	3.4
by "developing" countries	134.2	(21)	139.2	(48)	1.0
by 2 EEC countries	330.7	(50)	104.8	(36)	3.2
in eastern basin	91.5	(14)	91.2	(32)	1.0
in western basin	547.1	(86)	197.8	(68)	2.8
by 4 "central zone" countries	330.0	(52)	61.0	(21)	5.4
by Italy	288.0	(45)	53.7	(19)	5.4
as % of North-shore	(53)				
as % of "developed"	(57)				
as % of Western Basin	(53)				
as % of "central zone"	(87)				
by Tunisia	29.6	(5)	5.1	(1.8)	5.8
as % of South-Shore	(34)				
as % of developing	(22)				
as % of central zone	(9)				
by Turkey	166.9 (100)		35.6	(12)	
in Black Sea	112.5 (76)				
in Sea of Narmara	46.1 (20)				
in MS	8.3 (4)	(1.3)			0.2
by MS Countries	459.6	(72)	152.2	(53)	3.0

and Tunisia is of current interest. This group includes the leading country in the developed and "north shore" group—Italy—and the leading country in the developing and "south shore" group—Tunisia. The combined catch by the four countries is 52 percent of the Mediterranean total; of this amount, Italy takes 90 percent and Tunisia 9 percent.

Although ships of European countries fish on the southern side, they do not move far either westward or eastward. Apart from Turkey, countries which choose to fish far from their own shores do so outside the Mediterranean-Black Sea basin.

Of the 20 countries listed, 10 fish only in the Mediterranean and/or Black Seas; their catches, however, account for only 29 percent of the catches in these basins. Twelve countries (including the 10 above) fish only or mainly there; they account for 67 percent of the catch (1969 data). Similarly, of 17 countries (including Turkey) with Mediterranean coasts, eight fish only in the Mediterranean; they account for 16 percent of the Mediterranean catch. Ten of the 17 fish mainly in the Mediterranean and account for just over 70 percent of the catches there.

The total marine catch by Mediterranean and Black Sea countries in 1969 was 9.1 million tons, 17 percent of the world total. The Mediterranean countries took 3.2 million tons, 6 percent of the total. The Mediterranean and Black Seas catch was only 10 percent of the total catch by Mediterranean and Black Sea countries. The Mediterranean catch was 20 percent of the catch by Mediterranean countries. These percentages are, however, so very low because, in the first case, of the very large USSR catches elsewhere and, in the second, of the large French, Moroccan, and Spanish catches in the Atlantic. In fact, *all* the countries having coasts also on other sea areas fish mostly outside the Mediterranean and Black Seas. Of the others, Bulgaria and Romania fish mostly outside, while Greece and Italy mostly fish inside.

The catches per capita vary widely among countries. They are not closely correlated with GNP per capita. The demand by the Mediterranean countries for fish is not satisfied by their own fishing activity. Of the 16 countries for which FAO publishes data, 12 are net importers of fish products and six are net exporters (1970 data, fishery products of marine and inland origin not distinguished; see Table 9.4). The statistics for export and import of products are insufficient for detailed analysis. The destinations of exports are sometimes clear. For example, Moroccan exports, both of products for direct human consumption and of meals and oil, are mainly to France and thus are consumed in the Mediterranean region.

Most of the large imports of both groups of products are from countries other than the Mediterranean and Black Sea countries. Overall, the imports of all products exceed the exports by 425,000 tons, but if Black Sea countries

TABLE 9.4

FISH SUPPLIES, CATCHES, CONSUMPTION BY MEDITERRANEAN AND BLACK SEA COUNTRIES

	Catches m % m+f 1964–71	Tonnes $\times 10^{-4}$ Total 1970	Tonnes $\times 10^{-4}$ From MS and/or BS 1970	MS and/or BS–Total %, 1964–71	Population Early 1970s $\times 10^{-6}$	Catches per Capita Total (kg.)	Catches per Capita From MS and/or BS	GNP US \$ $\times 10^{-9}$	GNP per capita \$ $\times 10^{-2}$	Gross Value Total Catch m+f 1970 \$ $\times 10^{-6}$	Supply-Tonnes $\times 10^{-4}$ 1970, m+f total	Supply-Tonnes $\times 10^{-4}$ As food	Consumption (Supply per capita) m+f, kg. total	Consumption As food	Import Export of Products Tonnes $\times 10^{-3}$
France	(100)	764.4	45.6	(5)	51.1	15	0.8	100	20	237	1490.4	1042.4	29.2	20.6	I 1306.1
Spain	(99)	1483.3	124.3	(8)	33.2	45	3	23	7	378	1904.9	1169.4	57.4	35.1	E 61.6
Morocco	(99)	255.0	10.5	(4)	15.7	14	0.6	3	2	18	82.9	52.4	5.3	3.4	E 87.8
Italy	(95)	368.2	305.3	(83)	53.7	7	5	60	11	275	1278.6	710.6	23.8	13.3	I 1295.5
Yugoslavia	(62)	25.6	25.6	(100)	20.6	1	1	11	5		298.8	39.8	14.5	2.0	I 55.3
Albania	(100)	[4.0]	[4.0]	(100)	2.2	2	2	1	3						
Greece	(100)	91.3	58.0	(67)	8.9	10	7	6	7	7	244.1	184.8	27.4	20.6	I 35.8
Algeria	(100)	25.7	25.7	(100)	14.0	2	2	4	3	3	23.0	22.5	1.6	1.6	E 1.5
Tunisia	(99)	24.3	24.3	(100)	5.1	6	6	1	2	9	24.6	24.6	4.7	4.7	E 2.1
Libya	(100)	5.5	5.5	(100)	1.9	6	6	1	7	4	6.9	6.9	3.5	3.5	I 1.0
Egypt	(32)	[29.8]	14.8	(54)	33.9	1	0.4	5	2		103.9	103.9	3.1	3.1	I 4.3
Israel	(48)	10.3	3.0	(30)	2.9	4	1	4	12	5	158.2	36.7	54.6	12.1	I 29.3
Syria	(80)	1.0	1.0	(100)	6.2	0.2	0.2	1	2	2					I 2.7
Lebanon	(100)	2.3	2.3	(100)	2.8	1	1	2	5	4					I 5.0
Malta	(100)	1.2	1.2	(100)	0.3	4	4	0.2	6	1	8.6	2.6	25.0	8.1	I 1.4
Cyprus	(100)	1.4	1.4	(100)	0.6	2	2	0.5	8	1	4.4	4.4	7.0	7.0	I 2.2
Turkey Total	(94)	103.5	103.5	(100)	35.6	5	5	10	3		171.3	161.3	4.8	4.6	E 9.1
MS	(89)	7	7	[6]											
BS (incl.)		96	96	[94]											
Bulgaria	(89)	84.4	4.4	(13)	8.5	9	0.7	6	7		161.2	59.2	19.0	7.0	E 2.9
Romania	(39)	25.8	5.1	(29)	20.3	1	0.1	15	7		93.8	93.8	4.6	4.6	
USSR	(86)	302.5	302.5	(5)	242.6	24	0.6	235	10		7015.0	6083.0	28.9	24.9	E270.0
MBS countries	(89)	9706	1068	(11)	560.4	16	1.7	487	9		[13,080]	[9810]	[23]	[18]	1304
MS countries	(96)	3197	659	(21)	289.0	11	2.2	232	8	[1300]	[5810]	[3570]	[20]	[12]	1577
World	(87)	60,600	1068	(2)	3630	15					69,700	[29,800]	19	8	0

Catches and supplies given in equivalent round fresh weights. Supply equals catch plus imports plus exports.

"As food" is in direct human consumption; remainder for animal feeds, etc.

I = net imports of processed products; E = net exports. Number is thousands of tonnes (not export or import) of processed products (not corrected to equivalent round fresh weights).

174

(USSR and Bulgaria; no data available for Romania) are excluded, imports exceed exports by 700,000 tons.

The Indicative World Plan's estimates of potential fish yield from the Mediterranean and Black Seas are not as soundly based as we would wish. Few, if any, exploited stocks there have been subject to scientific assessment, as have stocks in, for example, the north Atlantic, north Pacific, and even in parts of the Southern hemisphere. The statistics of fish catches are weak, and the data for fishing effort are poor. The FAO report suggests that, "given the nature of the fisheries and the magnitude of the potential resource, the considerable effort required to bring up the level (in quality) of the statistics would not be worthwhile." If, however, we take into account the rather high value of the catches and the potential benefits from better management of heavily exploited stocks, we might reach a different conclusion.

Some demersal stocks off parts of North Africa and some pelagic stocks *might* still be lightly exploited. Although scientific proof is lacking, however, it is virtually certain that many stocks in the Mediterranean are now overfished and that a few of them have been for some time. International regulations are almost nonexistent; small mesh sizes are used in trawling; the illegal use of explosives and other destructive devices is prevalent; and national regulations are often not enforced. The wide disparity in participation in the fisheries by the more developed northern countries and the less developed southern countries perhaps contributes to a continuation of this unsatisfactory state of affairs. Only where national interests are more balanced and participation is by fewer fleets, as in the Adriatic, does it seem that much progress is being made toward more rational fisheries management.

Against this, we have in the Mediterranean an excess of international bodies concerned with the living resources. There are three intergovernmental bodies, including the Black Sea Fisheries Commission of the USSR, Bulgaria, and Romania. The General Fisheries Council for the Mediterranean (GFCM) was set up under the auspices of FAO in 1952. While being a valuable forum for scientific, technical, and economic discussion, the council has been extremely slow in coming to grips with resource assessment and management problems. A hopeful sign was the study by a GFCM working group, in the first half of 1973, of fishery management problems in the western Mediterranean. United Nations-aided projects in the area have been limited, partly because of the above-mentioned assumption that the Mediterranean fisheries were too small to be worth much assistance.

The International Commission for Scientific Exploration of the Mediterranean Sea (ICSEMS) is older than the GFCM. It is modeled on the International Council for Exploration of the Sea (ICES) in Copenhagen, but it has been much less significant than ICES in influencing fisheries policies. Its scope is limited to "science" and, under the influence of academic groups in the older member states, it has given much more attention to biological oceanography and marine biology than to scientific resource studies.

The GFCM and ICSEMS include most coastal states, but there is uneven participation in meetings. In particular, participation by the African states in recent ICSEMS meetings has been minimal. The GFCM receives its limited funds and secretariat from FAO. In theory, it covers the Black Sea, but the USSR, not being a member of FAO, is not a member.

A few years ago, the Intergovernmental Oceanographic Commission (IOC) of UNESCO, which also serves the other agencies of the UN system, launched as one of its series of "cooperative studies" a Cooperative Investigation of the Mediterranean (CIM), planned and executed jointly by IOC, GFCM, and ICSEMS, but states have been slow and niggardly in pledging their efforts (vessels and support) to it.

There being so much ignorance about this sea, the first plan for CIM was comprehensive but impracticable. It has been progressively sharpened and now focuses largely on pollution research. The CIM results should thus be relevant to fisheries but not sufficient in themselves for a leap forward in rational management. There is still the need both for more vigorous fishery research in the area and decisive management actions at national and international levels. Perhaps the time is now past when these could be expected from an intergovernmental body concerned only with fisheries. Such actions regarding fisheries now need at least to be related to pollution questions. Very soon they may not be possible without reference to oil exploration, extraction, and transport and to other uses of ocean space.

Several studies have recently been published on the state of marine pollution in the Mediterranean. Among them are the book edited by Ritchie-Calder, which contains some of the contributions of the second Pacem in Maribus Convocation,[5] and the GFCM *Studies and Reviews* No. 51 (1972). One might have expected the latter, since it comes from a fishery organization, to deal fully with the impact of pollution on the fisheries of the region, but the only references to the effect on fisheries are to the bad taste of fish from waters polluted by oil and the consequent effects on marketing—and even for that, no data are given. Other effects of various kinds of pollution on fish stocks (and on consumers of fish) are either not known or not documented. This, of course, does not mean they do not exist or are not important.

There have been a number of bilateral and multilateral intergovern-

[5] *The Pollution of the Mediterranean,* ed. Ritchie-Calder, Bern: Herbert Lang & Co., 1972. Ritchie-Calder's essay is included as Chapter 8 of this volume.

mental actions at the subregional level—for example, between Italy and Yugoslavia with respect to the Adriatic. In the "central zone," negotiations have begun since the third Pacem in Maribus Convocation and the meeting of Mediterranean states members of the UN Sea-Bed Committee, which followed it in Malta in July 1972. For example, during 1972, Malta and Libya began a joint resource survey, with Japanese assistance. Then in November, at a meeting of the Prime Minister of Malta with the Foreign Ministers of Italy, Libya and Tunisia, a seven-item agenda was agreed on for later discussions at the ambassadorial level, of which three items related directly to the sea—marine pollution, seabed problems, and fisheries.

. The importance of this central zone in the Mediterranean fisheries picture has already been stressed. The participating countries' interest in fisheries is in three cases exclusively and in one case mainly within the Mediterranean, and within the subarea in question. A proposal that they should jointly and continuously operate a vessel for monitoring pollution could be combined, if they so wish, with continuous monitoring of fish stocks and of related environmental parameters. If such an operation could be successfully mounted, the idea of such cooperation might spread elsewhere in the Mediterranean. Perhaps the most difficult question to arise concerns the conditions governing access to data. Detailed information about the distribution of fish in the sea can be used more effectively by some fisheries than by others. Equity in such situations is not achieved simply by making all data freely available or even by insuring participation by scientists of all concerned nations in the data collection. The problem is much the same in the debate about "freedom of scientific research" in the ocean.

In the Mediterranean area some scientists have become discouraged by the difficulties of getting prompt and effective cooperation through governmental channels. Much of their work is financed only indirectly, if at all, by governments. So some years ago a nongovernmental body was formed, the Mediterranean Association for Marine Biology and Oceanology (MAMBO). In its own way this remarkably fluid (some might say, disorganized) organization has done much to promote marine science in the region and, most important, to arouse interest among young people in the developing countries.

There are a number of other less broad, but significant, cooperative activities in the Mediterranean concerning the living resources and their environment. Among these are the Mediterranean Marine Sorting Center in Tunisia (a joint, continuing project of the Smithsonian Institution in the US and the government of Tunisia) and the Laboratory of Marine Radioactivity at Monaco (a joint project of the IAEA, the French Institute Oceanographique, and the government of Monaco, and now also of UNESCO). There is at least one marine laboratory in most Mediterranean countries. FAO headquarters are located on the Mediterranean, and nearly all UN agencies with ocean interests are based within easy access to the region. So there should be no dearth of international interest in the fisheries. There is still lacking a vigorous regional development and management body to marshal both the authority of all concerned governments and the enthusiasm of scientists—a body which would be able to deal with the fisheries themselves in their own right and with the increasing interaction of fishing with other ocean uses.

CHAPTER 10

Mediterranean Tourism: Some Geographic Perspectives

AMIRAM GONEN

Growth of Tourism and Vacationing

Spending a vacation in a foreign country or a different region is becoming a widespread phenomenon. On one hand, "an increased awareness of the outer world seems to lead to an increased readiness to leave one's habitat and to wander around temporarily."[1] On the other hand, tourism and vacationing are within the economic reach of more and more people, especially in the industrial countries of northwestern Europe and North America.

The major attractions for the tourists are cultural heritage and natural landscape for sightseeing and a pleasant physical environment for taking a rest. The Mediterranean countries, and especially the Mediterranean coastlands, are able to supply the needs of the millions of tourists originating in the urban-industrial concentrations to the north; as a result, each year they attract a substantial number of tourists. Table 10.1 shows the growth in international tourism in most of the Mediterranean countries between 1960

[1] Erik Cohen, "Toward a Sociology of International Tourism," *Social Research,* 39, no.1 (Spring 1972), p. 165.

TABLE 10.1

NUMBER OF VISITORS IN MEDITERRANEAN COUNTRIES, 1960–70

Country	No. of Visitors (thousands)		Percent
	1960	1970	Change
NW Mediterranean			
Spain	6,113	22,657	271
France	5,613	13,700	144
Italy	9,100	12,719	40
NE Mediterranean			
Yugoslavia	873	4,748	444
Greece	344	1,407	309
Turkey	94	446	374
Cyprus	26	127	393
SW Mediterranean			
Morocco	158	701	343
Tunisia	53	411	668
SE Mediterranean			
Lebanon	612	1,210	98
Israel	114	437	283

Source: *United Nations Statistical Yearbook.*

and 1970. In all of these countries, except for Italy, the number of tourists has at least doubled and in some even quadrupled.

Reasons for Growth

On the demand side, the main reasons for the growth of tourism are the increase in income and amount of free time. As income increases, the expenditure on foreign travel, as well as domestic vacation, increases. This is especially true in the case of paid vacations, whereby the increase in income is directly associated with taking a vacation or touring a foreign country. The arrangement by which paid vacations are part of the agreement between employers and employees has brought into the stream of tourists and vacationists a large number of people of moderate income formerly not within the economic range of tourism.

Conditions are also favorable for tourism on the supply side. The costs of spending a vacation in a foreign country have declined in relation to income, for a variety of reasons. The main development in this direction has taken place in the cost of travel, usually a substantial part of the total cost of taking a foreign vacation. With the development of package tours and group fares and especially with the spread of chartered air flights, the cost of travel has declined appreciably in the last two decades in relation to income. In addition to the decline in travel fares, accommodation has become cheaper. Mass tourism, in the form of large numbers of tourists being handled by large operators, introduced scale economies to the costs of accommodation. Package fares, block booking in hotels, and standardized services are important factors in lowering prices of tourist services. Moreover, with the increase in the number of middle- and lower-income tourists, cheap vacation facilities such as camping grounds have become widespread.

Associated with the rise in tourism is the increase in the magnitude of vacationing or domestic tourism, whereby large numbers of people flock each year to the countryside, resorts, and historic sites within the boundaries of their own countries. Going on a vacation, especially in the summer, has become important in European countries. This seasonal exodus from the large centers of population causes some basic changes in the distribution of the French population, during the vacation months.[2] Large, as well as small, cities are left by a large part of their populations, who tend to move to locations with some natural amenities or to those less densely inhabited. In Italy and Yugoslavia, as well, vacationing is an important phenomenon. In Italy it is strongly associated with the geographical pattern of income levels, the north having higher rates of vacationing than the south.[3] In Yugoslavia, about three-fifths of the visitors at tourist resorts are local citizens.[4]

In addition to the seasonal movement of vacationists, there is a growing tendency among affluent Europeans to keep a second home. Others settle in new homes upon retirement, usually outside the large cities. Although having a second home or changing residence upon retirement are not within the immediate scope of tourism, they are, nevertheless, strongly associated with similar locational attractions, namely natural and cultural amenities, and they too constitute an important factor in changing occupance patterns in recent years.[5]

[2]H. D. Clout, "The Great Summer Migration in France," *Geographical Review,* 61 (1971) pp. 535–36.
[3]Renée Rochefort, "Changements et permanences: géographie du travail et des vacances des Italiens," *Méditerranée,* 12 (1971), pp. 483–500.
[4]*Statistical Yearbook of the Socialist Federal Republic of Yugoslavia, 1970,* p. 237.
[5]H. D. Clout, "Second Homes in France," *Journal of the Town Planning Institute,* 40 (1969), p. 441.

The Growing Preference for the Coast

Formerly the Mediterranean countries attracted tourists mainly because of the rich historical heritage that has accumulated through the ages in the form of ancient towns, picturesque villages, monumental buildings, art objects, heroic battlefields, and archeological sites. But in recent decades there has been a growing preference among tourists coming to Mediterranean countries for coastal areas for their vacations. Having exhausted historical sites, north European tourists, especially those of the lower income brackets, are coming to the Mediterranean countries not so much to appreciate the cultural and historical heritage but to enjoy the amenities of the warm climate and the attractive beaches.

The Mediterranean coastal areas are an excellent foundation for developing a tourist region. The coasts provide a wide range of physical amenities and cultural attractions, as well as the necessary urban infrastructure of essential services.[6] The smaller coastal towns of the Mediterranean coasts constitute a basis for touristic activities by providing seaside amenities, an interesting past, a traditional architectural setting, and the old flair of a small fishing or commercial port. The desire to spend one's vacation on a sunny and sandy beach or in a small quiet resort town along the Mediterranean coast has become a major factor in the north-south flow of millions of Europeans.

In 1963 the proportion of nights spent by tourists in coastal resorts in Greece, out of the total number of tourist nights spent in the country, was 31.6 percent. In 1966 the share of coastal resorts was 41.3 percent.[7] In the same period the proportion of tourist nights spent in Athens declined from 44.1 to 38.7 percent. The data for Yugoslavia follow somewhat the same pattern. In 1960, 50.2 percent of foreign visitors in tourist resorts stayed in seaside resorts, while in 1969 the proportion rose to 55.5 percent, which consisted of over 2.6 million visitors.[8]

In Spain the growing preference for coastal locations among tourists has substantially changed the geographical pattern of tourism. During the 1950s and earlier, the main attraction for tourists coming to Spain were the cultural and historical endowments. The interior cities of the country, especially Madrid and its region, were the main focus of tourism in Spain. Nowadays the bulk of the tourist demand is for resort areas, mainly on the Mediterranean coast. In 1969 about three-quarters of all nights spent by

---

[6]John Piperoglou, "Identification and Definition of Regions in Greek Tourist Planning," *Papers, Regional Science Association,* 18 (1966), pp. 169–76.

[7]K. Car and A. Mandarić, "The Development of Tourism in Yugoslavia from 1958 to 1967," *United Nations Conference on Trade and Development (UNCTAD),* August 1971, p. 8.

[8]*Statistical Yearbook of the Socialist Federal Republic of Yugoslavia, 1970,* p. 237.

foreign visitors in Spain were at coastal centers, while only a tenth of such nights was spent in the region of Madrid, where cultural tourism prevails.[9] The attraction of the coast is emphasized in the Balearic Islands: Majorca, Iviza, and Minorca. In 1969 the Balearics accounted for one-third of all nights spent by tourists in Spain, while these islands account for only 1.5 percent of the country's population and less than 1 percent of its land area.[10] In the same year the Mediterranean coasts of Spain (Brava, Dorada, Azahar, Blanca, del Sol, and de la Luz) accounted for more than two-fifths of the tourist nights.[11] This data indicates clearly that Spain is now basically a coastal resort country, where tourists are coming mainly for relaxation on a sunny beach. Indeed, a survey of the Institut Nacional de Estadistica, conducted in August 1970, revealed that the main reasons for coming to Spain were climate and beaches. Only a tenth of the tourists in the survey quoted historical monuments as the main reason for visiting the country.[12]

In Corsica, too, most of the tourists stay along the coast, and only a few get to inner, mountainous areas.[13] The beaches are the main attraction for the tourists visiting this Mediterranean island. A string of coastal resorts has recently been developed around the island, most of them of the type of "sun-sand-sea" resorts.

Tunisia is being developed as a center for coastal tourism. Most tourist centers there are on the coast, and more are being developed in response to the growing demand in Europe. The ultimate expression of beach tourism in Tunisia is on the island of Jerba, where luxury hotels and bungalows are catering to an influx of west Europeans, mainly French, who come to the island almost solely for a beach vacation.

In Morocco the seaboard only recently has begun to be developed as a string of coastal resorts. Indeed, the main focus of the coastal tourism to Morocco is on the Atlantic coast (Tangier-Casablanca-Agadir), along which there is a network of camping sites. However, in the late 1960s the Rif road along the Mediterranean coast has been opened up and considerable investments have been made in resort complexes in the coastal region of Tetouan.[14] These were done in response to the growing number of Europeans coming for the sunny beaches of North Africa. Similar developments, but to a lesser extent, have recently been taking place along the Algerian coast.

In Turkey, too, an increasing share of the tourists are coming to coastal

[9]"National Report No. 2: Spain," *International Tourism Quarterly,* 1971, No. 2, p. 19.
[10]Ibid., p. 19.
[11]Ibid.
[12]Ibid., p. 14.
[13]Jannine Renucci, "La Corse et le tourisme," *Revue de Géographie de Lyon,* 37 (1962), p. 210.
[14]"Regional Report No.7: North Africa," *International Tourism Quarterly,* 1972, No. 4, p. 30.

resorts. Accordingly, most of the emphasis in the governmental planning for tourism is on coastal resorts. The Mediterranean, Aegean, and Marmara coasts of Turkey accounted for 90 percent of the investments planned for in the five-year plan of the early 1970s.[15]

The coastal areas attract tourists as well as local vacationers. The major vacation streams in France are from the interior cities toward maritime locations on the Atlantic and Mediterranean coasts, with only a minor stream of vacationers going to Alpine or Pyrenean resorts. The departments of Alpes-Maritimes and Var on the Mediterranean coast rank highest among French departments as receivers of hundreds of thousands of vacationers.[16] In southeastern France the coast is the main attraction for vacationists, as well as for owners of second homes.[17] In France, as is expected, most of the second homes are in rural areas, not too far from the urban centers, where two-thirds of such homes are located. However, about 20 percent of the second homes are by the sea, and only 10 percent in the mountains.[18] In Corsica the coastal areas are characterized by strips of second homes, mainly in the vicinity of larger towns. Some of these homes are owned by local residents of the island, while others are seasonally inhabited by residents of the continent.[19]

The growing preference for seaside resorts is related to the increasingly younger age of the tourists. Older tourists are not frequenting seaside resorts as much, in contrast to those less than 24 years old.[20] Nowadays the young tourists are a substantial part of the general stream of tourists, and their share among tourists visiting seaside resorts is tremendous. The preference for coastal locations among tourists has to do also with the lowering of the costs of vacations. As costs decrease, people of lower income enter the ranks of tourism, and there is therefore a growing tendency to include a sun-and-sand kind of tourism in one's itinerary or even prefer it to "cultural" tourism, often associated with higher income and higher education. The survey of tourists conducted in Spain in August 1970 showed that 47 percent of the tourists during that month were office employees and workers and 10 percent were students.[21]

---

[15]"National Report No. 3: Turkey," *International Tourism Quarterly*, 1971, No. 3, p. 19.

[16]Philippe Pinchemel, *France: A Geographical Survey*, London: G. Bell and Sons, 1969, p. 125.

[17]M.B. Barbier, "Logements de vacances et residences secondaires dans le Sud-Est méditerranée," *Bulletin de l'Association de Géographes Français*, Nos. 344-345 (1966), pp. 2-11.

[18]H.D. Clout, "Second Homes in France," *Journal of Town Planning Institute*, 40 (1969), p. 441.

[19]Renucci, "La Corse et le tourisme," p. 221.

[20]The relationship between age of tourists and the visit to seaside resorts was borne out in Israel in *Tourists Survey, 1970*, Tel Aviv: Otot-Sekarim (May 1971), p. 80.

[21]"National Report No. 2: Spain," *International Tourism Quarterly*, 1971, No. 2, p. 14.

The Impact on the Geography of Settlement

Before the rise of tourism and vacationing, urbanization was the major factor in shaping the geographical pattern of population distribution on the Mediterranean coastlands. Because of a maritime orientation, urban development was traditionally concentrated in coastal locations in many of the Mediterranean countries. Potential nuclei of urbanization existed along the Mediterranean coast where maritime trade supplemented the economy of numerous port towns. With the advent of industrialization and commercialization of agriculture, many of these port towns became bases for urbanization. The hilly areas in the interior were the main source of migration from the rural areas into the urban concentrations. Consequently the Mediterranean provinces experienced a drastic change in the geographic distribution of the population, with more weight given to localized areas, often on the coast. In some of the Mediterranean countries, however, the process of urbanization took place mainly in the interior locations away from the coast, as in countries where the coast is marginal to the economic and political heartland. Such is the case in France, Italy, Yugoslavia, Syria, and Morocco.

Because of its very nature, urbanization is characterized by the growth of particular nuclei of population. As a result, there are marked differences in the rates of change of population between the various districts and provinces of the Mediterranean coast. These differences are associated mainly with urbanization or the lack of it. The districts with high rates of population growth are generally those with large urban agglomerations. Decline of population is characteristic of rural districts with a few or no substantial urban centers. As a result, there are large segments of the Mediterranean coast that have lost population to a few small but densely populated clusters with fast-growing urban agglomerations.

The uneven population growth along the Mediterranean coast is exemplified in Greece. The main centers of population growth are the three metropolitan areas of Greater Athens, Salonika, and Larisa, as well as some other regional centers such as Patras.[22] At the same time, the maritime coast of the Peloponnesus and western Greece declined in population, mainly through migration into the large urban centers to the north and to the east.[23] The exodus from rural areas has resulted in increased abandonment of houses, villages, and fields.[24]

---

[22] *Statistical Yearbook of Greece, 1970*, pp. 24–26.

[23] A full discussion of the changes in the geographic distribution of population in Greece is included in Bernard Kayser, *Géographie Humaine de la Grèce,* Paris: Presses Universitaires de France, 1964.

[24] J.M. Wagstaff, "Rural Migration in Greece," *Geography*, 53 (1968), pp. 175–79.

Variation in population growth exists on the Italian coast, as well. The urban region of Rome (the provinces of Roma and Latina) stands out with high rates of population growth (27 and 20 percent, respectively) in 1961-70, while many of the other coastal provinces of Italy did not grow beyond 5 percent in the same period. The other provinces with relatively high rates of growth are those with major urban agglomerations such as Napoli.[25] Moreover, there is a marked difference between the western coast provinces and the eastern coast provinces in the rates of population growth. The western coast, in general, is a continuous strip of population growth, while in the east only part of the coastal provinces increased in population during the last two decades. The rural nature of the eastern coast and the small number of urban centers, as compared to the numerous large urban centers of the western coast, explain this difference in population growth between the two coasts. In southern Italy out-migration has strongly interfered with population growth in most of the provinces. However, even there the more urban provinces (and all of them are on the coast) have experienced relatively higher rates of growth due to regional migration within the south.[26]

On the Mediterranean coast of Spain the pattern of uneven growth is repeated. The province of Barcelona stands out with a growth rate of 30 percent during 1960-69. Relatively high rates of growth existed in the same period in the other northern provinces of the Spanish Mediterranean coast, where the provincial capitals developed as large urban centers. The southern provinces, however, with relatively small urban populations and small urban centers, had low rates of population growth.[27] Net migration in the southern provinces was negative. They were losing population to the more urbanized provinces of the north.[28]

In France the Mediterranean coast is a major attraction for internal migrants who come from all over France to settle in the pleasant Mediterranean environment.[29] Côte d'Azur ranks high in France, together with the Parisian region, in population growth and in positive net migration.[30]

Nevertheless, urbanization is not the sole factor in the relative high growth rates of the coastal areas of the Mediterranean. The development of tourism vacationing and retirement to pleasant communities along the coast contributed considerably to this growth as well, by creating a new

[25]*Annuario Statistico Italiano, 1961 and 1971.*

[26]Allan Rodgers, "Migration and Industrial Development: The Southern Italian Experience," *Economic Geography, 44* (1970), pp. 111–35.

[27]Yves Bravard, "L'Economie de L'Espagne," *Notes et Etudes Documentaires,* Nos. 3788-3789, Paris: La Documentation Francaise, 1971, p. 12.

[28]*Annuario Estadistico de Espana 1962* and *1970.*

[29]H.D. Clout, "French Population Growth, 1962-1968,"* Geography,* 1971, pp. 119-23.

[30]Pinchemel, *France: A Geographical Survey,* pp. 121-22. Also, *Annuaire Statistique de la France, 1969,* p. 64.

kind of economic base for the coastal regions. The millions of tourists and vacationers visiting the Mediterranean coasts of Spain, France, Italy, and Yugoslavia demand large quantities of goods and services and thus create new business and employment opportunities for many people.

However, the spatial patterns of tourism and vacationing vary markedly from that of urbanization. Tourism and vacationing are extensive users of space and tend to consume large tracts of land, in comparison to urban activities. One of the major reasons for going out on vacation is to leave the dense urban areas and to spend some time in remote, less-crowded localities where a restful vacation can be achieved.[31] As a result, there is a tendency among tourists and vacationers to spend their effects on the settlement distribution, as opposed to the concentrated effect of urbanization.

Tourists and vacationers are an integral part of the population and landscape of the Mediterranean coastal areas. They are consumers of space and especially of maritime-oriented space, seawaters as well as beaches. Space is consumed by the various facilities built to accommodate the large number of tourists and vacationers. Hotels, apartment buildings, weekend homes, vacation bungalows, camping grounds, facilities for sport, games, and leisure activities, as well as roads and other transportation facilities, are using large amounts of land along the Mediterranean.

The tourist population is not only a user but also a supplier of income and jobs.[32] Consequently, more local people are attracted toward the coastal settlements in order to take up a job or a business which is based directly or indirectly on the tourist economy.[33] The multiplier effect of the money spent by tourists along the Mediterranean coast results in increasing attraction for more people who are drawn into the coastal settlements and use more space and resources.

The seasonality of tourism is associated with a seasonal shortage in employment opportunities, especially for unskilled labor. In order to make up for this shortage or to take advantage of it, there is a tendency to develop alternative employment areas based largely on tourism. Various activities, mainly manufacturing of some seasonal nature, is being introduced to the tourist areas. This tendency is increasing even more the role of tourism as an important factor in bringing about economic growth and creating attractive urban centers.

[31]Walter Christaller, "Some Considerations of Tourism Location in Europe," *Papers, Regional Science Association*, 12 (1963), p. 104.

[32]See Jean-Bernard Charrier, "Le tourisme a Florence: la contribution directe et indirecte du fait touristique a la formation de revenues dans une grande ville," *Méditerranée* (1971), pp. 401-27.

[33]On the role of tourism in the regional economy of the Mediterranean provinces of Spain, see J. Naylon, "Tourism—Spain's Most Important Industry," *Geography*, 52 (1967), pp. 23-40.

188   THE TIDES OF CHANGE

During the tourist and vacation season the population of towns and villages in the tourist areas along the Mediterranean increases several times over. The town of Menton, on the Côte d'Azur, had 20,000 inhabitants in 1962. In the same year the town received more than 70,000 registered tourists. This figure did not include those who arrived without registering in tourist or vacation facilities or those who have a second residence there.[34] As a result, the land use pattern and the economic structure of the town is geared to the tourist season.

In much the same way, tourism has determined the demographic and economic fate of many agricultural communities along the Mediterranean coast. Those communities that do not take part in the recent development of tourism continue to decline in line with the general depopulation of agriculture and rural population. Those communities that are involved in tourism either grow or their decline is checked.[35] Where tourism was an important factor, the employment structure of communities was affected considerably, shifting the weight from primary to tertiary activities.[36]

In Spain the Mediterranean coasts are the target of the majority of foreign visitors. The sheer volume of tourism caused a transformation of the human landscape of the popular stretches of the Mediterranean coast in the Iberian peninsula as well as the Balearic Islands. Villages that were partly abandoned by their inhabitants are being occupied by tourists and by the facilities that cater to tourists such as hotels, residential buildings, and marinas. In Italy, as well, tourism has created areas with a new character, different in their landscape and economy from neighboring areas where tourism did not play an important role.[37]

The Adriatic coast of Yugoslavia is another example of the effect of tourism on the regional economy and human occupance of a coastal area. Prior to the advent of tourism, the towns and villages of the Adriatic coast, including the offshore islands (such as the Hvar group), were lagging behind the interior cities where industrialization and urbanization had concentrated. The Adriatic coast was for a long time a source of out-migrants leaving for other regions of Yugoslavia or even emigrating to foreign countries. Much of the out-migration was related to the scarcity of agricultural resources in the mountainous and rocky region. But with massive tourism to the Adriatic coast, a substantial change was introduced in the economy of the region, which had a considerable effect on population growth, espe-

[34]Léone Gueron, "Le tourisme a Menton," *Méditerranée,* 7 (1966), p. 51.
[35]B. Barbier, "Tourisme et emploi en Provence—Côte d'Azur," *Méditerranée,* 7 (1966), p. 216.
[36]Ibid., p. 220.
[37]Giovanni Merlini, "Problemi geografici del Turismo in Italia," *Bulletino della Società Geografica Italiana,* 9 (1968), p. 30.

cially in the urban centers associated with tourist activities.

Part of the Mediterranean space is made up of islands of various sizes which offer many attractions for tourism—seawaters, beaches, scenic landscape, historical sites, and a nonindustrial environment. Many of the islands are rocky and mountainous and not very attractive for agriculture. Their insularity does not provide a suitable location for industry. As a result, the economic fate of the Mediterranean islands is now dependent to a large extent on the development of tourism. Those islands that become important attractions for tourists continue to grow in population. Those that do not have any significant share in the rush of tourism to the Mediterranean are losing their population to the larger cities.[38]

Thus rural and nonmetropolitan communities which previously were negatively affected by urbanization, through the general drift from rural to urban areas or from many small towns to a few large cities, are currently undergoing a sort of economic rehabilitation in response to the increasing demand of tourists and vacationists for nonmetropolitan locations, especially along the coast. Tourism, then, is a weighty factor in the geographical redistribution of investments, jobs, and income and tends to favor rural areas, in contrast to the role of urbanization.

The Sprawl of a Tourist Corridor

Not much is known about the way tourists select the places where they like to spend some time. Even less is known about how tourists are distributed geographically.[39] Some broad generalizations are suggested here with regard to the Mediterranean coastlands.

With more people joining the stream of tourists and vacationers, the older places nearer to the place of residence of the tourists are becoming overcrowded. In order to satisfy the requirements for low density and extensive use of the coastal space for the purpose of vacationing, new sites are being sought along the coast. The result can only be described as a "tourist sprawl," from older, crowded, familiar resorts to new ones where there is still plenty of open space.

Another important factor in the sprawl of tourist resorts along the coasts of the Mediterranean is the shifting of popularity from one coast to another.[40] As older, familiar resorts are overtaken by tourists, new ones are

[38]For a detailed description of the development of population in the Mediterranean islands, see Y. Kolodny, "La population des îles en Méditerranée," *Méditerranée,* 7 (1966), pp. 3-32.
[39]Cohen, "Toward a Sociology of International Tourism," p. 179.
[40]Christaller, "Some Considerations," p. 104.

being "discovered" or developed, and the attention of the tourists turns to them.[41] The discovery of "new" places is not limited to nearby coasts. The low cost of transportation makes it possible for even remote resorts to become popular in certain years. Operators of resorts and travel services are able to build up the popularity of a resort area through a publicity campaign or very attractive prices.

The corridor-like pattern is caused by the overwhelming preference for seaside locations. It is the combination of sun, sand, and sea that attracts most tourists and vacationers, and the lack of any of these three components, but especially the sea, is likely to reduce the attraction of a location appreciably. Therefore there is a rather high degree of geographic concentration of tourists. But since there are other constraints, such as the requirement for some measure of low density or the shifting popularity of a site, the resorts tend to spread along the narrow strip of the coast.

The widespread use of the automobile and the development of a modern network of highways have been instrumental in the sprawl of tourism along the Mediterranean coast. The automobile is one of the factors that made possible the selection of a wider choice of sea resorts and beaches, and therefore, because some locations are getting overcrowded, the automobile makes it possible to move easily to others. The coastal highways, some constructed only in recent years, have added to the spread of tourism to remote locations as well as to locations between older centers of tourism. Land transportation links, with no difficulty and in a short time, the large cities of northern and western Europe with most of the coastal resorts of France, Spain, Italy, Yugoslavia, and to some extent even those of Greece.

Before the spread of the automobile, tourist resorts were relatively few and were largely dependent on rail and sea transportation. Only those towns with railroad service or a large enough port could develop as tourist centers, if other necessary conditions were right for the development of tourism. One of the first of these areas was the French Riviera.

A more recent development in transportation that has extended the accessibility of coastal resorts has been the construction of airports especially to service the tourist trade. Direct flights, mainly by chartered aircraft, bring tourists to remote resorts, thus overcoming the constraints of the existing network of land and sea transportation.

Increased use of package, or organized, tours brings to the map of tourism remote localities on the Mediterranean coast, localities the individual tourist would find it difficult to reach otherwise. The development of

[41]Walter Christaller, "Beiträge Zu Einer Geographie des Fremdenverkehrs," *Erdkunde*, 9 (1955), p. 1. Christaller emphasizes the claim that the destinations of tourists are subject to fashion.

large-scale operators organizing tours or vacations, often in resorts (or villages, as they are sometimes termed) run by the operators themselves, is instrumental in the spread of tourism to localities otherwise not visited by tourists.

The sprawl of tourism takes place within each country, as well as throughout the Mediterranean basin. The general direction of the sprawl seems to be from the northwestern coasts of the Mediterranean to the southern and eastern coasts, as is tentatively shown in Table 10.2. During 1960-65 many of the Mediterranean countries more than doubled the number of tourists visiting them. In the next five years (1965-70) only Cyprus, Lebanon, Tunisia, Algeria, and Morocco have retained this high rate of tourist growth. (Obviously, the data includes many tourists who do not visit coastal resorts, as well as those who come for reasons that have hardly anything to do with tourism. Moreover, tourism is subject to fluctuation due to political and military crises; therefore, in order to draw more specific conclusions from the data on tourist flows to the Mediterranean countries, one must make a more detailed analysis than is attempted here.)

The data in Table 10.2 suggests that northwest European tourists (as well as North Americans) looking for new tourist grounds and for a better bargain are moving from one tier of countries to another in a general southeasterly direction. From the old tourist centers of France and Italy, tourists are first moving to Spain, Yugoslavia, and Greece and have recently turned to the Middle Eastern and North African countries, as the data in Table 10.3 show. Authoritative, as well as comparative, studies of the prices of tourist services in the Mediterranean countries are not readily available, but there are enough indications to suggest that the spread of tourism to the southern and eastern Mediterranean is partly associated with differences in prices. To many of the tourists who flocked to Spain, price was the real persuader; currently it is the countries with lower service prices that attract many of the tourists. As Italy and France are becoming increasingly expensive for tourists, the less-developed countries, with substantially lower wages, are drawing the tourists, as are the operators of organized tours and developers of resorts. The competition of the less-developed countries in the Middle East and North Africa is increasing as travel fares decrease and the disadvantage of distance to these countries diminishes. The spread of tourism toward the southern and eastern Mediterranean coasts is not only a result of the search for less-crowded, yet unfamiliar coasts, it is also due to the desire to find more reliable coasts as far as climate is concerned. The southern and eastern coasts of the Mediterranean are characterized by a low incidence of rainfall, with virtually no rain in the summer, the height of the vacation season. Reliability of the weather is an important consideration in

TABLE 10.2

PERCENT CHANGE IN NUMBER OF TOURISTS IN MEDITERRANEAN COUNTRIES, 1960–65 AND 1965–70

Country	Percent Change		Country	Percent Change	
	1960–65	1965–70		1960–65	1965–70
Spain	133	59	Cyprus	29	281
France	98	23	Lebanon	−1	100
Italy	22	15	Israel	160	47
Yugoslavia	204	79	Tunisia	210	147
Greece	145	67	Morocco	186	55
Turkey	220	48	Algeria	—	116

Source: *United Nations Statistical Yearbook.*

TABLE 10.3

PERCENTAGE INCREASE OF NUMBER OF TOURISTS IN MEDITERRANEAN COUNTRIES, 1970–1971 (BASED ON JANUARY-SEPTEMBER COUNTS)

Country	Percent Change	Country	Percent Change
Algeria	−3.3	Libya	72.7
Cyprus	35.0	Malta	2.9
Egypt	18.0	Morocco	5.5
Israel	49.0	Spain	10.5
Italy	0.8	Tunisia	42.3
Lebanon	77.6	Yugoslavia	10.5

Source: International Union of Official Travel Organizations (IUOTO), *Technical Bulletin* 1972, BY/TS/1/72.

beach tourism, much more so than in cultural or even sightseeing trips. Also, from an economic point of view, operators of beach resorts are interested in spreading the tourist season for reasons of efficiency. This consideration offers some advantages to coastal resorts in the southern and eastern Mediterranean.

The Ecological Impact

In order to make the coast suitable for human occupance related to tourism and vacationing, the coastal environment has been transformed.

In the case of the draining of swamps infested with malaria, the transformation has had some positive effects. Due to the blocking of drainage on flat areas along the coast, swamps and malaria rendered these places inhospitable for human occupance and the development of tourism lagged behind. The growing economic returns from tourism and the crowding of older coast resorts have encouraged the draining of swamps and the eradication of malaria on such coasts. Along the lagoon coast of Languedoc in southern France, drainage projects and road construction were carried out during the 1960s, with the purpose of turning this formerly inhospitable and inaccessible region into a tourist area that would draw off vacation trade from the established but overcrowded resorts of the Riviera to the east.[42] In Corsica, too, new coastal areas were opened up for recreational use after efforts were made to remove the sources of malaria in the coastal swamps.[43]

In many other cases, however, the transformation of the coastal environment brought about by recreational activities is a source of anxiety to those concerned with ecological balance and the minimization of the deterioration of the natural environment. Because tourism entails a concentrated impact in a well-defined corridor along the shoreline, the ecological consequences of this growing population movement are intensified. A large number of tourists use large amounts of coastal space. In the process, the touristic uses of space compete with other uses that contribute to the quality of the coastal environment. Open beaches, clear swimming waters, seaside parks, and sand dunes give way to hotels, recreational facilities, and a multitude of boats that crowd the narrow strip of the Mediterranean coastline. Pollution of the sea, as well as the shore, is often the result.

The fact that tourism is a fast-growing industry and a major earner of foreign currency is related to its potential as an ecological problem. To this

[42]I. Cosgrove and R. Jackson, *The Geography of Recreation and Leisure,* London: Hutchinson University Library, 1972, p. 52.
[43]Renucci, "La Corse et le tourisme," p. 222.

reason one should add the rapid spread of touristic activity from one locality to another. The growth of the industry encourages entrepreneurs to quickly develop tourist facilities in a manner that is detrimental to the coastal environment. Local and national governments, in their eagerness to attract more tourists in order to develop the local economy, as well as to improve the balance of payments, are often ready to disregard zoning regulations and other qualitative standards. The results of such indiscriminate development are often ruined beaches, polluted coastal waters, and overloaded public services, as is the case along some parts of the Italian coast.[44]

It is often argued that cultural tourism did provide an economic incentive to preserve local traditional culture.[45] Without such an incentive, local, traditional landmarks would have disappeared or deteriorated. Moreover, it is maintained that "sightseeing is a product which can be sold over and over again without depletion of the resources."[46] However, this view disregards the required infrastructure that has to serve the sightseers. And with regard to coastal or seaside vacationing, as more and more tourists crowd along the Mediterranean coast, the natural environment is being depleted. Consequently, the cost-benefit calculations are different than for a nondepletive use.

The increase in international tourism has brought about an increase in the volume and proportion of the "mass" tourists. Mass tourists are often moving in groups and almost invariably visit or stay at the same places. They try to minimize the unfamiliarity of the microenvironment in which they move.[47] The necessary familiarity is usually provided by standardization of facilities such as hotels, buses, marinas, restaurants, beaches, stores, and other recreational facilities. Since the coastal countries or towns are eager to attract more of the group tourists, there is an increasing standardization of the tourist facilities even in remote regions. With a heavy concentration of group tourists on the Mediterranean coast there is not only a change in the economic base of towns and villages but also a transformation of their traditional color, way of life, and patterns of land use. On the Spanish Mediterranean coast there are sections that carry the flavor of the country of origin of the tourists or at best contain the standardized ubiquitous atmosphere of a tourist resort.

The large number of tourists can be a strain on local natural resources

    [44]Giuseppe Bozzini, "Processo al turismo Italiano," Vie d'Italia e del Mondo, vol. 1, no. 1 (1968), pp. 6–15.
    [45]S.K.Winters, "The American Tourist," The Annals of the American Academy of Political and Social Science, vol. 368 (November 1966), pp. 115–16.
    [46]Ibid., p. 113.
    [47]Cohen, "Toward a Sociology of International Tourism," pp. 166–67.

such as water, especially when they are in limited supply. In Yugoslavia, for instance, tourism is an important factor in the growing problem of water shortage. Adriatic towns and islands that have recently turned into centers of attraction for millions of tourists have to go to great efforts to supply water to the large number of tourists, in addition to the rise in the demand for water due to urbanization and a rising standard of living.[48] Similar problems exist with sewage. Systems were not planned to accommodate the growing number of temporary and permanent residents.

The increasing importance of seaside tourism accentuates the seasonality of tourism, especially in the northern Mediterranean which has a cold winter and cool spring or autumn. In Greece the concentration of tourists during the summer season (July to September) has increased in recent years. Between 1961 and 1970 the percentage share of the summer season in the total number of tourists grew from 46.6 to 50.9, which happened in spite of various efforts to diminish the high degree of seasonality.[49] The reasons for the high concentration of tourists, especially during the months of July and August lie, in part, in the perfect conditions of the weather (very sunny but accompanied by a cool sea breeze) along the Greek coast. The fact that the summer is a traditional vacation season is, of course, the main explanation. In Spain, 62 percent of the tourists arrived during the months July to September of 1970.[50]

The seasonal nature of tourism has had some impact on public services in areas where tourism is important. The large number of tourists necessitates the development of an excess capacity of public services such as water supply, sewerage, electricity, parking lots, and beach facilities. If tourists, vacationers, and even owners of second homes in some coastal areas are not differentially priced for these services, then, as peak users of public services, the seasonal consumers increase the costs of the services for the local residents. As such, the issue of excess capacity is a potential source of conflict of interest between the local population and the seasonal visitors.[51] The costs involved in excess capacity could be handled in the form of special prices for off-peak users or in a general tourist tax that would take care of the peak costs of a variety of public services. Alternatively, if differential pricing is not possible, excess capacity costs should be considered when benefits and costs of the tourist industry are weighed one against the other.

Added to the issue of excess capacity is the conflict over the use of scarce resources. Local residents in tourists areas are often forced to restrict

[48]Car and Mandarić, "Development of Tourism," pp. 49–50.
[49]"National Report No. 1.: Greece," *International Tourism Quarterly,* 1971, No. 1, p. 24.
[50]"National Report No. 2: Spain," *International Tourism Quarterly,* 1971, No. 2, p. 20.
[51]Clout, "Second Homes in France," p. 443.

their own use during the tourist season because of increased demand.[52]

The effect of tourism on the quality of the environment has become an important issue in the Mediterranean, so much so that the International Union of Official Travel Organizations has become concerned with the accusation that tourism "causes pollution and ruins cities." Indeed, in a press release in 1971, IUOTO claimed that deterioration of the coastal environment took place in spite of the effort of the tourist economy interests to protect the coastal environment, which is the "very stock-in-trade" of tourism. While this claim has some validity within the urban regions of the Mediterranean coast, where industries tend to be concentrated, tourists can hardly be considered protectors of the environment in the long nonurban stretches of the coast where industry does not have strong locational interests.

Conclusion

As long as urbanization was the major cause of population change on the Mediterranean coast, the geographic pattern of population distribution was that of increasing concentration in urban centers. However, with the advent of large-scale tourism and vacationing, the geographic pattern of settlement is increasingly taking on the shape of a coastal corridor. The sprawl along the coast caused by tourism is a result of tourists' preference for the shoreline and the extensive use of land which characterizes tourism. As the number of tourists coming to the Mediterranean grows, new coastal areas in the eastern Mediterranean and North Africa are being taken over for touristic land uses. The permanent residents of these coasts grow considerably due to the flow of income from tourism. Consequently, the ecological problems of human settlement along the Mediterranean are no longer limited to the urban agglomerations themselves but entail long stretches of the coasts that are not urbanized.

[52]Ibid., p. 442.

CHAPTER 11

Military Force in the Mediterranean

BERISLAV BADURINA

Introduction

Political conditions in the Mediterranean, making the framework for the existence, influence, and activities of military force, are quite complex. This region is exposed to the long-term interests of the US and USSR, first of all in the political and military-strategic fields, although those in the economic field (oil, maritime transport, etc.) are also significant. As mutually counteracting as they may be, there is within the wide range of these adverse interests one interest common to both sides: the wish to avoid a military confrontation that might result in catastrophic consequences to themselves and to a wider sphere. Each of these two powers will in the future endeavor to accentuate its presence in the Mediterranean while simultaneously making appropriate efforts to weaken its adversary's position.

Such a trend is favored by the protracted crisis in the Middle East. Certain unsolved matters within the field of interrelationships between the Mediterranean countries, as well as an unstable internal situation within some of them, might also serve as pretexts for an intensified interfering by non-Mediterranean powers in Mediterranean affairs, which might possibly result in the opening of some new hotbeds of conflict.

Although the presence of China in the Mediterranean is for the time being limited, an expansion of its political and economic relations with many Mediterranean countries should be expected, and the influence ex-

197

erted by China on developments in this region will probably grow.

However, the great powers' policies in the Mediterranean constitute only a part of their global policies and their global mutual relationship. Hence some of their proceedings and ventures in this region can be understood adequately only within the framework of their global activities.

The other side of this complex situation consists of the political, social, economic, and cultural heterogeneity of the Mediterranean. Sociopolitical systems, external political orientations, and levels of development of the Mediterranean countries show substantial differences, accentuated also by powerful influences exerted from outside the region.

Increasing Interest in the Sea

The second half of this century has been characterized by an increased interest in the sea, shown not only by great powers and littoral countries but by the entire international community. This has come about as the result of many factors, among them: increased demands for transport and communication in regional and global frameworks, the necessity of a more intensive utilization of natural riches which the sea hides within its depth, globalism of great-power policies and strategies, and the appearance and development of nuclear weapons and increasing militarization of the sea.

The over-all volume of the world exchange of goods increased in the 1960-71 period from 128.3 to approximately 340 thousand million dollars. In 1971 the exports from the western European countries alone reached the sum of 156 thousand million dollars. When one keeps in mind that an enormous part of world trade is handled by maritime transport, the exceptional importance of this communications medium, both in peace and in war, becomes obvious, particularly with regard to countries whose imports and exports are almost exclusively effected by sea routes.[1] This is also eloquently shown by data on the size of merchant fleets of individual countries, of the world merchant marine in general, and on the rhythm of their development.[2] One's attention is also drawn to the fact that in total

[1] In 1966, 1,810 million tons of goods were transported by maritime routes, of which some 950 million tons were of crude oil. Four years later (in 1970) these figures were 2,510 and 1,350 million respectively. The European Economic Community countries imported in 1970 745 million tons of goods by maritime routes and exported 178 million tons. "Problèmes economiques," La documentation française, February 2, 1972.

[2] By the end of June 1971 the tonnage of the world merchant fleet reached 238.2 million gross register tons, which constitutes an increase of 8.4 percent in comparison to the previous year. With the total tonnage of their merchant fleets, Japan, with its 29.5 million tons holds the second place in the world, Great Britain with 27.1 million tons and the USSR with 11.3 million tons, third and seventh place, respectively, and the US with 16.1 million tons, fifth place. Japan has planned to build in the 1969-75 period 28 million tons of shipping; the US

number and tonnage of ships, a significant place belongs to tankers, by which a lion's share of the world crude oil output is transported each year (in 1971 the world production of crude oil totalled 2,465 million tons).[3]

The sharp numerical increase of the world population, the urgent development needs of many countries, and the rising standards of living have accelerated the exploration of the sea, the seabed, and the subsoil thereof for the purpose of a larger and more complete use of the natural riches they hold.

Man has directed his exploration efforts, first of all, to the continental shelf, this direct extension of the land.[4] Situated under a water surface up to 200 meters deep or more, in cases where its exploitation proves to be possible, this shelf is presently accessible to the technologically developed countries but is also becoming a matter of dispute among different interests. Although the exploitation of deposits of coal, iron, copper, nickel, tin, etc., which this shelf contains, offers potential wealth, its main treasure consists of oil and natural gas.[5] Some 75 countries are exploring or participate in explorations and prospecting for oil in the continental shelf. In 1969 about 20 percent of the world crude oil production originated in deposits located within the seabed subsoil. It has been estimated that this percentage will double by the mid-1980s.

The sovereign right of the littoral countries to the exploration and peaceful uses of the seabed and of the continental shelf subsoil is creating international disputes. It is probable that military force may be used in the protection of seabed development rights in the future. Small countries find themselves in an unfavorable position in this respect, since their material limitations do not allow them either to enjoy their rights completely or to protect their interests effectively. By joining their efforts within regional or even wider frameworks, they would, however, improve their position.

Utilization of natural riches of the sea, situated beyond the existing limits set by national jurisdiction, constitutes, however, a separate problem, one giving rise to many difficulties and obstacles. These difficulties are a result of the arms race which is extending also to these underwater expanses

---

is planning to increase its merchant shipping within this decade by three to four times, while the USSR will build by 1975, some four million tons of shipping. Ibid.

[3]By the end of June 1971 the tonnage of tankers was 40.4 percent of the total world merchant shipping. The tanker fleet consisted of 4,200 tankers, with a tonnage totaling 164.7 million tons, recording an increase of 14.6 percent in comparison to the previous year. Ibid.

[4]The surface of the continental shelf amounts to 7.5 percent of the total surface of seabeds and ocean floors, or about 25 million square kilometers, that is roughly two-and-a-half times larger than the area of Europe. Edouard Gueit, "Le plateau continental: ressources et conquête," *Revue de defense nationale,* August-September, 1971.

[5]Almost half of the total space of the continental shelf is, by its geological composition, oil-promising, while on land such conditions are found only in one sixth of the total surface. Gueit, "Le plateau continental: ressources et conquête," *Revue de defense nationale.*

and of the unwritten "law of the stronger." Obstacles appear as a consequence of the present polarization of the world between the great and small, developed and developing, countries. From the exploration and exploitation of the seabed result far-reaching economic, military, and political implications. If these activities were regulated by international law, many confrontations and conflicts aggravating the instability existing in different regions and in the world in general could be avoided or prevented.

Great naval presence in the world ocean constitutes one of the basic attributes of the global policies and strategies of great powers. This role of the sea has been accentuated by the appearance of nuclear weapons.

When the Second World War terminated, the US remained in almost all of the seas where its forces had carried out naval operations, with an orientation to further augmenting and expanding its presence therein. Since in the course of the two following decades the US had no serious rival in these vast marine regions, a conviction grew that it must and could *dominate* the world sea, maintaining that this domination is of vital interest for its own security and well-being.

It seems that the Cuban crisis in 1962 was for the USSR a crucial moment in the development of its naval and general maritime concept. From then on, the USSR has oriented itself more firmly toward the development of its maritime forces in order to realize the idea of its presence in all seas. In the course of the past decade, the USSR has instituted an imposing development program of its maritime forces (navy, mercantile, fishing fleets, and hydrographic exploration ships). Its significant advantage over the US in this field is the "youth" of its warships and merchant ships. The USSR has finally left its littoral seas and taken to the open sea, with the intention of staying there. This process has been speeded up and facilitated by certain international developments such as the 1967 war in the Middle East and the events on the Indian subcontinent.

The encounter of these two great powers in the world sea constitutes a new stage in their mutual confrontation. The confrontation of their forces has thus been substantially expanded, while the inherent uncertainties in their relationships have been increased as well.

China has not taken to the world sea yet, but it is a realistic expectation that in the foreseeable future it will do so, first by building its submarine fleet and then by building a surface fleet able to remain for long periods in the open sea.

The development of nuclear weapons caused significant changes in naval strategies of the great powers. For their survival in a nuclear war, armed forces have much more favorable conditions at sea than on land. This has led to an acceleration in the construction of nuclear-powered submarines armed with high-efficiency missiles. Thus a substantial and in perspective decisive part of the strategic-offensive nuclear forces has been positioned at sea.

Once a relatively stable balance of nuclear deterrence between the US and USSR was established, the probability of a direct military confrontation and armed conflict in zones of vital importance—and thus the starting of a general nuclear war—were lessened. On the other hand the freedom and independence of small and medium-sized countries are increasingly endangered by local crises and conflicts in the "peripheral zones." Here one should keep in mind that in almost all the crises and conflicts that have taken place outside Europe since the end of the Second World War, naval forces have played a prominent, even decisive role, and that the main lines of supply to all the engaged forces were maritime.

The arms race has been extended to the sea. All types of warships are undergoing a significant evolution. There have been great changes in armament and equipment. Classical artillery is gradually being replaced by missiles. Beside the strategic ballistic missiles, surface-to-surface and antisubmarine missiles are being rapidly developed. With the appearance of new weapons, the land-sea ratio is being changed. While earlier naval forces were intended mostly for operations at sea and in coastal areas, they are now able to strike objectives far inland with missiles and with aircraft from aircraft carriers and missiles.

The criteria of force ratios have changed, too. Today no power, even if it had a numerical and qualitative advantage in warships, could covet general domination of the world sea or even limited sea space. Maritime might is a relative value, depending not only on the available number of ships and their armament but on many other factors.

The risk of an eventual conflict has attained such dimensions that deterrence and the wish to avoid mutual confrontation have become the basic preoccupation of great powers in their competition at sea. Any limited conflict between the powers carries the potential for escalation into a wider war.

Modern marine technology makes it possible for ships to operate on the high seas autonomously and for long periods. A major problem, however, remains that of resting ships' crews at land bases. A number of littoral countries offer various harbor and airport "alleviations and privileges" to fleets, and this is one way of basing them in foreign countries. But conventional naval and air force bases continue to be significant within the framework of the strategic concepts of certain great powers.

The peacetime role of these fleets is significant. Through their movements, maneuvers, and presence in specific regions and zones, they exert definite political and psychological influences, which could have far-reaching consequences. They are also a means of demonstrating military might and of supporting or exerting pressure on a government. Their flexibility and mobility enable them to appear quickly and in adequate force wherever it serves the political interests of their countries. Their movement and stay in international waters formally safeguards them from the political complications inherent in the stationing of land and air forces in foreign territories.

From all the above, the conclusion can be drawn that the significance of the sea is growing steadily. The sea occupies an increasingly prominent place in the policies, economies, and strategies of great powers. The development of small and medium-sized littoral countries and their international positions are increasingly tied to the sea. Somebody wrote that the winds of history blow toward the sea. I would add that from the sea also, many dangers may spring, not only for littoral countries but for the entire world.

Geo-Strategic Significance of the Mediterranean

With its 17 littoral and insular countries, the Mediterranean occupies a space of approximately 11.2 million square kilometers, with over 290 million inhabitants. This vast expanse enables a relatively favorable dispositioning and speedy maneuvering of armed forces. It also presents such forces with a favorable basis for carrying out operations. The substantial human resources of the region also play a role in any strategic concept.

Situated in an ideal, central position with regard to the strategic regions of continental Europe, the Middle East, the Indian Ocean, inner Africa, and the Atlantic Ocean, the Mediterranean can offer many advantages to a power intent on domination over it. A particularly significant fact is that the Mediterranean is connected with Europe and, via the Middle East, Suez Canal, and Red Sea, with the Indian Ocean. Actually, the Mediterranean and Europe constitute an integral strategic region, a fact brought about mostly by new military combat possibilities. The significance of the connection of the Mediterranean with the Indian Ocean results largely from the significance of Middle East oil, which is transported to other parts of the world via sea routes.

Gibraltar, the Suez Canal, the Bosporus, and the Dardanelles separate the Mediterranean Sea from the rest of the sea masses, and the passage between Sicily and Tunisia divides it into the eastern and western Mediterranean. The military significance of this geography is indisputable.

Continental Europe is connected with northern Africa by three natural geographic salients, extending, first, across Spain and Morocco, second across the Balkans and the Apennines, and third across the Middle East. The interest of non-Mediterranean powers in all three passages is evident.

The key geographical points of the Mediterranean in an east-west direction are, besides the sea straits and passages, the Pyrenean Peninsula with northwestern Africa, the Middle East, and in between them, the Balearic Islands, Crete, and Cyprus.

The strategic center of gravity of this entire wider region lies in the eastern Mediterranean and Middle East. This expanse, where three continents and three seas (Mediterranean, Black Sea, and Indian Ocean) meet, has exceptional strategic significance.

The Mediterranean is at the crossroads of the most important maritime and air routes, in peacetime and in war. It is the largest "sea corridor." To many Mediterranean countries, the sea is their principal connection with the world and to some, almost the only one.

The Mediterranean is also the crossroads for air routes that connect continents. As development of air transportation accelerates, this facet of the Mediterranean's significance will grow.

The Military Situation of the Mediterranean

A permanent increase of the military presence of non-Mediterranean powers, accompanied by the development of the military forces of some Mediterranean countries themselves, is a major feature of the postwar situation in the Mediterranean. The military presence of the US in the Mediterranean dates from the Second World War. Soon after the termination of the war, the US proclaimed, through the "Truman Doctrine" (March 1947), her resolute wish to become the guarantor of the interests of the West in this region, based primarily on American military force. This was followed by the creation of NATO, initiated by the US with the co-operation of Italy (since 1949), and Greece and Turkey (since 1952) in the Mediterranean. In February 1955 the Baghdad Pact was concluded between Turkey, Iraq, Iran, Pakistan, and Great Britain. Two years later this pact was joined by the US. It was succeeded in 1958 by CENTO. The US joined these pacts in concordance with the "Eisenhower Doctrine" (March 1957), which accentuated US interest in the Middle East. Thus the chain of US military-political measures was completed in this part of the world, with the explicit purpose of the encirclement of the USSR (the "policy of containment"). These multilateral arrangements were accompanied by bilateral agreements in which the US acquired military bases in Spain, Morocco, Libya, and Saudi Arabia. In this way the political foundation for installing the military force of the US in the Mediterranean and the Middle East was created.

The military presence of Great Britain in the Mediterranean and Middle East has moved in a descending line. Only recently has London shown a wish to stop the trend and safeguard its remaining positions (Gibraltar, Malta, Cyprus), which still occupy a prominent place within the framework of Mediterranean policies and the strategy of NATO (and the US in particular).

The Mediterranean countries of NATO started the renewal and development of their armed forces in the 1950s with substantial aid offered by the US. At the beginning of the 1960s they possessed a powerful military potential, which has increased, based in great measure on aid from abroad. France's withdrawal from the NATO military structure in 1966 was a sign of new trends within the NATO Pact and was not without consequence for its military possibilities in the Mediterranean.

Until the mid-1960s the military presence of the USSR in the Mediterranean was limited and sporadic. Prior to this time, however, Russia had decided to accelerate its naval build-up and to get to the world sea as soon as possible. One of the first steps in that direction was the sailing of the Soviet naval forces into the Mediterranean Sea, a maneuver precipitated by the June 1967 War. From that time on, Russian military force in the Mediterranean and Middle East has been growing constantly and shows a tendency to grow further.

June 1967 brought about a substantial increase in the armed forces of the direct participants. Military efforts of other Mediterranean countries move within limits set by their normal possibilities and needs.

Political trends and developments in the Mediterranean from the end of the Second World War to the present have been dynamic. During the first half of that period, 10 new states came into being (countries of northern Africa, the Middle East, Cyprus, and Malta), to be immediately confronted both with grave problems of their underdevelopment and with various pressures from abroad.

During this later period the political constellation in the Mediterranean was powerfully shaken and agitated by periodic tensions between some countries, by crisis and armed conflicts,[6] in which non-Mediterranean

---

[6]Intensification of tensions, crises, and conflicts in the Mediterranean, in its eastern part and in the Middle East in particular, started immediately after the end of World War II and have continued to the present. The civil war in Greece and the intervention of the armed forces of Great Britain and the US in Greece were not even terminated when the first armed conflict erupted in the Middle East between the newly established state of Israel and its Arab neighbors. From that time on, the Middle East crisis has become constantly more intense. In the 1945–54 period the "Trieste problem" caused severe tension in relations between Italy and Yugoslavia. During the 1950s Algerians and Cypriots fought for their liberation and the creation of their independent states, their valiant efforts being eventually crowned with complete success (the Republic of Cyprus was constituted in 1960 and that of Algeria in 1962). During the 1960s internal stirrings and disturbances in many countries of the Middle East and armed interventions of the US (in Lebanon) and of Great Britain (in Jordan and Kuwait) took place. A new hotbed of conflict has lately opened in Cyprus, while the questions of Malta and

factors almost always played an important role. The center of gravity of these unfavorable developments is situated in the eastern Mediterranean and Middle East, while their harmful consequences have far-reaching effects. The main battle is being fought between Israel and its Arab neighbors, although in substance this is a conflict between much wider interests.

One characteristic of the Mediterranean political scene is a state of internal instability in many countries, serving frequently as a pretext for intervention from abroad.

The main outcome of the political trends and developments in the Mediterranean during the past two or three decades can be described as the weakening of the influence of the West (the US, Great Britain, and the west European countries). This is due to a variety of reasons: Political inadequacy in the face of the emancipation of Mediterranean countries and wider positive changes in the world in general. An attempt to ascribe these profound changes to "communist subversion" has always been an expression of the failure of certain regimes to understand and respect the realities of life. How else could one explain the fact that the influence of the West in the Mediterranean reached its lowest level during the very period when its rapidly growing military presence in this region had almost no competition?

There is, at present, an enormous concentration of military power in the Mediterranean. It has been estimated that in 1971 military strength of the Mediterranean countries was over 2.8 million men and that their navies had some 360 larger warships (not counting minesweepers, minelayers, landing ships and craft under 100 tons). Some 13.5 thousand million dollars was spent for military purposes, while at the same time the gross national product of all the Mediterranean countries of North Africa and the Middle East amounted to 28 thousand million dollars. If to this are added the US and British armed forces stationed in the Mediterranean, it can be concluded that, besides Europe, this is one of the world regions wherein the largest armed forces are dispositioned.[7] What is more, in no other world

---

Gibraltar have recently also been included in the agenda. These are only some manifestations of tensions, conflicts and interventions in the Mediterranean and Middle East. The complete list of these occurrences and developments is much longer.

[7]The American Sixth Fleet was formed in June 1948 of naval units which had already cruised in the Mediterranean Sea. Within its organization the fleet presently has two to three aircraft carriers, with some 150 to 170 combat aircraft aboard, many of which are capable of transporting nuclear weapons over long distances, one helicopter carrier, two missile-cruisers, about 20 destroyers, several submarines, and a substantial number of landing and auxiliary ships—a total of about 60 ships. On board the landing ships there is a detachment of US Marines.

The Mediterranean Fleet of the USSR has 30 to 60 ships, their number depending on the current situation in the Mediterranean and the season of the year. It usually consists of one cruiser-helicopter carrier, two other cruisers (one of which armed with missiles), 10 to 15 submarines, 10 to 15 destroyers, frigates and corvettes, and about 20 landing and auxiliary

region do such powerful military forces (both conventional and nuclear) of the US and USSR directly confront each other in so limited a space (the eastern Mediterranean in particular).

The presence and relationship of the armed forces of non-Mediterranean powers give rise to some adverse assessments and conclusions. This is usually a result of a technocratic approach to the matter. Numerical data on the armed forces are displayed and compared; the technological advantages and disadvantages of one or the other side are analyzed; hypotheses on the ways and means of utilization of these forces in peacetime and in war are set forth; and on this basis, an unrealistic perception of their own abilities is built, only to be—not rarely—proved incorrect in practice.

Such an approach to the matter of military force does not permit the problem to be perceived and understood in its entirety and complexity. Ignoring such significant elements as political, economic, social, psychological and other factors, both Mediterranean and non-Mediterranean, inevitably leads to wrong conclusions. From there to the wrong action is but one step, made many times by some great powers in their Mediterranean policies. The most indicative example was the attempt of the British and the French to invade Egypt in 1956, based on their one-sided, and consequently wrong, estimate of the force ratio.

As in other parts of the world, in the Mediterranean the notorious truth of the might yet feebleness of military force finds its proof. Serving policies of interference, pressures, and domination, military force in this region has brought short-lived gains but long-lasting damage and harm.

The military presence of non-Mediterranean powers in the Mediterranean is a reality, as is their determination to rely more and more on military force in their future policies. It would be a mistake to expect that such trends could be altered by merely condemning the Mediterranean policies of the great powers and by demanding of them a lessening of their military forces in this region. It is indispensable that the international conditions, both regional and global, in which such policies can exist should be altered. An approach should be found in which it would be possible to build the interests and potential of the great powers into a positive program for fortifying peace and security and for developing international cooperation within the Mediterranean.

The non-Mediterranean factors are not the only cause of tensions and conflicts in the Mediterranean however. Within certain Mediterranean countries, or within the frameworks of their interrelations, there exist real

---

ships. On board the landing ships there is a detachment of the naval landing infantry.

Great Britain keeps a smaller fleet in the Mediterranean, which is reinforced as the need arises. On its bases in Cyprus, Malta, and Gibraltar, it has smaller contingents of army forces and several combat aircraft squadrons.

or potential hotbeds of crisis. On the other hand, there are active forces in the Mediterranean, which have the vision of the Mediterranean as a zone of peace and cooperation based on equal rights, and they are ready to join forces in finding ways to quickly and painlessly transform this vision into reality.

The Alternative to the Policy of Force

The only alternative to the policy of force in the Mediterranean is that of cooperation on an equal footing between all the countries of this region, a peaceful solving of existing problems, the building of a collective security system based on the principles contained in the UN Charter. This would require more constructive attitudes on the part of the big powers where Mediterranean problems and dilemmas are concerned.

An efficient, collective security system in the Mediterranean cannot be built on the basis of military premises and solutions. Experience has shown that there exist no dependable military-technological formulas for preserving and fortifying peace and security; nor do I believe that such a formula can be found in the future. Security is a function of a great number of interconnected, interdependent, and constantly changing factors with political, social, economic, scientific, technological, psychological, and military overtones. Within such a comprehensive framework the primary factor is political, the political will of states to resolutely move along the road of peace, security, and cooperation.

A system of Mediterranean security must be a general one, equally accessible and useful to all the countries of this region. A monopoly enjoyed by some, with discrimination against other countries would be contrary to the substance and basic objectives of the collective security concept. After all, collective security cannot even be mentioned if the security of each and every country is not guaranteed.

Here one should keep in mind that the Mediterranean is not, nor can it be, a closed region, a reservation within which only its internal forces would be active. This region is open to the world and particularly to the great powers, to Europe and Africa, which means that any realistic concept of security must also contain this dimension.

A reliable system of Mediterranean security should be based on the principles of sovereignty, independence, equality of rights, nonintervention in the internal affairs of other states, territorial integrity, abstention from the threat by force or from its application, and of the free political will of each nation. These principles should be strictly respected. Such behavior of states would contribute to a relaxation of tensions and to the development of a spirit of confidence among nations and states. This is the basic presupposition for a democratic resolution of the international problems that exist in this part of the world, for discontinuing the arms race, and for moving toward disarmament. A final solution of the Middle East crisis, which would satisfy the vital interests of all countries involved, would have exceptional significance.

The abandonment of the arms race should be made effective in all countries whose armed forces are stationed in the Mediterranean or carry out their activities therein. The same applies to gradual disarmament, which should be effected in a balanced way, so that in no stage thereof and in no part of this region, arms reduction would bring advantages to one side while jeopardizing the other. Respecting the principle of the free and peaceful use of the sea, the seabed, and the air space beyond the limits of national jurisdiction, a realistic program of gradual military disengagement, starting from limited and simpler measures, with a later application of wider and more complex ones, should be worked out. In a first stage, efforts might be directed toward limiting or eliminating such manifestations of military force as would hamper the slackening of tensions and the building of confidence among states (military maneuvers, movements of troops, introduction of new contingents of foreign armed forces, etc.). Along with this, a process of gradually diminishing the military presence of non-Mediterranean powers in the area should be started as soon as possible. This demand is all the more logical since these powers, thanks to new achievements in the field of military technology, can realize their basic goals and purposes in the Mediterranean even with a lowered level of military presence in the region.

The stopping of the arms race in the Mediterranean cannot be separated from wider international activities, particularly those taking place in Europe and within the framework of relationships between great powers. This, however, does not mean that a Mediterranean action in disarmament could be started only after certain positive results were attained in other regions of the world. Certain ideas on these matters have already come to the fore. Some initiatives for reducing the military presence of foreign powers in the Mediterranean have already been undertaken. If nothing else, this can serve as an impulse to deliberations, which could in certain conditions make possible the undertaking of the next step with less delay.

An important component of the collective security system in the Mediterranean is the acceleration and intensification of development in the developing countries of this region and of Europe. The UN has indicated ways leading toward the solution of this acute problem, which is, however, not only a Mediterranean one. The developed European countries could contribute significantly to the more rapid movement along this road, which could also serve their own interests. If the great powers should exchange military competition in the Mediterranean for competition in offering economic aid to the less-developed Mediterranean countries, the perspective of their development would be more favorable. Intensive economic cooperation between Mediterranean countries could also constitute a significant element of such development. This would constitute part of a wider cooperation between the Mediterranean and other countries, based on the principles of peaceful coexistence and mutual interests.

Only on such bases can a reliable regional system of Mediterranean security be built as an inseparable part of a general security system and as a significant contribution to world peace.

The present situation in the Mediterranean and its unfavorable future prospects point to the indispensability and urgency of action. Awareness of this is increasing in many Mediterranean countries, together with their readiness for action. It is indispensable that this awareness and readiness soon acquire an adequate organizational form.

CHAPTER 12

A Mediterranean Council to Combat Pollution

ELISABETH MANN BORGESE

A MODEL DRAFT AGREEMENT

WE THE PEOPLE of all Nations bordering the Mediterranean Sea, to wit:

Albania	Malta
Algeria	Monaco
Cyprus	Morocco
France	Spain
Greece	Syria
Israel	Tunisia
Italy	Turkey
Lebanon	United Arab Republic
Lybia	Yugoslavia

AWARE of increasing populations and advancing industrialization on our shores; of the growing intensity of maritime traffic in coastal waters and on the high seas; and of the progress of science and technology in exploring and exploiting marine resources;

FEARFUL that these developments, if unchecked, may further soil the natural beauty of our coasts and blight their vegetation; defile historical shrines; destroy archeological treasures; threaten the ecological balance of the region; endanger human and animal health; and, in the long run,

210

extinguish life in the Mediterranean Sea;

AFFIRMING that the Mediterranean Sea, the cradle of civilizations, is our common heritage which we feel duty-bound to transmit viable to future generations;

BEARING IN MIND that the Mediterranean, while raising special problems which call for special solutions, yet is a part of the world ocean system, which is an ecological whole;

BELIEVING IT ESSENTIAL that any regional solution therefor must be conceived as an integral part of the over-all international ocean regime;

ACKNOWLEDGING the existence of political, economic, and ideological divisions which may impose conflicting loyalties and obligations but need not interfere with the pursuit of the common cause of all the people of the Mediterranean basin to save the Mediterranean Sea;

RECOGNIZING that pollution is a symptom rather than a cause and, in the long run, can be controlled only in the context of systemic, positive planning;

ACKNOWLEDGING[1] the efforts of FAO, UNESCO/IOC, WMO, IMCO, and IAEA to combat pollution in the world ocean system; and the necessity to dovetail any special regulations for the Mediterranean with the universal standards and rules recommended or to be recommended by these organs;

TAKING INTO ACCOUNT[2] the activities of international organizations which have already dealt specifically with pollution in the Mediterranean, notably the FAO General Fisheries Council for the Mediterranean, the International Commission for the Scientific Exploration of the Mediterranean; UNESCO/IOC, the Cooperative Investigations of the Mediterranean, WHO, and others, and the need for harmonizing and coordinating these activities;

ORDAIN AND ESTABLISH, through our duly constituted governments
The Mediterranean Council to Combat Pollution.

General Principles[3]

1. The Mediterranean Council to Combat Pollution (referred to hereinafter as "the Organization") shall seek to prevent any new form of marine pollution or any increase in the degree of existing pollution which would

---

[1]This paragraph was added in accordance with Lord Kennet's remarks.

[2]This paragraph corresponds to paragraph (9) of Annex VII, Note on the Advisability of a Regional Agreement on the Control of Marine Pollution in the Mediterranean, A/Conf.48/PC/IWGMP.I/5 Prov.

[3]These principles have been adapted from a statement by Thomas Busha, Deputy Head, Legal Division of IMCO.

injure the marine environment or cause injury to another state.

2. The Organization shall abate existing marine pollution causing injury to the marine environment or to another state.

3. States should be held responsible for environmental control and conservation in the areas within their trust and for causing pollution injury to another state, for which compensation should be given.

4. The prevention and control of pollution by national and international legislative means shall proceed side by side with the scientific determination of the causes and characteristics of the problem.

5. The measures for implementing and amending all laws and regulations, national and international, shall be sufficiently flexible to progress in harmony with scientific and technological advances.

6. In making its regulations, the Organization shall take into necessary account the ecology of the entire area and basin, the economic and social needs of the states concerned, and the amenities, recreational facilities, and historical uses of the coastal areas and waters therein.

7. The Organization shall make regulations applying uniform standards to determine the level of marine pollution above which injury to the environment or to another state would predictably result, and these standards shall be based on factors or determinants applicable to each area of the region.

8. All states concerned with the region shall provide by cooperative effort a reasonable probability of detecting violations of their own and their neighboring states' laws and regulations, and shall provide adequate penalties for such violations, in particular, violations of agreed-upon prescriptions in multilateral conventions dependent on national law for enforcement.

9. In legislating nationally or internationally for the seabed and the water column above it, adequate account shall be taken in matters of pollution of the distinction between them, namely, the free movement of the water masses as contrasted with the more stationary ocean floor.

10. All states concerned with the region shall cooperate in developing uniform standards for processing, handling, transporting, or disposing of polluting and toxic materials of all kinds, including the provision of adequate shore reception facilities for oily mixtures retained on board tankers, the equipping of ships with efficient oil-water-separating equipment and oil content meters and the means of safe transport of other noxious and hazardous cargos, and the development of methods of tank cleaning and ballasting whereby no reason for discharge of oily mixtures into the sea will remain.

11. The Organization shall provide for cooperative measures for monitoring, focussed on biological changes to the ecosystem of the region, including systematic and continuing ecological baseline studies at selected locations; similar measures shall be envisaged for surveillance of the region,

including aircraft and satellite observation, for data exchange, and for an international registry of wastes discharged into the environment.

12. All regulations should be prepared in such a way as to conform with wider, multilateral, conventional systems aimed at prevention and control of marine pollution, and each state concerned shall without delay undertake the obligations of those systems and accept such amendments as may be agreed upon to assure their current application.

13. Due account shall be taken in all arrangements and regulations of the difficulties faced by developing countries in acquiring information on the distribution and concentration of pollutants, in acquiring expertise and training for their nationals, and in establishing facilities, for example, for monitoring and detection of pollution or for accident reporting.

14. Recognizing that intensified use of the waters and coastal areas of the region will inevitably be accompanied by accidents resulting in pollution, all states concerned shall cooperate, on the widest possible scale, in the creation of a new corpus of international law in the field of prohibition, prevention, and redress (liability and compensation) for damage caused by accidental pollution whether resulting from misadventure to vessels, offshore drilling rigs (including pipelines for transporting oil to the shore) or other equipment in the marine environment.

Composition

The Mediterranean Council shall consist of the

> Mediterranean Committee
> Mediterranean Bureau
> Mediterranean Institute.

A. The Mediterranean Committee

shall consist of representatives (plenipotentiary ambassadors) of all member nations. The Committee shall meet twice a year. It shall elect its own chairman from time to time. The Committee shall discuss all recommendations and proposals issued by the Bureau and adopt, or return them to the Bureau with its recommendations. It may also request studies and take such other initiatives as it deems useful. Decisions of the Committee shall be made on a consensus basis.

Among other things, the Committee shall adopt standards, rules, and regulations:

214 THE TIDES OF CHANGE

To control dumping; to prohibit the dumping of atomic wastes and other persistent toxic material in the Mediterranean and to ration other dumping by substance and place for each country; to provide for the necessary inspection of dumping, including onboard inspection; and to keep a register of all dumping.

To control the discharge of industrial and domestic effluents (pipelines or rivers).

To reduce as far as is technically feasible the discharge of oil from tankers and other ships (military and civil) into any part of the Mediterranean.[4]

To ensure that the installation of slop reception facilities should be required where they are desirable and installed by appropriate technical means.

To encourage harbor and canal authorities to frame their regulations so that the condition of "gas-free" should not be a pretext for disposal of slops at sea.

To fix shipping lanes in restricted waters.

The Committee shall codify national and international legislation on pollution; assess the performance of nations and industries with regard to such legislation; and arbitrate disputes, assess damages, and fix reparations.

B. The Mediterranean Bureau

shall be a new type of organ,[5] corresponding to the new needs of environment management. It shall consist of a *secretariat* staffed by international civil servants and directed by a *board* composed of representatives of civic bodies such as water commissions, departments of interior or health, environmental agencies or councils of member nations, as well as representatives of the major industries active in the Mediterranean area; and representatives of the Mediterranean Institute. These shall be appointed in a manner to be determined. They shall serve for three years. They shall elect their own director-general. The Bureau shall function in continuation except for determined periods of recess; it shall deliberate on all matters within the scope of the Council and make recommendations to the Committee.

[4]Taken over from "A Statement of concern," proposed by Thor Heyerdahl and Arthur Bourne.
[5]The organization of the Council is based on the conviction that governments must control decision-making, whereas there must be a transnational input in policy-making concerning transnational issues. Such an input can best be provided by industry and science.

C. The Mediterranean Institute

shall consist of a *faculty* and a *supporting staff*. The faculty shall be appointed by member states on the recommendation of universities and oceanographic institutes in each member state. The faculty shall also include experts from the Mediterranean Commission of Scientific Research, the Council for the Scientific Exploration of the Mediterranean, the General Fisheries Council of the Mediterranean, MAMBO, the Cooperative Investigations of the Mediterranean, IMCO, IAEA, WMO, WHO and GESAMP, with all of which the Institute shall maintain close cooperation and coordination of activities. The faculty shall elect its president and other officers. The president shall appoint the supporting staff.

The Institute shall create and maintain the scientific basis for the Council's activities, and it shall engage in any research deemed essential to this end. The Institute's research program shall be determined by the faculty. The Institute shall have absolute freedom to publish reports, press releases, make films, and prepare television documentaries.

Fiscal Measures[6]

The Bureau and the Institute shall prepare annual, two-year, five-year, and ten-year budgets and submit them to the Committee for approval.

Budgets must remain within the over-all limit of 1 percent of the revenues from the total gross maritime product of all Mediterranean nations.

[6]There can be no doubt that the cost of cleaning up the Mediterranean and keeping it clean is considerable. This cost will include research, application of antipollution measures, administration and measures to keep industries in Mediterranean nations capable of competing on world markets. Cf. "Rapport Preliminaire sur un schéma operationnel de lutte contre la pollution marine en Méditerranée," Centre National Pour l'Exploitation des Océans: "Il n'y a aucune illusion à se faire: les actions proposées, les mésures techniques qu'elles conduiront à prendre, impliquent un effort financier considerable, qu'l faut chiffrer."

The Draft Convention Presented by the US on the *Regulation of Transportation for Ocean Dumping Convention* A/CONF.48/PC/IWGMP.I/5 Prov. Annex V, provides in Article VI that, "The Secretariat shall submit to the General Conference budget estimates for expenses it may incur on behalf of the General Conference and for other expenses of the General Conference. The General Conference shall apportion the expenses among the Parties in accordance with a scale to be fixed by it, following as nearly as possible the principles adopted by the United Nations in assessing contributions of Member States to the regular budget of the United Nations. No Party shall be assessed more than one-third such expenses."

No agreement to combat pollution in the Mediterranean should be proposed without provisions for the raising of the necessary funds. Whether the criteria adopted by the United Nations in assessing contributions of member states to the regular budget of the United Nations are the ones most suitable here is rather doubtful.

The measures proposed here, criticized in particular by the representatives of the Soviet Union, are based on the concept of the Common Heritage of Mankind, the use and exploitation of which must be for the benefit of all.

Contributions shall be assessed to nations on the basis of their use of the Mediterranean Sea and shall amount to not more than 1 percent of revenues from:

Large-scale commercial fishing[7] (employing vessels over____ tons)
Passenger shipping (based on the sales price of tickets)
Freight (cargo miles)
Military uses of the Mediterranean Sea (ship days)
Offshore oil
Desalination and in-solution mining
Recreation (on the basis of a tourist tax)
Dumping
Industrial and domestic waste
Cables (based on the price of messages).

Contributions shall be weighted by per capita income as calculated by the United Nations, in a standard currency. Nations with a low per capita income thus will pay less than 1 percent, but no nation shall pay more than 1 percent.

Nations not members of the Mediterranean Council shall be charged equally for their uses of the Mediterranean on the same basis, on penalty of being refused access to landing, repair, and fueling facilities.

Nations with "soft" currencies may pay their contributions in services and goods.

The fiscal scheme for financing pollution control in the Mediterranean shall be incorporated in and adjusted to any larger scheme for an ocean development tax, if and when such a scheme is adopted by the International Ocean Regime.

Immunities[8]

The Organization and its organs shall enjoy such privileges and immunities as are necessary to carry out the purpose of this agreement, provided that nothing herein shall reduce the privileges and immunities to which any nation might otherwise be entitled.

[7]This provision has been added in response to comments made during the discussion of the ocean development tax project.
[8]The remaining paragraphs have been adapted from the US Draft Convention on Dumping.

Amendments

Amendments to this agreement may be proposed by any member nation. Any such amendment shall be circulated to all member nations by the Bureau not less than 90 days before its consideration by the Committee. If an amendment is approved by the Committee, it shall be submitted to the member nations for acceptance in accordance with their respective constitutional processes. An amendment shall enter into force for the member nations accepting it when accepted by two-thirds of the members. The amendment shall enter into force for the members accepting it thereafter upon the date of such acceptance. Acceptance shall be effected by deposit of an instrument of acceptance with the depositary governments.

Withdrawals

Any member may withdraw from this agreement by instrument delivered to the depositary governments, which shall promptly inform all other members. Withdrawal shall not affect a member's budgetary obligations for the year in which it withdraws.

Signature

This agreement shall be open for signature by_____ for a period of _____ from _____. States shall become party to this agreement by deposit of an instrument of ratification, acceptance, or approval. This agreement shall enter into force when instruments of ratification, acceptance, or approval have been deposited by _____ states.

The depositary governments shall be the governments of _____. They shall promptly inform all states signatory or party to this agreement of the date of each deposit of an instrument of ratification, acceptance, or approval, and of the date of entry into force of this agreement.

The depositary governments shall register this agreement pursuant to Article 102 of the Charter of the United Nations.

PART IV

THE DEVELOPMENT OF THE CARIBBEAN

The Project on the Development of the Caribbean Sea was initiated in 1972 with the aid of a grant from the General Service Foundation. It was directed by Sir Egerton Richardson, formerly Ambassador of Jamaica to the United Nations and the United States, now Councillor to the Ministry of External Affairs of Jamaica.

There are obviously great differences between the Caribbean and the Mediterranean Seas. These range from ecological to cultural conditions. For instance, all Caribbean nations are developing nations; nevertheless, the pattern established by the IOI's Mediterranean Project proved helpful in organizing this second regional study. The problems raised by conflicting uses of ocean space and resources are similar. The analyses of fisheries, shipping, mineral potential, tourism, urbanization, industrialization, and military uses offer many analogies.

In contrast to the history of the Mediterranean, that of the Caribbean is rich in attempts to establish regional organizations to cope with common problems. Some of these precedents are indicated in Dr. Mathew's historical account. All of them, however, have been distorted by a *continental* orientation, usually leaving the bonds with present or former metropolitan administrations and interests stronger than the new oceanic bonds. In this respect, the proposal for a *Caribbean Community* at the end of this section differs essentially from past proposals, for it is genuinely ocean-oriented, aiming at the development of this common heritage.

The article on the sea-level canal raises a specific problem with general implications: What happens to the *sovereignty* of Caribbean nations whose ecology and economy may be basically altered by a decision—to build the canal —made *outside,* that is, by the United States and a client country? Can states be said to be *sovereign* when decisions directly affecting the livelihood and well-being of their citizens are *beyond their control?* It would seem that only through the establishment of an international forum, through which they could participate in such decision-making, could they reassert their sovereignty. Or, as Arvid Pardo put it in his article in Part VI, "Comprehensive international institutions for ocean space do not contradict sovereignty but rather strengthen sovereignty and give to this concept a more contemporary interpretation. A nation whose ecological and economic base is determined by the decisions of others—and in the oceans this is increasingly true of all states and particularly of small nations—has for all practical purposes lost control of much of its sovereignty. It can regain its sovereignty only through effective participation in the making of decisions that directly affect it. Far from restricting national sovereignty, comprehensive international ocean space institutions are the only way to safeguard and guarantee national sovereignty."

Reynaldo Galindo-Pohl clarifies the concept of the "patrimonial sea." By suggesting the merger of these ocean zones into a "matrimonial sea" or integrated economic zone, he proposes an ideal territorial basis for a regional management system apt to articulate and harmonize national, regional, and global interests.

220

There is, at present, more oil in the Caribbean than in the Mediterranean Sea. How much, is not known at this time; the geophysical exploration of the area is incomplete. One of the practical results of the IOI's Caribbean study has been a cooperative project, initiated by the Woods Hole Oceanographic Institution and the IOI, to explore the geophysical foundation of the Caribbean and its mineral resources. The project will take two years. A regional secretariat, directed by Sir Egerton Richardson, has been established in Jamaica to coordinate the project and organize the participation of all Caribbean nations, if possible. It is anticipated that this ad hoc organization will be further used for joint efforts in ocean exploration and exploitation.

Dr. Thomas Mathews is director of the Institute for Caribbean Studies at the University of Puerto Rico. Professor K.O. Emery and Elazar Uchupi are from the Woods Hole Oceanographic Institution. Dr. Ira Rubinoff is a senior scientist of the Smithsonian Institute in the Canal Zone in Panama. Reynaldo Galindo-Pohl is Ambassador of El Salvador to the United Nations, and Dr. David Krieger, formerly at the Center for the Study of Democratic Institutions, is now engaged in writing and free-lance writing on international problems.

The Caribbean project is the second in a series of regional studies of the IOI. Further such studies, on the Arctic and on the Central Pacific, have been initiated.

CHAPTER 13

Historical Patterns of Caribbean Communication

THOMAS MATHEWS

Throughout the almost 500 years of western man's knowledge of the existence of the Caribbean Sea, his mental image of this body of water and the broken and unbroken land barriers that define it has been conditioned by the political and economic interests which focussed his attention on the region. The image of the sea which has dominated thought about the area has been that which was conceptualized by the European explorer, colonizer, and trader. This image was not significantly modified when the European was joined by his North American counterpart whose political and economic interests were not much different from those of the original colonizer.

Variants of the image, however, did exist, and it will be my purpose in this article to explore these variants, as well as to explore the patterns of communication that correspond to the image to which I have alluded. A second image of the Caribbean Sea and the communities which sprung up around it had surfaced for limited periods of time during the 400 years prior to the present century. In fact, if we were able to explore the minds of the original inhabitants of the region, the picture of the Caribbean we would find would correspond more to the second image than to the first. The image held by a native of the Caribbean would have reflected not only his point of observation but, more importantly, the mental concept he had of his homeland and the relationship of that homeland, whether a coastal city or an island, to its immediate surroundings in the Caribbean region.

222

This is not to say that the holder of the second image believes the region exists in isolation; rather, the region is foremost in his mind, while outside relationships, although vital, are of secondary importance.

Recognition of the existence of the two images is important for analysis of problems in the social and political sphere of the Caribbean region. My focus will be on the lines of communication, and, since we are concerned with the Caribbean, our attention will be primarily marine-directed but not exclusively; air, wire, and space communications will be referred to as we approach the modern period.

The View from Without

For the European, whether Spaniard, Dutchman, or Englishman, the Caribbean Sea has been a place where products could be found and exploited for profit in the European markets. The Spaniard was the first to exploit the area and enjoyed a monopoly on exploitation for most of the 16th century, first exhausting the gold and silver and then shifting his attention to other products. In the first years of discovery the islands detained him. Then as the coastal areas at the far reaches of the Caribbean Sea, in Mexico and later in Peru, were discovered to contain instant wealth, the Spaniard came to look upon the communities in the broken chain of islands which defined the eastern extremities of the Caribbean no longer as centers which offered exploitation but rather as first lines of defense, which protected the approaches to the land depots such as Vera Cruz in the Gulf of Mexico and Portobelo in the southwest corner of the Caribbean. In such locations, the mineral wealth of Mexico and Peru was accumulated.

At enormous human and material cost, formidable fortresses were built to guard the harbors of San Juan, Puerto Rico, Havana, Santiago, Cuba, and Cartagena, Colombia. The Spaniards devised a system of *flotas y galeones,* which congregated into two great convoys the merchant ships bound yearly for the Caribbean port of Portobelo and the Gulf port of Vera Cruz [Haring, esp. Chap. 9]. The routes of these convoys were designed to permit a combination of maximum speed with maximum protection. Lookout posts along the route were to keep the authorities informed on the movements of marauding ships from enemy nations or later from the attacks of pirates in the Caribbean itself. The Spaniards attempted to maintain lesser outposts in places such as St. Martin in the northeast corner of the Caribbean, Trinidad in the southeast, and La Nueva Providencia in the western Caribbean, but outposts languished from lack of attention or were given up completely as the power of Spain declined [Naipaul; Mathews, 1969].

Less well known is the long history of the attempt of local Caribbean authorities, concerned for the welfare of Spanish interests in the region, to organize and maintain a Caribbean squadron, known generally throughout the 17th century as the *Armada de Barlovento* [Wright]. The plan was for the armada to be based in the eastern Caribbean, in Santo Domingo or Puerto Rico, from which it would circulate through the islands of the Lesser Antilles chain. During the very few years in which it did manage to function, it operated out of Havana, Cuba. The armada was never really allowed to function as planned, because the ships, which had to be built in Caribbean shipyards, were usurped by the King of Spain who ordered that they be incorporated into the depleted ranks of his own Spanish-based merchant fleets. There was also the fear that the boats of the armada, if left in the Caribbean, would develop their own points of contact for the carrying out of clandestine trade.

Most of the convoy ships did not carry on trade with the islands of the Caribbean (with the exception of Cuba, where they convened at Havana for the return trip to Spain). Certain merchant ships which had permission to trade in ports on Puerto Rico, Spanish Jamaica, or other islands separated themselves from the convoy at the appropriate time. The protection offered by closed harbors, such as that enjoyed by San Juan, was a disadvantage to the Caribbean convoy because of the difficulty of maneuvering in and out of a harbor. The fleet preferred to stand off a protected point, such as that of the northwest corner of Puerto Rico, or to drop anchor momentarily in a quiet passageway such as the Mona Passage to take on water or send ashore the *llovidos*.[1] From such anchorage the fleet could slip away quickly should enemy sails appear.

In order to sustain its island guardian posts, Spain had to authorize substantial amounts as yearly subsidies. Smaller ships thus regularly plied between either Mexico and the islands or Cartagena and the Greater Antilles. The small, armed, exclusively male, unit which guarded St. Martin was served with food and munitions from San Juan and with arms and occasional female companionship from Santo Domingo [Mathews, 1969]. The lack of any Caribbean-based armada and the inability to foster any local shipping resources, except in the port of Havana, effectively curbed any development of interisland communication.

In the later centuries of Spanish control, the monopolistic domination of Andalusian ports was broken and mercantile centers in other regions of Spain began to develop trade with the islands of the Caribbean. Well known is the development of the trade with the coast of Venezuela carried out by the Basque Guipuzoa Company [Hurssey]. Lesser known is the fact that a mercantile company working out of Barcelona was authorized to develop

---

[1]These were the stowaways who were put ashore at the first landfall in the New World, thus putting an end, momentarily at least, to their hopes for fortune in the Indies.

trade with Puerto Rico and Santo Domingo. In contrast to the success of the first venture, the second produced little economic activity.

The Dutch interest in the Caribbean, at least in the beginning, was purely commercial. Later, it developed into pure and simple pirating. The Dutch West Indian Company never did manage to establish its claim over any substantial land area except that north of Brazil on the Wild Coast, which is somewhat out of our range of interest [Goslinga]. Salt was the commodity that brought the Dutch into the Caribbean and led them to locate areas of influence, the first one on the eastern section of the Caribbean coast of present-day Venezuela [Sluiter]. The Paria peninsula, where salt is still produced, and the area around Cumana, were centers of conflict between Dutch salt fleets and Spanish administrators. Claim was laid to the deserted island of St. Martin, where a great salt flat existed, and Spain was forced to establish a garrison on the island to defend her sea routes. The Governor of Puerto Rico complained that the Dutch could launch an attack on Puerto Rico from St. Martin within 24 hours, due to the favorable wind position of the smaller island. On the other hand, to attack St. Martin from Puerto Rico would have required a sailing time of 7 to 10 days, depending on the direction and strength of the opposing wind. It was far easier to approach the island from Spain.[2] Such were the problems of ship maneuvering in a time when the wind was the only source of power.

Scourged from Paria and checked at St. Martin, the Dutch moved into the island of Curaçao, which contained nothing of material importance but did have one of the best harbors in the Caribbean. The Dutch held onto this island and moved out to include Aruba and Bonaire in their area of influence. With the peace of 1648 between Spain and Holland, St. Martin was returned to the Dutch and the neighboring islands of Saba and St. Eustatius were added to the area of Dutch influence in the north. Since salt could be picked up freely from almost any of the Caribbean islands, the commercial and trade potential of the port of Curaçao monopolized the attention of the Dutch West Indian Company. Willemstad, the port of Curaçao, rapidly became an emporium or warehouse for the Spanish Caribbean, setting up patterns of trade with Santo Domingo, Puerto Rico, and the coast of Venezuela and Colombia, which still survive. Of course, in the 17th century, the prime product was human cargo brought from Africa and distributed through the Caribbean once the period of conditioning had been carried out on the healthy and dry island of Curaçao [Hoetink].

In the next century the island of St. Eustatius became an important center for distribution, not only to the Caribbean but also to the colonies of the coast of North America [Hartog, 1964]. With local centers of distri-

---

[2]See Morales Padron, 1952, for comments on problems of communication with the lesser Caribbean colonies.

bution for the Caribbean region, the Dutch lines of trade obviously differed from the pattern developed by Spain. Nevertheless, the basic over-all pattern was not changed, since local centers depended on lines of communication with the European power and were not self-sustaining.

The English, and, as Eric Williams [1970] correctly adds, the French and also the North American Colonies, developed a triangular trade pattern in their commercial ties with the colonies of the West Indies. Shipping lines went to three centers in the Caribbean. Jamaica was the most important, followed by the Leeward Islands in the Lesser Antilles, and finally, Barbados, to which were added the Windward Islands when they came under the British crown in the late 18th century. Maneuvering large sailing vessels among the islands was not easy and took time. Thus such islands as Barbados and Antigua, with good roadsteads positioned near the open sea, were favored as collection centers for the surrounding islands. Overshooting the entrance to a narrow harbor could mean the loss of a day in preparing for a second approach. In the case of missing the narrow and current-ridden entrance to the harbor at Curaçao, it could mean the delay of two or even three days.

With the introduction of steam, the patterns of navigation changed somewhat. First of all, the vessels became larger, carrying more cargo and drawing more water. Smaller harbors lost importance and smaller islands found themselves excluded from the regular routes. Steam was introduced in the interocean routes and soon monopolized trade into the Caribbean from Europe and North America. Sailing vessels continued for many decades, even up to the present, to ply the trade routes between the islands. Free ports such as St. Thomas continued to be centers of trade and with the advent of steam-driven vessels became coaling stations. The English writer Anthony Trollope, who visited the Caribbean shortly after motor-driven ships came into wide use, about the mid-19th century, commented that he was frequently forced to journey to St. Thomas in order to get from one British island to another [Trollope]. It hurt his English pride and must have seemed contradictory that the Queen of the Seas in the Caribbean could not command what was obviously the busiest port of the Caribbean.

With the decline of sugar, the abolition of slavery in all of the islands, and the trend toward freer trade, the interest of European powers in the Caribbean declined somewhat. However, with that decline arose the interest of the United States, which replaced Spain as an imperial power in the region. United States interest dated from colonial times in the 17th century and was probably initiated by Dutch traders, first from Curaçao and later from St. Eustatius. The bond between New York and Curaçao was an early relationship, of rarely recognized importance except by Dutch historians [Hartog, 1968]. US interest in the region was solidified with the acquisition of Puerto Rico, the protectorate over Cuba, the construction of the Panama Canal, and the purchase of the Danish West Indies.

With the opening of the Canal in 1920 the image in the mind of the European of the Caribbean Sea acquired a new variation. It was now no longer just the terminal point for ships seeking West Indian products for the mother countries. The Caribbean came to be seen also as a water passageway between the two principal oceans. In the past the bridging of the land barrier had frequently been preferred to the long haul through the Straits of Magellan [Phelan]. Spain's official route to the Philippines had been overland through Mexico to the port of Acapulco on the west coast. A more practical route was developed later through the Tehuantepec peninsula. All of this increased use of the Caribbean naturally augmented the importance of the ports in the region, but it did not basically change their relationship to, nor the image of the Caribbean in the mind of the European or North American. Indeed, as we shall see when we turn to communications in this century by the military in the region, the concept held by Spain from the earliest times was taken over with very little variation by the US military strategists.

The View from Within

When emphasis is placed on the second image of the Caribbean, it is conceived of as a completely different body of water. We might consider the Caribbean as a town square, *la plaza mayor,* with the Gulf of Mexico serving as *la plaza menor*. The community is then built around the plaza or square and trade and communications transverse it frequently in all directions.

As suggested above, the indigenous inhabitants of the Caribbean undoubtedly were the first to have this image of the Caribbean, but their modes of transportation and communication were too primitive to be significant in this discussion.

Undoubtedly the second image was most prevalent in the little-known 17th-century Caribbean. Spain's power in the new world was on the decline, but other European states were either not powerful enough to fill the vacuum left by Spain or were too concerned with problems in Europe to direct much energy or capital to developing extensive colonial systems. As a result, the seaways of the Caribbean were dominated at that time by local residents of the region. Some built communities which owed loyalty to no flag but their own, and the Spaniards classified them as pirates and buccaneers [Esquemelina]. The settlement on Tortuga, off the northwestern coast of the island of Santo Domingo, was such a community. But the regular law-abiding colonists on the small and even on the large islands, both Spanish and English, also had to take to the sea for their own welfare and survival, rather than depend on the long-awaited ships from Europe.

Those on the Spanish islands of Santo Domingo and Puerto Rico, as well as those on the British islands of Barbados and St. Kitts, came out of necessity to know and use the Caribbean as an integral part of their community. Thus local ports which served subregions within the Caribbean, such as Charlotte Amalie in St. Thomas or Willemstad in Curaçao or Port Royal in Jamaica, became important as essential regional trading centers. St. Thomas served the northeastern corner of the Caribbean, Curaçao the Venezuelan and Colombian coast as well as Santo Domingo. Port Royal served the coast of Central America and the smaller islands of the western Caribbean.

Precisely because this was a period of local, regional importance, the history of the 17th century is little known and even less appreciated. Up to now histories have been written about the Caribbean either from the metropolitan point of view or by West Indian nationalists. Dr. Eric Williams and C.L.R. James were among the first of these, but they too used metropolitan resources [Williams, 1944; James; Bosch]. No one has attempted to write, as yet, a history of the Caribbean with the second image foremost in mind.

In the 18th century, focus on the Caribbean was again determined by European control and the second image declined in importance. France and England dominated the area, as Spain had in the 16th century. Port Royal was destroyed by natural forces, but England would have been just as destructive in bringing it under control. Tortuga disappeared as a center of illicit trade, and France developed its national and colonial interests out of Port-au-Prince. While Curaçao and St. Thomas continued as regional trade and communication centers for the Caribbean, their status as terminals for European shipping increased in importance.

With the revolt of the mainland colonies in both North and South America, the importance of these somewhat independent ports of the Caribbean was fully recognized. The disastrous fate of the small but important port located on the island of St. Eustatius only underlines the role played by these trading centers. They served not only as ports of supply for the rebelling armies but also as exile or refuge communities for both sides in the conflict. The populations of Puerto Rico and Cuba were augmented substantially by Spanish officials and royalists and their families who were forced to relocate.

With the introduction of steam-driven vessels, the Caribbean-centered image of the Sea was modified somewhat. Sailing vessels [Kingsley, esp.

chaps. 1 and 2] or schooners were still used for local or regional communications, while steam-driven ships were primarily used for interocean travel. St. Thomas and Curaçao continued to be important trading and communication centers by serving as coaling stations, particularly for ships of those nations not possessing colonies in the Caribbean, such as Germany, Italy, and up to 1898, the United States.

The increased use of steamer service took trade and products more frequently out of the Caribbean, rather than stimulating trade within the region itself. This result was a source of regret to some islanders.

There were other adverse effects, such as the decline in the importance of the smaller or lesser ports on the various islands and the permanent destruction brought about by the necessary modification of the principal ports to allow larger vessels with deeper draft to use the harbors. The case of the dynamiting of the coral barrier which limited the entrance to the harbor for the city of Santo Domingo is perhaps the most important example of this destruction [Barrett, p. 65].

In this century steam-driven vessels were finally introduced into the strictly regional trade of the Caribbean. The Dutch were probably the first to maintain constant regional communications among their widely separated islands. A schooner with a supplementary motor was functioning as late as about 1950, connecting Curaçao with the three Dutch islands in the Leeward Island group on an average of twice a month.[3]

Caribbean resources provided steam-driven vessels for the English-speaking islands. The fleet consisted of five small passenger ships, which also carried light cargo, and six freighters, which carried heavy cargo and some passengers. It operated between Montreal and 10 Caribbean ports, including Georgetown in British Guiana, which lies outside of the Caribbean proper. The operation lost money, in spite of—or, it has been suggested, because of—its ties with Canada [Levitt and McIntyre].

The service faltered in 1952 and was terminated in 1958. With the creation of the West Indies Federation, Canada again came bearing gifts— two new ships, considered by some to be white elephants. The argument was that Canadian shipyards realized more profit from their construction than the West Indies did from their costly operation. With the demise of the federation, a Regional Shipping Council came into existence and has met from time to time to handle urgent transportation problems. The most urgent is the debt created by the continued operation of the vessels. The ships are operated by the West Indian Shipping Corporation. Recent press

---

[3]These are Saba, St. Eustatius, and St. Martin (half of which is French). They are called the Dutch Windward Islands, although they lie within the Leeward Island group of the English-speaking islands. This confusion of nomenclature is a carryover of sailing terminology to the modern era, although the designation is no longer meaningful.

reports indicate that one of the vessels is to be sold.[4] This could seriously affect the service, and the Council may direct the Corporation to rent or charter services for the West Indies until a new ship can be purchased.

Worthy of some study for the islands of the Caribbean is the ferry system being considered in the Hawaiian Islands. Two types of vessels may be used: high-speed hydrofoils for the rapid transportation of passengers among the islands, and larger vessels for the transportation of cars and freight as well as passengers.

Hovercraft of various kinds have been used with varying degrees of success in the Caribbean. Ferry service has been attempted between Puerto Rico and the Virgin Islands, among some of the Windward Islands, and between Curaçao and Venezuela, but the service has not been offered on a sustaining basis and, at least in the first example, has served primarily the tourist trade.

The governments of some islands, such as the Dominican Republic and Cuba, have had their own shipping companies. In late 1972 a new shipping company was established in Puerto Rico, with plans to limit its operation strictly to the Caribbean area. While these companies free the Caribbean nations from complete dependency on European or North American shipping facilities, they do not necessarily provide increased inter-Caribbean trade.[5]

What is needed is a regional shipping authority which would service all of the communities of the Caribbean. This could be established only through cooperation of all of the governments at an international level. The likelihood of such an authority is remote until national interests become subordinated to regional interests. What could reasonably be expected is the establishment of a regional international agency which would supervise the use of the Caribbean Sea, with authority to safeguard the region from pollution of the marine environment. Such an authority could require, for example, all oil cargo ships using the Caribbean waterways to "tag" their cargo with magnetic dust for identification purposes so that spills might be identified and responsibility fixed for clean-up and payment of fines.[6] Other types of shipping, including tourist cruise ships visiting the islands of the Caribbean, would be under the supervision of this authority, which could also levy the tourist tax assessment for the region.

[4] *Trinidad Guardian,* October 25, 1972, p. 10.

[5] To gauge the amount of trade within the English-speaking Caribbean at present and for the immediate future, see E.C. Emerson, "Transportation and Economic Development in the Caribbean" *West Indies Chronicle,* July 1969. Mr. Emerson, who worked for Transport Research Program of Earth-Air Space and Advanced Military Systems, Ltd., projects the effect of containerization and jumbo jets on Caribbean transportation problems.

[6] *San Juan Star,* October 16, 1972, p. 6.

The control of the shipment of oil through the Caribbean takes on greater importance in the light of a recent proposal by the outgoing governor of Puerto Rico, Luis Ferré, who has suggested that the uninhabited islands of Mona, located between Puerto Rico and the island of Santo Domingo, be the site of a huge oil reception, storage, and distribution port. In making the announcement, an aide to the governor revealed a rather limited perspective by indicating that such a center would not threaten the coast of Puerto Rico with pollution, since the ocean currents and prevailing winds would direct the spills and fumes to other Caribbean shores.[7] The creation of such a center would also serve as a transshipment port for the large (500,000 ton) tankers which will be used in the future for transoceanic oil shipping but which cannot enter continental ports.[8] Obviously such a facility located in one of the major passages of the Caribbean should be a concern of the whole region and not just of the polity which happens to have sovereignty over the island in question. This concern could be channeled through such a regional or international authority as that suggested above.

Cable and Air Communications

For the most part, the history of the development of cable and air communications within the Caribbean follows the same pattern as that for maritime communications. Fort de France in Martinique and Point a Pitre in Guadeloupe were connected with Paris. London was linked with the capital of its colonies in the Caribbean. While the decline of Spanish power in the Caribbean slowed the development of modern communication with Spain's overseas colonies in the Caribbean in the 19th century, cable links with the United States were developed at a faster pace with the former colonies of Spain in the 20th-century Caribbean than any links of communication between the islands themselves.

Thus communication between islands belonging to the same flag within the Caribbean was cumbersome, having to be connected by way of the imperial capital. Telephone or telegraph communication across lines of sovereignty were virtually impossible unless the trunk cable between London and Paris was used. Such circumstances are ironical in light of the fact that the founder of International Telephone and Telegraph was from the island of St. Thomas, and that Samuel F.B. Morse carried out some of his early experiments on the island of Puerto Rico.

In the case of air communications, the development was somewhat

---

[7]*New York Times,* November 12, 1972.
[8]*San Juan Star,* December 13, 1972.

different, since early transportation of passengers by air required short intermediate hops over water. Thus Pan American Airways, which was the first to develop air service in the Caribbean, of necessity linked up the islands regardless of national sovereignty. After the Second World War, however, the pattern reverted to the more common one of imperial development. Air France, the British Overseas Airways Corporation, and KLM, Royal Dutch Airlines each developed lines of air communication first with its country's own colonies. Later, regional carriers were encouraged to develop, and the British West Indies Airways (BWIA) and Caribbean International Airways (Caribair) emerged as regional carriers, operating out of Trinidad and Puerto Rico, respectively. Rather than developing into solid regional companies serving the Caribbean, these two airlines have barely survived to date. Caribair will succumb to the competition of the large corporations in the United States which have found the Caribbean to be a source of lucrative trade. BWIA will find it increasingly difficult to survive against the growing national airlines that are being developed by each island government as almost an essential, but futile, gesture of national sovereignty.

Nearly every island of the Caribbean now has an air field. Even the volcanic rock of Saba, with no beach and no port, now has an uphill runway which can accommodate planes designed to take off and land in short distances. Only a few of the islands have runways of sufficient length to accommodate jumbo jets such as the Boeing 747. In the air, as on the sea, the use of larger and thus cheaper-per-unit vehicles of transport operates in favor of the metropolitan-based companies and to the detriment of the regionally based corporations that attempt to serve the Caribbean.

Modern Telecommunications

Scientific improvements have also provided "bigger and better" instruments in the area of verbal communications. While it is true that lines of communication have recently been improved somewhat in the Caribbean and that the distorted patterns indicated above are no longer the only existing ones, such improvement has been long overdue. Thus only in 1972 did it become possible to dial directly from Puerto Rico to Jamaica. However, this improvement is an illusion, because the connections allowing direct dialing are still made outside of the Caribbean.

Since 1965 a new method of intercontinental communication has been made possible through the use of earth satellites. At least eight nations now belong to the International Telecommunications Satellite Consortium. In this group are Puerto Rico, Jamaica, Barbados, Venezuela, and Colombia from the Caribbean region. The consortium uses the Intelsats, which are launched from Cape Kennedy by the Comsat Corporation. Such a system of satellite communications obviously simplifies the problem of communication within the Caribbean as more and more islands have their own earth-receiving station, but again it is the tie-in with large continental units such as North America and Europe that makes this system a working reality, and the benefit to the smaller region is only a by-product of the system. The system is expensive for impoverished countries. The price of admission to the consortium is $15,000 a year, and the cost of construction of an earth-receiving station is about $6 million.[9]

The Caribbean does have available theoretically an alternative to sole dependence on the launching programs of Cape Kennedy under the control of the United States. This is the space center at Kourou in French Guiana, which is supposed to be capable of putting into orbit satellites for communications between Europe and South America. The French have had some financial and scientific setbacks with the operation of the launching station and have fallen behind greatly in the planned operation of the center.[10] There is no reason, however, to think the station will not continue to operate and eventually achieve success and thus offer an alternative in the Caribbean. The recommendation suggested in the area of telecommunications for the Caribbean would be the construction of a satellite to serve the communities of the region exclusively. The launching of such a satellite could be from the United States or from the French space center. The benefits for the unification and communications of the area are incalculable. But it would take an imaginative government or consortium of governments to provide the rationale for such an operation. The current models contain, in addition to telephone facilities, 12 television channels. Such a communication facility could be put into immediate use by the Association of Caribbean Universities. It could also serve to renew Caribbean ties with Africa and Asia, the mother continents of the people of the Caribbean. In contrast, current satellite connections link the area with North America and Europe.[11]

The use of satellites for purposes other than that of communications is already being explored in the Caribbean region. Early in 1972 the first of a series of satellites designed to monitor and detect ecological changes was launched. These are the Earth Resources Technology Satellites

[9]*Caribbean Sun,* December 17–30, 1972.

[10]*Le Figaro,* October 8, 1972. Compare the current stage of operation with the projected planned development as indicated in Mathews [1966].

[11]See the Report of the Secretary-General of the Association of Caribbean Universities, Sir Phillip Sherlock, 1972 (Spanish version, San Juan; English version, Kingston). His proposal is a realistic and practical one; it only needs to be modified slightly to realize the benefits of satellite communications.

(ERTS), whose cameras photograph every section of the earth once every 18 days. Water pollution from oil spills can be readily detected, as well as any significant change in foliage. ERTS II, launched in 1973, will be capable of monitoring the temperature change of coastal waters, and ERTS III will increase that coverage up to a depth of 10 feet. The importance and significance of this satellite-surveillance system has been understood by the university scientists of the Caribbean, who are cooperating with the project and utilizing the material the cameras are producing or will produce.

The importance of this type of monitoring for the Caribbean is obvious, since it would provide quick detection of oil pollution from ships passing through the Caribbean Sea. The authority suggested previously could use satellite pictures as a means of detecting violations of regulations governing the use of the international waterways under its supervision.

Military Significance of the Caribbean

United States interest in the Caribbean has been dealt with extensively in several authoritative works. Admiral Mahan is usually the authority cited in reference to the military necessity of control over the Caribbean [Morse, p. 155]. The vital interocean link through the Panama Canal and the movement of oil from Texas, as well as the location of the entrance to the water artery which cuts through the center of Panama are sufficient reasons for an American concern for a strong first-line-of-defense system throughout the Caribbean. As mentioned above, the United States had to modify only slightly the basic plan of defense designed by 16th-century Spanish strategists, when it replaced Spain in the Caribbean. Guantanamo Bay replaced Havana in military importance. The Gulf entrance could be controlled more effectively from the continent, whereas the naval base at Guantanamo—located on the Windward Passage, into the Caribbean—provided an excellent sentinel post at the front door.

Puerto Rico eventually bristled with military bases. The Air Force built Ramey field on the northwestern tip of the island, thus providing another sentinel post for Mona Passage, a sidedoor entrance into the Caribbean. Roosevelt Roads Naval Base complex, spread out from the southeastern shore of the island to the two adjacent smaller islands of Vieques and Culebra, provided, once the Virgin Islands were secured from Denmark in 1917, sufficient protection for the Anegada Passage, the entrance from Europe to the Caribbean.

The Lesser Antilles are dotted with formidable stone forts from the 17th and 18th centuries. Today Brimstone Hill on St. Kitts provides a magnificent view of adjacent islands to the north, but the spiked cannons jutting from its redoubts arouse only curiosity. Nelson's dockyard in nearby Antigua, although located in a well-protected natural harbor, has no military use in modern-day warfare.

During the Second World War the islands came into military prominence when the United States negotiated with Great Britain for the long-term (99-year) use of air fields from Antigua to Trinidad in exchange for badly needed cargo ships to supply a besieged Britain. With the possible exception of Charguaramos Bay in Trinidad, these facilities are still available to the United States, and some, like those in Antigua and St. Lucia, are in current use as Air Force and/or NASA tracking stations or radar facilities.

During World War II, when France fell to Germany and the French islands of the Caribbean came under the control of the Vichy government, the military presence of supposedly neutral naval power in the roadstead of Martinique was cause for a great deal of concern. At one point an expeditionary force was planned, to put the ships out of possible action [Tugwell]. German submarines may not have been serviced in the larger islands, but there is now ample evidence to indicate that they were fueled and serviced in the quiet out-of-the-way port of Gustave on the French island of Saint Bartholomew. Thus once friendly and supposedly neutral ports in the Caribbean substantially weakened the iron ring the United States tried to forge around the Caribbean.

When one turns to the military aspect of the Dutch presence in the Caribbean, there are incidents which verge on the opéra bouffe. In this century no less, the Dutch island of Curaçao fell under the complete control of an exiled Venezuelan politician who schemed to recover his lost presidency from the offshore island [Baptiste]. The fact that this could be done by an amateur was serious cause for concern to the British and US forces during World Wars I and II. German submarines managed to inflict significant damage on the oil refinery of Aruba in the spring of 1942.

The pressures of war, coupled with the problem of feeding island populations when ships could no longer freely navigate the waters of the Caribbean, gave rise to new ideas. One of the most imaginative was that of constructing a highway through the West Indies. Utilizing the central highway which cuts down the length of Cuba, the only missing link would have been the connection through the island of Santo Domingo [Tugwell]. In length the highway would have covered 1,025 miles overland and 505 miles of sea. Rexford G. Tugwell, one of the originators of the idea, felt that fast electric ferries could bridge the three water gaps. Today the use of the hydrofoil makes the idea even more practicable. Certainly the construction of such a highway would be of great benefit to the communities of the Caribbean, even though its reason for being might first have been the exceptional circumstances of war. However, it is highly doubtful that such a scheme would be carried out, even between Puerto Rico and the Virgin Islands, where the amount of deep water to be spanned is minimal.

Modern scientific equipment now available to the military forces of a wealthy nation like the United States allows extensive areas such as that encompassed by the Caribbean Sea to be placed under complete surveillance with little awareness on the part of those being watched. The silent satellite as it passes 500 miles overhead bothers few people. There is little occurring on the surface of, for example, Cuba, which is overlooked by the cameras. Beneath the surface is another matter, but even here, as far as the sea is concerned, modern equipment has apparently provided the necessary information for the military mind. Although little is known about the nature of its operation by even the informed public of the Caribbean, there is apparently in operation an undersea surveillance system known as SOSUS [Crassweller], which can detect and locate submarine penetration of the Caribbean. With naval and air reconnaissance units, and satellite surveillance, the military has the Caribbean sewn up fairly tight. The implications of such a complete system of surveillance over an area in which there are 25 million people, six sovereign states, and international water and airways utilized by all nationalities should be reason for concern on the part of the citizens of the region.

The Caribbean as a Region

The only way such concern could be expressed effectively would be to channel it through a regional organization that could speak with authority, assuming it could approach some sort of agreement as to the posture to be taken. At the very least, such a regional organization could mobilize public opinion in the area to bring moral pressure on those who might violate agreed-upon norms of operation. The degree of effectiveness such pressure might have on the use of land within the boundaries of national sovereignty might be questionable, but certainly it is not too late to establish norms over international skies, seas, and ocean beds. If a small region such as the Caribbean, where there are so many diverse national entities competing for the use of a common sea, cannot get together for its common good and self-preservation, then international cooperation at any level is unrealistic. By now it should be clear to those who live on the islands of the Caribbean that an island is not isolated by the sea but rather is a vital part of a regional community intimately integrated by means of the sea that surrounds it. The sooner this is understood and acted on the better the chances for survival of the Caribbean communities will be.

References

Baptiste, Fitz A. 1973. *The seizure of Curaçao, June, 1929.* Caribbean Studies.

Barrett, W. 1962. *Emerged and submerged shorelines of the Dominican Republic.* Revista Geogràfica 30, no. 56.

Bosch, Juan. 1970. *De Cristobal Colon a Fidel Castro.* Madrid: Graficas Cardel.

Crassweller, Robert D. 1972. *The Caribbean Community.* New York: Praeger.

Esquemelina, J. 1967. *The Buccaneers of America.* New York: Dover.

Goslinga, C. 1971. *The Dutch in the Caribbean and on the Wild Coast, 1580–1680.* Gainesville: Univ. of Florida Press.

Haring, Clarence H. 1939. *El comercio y la navegación entre España y las Indias en época de los Habsburgos.* Paris: Brujas Desclée, de Brouwer.

Hartog, J. 1964. *De Bovenwindse Eilanden.* Orangestad, Aruba: de Wit, Inc.

_____. 1968. *Curaçao.* Orangestad, Aruba: de Wit, Inc.

Hoetink, H. 1958. *Het Patroon van de Oude Curacaose Samenleving.* Assen: Van Gorcum.

Hurssey, Roland D. 1934. *The Caracas Company, 1728–1784.* Cambridge, Mass.

James, C.L.R. 1963. *Black Jacobins: Toussaint L'Ouverture and the San Domingo revolution.* New York: Vintage Books.

Kingsley, Charles. 1887. *At last: A Christmas in the West Indies.* London: Macmillan.

Levitt, Kari and McIntyre, Alister. 1969. *Canada-West Indies Economic Relations.* McGill University, Center for Developing Area Studies.

Mathews, Thomas G. 1966. "The Three Guianas," *Current History,* December.

_____. 1969. "The Spanish Domination of Saint Martin, 1633–1648," *Caribbean Studies* 9, No. 1.

Morales Padrón, Francisco. 1952. *Jamaica Española.* Sevilla: Escuela de Estudios Hispano-Americanos.

Morse, Richard M. 1967. "The Caribbean: Geopolitics and Geohistory." In *Caribbean Integration,* Thomas G. Mathews and Sybil Lewis, eds. Rio Piedras: Institute of Caribbean Studies.

Naipaul, V.S. 1969. *The Loss of El Dorado, A history.* London: André Deutsch.

Phelan, John L. 1959. *The Hispanization of the Philippines: Spanish Aims and Filipino Responses, 1565–1700.* Madison: Univ. of Wisconsin Press.

Sluiter, Engle. 1948. "Dutch-Spanish Rivalry in the Caribbean Area, 1594–1609." *Hispanic-American Historical Review* 28:165.

Trollope, Anthony. 1860. *The West Indies and the Spanish Main*. Leipzig; Bernhard Tauchnitz.

Tugwell, Rexford G. 1947. *The Stricken Land, the Story of Puerto Rico*. Garden City: Doubleday.

Williams, Eric. 1944. *Capitalism and Slavery*. Chapel Hill: Univ. of North Carolina Press.

_____. 1970. *From Columbus to Castro, The History of the Caribbean, 1492–1969*. London: André Deutsch.

Wright, Irene A. 1919. *La Armada de Barlovento*. New York: La Reforma Social.

CHAPTER 14

The Oil Potential of the Caribbean

K. O. EMERY AND ELAZAR UCHUPI

The distribution of favorable source sediments and of shallow water in the Caribbean Sea and the Gulf of Mexico indicates that the best areas for production of oil and gas are those adjacent to North America and South America, at opposite ends of the region. Figures for production and reserves support this conclusion. Although about one-sixth of the world's petroleum comes from the continental shelves and adjacent land of this region, pollution of the shores appears to be minimal, perhaps because of the extensive use of pipelines to bring oil ashore, the departure of tankers in full condition, and the low population density along most shores.

Geological History

The Caribbean Sea and Gulf of Mexico are a region of complex topography linking North America and South America. The region contains six large physiographic units (Gulf of Mexico, Yucatan Basin, Cayman Trough, Colombia Basin, Venezuela Basin, and Grenada Trough) and several smaller deep basins (Fig. 14.1). All are separated by irregular structural ridges and bordered by flat continental shelves and bank tops.

Most geologists believe that the topography of the region is the result of the separation of North America from a unit consisting of both South America and Africa about 180 million years ago and by the separation of South America from Africa about 130 million years ago. These movements led to the entrapment of the narrow Caribbean crustal plate between the

239

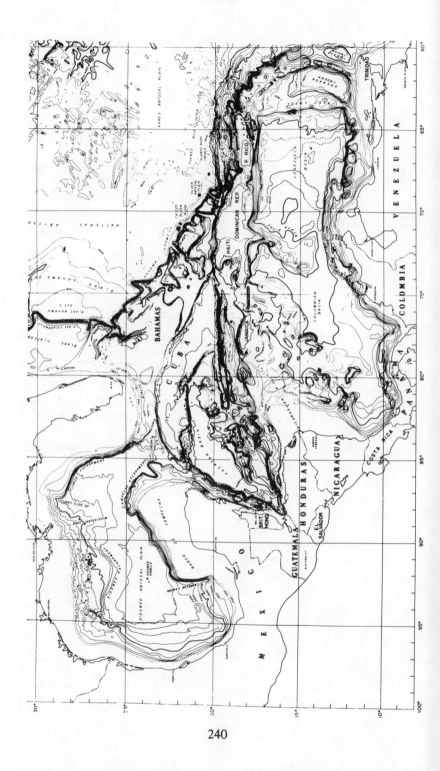

240

westward-drifting North American and South American plates (Fig. 14.2). Underthrusting at the Lesser Antilles sealed off this ancient oceanic fragment from the Atlantic Ocean floor. The enclosure by the American continents and the underthrusting zone to the east led to the development of the Greater and Lesser Antillean Island arcs and the structural ridges along the southern and western margins of the Caribbean and in the central part of the sea. Prior to and during the initial separation of the continents in latest Triassic-Middle Jurassic time, thick strata of salt were deposited in the western Gulf of Mexico. With continued separation of the continents, the Gulf of Mexico underwent considerable subsidence, accompanied by the deposition, at Early Cretaceous time at the latest, of a very long coral-algal reef along the periphery of the ancient Gulf of Mexico (Fig. 14.2). Carbonate deposition landward of the reef formed the Florida and Campeche platforms in the eastern and southeastern Gulf of Mexico. The ancient oceanic crustal plate enclosed by the drifting continents received enormous quantities of silt and clay, particularly along the seaward edges of the continents. Incorporated within the land-derived silts and and clays were remains of planktonic and benthic organisms. This organic matter was largely preserved in the sediments of the continental shelves, slopes, and upper rises. However, it was oxidized and removed from the more slowly deposited sediments on the floors of the deep basins and on the ridges that separate the basins. Similar destruction also occurred in areas that underwent intense metamorphism and igneous activity caused by the drifting continents. Such analyses of the tectonic evolution of the Caribbean Sea and the Gulf of Mexico, plus results of drilling, have been used to delineate the petroleum provinces of the area [Meyerhoff; Paine and Meyerhoff; Arden; Jacobsen and Neff].

This summary of the geological history of the Caribbean Sea and the Gulf of Mexico indicates that the most likely places for large concentrations of oil and gas are in the regions of thick organic-rich, land-derived sediment at the northern and southern ends of the region (Fig. 14.3).The broad belt between these places is unfavorable for large accumulations because of the low content of organic matter in the calcareous sediment of the platforms (owing to original low content of organic matter as well as to subsequent nearly complete oxidation of it) and on the ridges and the floors of the basins (due to a slow rate of deposition and the resulting destruction of organic matter). Slow uplift of the continents has elevated some of the organic-rich sediment above sea level, where concentrations of oil and gas in fault zones, folds, and other local structures are easily accessible. In part of the land area, as well as offshore, these sediments are underlain locally at shallow depth by igneous and metamorphic rocks and thus are unfavorable for large accumulations of oil. Most of the organic-rich sediment still lies beneath the

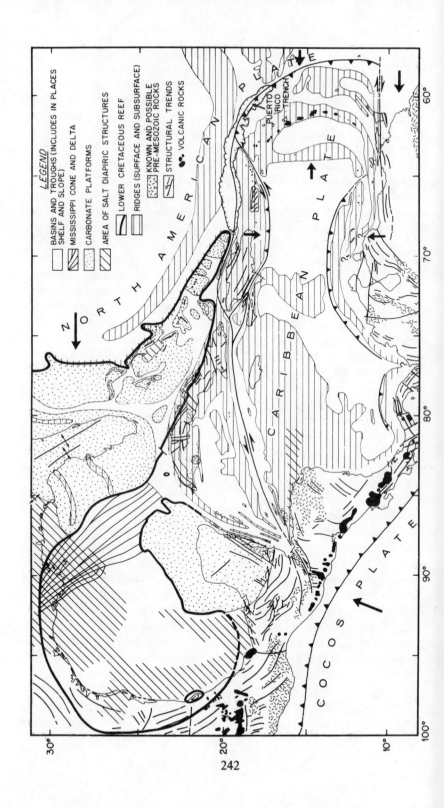

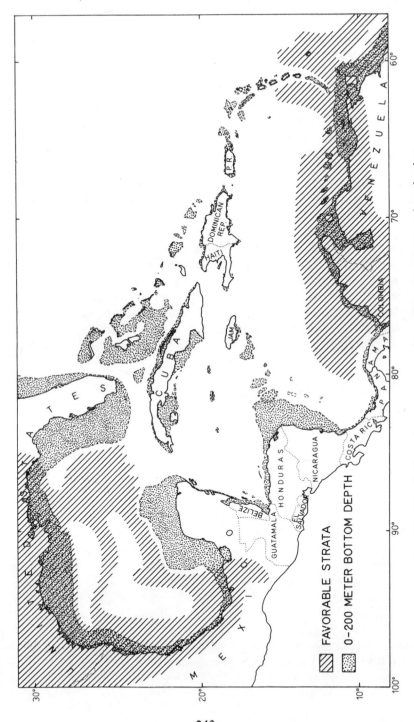

Fig. 14.3 Distribution of two parameters favorable to occurrence and production of petroleum: thick sediments of high organic content and water depths shallower than 200 meters. Simplified from Figures 14.1 and 14.2.

FAVORABLE STRATA

0–200 METER BOTTOM DEPTH

243

ocean. That which is under the continental shelf or other areas of shallow water can be drilled much more cheaply than that at greater water depth. As shown in Figure 14.3, the most favorable areas for offshore recovery of oil and gas are limited by both the kind of strata and shallow water depth to a very small percentage of the entire Caribbean Sea and Gulf of Mexico. Here, the chief problem is that of locating suitable geological structures, or traps, that have concentrated the oil and gas sufficiently for economical extraction.

In spite of the limitation of major oil potential to the continental shelves off the United States, Mexico, Colombia, and Venezuela, large tracts of the intervening area of low potential but shallow depth have been leased and drilled (Fig. 14.4). Especially large leases are typical of the less favorable areas, particularly of the Bahama Banks, Honduras, and Nicaragua. In contrast, the leases off the United States are small and highly selective (owning to the large bonus payments required), and the shelves off Colombia and Venezuela have been explored only slightly, possibly because of large previous discoveries on land and in Lake Maracaibo. The shelves off Mexico, Cuba, and Venezuela are also reserved for development by national organizations, whose activities require no published boundary or demarcation restrictions.

Oil Production and Reserves

The favorable-versus-unfavorable parts of the region are well illustrated by annual production figures for oil (Fig. 14.5). Thus 1,452 million barrels of oil were obtained during 1971 from the parts of the United States and Mexico that lie within the limits of the map. Almost the same amount came from the South American countries that border on the Caribbean Sea, (Venezuela and Colombia, and Trinidad, which in a sense occupies part of the shelf off Venezuela). Less than 1 million barrels are reported (Cuba) from the more than ten times larger intervening region. The total 1971 production of the whole region is one-sixth of the world production. Production in most of the countries has declined during the past several years from peaks reached in 1966 for Trinidad, 1968 for Venezuela and Mexico, and 1969 for Colombia. A steady rise in production up to and including 1971 has characterized that part of the United States shown within the area of Figure 14.5.

Similar relationships are exhibited by the proved reserves, with 11,476 million barrels reported for this part of the United States and Mexico, and 16,419 million barrels for Venezuela, Colombia, and Trinidad (Fig. 14.6). Only 11 million barrels of oil reserves are indicated for the rest of the region.

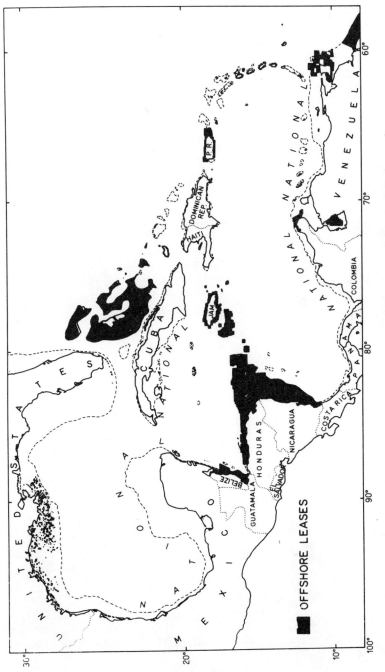

Fig. 14.4   Areas of offshore leases in the Caribbean Sea and Gulf of Mexico at the end of 1971. Note that the ocean floor off Cuba, Mexico, and Venezuela is reserved for national petroleum organizations and that the areas of activity are not demarked. (From Anonymous [1968, 1970, 1971a], Castano [1969], and Jacobsen and Neff [1972])

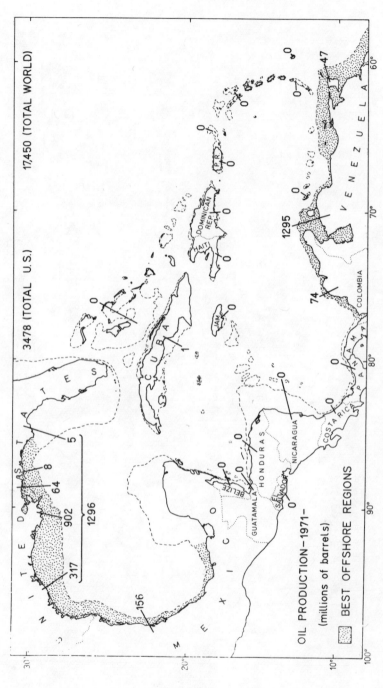

Fig. 14.5 Oil production during 1971 by each country of the region. For the United States only the production in southern Texas, Louisiana, Missi...

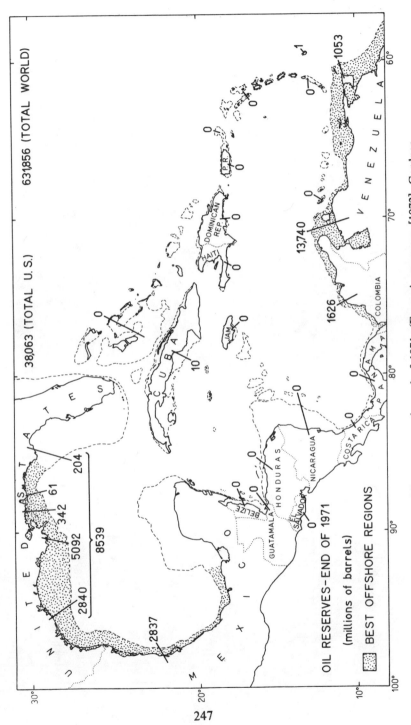

Fig. 14.6 Oil reserves at the end of 1971. (From Anonymous [1972], Gardner [1971], and Kliewer [1972])

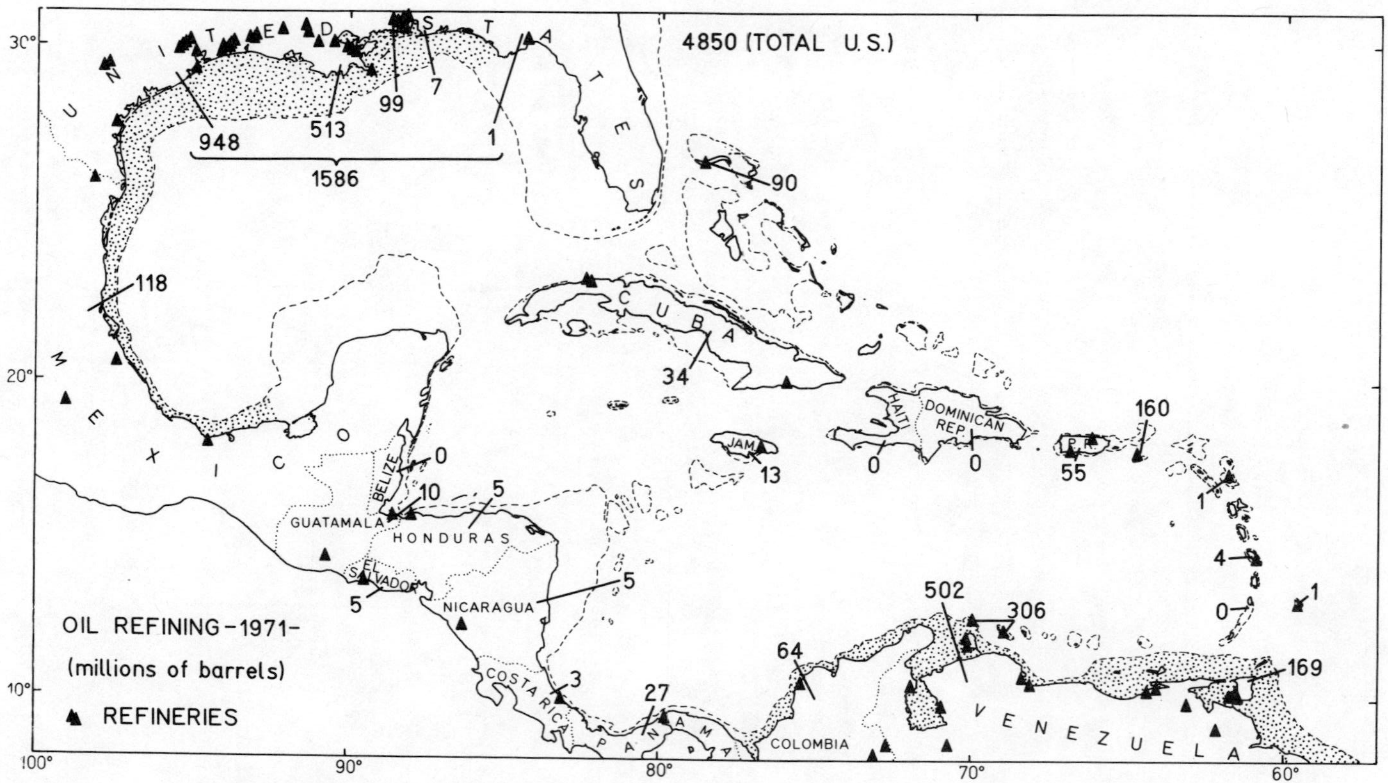

OIL REFINING–1971–
(millions of barrels)

▲ REFINERIES

Fig. 147 Oil refined during 1971 (From Anonymous [1971b] and Cantrell [1972])

The present reserves are only 4.4 percent of the total world reserves, most of which are in the Persian Gulf and vicinity. After the exploration of the continental shelves of the United States, Mexico, Venezuela, and Colombia is more complete, the reserves of the region will probably be found to be much greater than presently indicated.

Refinery capacity is more widely distributed than are production and reserves. The part of the United States and Mexico within the limits of Figure 14.7 refined 1,704 million barrels of oil during 1971 (more than the production), and Venezuela, Colombia, and Trinidad refined 735 million barrels (about half their production). The other half was shipped for refining in the United States, Curaçao, Aruba, Virgin Islands, Bahama Islands, Puerto Rico, Cuba, Panama, Jamaica, Guatemala, Honduras, Nicaragua, Martinique, Costa Rica, Barbados, and the Leeward Islands. Nearly all of the countries in the region have refineries, even though crude oil must be imported for most of them. Perhaps these relationships indicate that the nonproducing countries are less fearful of pollution than of missing an opportunity to industrialize.

Pollution

Most pollution by oil in the world oceans appears to be from numerous unspectacular causes. Most important are waste disposal and the washing of tanks at sea. Pollution from this source could be reduced 99 percent by modern tankers using the load-on-top method. Next most important is the loss of oil through collision or grounding of tankers, and least is direct loss through drilling operations. Both of these losses receive a disproportionate share of news coverage. Once the oil reaches the ocean surface, it is subject to drifting by winds and currents. Winds in the Caribbean Sea are the steady trades that blow from the northeast or east (Fig. 14.8) about 90 percent of the time and with an average speed of about 25 kilometers per hour. Owing to the earth's rotation, this wind drives the surface water in the Caribbean Sea westerly and northwesterly (Fig. 14.9) one to two kilometers per hour. Eddies exist in broad coastal indentations between Colombia and Nicaragua, Honduras and the Yucatan Peninsula of Mexico, and Jamaica and western Cuba. These are the chief, likely sites of shore pollution by floating oil and tar, but most are only thinly inhabited.

Probably a small amount of the pollution escapes the Caribbean Sea and enters the Gulf of Mexico, where both the winds and the currents are variable in direction and slower than in the Caribbean Sea. Oil pollution from shipping, refining, and drilling in the Gulf of Mexico can move either easterly or westerly depending on the position of the source and the season.

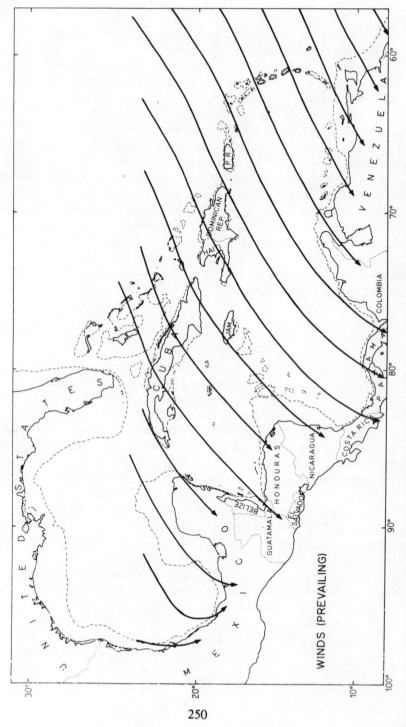

WINDS (PREVAILING)

Fig. 14.8 Prevailing winds in the Caribbean Sea and Gulf of Mexico. (From United

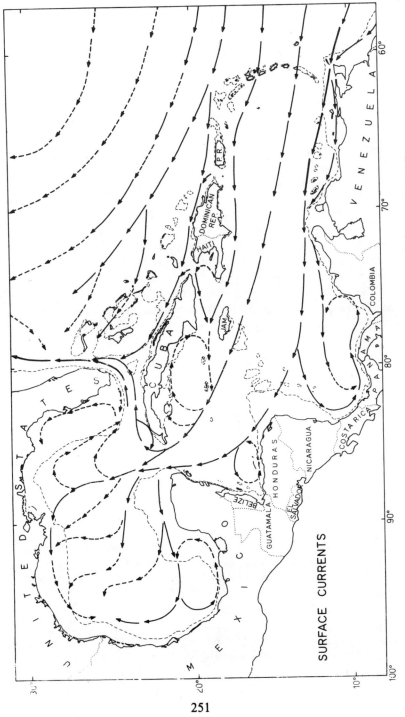

SURFACE CURRENTS

Fig. 14.9 Surface currents. (From United States Navy Oceanographic Office, January 1969 chart)

251

Some of it must end in lightly inhabited mangrove and deltaic swamps; however, there appear to be anomalously few complaints about polluted beaches in either the Caribbean Sea or the Gulf of Mexico.

One might attempt to rationalize the apparently small amount of pollution by considering that most of the tankers which arrive at the South American ports are modern ones using the load-on-top method or they come from distant ports and their tanks have been washed far from the Caribbean Sea. These ships leave the Caribbean ports with full tanks of crude oil; thus they need no washing. Most of the oil from the shelf off the United States is shipped to shore via pipeline, and probably most of the tankers that do bring crude oil leave with refined oil, because nearly 500 million barrels of refinery products were shipped during 1970 from Gulf Coast to West Coast and East Coast ports [Kirby and Moore, pp. 839–40]. Such a situation is far different from that in New England and in the Mediterranean Sea, with their heavier tanker traffic. Neither of the latter areas produce much oil as yet, and much crude oil is brought to both of them by tankers that leave empty and ready to wash tanks, thus accounting for the apparently greater pollution of the shores of New England and the Mediterranean Sea than of the Caribbean Sea and the Gulf of Mexico.

References

Anonymous. 1968. Upper Texas continental shelf Gulf of Mexico offshore lease map showing oil and gas fields, oil and gas pipe lines, and water depths. *Offshore Magazine,* supplement to July issue. 1970. "Lo más destacado de la Cuenca de Maracaibo." *Petroleo Interamericano,* December, pp. 34–35. 1971a. Louisiana offshore Gulf of Mexico map showing leases and platforms. *Offshore Magazine,* supplements to February issue. 1971b. "Worldwide refining." *Oil and Gas Journal* 69, No. 52; pp. 75–86. 1972. "Big Drilling Expansion Predicted." *World Oil* 175, no. 3, pp. 61–64.

Arden, D.D., Jr. 1971. "Petroleum Prospecting in the Caribbean Area." Symposium on Investigations and Resources of the Caribbean Sea and Adjacent Regions, UNESCO, Paris, pp. 205–13.

Cantrell, Aileen. 1972. Annual Refining Survey. *Oil and Gas Journal* 70, no. 13, pp. 135–62.

Castano B., Leopoldo. 1969. "Colombia to Get Exploratory Wells." *Oil and Gas Journal* 67, no. 15, p. 153.

Gardner, F. J. 1971. "Price, Nationalization Jitters Plague International Oil World." *Oil and Gas Journal* 69, no. 52, pp. 67–74.

Jacobsen, P., Jr. and C.H. Neff. 1972. Review of 1971 Petroleum Developments in South America, Central America and Caribbean Area. *American Association of Petroleum Geologists Bulletin 56.*

Kirby, J.G. and Betty M. Moore. 1971. Crude Petroleum and Petroleum Products. *Minerals Yearbook 1969,* vols. I-II, Metals, Minerals and Fuels, Bureau of Mines, pp. 795–906. Washington, D.C.

Kliewer, Gene. 1972. "World Drilling Rise Forecast." *World Oil* 175, no. 3, pp. 57–60.

Meyerhoff, A.A. 1967. Future Hydrocarbon Provinces of Gulf of Mexico-Caribbean Region. Gulf Coast Association of Geological Societies, *Transactions* 17:217–60.

Paine, W.R. and A.A. Meyerhoff. 1970. Gulf of Mexico Basin: Interactions among Tectonics, Sedimentation, and Hydrocarbon Accumulation. Gulf Coast Association of Geological Societies, *Transactions* 20:5–44.

Uchupi, Elazar. 1971. Bathymetric Atlas of the Atlantic, Caribbean, and Gulf of Mexico. Woods Hole Oceanographic Institution, Ref. No. 71–72.in press. "Physiography of the Caribbean and Gulf of Mexico." In *Ocean Basins and Margins III, The Caribbean and Gulf of Mexico.* A.E.M. Nairn and F.G. Stehli, eds. New York: Plenum Publishing Co.

United States Navy Oceanographic Office 1969 Atlas of Pilot Charts: Central American Waters and South Atlantic Ocean. Pub. No. 106, Washington, D.C.

CHAPTER 15

A Sea-Level Canal in Panama

IRA RUBINOFF

A sea-level canal across Central America has been sought for more than four centuries. Now there are no longer technical obstacles to its successful construction and operation. This possible uniting of the two oceans is one of the most fantastic environmental manipulations seriously contemplated by man. If it is done, the results are very likely to be long in developing and far-reaching.

The potential biological consequences of a sea-level canal have been the subject of considerable controversy, not all of it particularly rational. Based largely on their own intuition, some biologists have viewed the potential effects benignly, while others have prophesied a great and widespread ecological catastrophe. Too few have analyzed the situation objectively, with an eye toward increasing our knowledge of the area so that a more precise and reasonable assessment can be made.

The Present Panama Canal

For purposes of this discussion, one must understand the contrast between the proposed level canal and the present Panama Canal. An examination of the present canal can conveniently be made from the point of view of a ship transiting from the Atlantic to the Pacific. Because of curvature in the isthmus, the canal does not run east and west, but nearly north and south. It is 50 miles from coast to coast. Principal features include locks at either end, a man-made lake on which ships cross

254

the isthmus, and a cut through the continental divide.

Starting at the Caribbean end of the canal, a transiting ship first enters Limon Bay. The ship proceeds up a channel for five miles until it arrives at Gatun Locks, where it is raised approximately 85 feet to the level of Gatun Lake. Each lock chamber is 110 feet wide and a little over 1,000 feet long. All the lock series have double chambers, and the canal channels are wide enough so that ships can pass in opposite directions. The water to raise or lower the ships in the canal moves by gravity; there is no water pumped. Each lockage allows 52 million gallons of fresh water from the lakes to flow into the oceans. The amount of water used by the canal in a day equals the consumption of a city the size of Rochester, New York, for six weeks.

The route of the canal across the 23 miles of Gatun Lake follows the riverbed of the old Chagres River. At the southern end of the lake a ship heading toward the Pacific enters the Gaillard Cut, a nine-mile excavation through the continental divide. As originally constructed, this cut was only 300 feet wide, but it has recently been widened to 500 feet, an improvement. At the end of the cut, a Pacific-bound ship arrives at Pedro Miguel Locks where it is lowered 27 feet. After leaving Pedro Miguel Locks, the ship passes the one-mile-long Miraflores Lake, then enters Miraflores Locks where it is then lowered in two steps the remaining 54 feet to the Pacific Ocean level.

The Panama Canal is too small to accommodate approximately 1300 of the present ships afloat. Another 1700 cannot pass through fully laden, particularly during the dry season (January-April) when the lake level is reduced through evaporation and lockages. Fresh water is the principal limiting factor of the present canal. At present, 14,000 ships can transit a year, and certain improvements could increase this capacity somewhat, but in any case a maximum would definitely be reached by the end of this century.

Proposed Sea-Level Canal Routes

In 1964, the U.S. Corps of Engineers, the Atomic Energy Commission, and the Panama Canal Company completed a preliminary study of 30 prospective routes for a sea-level canal constructed by nuclear means. In 1965, President Johnson appointed the Atlantic-Pacific Interoceanic Canal Study Commission to study the situation and make final recommendations for the site of a new canal. The Commission devoted most of its five-year, $24-million-dollar effort to evaluating nuclear routes. By the fall of 1969, after most of the data was gathered, the commission publicly announced that the techniques of nuclear excavation were not yet proven feasible. In

256   THE TIDES OF CHANGE

1970 they presented their completed report to President Nixon. Some of the conclusions of this study are:

1. An adequate isthmian canal is of great economic value to many nations, but especially to the United States, since approximately 70 percent of the tonnage through the canal in recent years has been to, from, or between that country's ports.

2. The annual demand for transits through the present canal will probably exceed its estimated maximum capacity of 26,800 transits during the last decade of this century. To reach this figure additional water supply for lock operation must be found.

3. A new plan is needed for a waterway to accommodate 35,000 annual transits, and such a plan should have provisions for progressive expansion, to double or even triple this capacity.

4. A sea-level canal would provide significant improvement in the ability of an isthmian waterway to support military operations. The military advantages of a sea-level canal, together with its greater capacity to meet future transit needs, and its lower operating costs, would more than compensate for the lower construction costs of building larger locks into the present canal.

5. The technical feasibility of the use of nuclear excavation devices has not been established.

6. A conventionally excavated sea-level canal in Panama is technically feasible on either Route 10 or Route 14 (Fig. 15.1). Route 14 represents a conversion by conventional means of the present canal to sea level. It would require the construction of numerous temporary dams, but the engineers feel it could be accomplished with only brief interruptions in the operations of the canal. This site has the advantage of being near population centers and engineering support facilities. It is also completely within the present Canal Zone controlled by the United States.

Route 10, built by conventional means, would require construction of some additional support facilities, but it would have the distinct advantage of not interrupting the operation of the present canal. Since a new canal in this region is likely to have initial problems with slope stability, having two canals insures a continuous waterway in case of major slides. Route 10 is the most advantageous sea-level site.

7. A conventionally excavated sea-level canal on Route 10, with tidal gates and capable of accommodating at least 35,000 transits each year, would require $2.88 billion at 1970 costs.

8. In regard to ecological effects, the Commission report

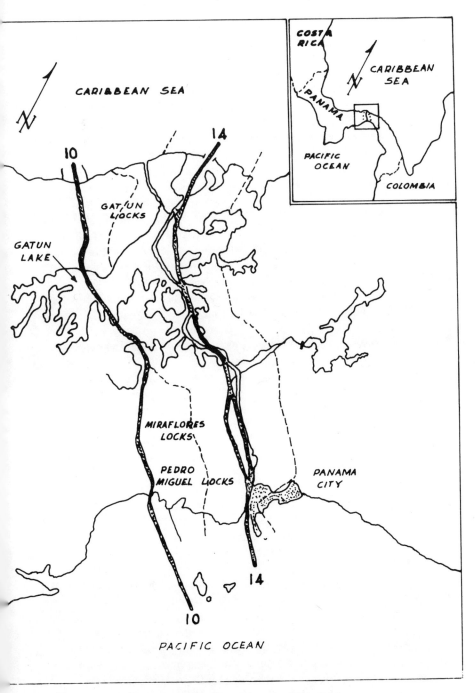

Fig. 15.1 Sea level canal routes 10 and 14

257

states: "So far as the Commission is able to determine on the basis of limited studies, linking the oceans at sea-level would not endanger commercial or sport fish on either side of the American Isthmus. No significant physical changes to the environment appear probable outside the immediate areas of excavation and spoil disposal. Tidal gates could be used to eliminate substantially the flow of water between the oceans, and the water between the gates would have incidental temperature and salinity differences from either ocean that would constitute a limited barrier to transfer of marine life. A definitive and reliable prediction of all ecological effects of a sea-level canal is not possible. The potential for transfer of harmful biota and hybridization or displacement of species in both oceans exists but the risks involved appear to be acceptable. Long-term studies starting before construction is initiated and continuing many years beyond the opening of a sea-level canal would be required to measure ecological effects."

9. A decision to construct a sea-level canal should allow for planning and construction lead time of approximately 15 years.

Some biological and physical background is helpful in evaluating the report of the Commission. The marine species of the tropical Atlantic and Pacific Oceans have been separated for about two million years. The present canal, with its fresh-water lake, is still a formidable barrier to most marine forms. A postulation of the possible results of allowing Atlantic and Pacific species to intermix is dependent on some aspects of the physical environments on the respective coasts.

The Atlantic and Pacific coasts of Panama experience pronounced seasonal changes in climate. These changes are primarily related to the relative position of the Intertropical Convergence Zone (ITCZ). A southward migration of the ITCZ, usually from January through April, is characterized by high winds and a cessation of rains. The Caribbean shores of Panama are buffeted by high winds, receive about twice as much rainfall as the Pacific coast and are subject to greater seasonal variation in cloud cover. The most conspicuous hydrographic difference between the two coasts is the dry season initiation of upwelling in the Gulf of Panama, the result of displacement of surface waters by northerly winds. Sea surface temperature may vary from 27 to 18 degrees centigrade in a 24-hour period. The upwelling produces an enrichment of nutrients in plankton and higher trophic levels. For example, the mean primary productivity expressed in $gC/m^2/day$ is 0.75 grams for the Gulf of Panama and only 0.18 for Jamaica, which is presumably close to the value for the Atlantic side of Panama. The southwestern section of the Pacific coast of Panama is protected from the effects of the ITCZ by the Central Cordilleras and does not experience the thermal extremes of upwelling. The tides in Panama Bay are semi-diurnal, high amplitude, and predictable. The Caribbean tides are mixed-diurnal, low amplitude, irregular, and greatly influenced by local meteorological conditions.

It is obvious that there are major differences in the physical environments on either side of the Isthmus. The extent to which these physical factors affect marine life is less obvious. Of the several thousand Western Atlantic and Eastern Pacific tropical shore fishes, only about 1 percent of the species are still considered identical on both coasts. The different environments are obviously exerting different selective pressures on these populations. Even if the biota of this region were better known, it would still be difficult to estimate the specific outcome of any pair of interactions, much less the final equilibrium position of the entire biota.

I do not wish to discuss the engineering, geological, meteorological, or nuclear aspects of a sea-level canal but rather to cast a critical eye on the various views which have been expressed concerning the possible biological consequences of mixing Atlantic and Pacific biota.

Shortly after the Commission was appointed in 1965, it contracted the Battelle Memorial Institute to carry out a number of environmental studies, most of them directed at potential problems of radioactive materials in the complex tropical food chains. As a result of growing public concern over the environmental consequences of a new canal, the studies were to cover the potential exchange of marine life through a sea-level canal. The Commission also requested that the National Academy of Sciences appoint a committee of biologists to review what had been accomplished and to make recommendations with regard to the ecological problems surrounding a sea-level canal. This Committee of Ecological Research for the Interoceanic Canal (CERIC) was charged with the responsibility of examining the ecological issues implicit in constructing a canal, outlining a program of needed research, and recommending methods of minimizing possible danger.

After reviewing the findings of the Battelle Institute and the CERIC committee, the Commission's report to the President stated: "So far the Commission is able to determine on the basis of limited studies, linking the oceans at sea-level would not endanger commercial or sport fish on either side of the American Isthmus. . . . The potential for transfer of harmful biota and hybridization or displacement of species in both oceans exists but the risks involved appear to be acceptable." One wonders on what basis they arrived at this conclusion?

The Battelle report clearly states that existing knowledge of the region does not permit precise ecological predictions. It advises that there is "no evidence for predicting ecological changes that would be economically deleterious to commercial, sport or subsistence fisheries" and "no evidence to support the prediction of massive migrations from one ocean to another followed by widespread competition and extinction of thousands of species," but deep in their report they also admit that it is "clearly possible that successful invasion followed by explosive population growth of invading species could cause significant disruption of established ecological patterns and processes and that this could result in the displacement of desirable or economically important species in the native fauna by undesirable or dangerous invaders."

Possibly multiple authorship and inadequate editing may explain the inconsistencies in Battelle's report. What cannot be explained is the Commission's attitude that the risks of adverse ecological consequences stemming from construction appear to be acceptable. This is an absolutely unsupportable statement in view of the CERIC report, which considered an unrestricted breaching of the Panamic Isthmus as totally unacceptable.

According to the CERIC report, the transfer of undesirable organisms is a distinct possibility. The yellow-bellied sea snake and the crown-of-thorns starfish are two conspicuous Pacific forms that might get into the Caribbean through an unrestricted canal, but inconspicuous parasites or microscopic forms could in the long run be potentially more troublesome.

Needless to say, the members of the CERIC committee were appalled by the Commission's attitude that the "risks are acceptable." At a recent symposium on the Panamic Biota, one member of CERIC accused the executive secretary of the Commission of having "had an elastic collision with knowledge in his argument that the crown-of-thorns starfish already would have established itself in the Caribbean were conditions there favorable for it. Such a statement only displays an ignorance of the facts and the principles of zoogeography and elementary ecology." I think this pointed remark illustrates the frustrations of many biologists in obtaining an unbiased forum before the Commission. None of the commissioners has any ecological or biological background. Their study was designed before the ecological awakening of the late 1960s, before ecology became a household word. I cannot imagine such a commission being appointed today.

Although the controversy continues, any biologist realizes that precise predictions are impossible. Panama, like most other regions in the lower latitudes, is in need of a more thorough biological inventory and greater emphasis on ecologically oriented studies designed to evaluate seasonal and long-term fluctuations. Both the Battelle and CERIC reports emphasized the need for further research, if for no other reason than to document the natural fluctuations in biota at the termini of the canal so that any future changes are not a priori blamed on the canal.

An Alternative Proposal

The present Panama Canal may outlive its usefulness by the end of this century. It will be necessary to either increase its capacity or replace it with a sea-level version. Plans for a sea-level canal have been criticized because such a canal would present an unimpeded pathway for the migration of marine organisms from one ocean to the other. The plans to increase the efficiency of the present canal by pumping seawater during Panama's dry season have also been criticized, because any salinization of Gatun Lake will decrease its current effectiveness as a barrier to marine life.

I would like to suggest a plan which would eliminate many of the fears and uncertainties expressed by biologists. A solution is apparent which would preclude the need for digging a sea-level canal and would also make it unnecessary to flood additional areas of Panama's valuable real estate in order to store additional fresh water for a more efficient lock-canal. I suggest that a third set of locks be constructed, large enough to accommodate the world's largest ships. Water to operate these locks could be pumped from the ocean. A set of gates could be installed in the present Guillard Cut or other restricted area of the canal. The area between these gates could then be filled with a toxic material to prevent the passage of marine life through the canal. A compound could be used with a short half-life or one that is quickly oxidizable so that its effects do not spread throughout the remainder of the lake. Alternatively, a biotic barrier could be created by heating the the water between the gates. A biotic barrier in the context of a lock-canal could be maintained with more reliability and with less expenditure of energy than would be needed in a sea-level canal where currents are predicted to, at times, exceed four knots. The advantages of such a system combining locks, salt-water, and a biotic barrier are:

1. Accommodation of ships of all sizes.
2. Elimination of marine biotic transport through the present canal.
3. Elimination of the greater threat of interoceanic marine biological transport from a sea-level canal.
4. Elimination of the need for constructing new dams and larger lakes.
5. Much lower construction cost than a sea-level canal.
6. Ships passing through the toxic barrier would have their bottom fouling killed.
7. The distinctive biota of the two oceans would not be threatened.

Conclusion

In conclusion, there are considerable uncertainties concerning the nature of the biological interactions which may occur if a sea-level canal is constructed. Before the United States can construct a sea-level canal, a thorough environmental impact statement must be made. To meet this requirement, many additional long-term biological studies will be necessary.

The decision on whether or not to build a new canal will not be made by biologists. A number of factors that are likely to change by the end of the century may alter our current evaluations of the need for a new canal —transportation methods may be revolutionized; world markets may change dramatically; military requirements may alter or become obsolete; the costs of construction may no longer be economically justifiable; the attitude of the United States Congress toward ratification of a new treaty is uncertain; and international law may require at least regional concurrence before a canal is built.

I hope ecological impact will be given at least as much weight in the final decision as some of the other considerations. It is time for the sea-level canal to be considered *together* by lawyers, biologists, engineers, economists, and politicians and not just *individually* by these disciplines with their limited perspectives.

References

Atlantic-Pacific Interoceanic Canal Study Commission. 1970. Report of the Atlantic-Pacific Interoceanic Canal Study Commission. Washington, D.C.

Boffey, P. 1971. "Sea-Level Canal: How the Academist's Voice Was Muted." *Science* 171: pp. 355–58.

Graham, J.B., I. Rubinoff, and M.K. Hecht. 1971. Temperature Physiology of the Sea Snake *Pelamis Platurus:* An Index of Its Colonization Potential in the Atlantic Ocean. *Proceedings of the National Academy of Sciences* 68, No. 6, pp. 1360–63. Washington, D.C.

Jones, M.L., ed. 1972. The Panamic Biota: Some Observations Prior to a Sea-Level Canal. Biological Society of Washington, *Bulletin No. 2.*

Rubinoff, I. 1968. "Central American Sea-Level Canal: Possible Biological Effects. *Science* 161: pp. 857–61.

Rubinoff, R.W. and I. Rubinoff. 1971. "Geographic and Reproductive Isolation in Atlantic and Pacific Population of *Bathgobius. Evolution* 25, No. 1, pp. 88–97.

United States House of Representatives. 1972. Hearing before the Subcommittee on Panama Canal of the Committee on Merchant Marine and Fisheries. 92nd Congress, No. 92–30.

CHAPTER 16

Pacem in Maribus in the Caribbean

REYNALDO GALINDO-POHL

El Salvador is committed by its constitutional law to new concepts and regulations in the law of the seas. My early approach to the problems of the seas as representative of El Salvador was directed solely by the national policy of protection, defense, and recognition of an area of 200 miles under national jurisdiction. This was a mandatory position dictated by the political constitution of my native country and homeland. I made every effort, and I continue to make it, to support the national claim.

Political and legal arguments to support national policies on the seas have been developed in Latin America during the last 25 years. The fact that more than 40 countries from all continents now look favorably on the establishment of a special economic zone beyond the traditional territorial sea indicates that some concepts of Latin American origin are attractive to the less-developed countries. Moreover, the trend among big maritime powers toward recognition of a special economic zone up to 200 miles reflects the influence of Latin American ideas and ideals, worked out from the needs, realities, and aspirations of the Third World. Through their energetic claims and inexhaustible efforts, these countries, now associated with some states from Asia, Africa, and Europe, have promoted creative thinking and stimulated the academic circles of developed and underdeveloped nations.

During my years as Permanent Representative of El Salvador to the United Nations and chairman of one of the subcommittees of the Committee on the Sea-Bed, I have realized that a strict national approach will not solve the problems of the seas on a rational and up-to-date basis. If we divide the seas among national states, even though a big share may go to the developing countries, we would still fall short of serving the fundamental interests of mankind and consequently of the peoples in national states.

The national approach is valid but insufficient. Coherent and institutionalized collective action and the integration of rights and interests seem the best way to serve national interests in this era of advanced technology, swift communications, and interdependence. This more comprehensive approach does not destroy the rightful and sound claims of developing nations to a fair share in the exploitation of the seas through setting wider limits to national jurisdiction over adjacent waters. This fair share has the principle of free competition which in practice has meant a bigger share going to the few powerful nations having capital, skill, and technology.

The problems of the sea require an *oceanic* solution—huge, deep, magnificent, even astonishing in its novelty. No temporary expedient will be appropriate to the complex and challenging issues that the sea poses to the contemporary mind.

A New Approach to the Problems of the Seas

My starting point is that the oceans are a physical and ecological unity and that all maritime boundaries are artificial, established to take into account such political facts as the existence of national states and the international community. The challenge to the traditional law of the seas, beginning with the claim of states to wide, adjacent coastal areas, had its beginning in Latin America in the late 1940s and early 1950s. The intent was to assure to developing countries the exclusive rights to exploit a protected zone without overwhelming competition, which had sometimes resulted in the total annihilation of living resources. The disappearance of the whale from Chilean waters is an example. The security zone around the American continent during World War II and the Truman Proclamation of 1945, had a catalytic effect on ocean policies. It was not difficult to shift attention from security and temporary considerations to economic and permanent ones, from the needs of war to the expectations of peace, from the sea bed to the superjacent waters.

Unilateralism has been presented as the evil. But as a matter of fact, international law evolves through unilateral acts. Claims and declarations by themselves are a valid source of international law. Unilateral acts may or may not be converted into a source of international law, however; unilateral claims are not per se sources of international law. Unilateral declarations have the effect of breaking the status quo ante, of shocking the conscience of public opinion, and of pointing out neglected issues which come from changes in historic circumstances. Attitudes change when facts change.

Sometimes unilateral claims are imprecise, such as the claim that several Latin American countries put forward in the early fifties concerning the right of each country to fix the limits of the zone under its jurisdiction, taking into consideration economic and social factors of which each country is the sole judge. That principle, appearing in the Declaration of Montevideo, needs to be completed and made precise. It had an important role as a device to break down the status quo, as the big cannon of the Venetian mercenary broke down the walls of Constantinople. But the time has come for a more precise statement of the principle which served in the fifties to establish the economic zone. A maximum limit must be put, not an obligatory limit but a maximum one.

Thinking and policy evolve at the pace of social change. It would be an aberration for the law of the seas to remain static in a time of accelerated change. It is easy to realize that the mere widening of national limits and jurisdiction within the traditional concepts and regulations of the seas will not sufficiently protect the international community and peoples of the world. The new economic zone has to evolve into a completely new regime of the seas in accordance with the present stage of the international community and the development of science and technology.

It is no longer possible to isolate and protect an area of the sea. Modern communications, new technology, and maritime currents make ineffective whatever determination a national state might make on the exploitation and preservation of its economic zone. If we repeat with the seas in the last decades of the 20th century what our ancestors did with the land at the beginning of the modern age, we will demonstrate that we have neither understood nor learned the lessons of history and that we are not mature enough to handle the potentialities—and the risks—of advanced technology. A mixture of both national and international interests and organizations, mutually limited and conditioned, would provide the scheme for a mature international community. I go as far, sometimes, as to talk of sovereignty in generic terms, not as pertaining exclusively to the state but in some way to the international community, and I distinguish between national and international sovereignty; but this is not the right place to elaborate on these ideas.

Now that the entire regime of the seas is to be discussed in a world conference we are presented with several opportunities. One is to establish the machinery to direct the rationalized exploitation of the seas, both of the waters and the sea bed and its subsoil. Another is to deduce new principles and agree on new rules of law. We have the opportunity to conceive and put into operation a system of international distributive justice—to create international social justice. And we may redefine the freedoms of the high seas more by content than by form.

The negotiations on the new regime of the seas will be the most ambitious and decisive ones of the 20th century and will constitute a direct challenge to the lack of attention by national states to the trends and conditions of this precise moment in history. The new regime, consolidating the international community through a strong machinery for exploration and exploitation of the resources of the seas in general and the sea bed in particular, could lead to an enlightened policy of development, and could provide the opportunity to mix and blend the interests and rights of national states into integrated maritime zones. At the same time, appropriate rules of management, protection, and international law may be developed.

It is not an exaggeration to assert that the Third Conference on the Law of the Sea will be the most important conference in the remainder of the present century. In my opinion it will be a pity if the Third Conference confines itself to a confrontation between the maritime powers and the developing countries. It will be a success if, going further than the mere redress of inequalities coming from the traditional international law of the seas, it establishes sound international cooperation on this last frontier of human hopes and natural resources, assures a viable scheme of world development, and, considering the oceans as a unity, translates this unity into policy and into rules of international law.

Some Presuppositions on the Future Regime of the Seas

At the present stage of the preparatory work for the Third Conference on the Law of the Sea, there is enough background to assert that important changes may take place in the regime of the seas and that original rules and institutions of international law may appear. The First and Second Conferences on the Law of the Seas (Geneva, 1958 and 1960) were devoted mainly to the codification of traditional maritime law, European by origin, and adapted to a world dominated politically and intellectually by Europe. Those conferences marked the apogee of traditional international law, dating from the 17th century, and were devoted to giving precision to the *lex lata*. The Third Conference must be devoted primarily to the *lex ferenda*, or it will be a complete failure. The quality of the results of the Third Conference will not be measured by the number of votes approving a resolution; the resolution will be evaluated by its content. If the conference confines itself to a redistribution of the shares of the seas along the lines of traditional law and concepts, no matter how just the distribution may be, the conference will have lost the opportunity to push the international community into a path worthy of the spectacular technological achievements in our time.

Present Trends which May Be Reflected in Decisions of the Third Conference

It is impossible to foresee the amount of change that will be agreed upon (I pass the exact prediction to the computers), but as some working hypotheses are needed, I assume that some trends now discernible may by then be mature and ready for conversion into new rules and institutions. The following positive trends may have reached maturity at the time of the Third Conference:

Continental Shelf

A precise limit may be established to the continental shelf under national jurisdiction, putting an end to the uncertainty of the Geneva Convention on this matter. This limit could be determined by geographical or geological criteria. Some countries would maintain that the continental rise should be recognized as the exterior limit of the national continental shelf. It could be taken for granted that nations would not agree to fewer rights than those agreed upon by the Geneva Convention and that consequently they will stick to the term "sovereign rights" to designate the kind of jurisdiction and power a nation could exercise on its continental shelf.

Territorial Sea

The territorial sea, understood in the narrow and traditional sense, would be fixed at 12 miles, provided that a larger economic zone was recognized, as well as a regime for the passage through international straits agreed on. The coastal state would assure the exclusivity of the exploration and exploitation of the territorial sea, in addition to civil and criminal jurisdiction. Innocent passage would continue to limit the sovereignty of the coastal state.

A Wide Area of Limited Jurisdiction

A wider area beyond the territorial sea would be recognized, where the coastal state would have exclusive or preferential rights of exploration (exclusive rights according to the developing nations, preferential rights according to the developed ones). The coastal state would not exercise civil and criminal jurisdiction in that wider area, and freedom of navigation through it would be the right of all nations.

This zone would be designated by different names. Some countries might adopt hard positions concerning names, in order to conform to their national legislation. The question of names could be a real problem, on the basis of national legislation. One way to solve or avoid it is to declare that each nation has the right to decide about names. It seems that the question of the name of the wider area beyond the territorial sea has been settled for the countries bordering the Caribbean Sea, as the Conference of Santo Domingo adopted the term *patrimonial sea.* Some countries of the Pacific and Atlantic coasts of Latin America would hardly accept a name different from *territorial sea* to designate that wider area. The name *national sea* will promptly come into the game, and other names could appear in the near future.

I point out that El Salvador's constitution does not use the term "territorial sea"; it declares that the adjacent sea from the coast out to 200 miles is part of the national territory. It puts aside the question of terms as it is not involved with the meaning of the term territorial sea, which has a definite meaning in traditional international law. The constitution of El Salvador fully recognizes the freedom of navigation. The historical background of that constitution demonstrates that its main and sole purpose was to claim an economic zone.

My personal choice of names is a neutral descriptive term, such as "economic zone," so as to avoid the civil law overtones of "patrimonial sea" and the traditional meaning behind "territorial sea." If "territorial sea" is preferred it can be used in two senses, the narrow, traditional one and the new economic one. The countries wanting to use "territorial sea" in a new way could divide the territorial sea into two parts, one of traditional content and the other with the features that would be agreed to about the adjacent zone, in this case more than a mere economic zone. Countries fighting for "territorial sea" are seeking to have an adjacent zone over which they would have more than economic rights. This is another reason to hold that the problem of names is a fundamental one as the names represent more extensive or more narrow claims and rights.

The name could be converted into an issue by itself, if there were a trend to give a definite but controversial name to the zone. In some meetings of the Sea-bed Committee the name has been an underlying issue. I remember the days when it was forbidden, by tacit agreement, to mention the territorial sea or to talk about limits and so on. The Sea-bed Committee has slowly and gently destroyed many taboos. The time of taboos is over, and nothing now escapes critical examination and free discussion and negotiation.

I expect that the real issue concerning the economic zone will be its content and not its name. I believe a majority of countries, including many developed countries, favors the recognition of an economic zone beyond the traditional territorial sea. I am not sure whether a zone of exclusive or of preferential rights will be preferred. This may be one of the grounds for conflict between developed and developing countries. I foresee that some landlocked countries, both developed and developing, will side with the maritime powers in trying to establish limited or preferential rights for coastal states, with strong international elements in the national economic zone.

I assume that a redefinition of the freedom of navigation, both on the high seas and in the economic zone, might be worked out. A redefined freedom of navigation would apply on equal terms to the high seas and the economic zone and would be drawn on the basis of technical approaches to preservation of the seas.

International Zone of the Sea Bed

An international authority may be established to handle the problems of the exploration and exploitation of the international zone of the sea bed—the part of the sea bed that was declared the common heritage of mankind by the United Nations. There is agreement, at least in principle, that an international machinery should be established, but wide disagreement exists on its structure, functions, and responsibilities. The Latin American proposal offers a middle ground between the licensing machinery proposed by some Western countries, and the African proposal involving complete control by states. It mixes state control and policy making and private expertise and technology. I realize that this proposal has not been sufficiently explained and developed. Regional enterprises could complement or constitute the specific arms of the "enterprise" of the Latin American proposal. I intend to elaborate in the future on the philosophy behind the "enterprise" and to demonstrate that it is a kind of compromise among different proposals.

Controversial Proposals which May Be Considered by the Third Conference

It is impossible to know how much support a number of controversial suggestions will receive at the forthcoming conference. There is now no definite trend toward their acceptance, but they could, nevertheless, constitute a set of important features of a future regime. Their favorable consideration would place the forthcoming conference in a sound creative role. The conference may receive proposals on the following ideas:

Ecological and economic considerations. Limitations may be suggested on the rights of coastal states in the use of traditional territorial seas in order to preserve the marine environment, ecological balance, natural purity of waters, and survival of marine species. In addition, an economic zone would imply obligations for the state concerned.

Recognition of the traditional territorial sea of 12 miles and of an adjacent economic zone would in itself be insufficient to meet the best and most far-reaching interests of the international community and of peoples distributed into national states if that recognition were to follow the old patterns of international politics and law and reduce the problem of the seas to a question of limits. The future regime of the seas requires more than simply a reversal of the advantages that the developed countries have under traditional maritime law. It requires a thorough reappraisal of the entire regime—of the seabed and the waters, of the coastal areas and the high seas. An easy way to conduct the forthcoming conference would be to reduce it to the settlement of limits, but the constructive way lies in a comprehensive approach to the problem of the seas.

National obligations. The explicit and emphatic recognition that obligations normally flow from rights, that abuses in the exercise of rights must be checked, and that all principles and rules of the regime constitute a whole for interpretation, application, and management seems easy to agree on. But in practice, only the rights are in the game. A clear outline of obligations derived from rights, including those associated with the traditional territorial sea, should receive careful consideration. The coastal state should be entitled to qualified rights, within the interests of the international community. This should include interior waters in regard to measures for the protection of marine ecology and for the fight against pollution.

Resources. It may be proposed that the resources of the seas be assessed on a worldwide basis, with regional and subregional exploitation taking into account world economic trends.

Combined or integrated economic zones. A combination of the economic zones of neighboring states would be convenient in order to avoid controversies and strenghthen the capacity to exploit resources. This would be of special interest to common markets, free-trade zones, and programs of integration. It would help to avoid controversies and complex problems of collateral delimitation, when national coastlines are relatively short although the seas are open, as happens in the Pacific coast of Central America. I find it unavoidable in the very complex geography of the Caribbean Sea. The division of zones could lead to interminable disputes, and the advantages of the new regime might be jeopardized by the complexity of the problems related to the protection of national fleets.

There would be two basic ways to reach this result. One would be to apply the agreed-upon general rules on delimitation, identifying each national economic zone; afterward, the states concerned could put their economic zones together. In this case, many problems of negotiations would arise; in the event that one or two states refused to join the integrated economic zone, the entire project might suffer a deadly blow. This would be the procedure most in accordance with the philosophy and policy of national states.

The other way would consist of creating an integrated zone from the very beginning. *An integrated economic zone might be recognized instead of national economic zones.* None of the states concerned would have title to a zone, and none could act unilaterally. All the states would hold title in common and all would act multilaterally. The international community would proclaim and recognize integrated economic zones, not national zones. This would take place in selected areas of complex geography, notably the Caribbean region, the Pacific Coast of the Central American States, and the Mediterranean Sea.

The new rules set forth by the conference might provide a concrete scheme for *economic integrated zones.* The international community should not leave this very important issue to the erratic views of the states concerned but should establish such zones whenever the geography demands it. This should be by decision of the international community through the Third Conference, not by the convention of sovereign states. I advance the idea of moving from the recognition of economic zones in selected areas to the acceptance of integrated economic zones by the states concerned. This would be far ahead of the old patterns of international law and politics.

International development fund. The exploitation of every area of the seas, even those close to the coasts, should imply an obligation to contribute to an international fund devoted to development. There are no isolated areas of the seas, as each one receives physical and biological influences from great distances. It is true that the coastal area is dependent on the mainland, but it is also dependent on the rest of the sea waters.

A system of voluntary contributions and taxes might be devised. Voluntary contributions would come from the exploitation of the territorial sea; taxes would come from the economic zone and the high seas, in the first case on the basis of agreement between a coastal state and the competent authority representing the international community, and in the second, by agreement among all nations. Principles and rules of international taxation would be devised to assure fair treatment for all concerned.

Taxes would be based on revenues, as a simple and expedient device. If revenues were managed by an international authority, a complex and expensive machinery to supervise exploitation would be necessary, and revenues might disappear through expensive management. Taxes would avoid many problems of management and would represent the interests of mankind as a whole—the physical unity of the ocean waters and the solidarity of all nations regarding the programs of development.

Problems of the Economic Zone

it seems that there is a kind of irreconcilable difference between national claims and the interests of the international community as a whole, namely, between the new economic zone of individual states and the concept of an international zone as a common heritage of mankind.

This is a real issue, and it needs some explanation. In the first place, it should be noted that the zone recognized as the common heritage of mankind in the United Nations Declaration on the Sea Bed and Subsoil Thereof is the deep ocean floor and not the superjacent waters. The concept of common heritage has not yet been applied to the waters overlying the international zone. Maybe the time has not yet come to extend the concept of common heritage to the overlying waters. It is my feeling that such an extension is worth a diplomatic effort, as it would help to solve many problems and put all principles and rules of maritime law under a brighter light.

The concept of the common heritage contains the following notions: (1) a zone and its resources; however, there may be a point of disagreement here, as some commentators would assert that it concerns only resources; (2) a zone subject neither to appropriation nor to the sovereign jurisdiction of any state in particular; (3) resources which may and should be exploited in such a way that all mankind can derive some benefits from them; consequently, a regime for the distribution of benefits would be established; (4) a kind of common management to assure the rational exploitation of resources, the equitable distribution of benefits among all concerned, and the preservation of the marine environment in an ordered use of the zone; (5) some kind of partnerships among states, as states represent humanity; (6) resources which, though exploited according to international rules, may be subject to particular appropriation and specific use.

Would states be ready to establish a similar regime for fishing? It is doubtful. But is there any sufficient reason to avoid a serious and meaningful proposal on the matter? Why don't we extend the common heritage concept to the resources of the waters beyond the territorial sea and the economic zone? Why don't we try to do it? National claims may be eased insofar as commonly shared benefits could emerge from the exploitation and use of the sea.

Other means to ease the competition between national claims and common interests are international taxation and the recognition of international elements and interests in national economic zones and even in territorial seas. For example, El Salvador has officially advocated a broad system of international taxes on resources, both living and mineral, renewable and non-renewable.* All of these means could constitute compromise solutions that might have their most significant impact combined with a broadening of the common heritage concept. Each compromise solution could work separately, but it would be most effective in combination with others.

One of the weak points of the concept of the economic zone is that if waters are divided among national states, the distribution of living resources is unequal. In the Caribbean region, the concept of an integrated economic zone deals with this problem and introduces an element of fair distribution and exploitation. Worldwide, the economic zone would give an important degree of access to living resources to a large number of developed countries. The argument that they would receive a large amount of the produce is correct; but to argue that this is against the interest of the developing countries is inappropriate. The issue is not a matter of excluding the developed countries from access to the resources of the seas, but one of giving to all countries real access to those riches. Comparing the present situation, in which the great powers ravage the seven seas without any obligation, to an eventual situation in which an important share of resources may go to the developing countries, the choice is clear.

The economic zone neither makes all states equal nor all states happy. Many differences would remain among states and peoples in relation to the exploitation and use of the sea, but it would diminish the inequalities resulting from the present system of complete freedom, in which a few developed states are the real and sole beneficiaries of the resources of the seas.

The mere establishment of the economic zone would not solve all problems, although it would attenuate the existing inequalities. What is included in the economic zone is the real issue. How the economic zone is reconciled with the interests of the international community as a whole will be one of the most delicate enterprises of diplomatic negotiation. How the economic zone combines with the territorial sea and the common heritage is another crucial issue.

*See the statement of the Minister of Foreign Affairs of El Salvador, United Nations A/PV. 2061, 10 October 1972.

How to measure the economic zone is one of the hottest points. One way would be simply to apply the base line criterion, with the rules laid down in the Geneva Convention on the Territorial Sea. But it seems that some specific criteria should be worked out to measure the economic zone. A continental state having an island in mid-ocean presents a problem, for example; would that dependent island be entitled to an economic zone? Insular states would receive treatment similar to coastal continental states; but would it be fair to give the same treatment to islands dependent on continental states?

And what about land-locked countries? The economic zone would diminish the ocean space actually open to their economic activities. There is, of course, a deep difference between the developed and the developing, land-locked states. The latter would have a right that would be meaningless in reality, as they do not exploit the sea anyway. A form of regional arrangement may constitute a fair solution to the problem; perhaps the land-locked states should have rights in the economic zone of the states in their region.

Another problem of the economic zone may be under-exploitation. As a matter of fact, most developing countries may be unable to directly exploit that zone. Provisions for concessions, particularly for short-living fish, may be instituted. Special provisions may be drafted for highly migratory species.

The Caribbean Region at the Crossroads

I refer to the Caribbean Sea as defined by the Sixth Conference of the International Hydrographic Bureau in 1952, a definition adopted by the Santo Domingo Conference in 1972. The Caribbean region has been the scene of bitter disputes since the early settlement of Europeans in the New World. An agitated history of alliances and wars, collaboration and competition, has left a mosaic of languages, races, nations, and states. The main feature of the region is that it is a crossroads of cultures, languages, and peoples. There are big and small countries, largely developed and very poor peoples, wonders of natural beauty, remarkable human accomplishments, and a will to progress. This crossroads, with its contrasts and similarities, may be the most appropriate place to establish a sound regional cooperation in accordance with recent trends toward internationalization and inter-dependence.

It is no longer the time for isolated political communities. It is evident that modern technology calls for large economic spaces and masses of consumers. In the past, economic spaces followed the political spaces constructed through conquest and domination. To construct by force a large economic space is quite impossible at the present stage of the international community. Negotiation and agreement, understanding and cooperation are the sole means by which we can build the large economic space needed by modern technology, and cultivate high standards of living and the pleasures of leisure and art.

Our time has among its features a trend toward integration, notwithstanding the occasional and temporary setbacks we observe in regions such as Central America. Linked with integration, a redefinition of the structure and functions of the national state ought to take place. A political approach and conception has been lacking in some schemes of integration which reduce them to mere joint ventures; that was the case of the Central American Common Market. If the economy has been the battleground of nations during many centuries, it would be a miracle for the economy to become the indestructible link among national states in the 20th century. In some regions the economists thought they would be able to solve some problems without the cooperation of the politicians. What is needed is statesmanship that would promote synergy between economics and politics.

A sense of interdependence is pervading the world. The feeling of proximity, of interrelated interests, and even of a common destiny is increasing with communications, tourism, and joint economic ventures. It is known from ancient times that traveling plays a large part in change of mentality. The traveler is a potential internationalist. The necessity of faithful and reasonable cooperation is as evident at the present stage of the international community as is the best-demonstrated law of physics.

The Caribbean region is particularly fit to develop a special kind of cooperation and association. The conference held by the Caribbean countries at Santo Domingo referred to a common policy of the incumbent states concerning scientific research, pollution, conservation, and exploitation of marine resources.

The Caribbean region needs more than a common policy and an institutionalized cooperation; it needs association and integration. The Declaration of Santo Domingo does not make entirely clear whether the intended common policy refers to the period of negotiation preceding the establishment of the new regime of the seas or whether it covers the application of the new regime as such. It might be interpreted that the Declaration covers the two possibilities mentioned above, as reference to conservation and exploitation of marine resources is likely to be at its best when the new regime is in force.

A Subregional Regime of the Caribbean Region

Here I refer to the Caribbean region, excluding the Gulf of Mexico, as I understand that the problems of the Gulf of Mexico are different. The Gulf of Mexico is not as complex as the Caribbean Sea. Three countries have direct interests on it: the United States, Mexico, and Cuba.

Various avenues of cooperation and association could be outlined for the Caribbean Sea: (1) a common policy (the weakest of all); (2) cooperative institutions such as the Oceanographic Institute, which was left for further study by the Conference of Santo Domingo; (3) the establishment of an integrated economic zone; the alternatives are between exploitation of resources on a purely national basis, under the criteria of delimitation and partition that would be devised by the Third Conference, and exploration, preservation, and exploitation on an integrated regional basis.

A loose cooperation might benefit the countries concerned from the point of view of technological know-how, investments, and so on. But association would be the soundest way to deal with the complexities of the region. I do not doubt that the states are ready to cooperate in fields as obvious as pollution, scientific research, preservation of marine species, and renewable resources. The crucial political decision must be made about a meaningful and effective association. National exploitation or integrated exploitation is the dilemma. Reason and reasoning are the main factors in the decision of the states concerned, because they sometimes have scanty knowledge of each other.

In the Third Conference, agreement might be on ways to apply universal rules. Regional and subregional management of the exploitation of resources, including those of the sea bed and its subsoil, ought to be considered within the great framework of a world organization. The Latin American draft on machinery needs further elaboration and refinement in various ways and in particular concerning the decentralization of the "enterprise" through regional and subregional agencies.

Before the Third Conference a period of enlightenment by the academic community may be the best way to prepare, on a rational basis, for the crucial political decisions to be taken. Much is to be gained from the cross-examination of problems and issues by persons representing different cultures and ways of thinking. It may be most useful to have a conference devoted to new trends in international relations and new features of the international community.

CHAPTER 17

A Caribbean Community for
Ocean Development

Applications of the Latin American Seabed Draft Treaty to Ocean
Development in the Caribbean[1]

DAVID KRIEGER

An ocean development community is herein defined as a regional organization with the prime function of developing ocean resources for the common
benefit of the littoral states. The concept of regional organization around
ocean space is relatively new. Generally, regional organization has been
bounded by land masses, but there is no reason for us to restrain our vision
to territorial limits. In fact, technological advances in ocean exploitation are
making it imperative to at least control the negative side effects of ocean
development, if not imperative to channel the positive effects into regional
development programs.

   While in the next few years we can expect international agreement on
a new Law of the Sea, it is becoming increasingly apparent that although
the law may extend coastward of the boundaries of national jurisdiction, the
coastal nations will probably be successful in retaining exploitation rights
to the ocean resources to a boundary of 200 miles. The Latin American
nations have, in fact, been leaders in exerting claims to a 200-mile boundary.
They have introduced into the discussion of national jurisdiction the con-

---

[1]The official title of the Latin American document is: "Working Paper on the Regime for
the Sea Bed and Ocean Floor and Its Subsoil Beyond the Limits of National Jurisdiction."
It was submitted to the United Nations Committee on the Peaceful Uses of the Sea-Bed and
Ocean Floor Beyond the Limits of National Jurisdiction on August 4, 1971 by Chile, Colombia, Ecuador, El Salvador, Guatemala, Guyana, Jamaica, Mexico, Panama, Peru, Trinidad
and Tobago, Uruguay, and Venezuela.

cept of *patrimonial sea* which would allow the adjacent coastal state exclusive rights to all living and nonliving resources to a maximum distance of 200 miles from the coast.

The application of the patrimonial sea concept could lead to an important experiment in regional cooperation for ocean development *if it were to be applied creatively;* that is, if the nations surrounding a semi-enclosed sea were to claim jurisdiction over a patrimonial sea to a maximum limit of 200 miles and then create an organization that would manage the major portion of this area for the common benefit. This concept has already been put forward in the Caribbean by Jamaica, which has called for a matrimonial rather than patrimonial sea beyond territorial waters. The matrimonial sea is an attempt to give regional embodiment to the concept of the oceans as the common heritage of mankind. While there is as yet little political support for creating a matrimonial sea or regional community in the Caribbean, the regional benefits of such a proposal deserve far more serious consideration.

If the regionalization of the Caribbean Sea were to be implemented so that all of the littoral states created a regional community to manage the area beyond the 12-mile territorial sea, it would add a second dimension to the experiment, that of regional cooperation for development among the developing. This could set an important precedent for other developing regions.

While regional organization around an ocean area may bring together states which are socially, culturally, and economically diverse, there are a number of good reasons for believing that this form of organization would be mutually beneficial to the countries concerned. We will consider some of these benefits below under the following four headings: (1) planning for the rational development of the area; (2) participation in cooperative projects for which any one state would lack sufficient capital; (3) establishment of regional norms of conduct in the area; and (4) collective bargaining with large corporations.

Planning for Rational Development

Planning for rational development in a region would include, as a first stage, gathering systematic data on the living and nonliving resources of the region. Only after ascertaining the region's potential is it possible to plan rationally for its exploitation. A second stage of planning would require cost-benefit analyses of resource development. Some minerals, for example, might be too expensive to exploit and process to compete on the world market. In both of these planning stages there would be considerable saving to the region as a whole by elimination of overlapping research and development projects. These could be coordinated through a regional institute.

A third stage in the planning process involves the harmonization of the various uses of the area. This would include assessment of the impact of each of the activities carried on in the region on every other activity. Thus, for example, the effect of deep-sea mining on fishing, transportation, communication, and tourism would require consideration. It would be possible to construct a matrix of present and future interaction effects throughout the region. Planning must take into account the effects of negative interactions such as pollution on tourism, and attempt to construct programs where negative actions lead to positive interactions—an example is the use of sewage as fertilizer for fish farming. With regional planning it will also be possible to set aside certain areas for experimental programs in fish farming, desalinization, mineral extraction, etc.

Harmonization of the uses of the area would be important in resolving potential conflicts at the planning stage rather than at the stage of implementation. As technology allows for greater exploitability of ocean resources, increased conflicts are to be anticipated without prior regional, and indeed, global planning. It is crucial that nations perceive their interests in cooperative, as opposed to free-for-all, terms.

Participation in Cooperative Projects

There are any number of potential projects which individual states, particularly developing states, are prevented from pursuing because of the cost involved. Regional cooperation could expand the scope of activities accessible to participatory states. Some of the important projects that fall into this category are:

1. The creation of an institute to conduct exploration of the area, organize data and create information-retrieval systems, and train indigenous personnel in the ocean sciences.

2. The purchase or lease of equipment for mining and processing deep seabed minerals.

3. Access to advanced technologies such as satellites, which would aid exploration of the area's resources.

4. In the future, the creation of combined fusion energy and desalinization plants, which would use deuterium from salt water as "fuel."

In addition to being able to raise more capital among themselves for cooperative projects, regional organization should also make it easier to raise capital from international banks and development funds. There are two reasons why this would appear to be so. First, cooperative regional projects would allow for the raising of increased capital for matching funds, and second, it is more likely that research will be more adequate when done with the resources made available through regional cooperation.

Establishment of Regional Norms

Regional norms would, for the most part, be regional applications of the new Law of the Sea, but in some instances they would supplement international law as required by regional conditions. As technology makes possible increasing uses of the area, there will be an increasing need for ongoing consideration of normative behavior in order to minimize conflict in the seas. It will be necessary to place restrictions on certain activities such as dumping and set aside some areas for special purposes.

Collective Bargaining

A final area in which I see benefit in regional organization over individual state action is that of collective bargaining with the large corporations. Let us assume that in a region such as the Caribbean, the same resource will be available to more than one of the coastal states. If a technologically advanced corporation opts for developing this resource, it will be able to do so less expensively if the situation is such that one nation bids against another for bringing in the corporation. If the region presents a united front, however, it will then be necessary for the corporation to come in on regional terms, in which case the price would not be driven down by competing states.

There has already been some consideration of regional organization for ocean development in the Mediterranean. A series of conferences have been held on this subject, including a follow-up conference to Pacem in Maribus III of representatives to the United Nations Sea-Bed Committee from Mediterranean nations. At this meeting the Mediterranean diplomats were able to reach unanimous agreement on the following points:

1. The Mediterranean Sea contains a heritage of civilization and culture which must be protected, and the Mediterranean states must work toward peace based on justice in the region. For this purpose further meetings are to be held.

2. Most intense cooperation is urgently required on the serious problems of sea pollution.

3. Regional cooperation is required in the field of fisheries, with the object of preserving the biological resources of the Mediterranean.

4. The governments represented at the conference are to cooperate for the protection of submarine archeological and historical treasures in the Mediterranean Sea beyond the limits of national jurisdiction.

5. Another field of regional cooperation which is to be strengthened is that of scientific research and the training of experts and technical personnel and exchange of information in various fields related to the sea, with benefit for all the countries represented at the meeting and particularly for those less expert and technically advanced.

The areas of primary concern in the Caribbean will most likely differ to some extent from those in the Mediterranean. The important point in referring to the Mediterranean is simply to indicate that there were areas in which the need for regional cooperation for mutual benefit was unanimously agreed on. The recognition of common interest serves as a point of departure for the development of programs of regional cooperation.

Before turning to a consideration of the specific characteristics of the Caribbean region and supplying a definition of the area, I will add one argument to those set forth above, in favor of regional organization for ocean development. This derives from the position taken in the Latin American Sea-bed Draft Treaty. In Article 14(g) the draft treaty specifically empowers the Sea-bed Authority "to make, on the initiative of interested states or in agreement with them, such regional or subregional arrangements, including facilities, as it deems necessary for the exercise of its functions." Thus there is explicit approval of states taking the initiative to establish regional organizations based on ocean space. This principle clearly allows for states to begin planning for regional structures which would be linked to a future ocean authority.

Any regional organizations that were implemented in the interim prior to the establishment of a global ocean regime would, in important respects, serve as models for the global machinery. As we shall see when we discuss the Latin American concept of a Sea-bed Enterprise, this may be a matter of considerable importance in the design of the global Ocean Regime. If a Caribbean Community can prove the viability of an Ocean Enterprise, the developing world generally should have a far stronger position of argument for the implementation of this structure at the global level.

The Latin American Sea-bed Draft Treaty is considered a document of prime importance in providing guidelines for a regional community in the Caribbean, as 7 of the 13 signatory states border on the Caribbean and two of the other signatories have close ties with the region and would be considered for regional membership in a Caribbean Community. I will make reference to this document when applicable in the design of the structural model for the Caribbean Community for Ocean Development which will be discussed following a description of the Caribbean region.

The Caribbean

The Caribbean is a mixture of West and East Indian, European and African cultures blended in an American cauldron. Of the five colonial powers which once dominated the region, only Spain is no longer present. Great Britain, France, the Netherlands, and the United States remain involved, but all dependencies now have a considerable degree of local autonomy. Of the 123 million people in the region, only some 5 million now live in dependencies,[2] yet ties of trade and custom still cause the nations of the region to look outward.

There are 14 sovereign states in the Caribbean and 16 dependencies, if the region is defined in the north by the Yucatan Channel and in the south by Colombia, Venezuela, and Trinidad and Tobago. This includes the southern portion of Mexico but excludes the Gulf of Mexico and therefore the United States. The other nation in the Gulf, Cuba, also borders on the Caribbean. For purposes of regional organization I felt it best to define the region so that the inclusion of the United States did not overpower the organization. As I will point out below, one of the characteristics of the region is its shared need for development. The priority of problems in the Gulf of Mexico differ from those in the Caribbean, and in my opinion would be subject to the most advantageous resolution through bilateral agreement of the two powers that dominate 95 percent of the area, Mexico and the United States.

Beginning with Mexico and moving clockwise around the area, the nations of the Caribbean are: Mexico, Cuba, Jamaica, Haiti, Dominican

---

[2]The term *dependency* is used here to indicate entities associated with an external power that has responsibility for defense and foreign policy decisions. Most dependencies in the region have considerable control over matters of internal policy, particularly the Commonwealth of Puerto Rico which has the status of a "free associated state."

Republic, Barbados, Trinidad and Tobago, Venezuela, Colombia, Panama, Costa Rica, Nicaragua, Honduras, and Guatemala. Three other nations which do not border on the Caribbean but which have traditional ties with the region are El Salvador in Central America; Guyana, a member of several regional organizations in the eastern Caribbean; and the newly independent Bahamas. Because of their traditional ties to the region, it is felt that these states should be considered for inclusion in a regional organization.

The largest of the dependencies in the region is Puerto Rico, the possession of the United States, along with the US Virgin Islands. There are six British Associated States: Antigua, Dominica, Grenada, St. Kitts-Nevis-Anguilla, St. Lucia, and St. Vincent. Other British possessions in the area are: Cayman Islands, Montserrat, British Virgin Islands, and British Honduras (Belize).

The Dutch Caribbean is composed of the Netherlands Antilles, islands off the coast of Venezuela,[3] and Surinam on the eastern border of Guyana, which is actually outside the borders of the Caribbean Sea. The last of the dependencies in the region, the Islands of Guadaloupe and Martinique, are Overseas Departments of France. A third French dependency, French Guiana, located beyond the region, may also be considered for inclusion. Because all of the French dependencies, however, are considered to be a part of France proper, it may be preferable to omit them from consideration in the formation of a regional organization if their inclusion would bring in the metropolitan power.

In all, there are some 2 million square miles of territory, but most of it is broken up into small pieces. Of the total, nearly 80 percent is accounted for by the region's "big three"—Mexico, Colombia, and Venezuela. These three also account for 70 percent of the region's population and more than 75 percent of the total gross national product of approximately 82 billion dollars. At the other end of the continuum from the region's "big three" are eight territories which cover less than 200 square miles each. The smallest dependency I have included is Montserrat, with only 38 square miles, and the smallest state is Barbados which covers 170 square miles.

The lands of the Caribbean are a diverse group—diverse in size, cultural heritage, and political form—but they have in common two important factors. The first is their universal need for development. In more than half of the territories childhood mortality between the ages of one and four is 10 to 20 times as high as in the United States. In most of the nations there is only one doctor for every 3,000 inhabitants. In Haiti and Honduras there

[3]The three islands are Curaçao, Aruba, and Bonaire. There are also three small islands east of Puerto Rico with a combined population of 6,000.

is less than one doctor per 10,000 people. Other statistics of the region show that average calorie consumption, per capita income, and literacy rates are generally low. The great challenge confronting the nations of the Caribbean is to raise the quality of life of their people.

Other than the general need for development, the Caribbean territories share the common linkage of the Caribbean Sea. All are washed by the waters of this semi-enclosed sea, all are potential partners in the wealth of the sea. The sea is a common ground for fishing and transportation. In the coming decades it will become common ground for mining, farming, and perhaps living as well. The potential of the sea for the development of power, protein, mineral and hydrocarbon wealth remains to be thoroughly explored. The Caribbean Sea is approximately one million square miles; the cubed mileage staggers the imagination.

The question of greatest import to the lands of the Caribbean is whether it is possible to organize for development around a new concept of regionalism defined by ocean space. Coming from diverse social and cultural backgrounds, can the Caribbean peoples forge a creative force for common benefit from their two points of convergence—the need for development and their relationship to the sea? A model for this pioneering form of regional organization, consonant with the Latin American Seabed Draft Treaty, is the subject of the next section.

A Model for the Caribbean Community

With relatively few adaptations, the Latin American Seabed Draft Treaty could serve as a model for a regional organization for ocean development in the Caribbean. My purpose in this section will be to discuss this model in terms of the following categories: functions, membership, organs, and fiscal measures. Following these considerations we will turn to an interim procedure for establishment of the Community.

Functions

The functions of the Caribbean Community basically should be consonant with those outlined in Article 14 of the Latin American Seabed Draft Treaty. The modifications in these items would simply take into account the regional rather than global nature of the organization. The functions, with modifications, would be as follows:

To provide for the orderly and safe development and rational management of the area and its resources for the benefit of the

people of the Caribbean, with due regard for the welfare of suc-
ceeding generations [In this item "the people of the Caribbean"
has been substituted for the word "mankind"; the final phrase
beginning, "with due regard . . . ," has been added.]

To undertake scientific research in the area.

To undertake exploration of the area and exploitation of its
resources as well as all activities relating to production, processing, and marketing.

To provide for the equitable sharing of benefits deriving from
the exploration of the area and the exploitation of its resources,
taking into account the special interests and needs of the developing countries, whether landlocked or coastal, in accordance with
precise criteria to be established by the Assembly. [The qualifica-
tion "taking into account the special interests and needs of the
developing countries, whether landlocked or coastal" can be omit-
ted since all regional members of the Caribbean Community will
be developing.]

To take all necessary measures, including control, reduction,
or suspension of production or fixing of prices of products obtained from exploitation of the area, whenever it deems that such
production may have adverse economic effects for developing
countries, exporters of raw materials [This item should remain a
principle of planning for the region.]

To take measures to prevent, mitigate, or eliminate pollution
or the threat of pollution as well as any other hazardous occurrences resulting from or caused by any activities in the area [While
there has been a generalized downgrading of the importance of
pollution-control measures in developing areas, this item has important implications for the development of the Caribbean region
due to the economic potential of tourism in much of the area.]

To coordinate in all matters of common concern with the
appropriate organs of the global ocean authority [This item has
been substituted for the item quoted earlier in this article on the
establishment of regional or subregional facilities.]

To take measures to ensure the implementation of the principles and provisions of this convention.

Membership

I conceive of two classes of membership in the community, regular and
associate.

Regular membership would be open to all nations and dependencies in the region and would carry with it the right to choose representatives to the Assembly. To qualify for regular membership, a dependency would have to guarantee its right to local autonomy in regional matters.

Associate membership would be open to scientific organizations and organizations and associations concerned with the use of the sea for the development of living and nonliving resources, transportation, communication, and tourism. Associate members would serve as nominators for the scientific and industrial representatives to the Assembly.

Organs

The Caribbean Community for Ocean Development shall consist of:

the Assembly
the Council
the Enterprise
the Institute
the Secretariat
the Tribunal

Each will be discussed in turn below.

The Assembly. The Assembly shall be the supreme organ of the Caribbean Community for Ocean Development.

All states and dependencies which are Regular Members of the Community shall be represented in the Assembly.

In considering the manner of voting in the Assembly, there are three possible choices: unanimity, one vote to each state, or an attribute-based voting allocation by state. I would reject unanimity or a rule of consensus in a group with interests and backgrounds as diverse as in the Caribbean. With such a severe decisional rule as unanimity, I would fear that the amount agreed to would be minimal, thus minimizing potential benefits from regional organization.

The Latin American Seabed Draft Treaty allows one vote to each member of the organization. In this case, however, I would not follow the draft treaty. This is primarily because of the large differences in the population and area sizes of the states and dependencies of the region. To give each of the British Associated States and Colonies one vote in the Assembly would be to weight the voting heavily in favor of the small dependencies, and thereby probably doom the organization to failure at the outset. The larger states in the region, particularly the big three of Colombia, Mexico, and Venezuela, would be unlikely to enter an organization in which they would be consistently outvoted by a collection of colonial dependencies; in fact, it would seem likely that all independent nations in the region would adopt this perspective.

The final alternative is that of an attribute-based voting allocation. In this method certain attributes of members are given prime consideration in determining the allocation of Assembly votes for each member. While this method in no way impugns the principle of state sovereignty, it does allow salient characteristics with regard to the proposed Community to be emphasized in the allocation of votes.

There is precedent for this method of allocating votes in the European Economic Community, in which the original voting allocation was: Belgium, 14; France, 36; Germany, 36; Italy, 36; Luxembourg, 6; and the Netherlands, 14. As the EEC is primarily an economic organization, the allocation of Assembly votes was based on economic attributes. Because of its different function, I would allocate votes according to other criteria in the Caribbean Community.

The two attributes I would select in forming the voting model for the Caribbean Community are population and shoreline in the area. These attributes would balance representation in the Assembly by emphasizing the size of the entity involved in terms of its inhabitants and its relationship to the area as measured by its shoreline on the Caribbean. The first criterion, while recognizing sovereignty, places voting emphasis on the number of people represented. The second criterion allows a balancing factor for the degree to which an entity is connected to the area. For example, this criterion allows for a state like Mexico, with a large population but a relatively small shoreline on the Caribbean, to be allocated less votes in the Assembly than a state with a large population and a large shoreline in the region.

Table 17.1 shows the voting allocation for each state and dependency in the region, based on the two attributes discussed above. I have used a four-point scale (1–4) for population, and a five-point scale (0–4) for shoreline. I attempted to make divisions at what seemed like natural cutoff points separating clusters of entities, but undoubtedly there has been some arbitrariness to my decisional points. My feeling is that final decision on matters of scaling is a relatively small point, and the achievement of some consensus on attributes is what is most crucial. Entities are assigned a zero on shoreline if they do not border on the region; only those states and dependencies are included in this category which, as we discussed earlier, have some traditional connection with the region (the Bahamas, El Salvador, French Guiana, Guyana, and Surinam).

In all, there would be 97 votes in the Assembly if all states and dependencies, including the French territories, joined the organization. Seventy-eight, or roughly three-quarters of these, would be controlled by

AN ATTRIBUTE-BASED VOTING PLAN FOR THE CARIBBEAN COMMUNITY ASSEMBLY

State	Population[a]	Population Voting Allocation[b]	Shoreline[c] (miles)	Shoreline Voting Allocation[d]	Total Voting Allocation
Barbados	301,000	1	30	1	2
Bahamas	148,000	1	0	0	1
Guyana	721,000	2	0	0	2
Trinidad and Tobago	1,100,000	2	175	2	4
Panama	1,500,000	2	340	2	4
Costa Rica	1,800,000	2	115	2	4
Jamaica	2,000,000	2	290	2	4
Nicaragua	2,000,000	2	260	2	4
Honduras	2,700,000	3	330	2	5
El Salvador	3,400,000	3	0	0	3
Dominican Republic	4,300,000	3	175	2	5
Guatemala	5,100,000	3	50	1	4
Haiti	5,200,000	3	450	3	6
Cuba	8,400,000	4	950	4	8
Venezuela	10,800,000	4	1,080	4	8
Colombia	21,116,000	4	576	4	8
Mexico	50,700,000	4	225	2	6
Total		45		33	78

Dependency

Puerto Rico and U.S. Virgin Islands	2,700,000 (130,000)	3	150	2	5
Surinam	425,000	1	0	0	1
Netherlands Antilles	214,000	1	—	1	2
British Associated States and Smaller Colonies[e]	550,000 (approx)	2	—	3	5
British Honduras	106,000	1	—	2	3
Guadaloupe/ Martinique/French Guiana	750,000	2	—	1	3
Total		10		9	19
State and dependency total		55		42	97

[a]Population statistics taken from the *New York Times Encyclopedic Almanac, 1971.* Figures are generally 1970 estimates. While these figures may be slightly low, they are sufficient, since the concern here is more with relative than absolute population.
[b]The following cutoff points were used in determining the voting allocations:

$$0-500,000 = 1$$
$$500,001-2,500,000 = 2$$
$$2,500,001-7,500,000 = 3$$
$$7,500,001 \text{ and above} = 4$$

[c]Shoreline statistics are taken from Robert D. Hodgson, "The American Mediterranean: One Sea, One Region?" *Gulf and Caribbean Problems: Law of the Sea Workshop* (Kingston, R.I.: Law of the Sea Institute, 1973), pp. 7–15. Figures on the shoreline lengths of dependencies were not supplied, and the voting allocations listed on these are thus rough estimates and may require alteration.
[d]The following cutoff points were used in determining voting allocations:

$$1-99 = 1$$
$$100-349 = 2$$
$$350-549 = 3$$
$$500 \text{ and above} = 4$$

[e]The smaller colonies include the British Virgin Islands (59,000), the Cayman Islands (9,000), and Montserrat (15,000).

the states in the region, and the remaining quarter would be controlled by the dependencies. This is pointed out to show how the attribute-based voting alters the situation from one in which the dependencies would have a majority of votes on a one state-one vote basis. I would add, however, that there is no reason to expect that any coalition would form along the lines of states versus dependencies.

Cuba, Venezuela, and Colombia would all have the maximum number of votes possible—eight—while at the other end of the spectrum, Surinam and the Bahamas would have one vote each. The British Associated States and smaller colonies would have a total of five votes among nine dependencies. The largest of the dependencies, Puerto Rico, would have a total of five votes, on a par with Honduras and the Dominican Republic. Twelve of the 23 entities listed in Table 17.1 would have between four and six votes in the Assembly; eight entities would have three or less votes, and the remaining three would have eight votes each.

Each state and dependency should be allowed to send one delegate to the Assembly for each of its allocated votes. The selection of delegates to the Assembly should be made by the parliaments of each regular member. In the case of a cluster of dependencies such as the British Associated States and smaller colonies, the delegates should be selected by a meeting of parliamentary representatives of all entities included in the cluster.

The first delegate from each state or dependency should be a member of the parliament from which he is chosen. The second delegate should be chosen by the parliament from a list of nominations put forward by either the scientific associate members in that country or by the industrial associate members in that country. If the second delegate is a representative of science, the third delegate should be a representative of ocean industry (fishing, mining, transportation, tourism, etc.). This process of rotation should be continued for the choice of all delegates.

With the exception of the rules for voting and for the choice of delegates discussed above, the Assembly should operate in basically the manner described in the Latin American Seabed Draft Treaty. It should meet in ordinary session annually and be called into extraordinary session in the manner described in the draft treaty; that is, by the secretary-general at the request of the council or of a simple majority of the members. Decisions should be taken in the Assembly by a majority of the members present and voting.

The powers of the Assembly would correspond closely with those outlined in Article 24 of the draft treaty:

> To elect the president and other officers.
> To elect the members of the council after having determined

the group to which each contracting party will belong for the purpose of those elections, in accordance with the terms of Article _____ on the distribution of seats. [This item would be altered to read as follows: "To elect the members of the council from among its own membership. The council must include at least three parliamentary representatives, three representatives of science, and three representatives of industry. No two members of a single state or dependency may serve on the council at any one time."]

To determine its rules of procedure and constitute such subsidiary organs as it may consider necessary or desirable.

To decide on questions of contribution.

To approve the community's budget.

To consider the annual reports from the council and the secretary-general, as well as any special ones which it may receive, including those submitted upon its own request.

To approve the regulations proposed by the council relating to the formation of contracts and joint ventures with juridical persons, duly sponsored by states for the exploitation of the area.

To approve the report of the Enterprise, submitted through the council.

To adopt precise criteria for the sharing of benefits as well as approve annually the plan submitted by the council on the basis of such criteria.

To decide from time to time which parts of the area are open to exploration and exploitation, and to establish, as may be deemed necessary for the orderly development of the area and preservation of the marine environment and its living resources, reserve areas free from exploration and exploitation.

I would add the following three items to the functions of the Assembly:

To elect five directors of the Ocean Enterprise from among nominations put forward by the Industrial Associates.

To elect a five-member advisory board of the Institute from among nominations put forward by the Science Associates.

To ratify the appointment of members of the tribunal.

The Council. The Council shall be composed of 11 members chosen by the Assembly from among its own membership and shall include at least three representatives each of parliaments, science, and industry. Members of the Council shall serve for a period of three years, as specified in the draft treaty and be eligible for reelection. No two members of a single state or dependency shall be allowed to serve on the Council at any one time.

The primary function of the Council shall be to prepare for the Assembly an annual planning proposal. This proposal shall consist of a short-range (one-year) plan for ocean development in the Caribbean, and medium-range (five-year) and long-range (10-year) plans, which, after the initial proposal shall be annually revised and updated. The Council should incorporate into the annual proposal activities to be undertaken by the Institute and Enterprise. The annual planning proposal, as with all other substantive decisions made by the Council, shall require affirmation by a two-thirds majority of the Council members present and voting.

The powers and duties of the Council, in addition to preparing the annual planning proposal, should be basically those articulated in Article 32 of the draft treaty.

To submit annual reports to the Assembly as well as special reports which it may deem necessary or when requested by the Assembly.

To determine its rules of procedure.

To propose to the Assembly the establishment of subsidiary organs, as may be necessary or desirable, and the definition of their duties.

To make recommendations to the Assembly as to the contribution of member States.

To submit proposed budgets to the Assembly for its approval and supervise their execution.

To issue regulations pertaining to all activities undertaken in the area, including those related to the resources thereof, and supervise those activities in accordance with such criteria as may be laid down by the Assembly.

To submit to the Assembly proposed rules and regulations on the formation of joint ventures with juridical persons, duly sponsored by States, for the exploration and exploitation of the area.

To submit to the Assembly the scale of distribution among contracting parties of benefits from activities in the area.

To authorize scientific research in the area.

To set rules and standards for the prevention of pollution and contamination of the marine environment from seabed activities.

To adopt, for the benefit of developing countries, measures designed to attain the aims set forth in Article 16 [This item need not be retained since all countries in the region may be classified as developing.].

To make recommendations to the Assembly with respect to reserve areas [as provided for in Article 24(j)].

I would add the following function to the work of the Council:

To appoint the members of the Tribunal subject to the ratification of the Assembly.

The enterprise. One of the most innovative aspects of the Latin American Seabed Draft Treaty is its inclusion of a Seabed Enterprise. The Enterprise would serve as the organ of the authority "empowered to undertake all technical, industrial, or commercial activities relating to the exploration of the area and exploitation of its resources (by itself, or in joint ventures with juridical persons duly sponsored by States)." This would allow the Authority the ability to engage in direct exploitation of the area and mitigate the necessity of bringing in outside corporations for this purpose. The option of bringing in outside corporations to work in conjunction with the Enterprise would not, however, be foreclosed.

The major advantage of the Enterprise at the global level would be that it would allow for greater control over resource exploitation. The ocean authority could take the precautions necessary to protect the less-developed nations from economic injury which could result from ocean exploitation of a mineral which was exported by an underdeveloped area. While this would probably be of only marginal importance for a regional Enterprise in an underdeveloped area such as the Caribbean, the creation of a regional Enterprise in the Caribbean could serve as a model for a global Enterprise when the machinery for a global Ocean Regime is established.

While the Latin American Seabed Draft Treaty limits the activities of the Enterprise to the Seabed due to the context of the UN Seabed Committee discussions, there is no reason that the work of the Enterprise should be conceived of in this limited way in the Caribbean. It would be possible, for example, for the Enterprise to undertake projects in offshore hydrocarbon exploitation, deep-sea mining, aquaculture, intra-Caribbean tourism and transportation, ocean energy, etc. At the request of a regular member of the Community, the Enterprise could also enter into contract with that member for the development of resources within the territorial sea of the contracting party.

The criteria for undertaking Enterprise projects would be regional need and profitability. The decision to undertake specific projects would ultimately be that of the Caribbean Community Assembly.

The Enterprise would be run like a business corporation. Control of the Enterprise would be maintained by the Caribbean Community. Directors would be appointed by the Assembly in accord with the percentage of the Enterprise controlled by the Community. At no time could the Community control less than 51 percent of the stock in the Enterprise, and at least five of the nine directors. However, the Community may control as much as 100 percent of the Enterprise. The decision on this matter would be that of the Assembly.

The sale of stock in the Enterprise would be one method of raising capital for Enterprise projects. It would also provide a method of bringing in outside corporations with needed technical expertise without allowing them a controlling interest in the exploitation of any portion of the area.

The directors of the Enterprise will submit an annual report of activities and earnings to the Council. They will also submit to the Council an annual budget request. A representative of the Enterprise will coordinate closely with the Council in the preparation of the annual planning proposal.

The Institute. The establishment of oceanographic institutions on a regional basis is proposed in the Latin American Seabed Draft Treaty for "the training of nationals of developing countries in all aspects of marine science and technology." I would suggest that the Institute be given broader functions and conceived of as an ocean, rather than oceanographic, institution. Among the functions for the Institute, I would include:

Performance of scientific investigations at the request of other organs of the Community.

Compilation of statistics on ocean development in the region.

Organization of information-retrieval systems of all scientific work related to ocean development in the region.

Conducting of experiments in mariculture.

Testing for pollution in the area.

Participation in conferences on marine development located in other parts of the world.

Sponsorship of conferences on marine development in the Caribbean.

Coordination with other regional institutes.

At the outset, the Institute could be organized around a small, interdisciplinary faculty and a small number of graduate students. It is felt that connection with one of the universities in the region would be essential to the success of the Institute in providing facilities for its staff without a large capital investment.

The Institute shall have a five-member advisory board chosen by the Assembly from among nominations from the Science Associates. The advisory board shall name a director of the Institute who shall appoint a staff in accord with rules approved by the Assembly.

The Institute's research program shall be determined by the director and the faculty. They shall also perform research requested by the Assembly or Council.

The Institute shall have absolute freedom with regard to all publications and news releases.

The secretariat. The Secretariat shall be an international civil service responsible for administrative functions within the Caribbean Community. The chief administrative officer, the secretary-general, shall be elected by the Assembly for a five-year term. The duties and functions of the Secretariat and the Secretary-General are outlined in Articles 36 to 45 of the Latin American Seabed Draft Treaty:

> There shall be a secretary-general elected by the Assembly for a term of five years. The secretary-general shall be the chief administrative officer of the Authority (Community).
>
> The secretary-general shall act in that capacity in all meetings of the Assembly and the council and shall perform such other duties as are entrusted to him by these organs. He shall make an annual report to the Assembly on the work of the Authority (Community).
>
> The secretary-general shall act in an advisory capacity to the Enterprise.
>
> The secretary-general shall be responsible for the distribution of all information obtained from scientific research in the area.
>
> The secretary-general shall draw the attention of the council to any matter which in his opinion may require its urgent consideration.
>
> In the performance of their duties the secretary-general and the staff shall not seek or receive instructions from any government or from any other authority external to the Authority (Community). They shall refrain from any action which might reflect on their position as international officials responsible only to the Authority (Community).
>
> Each member of the Authority (Community) undertakes to respect the exclusively international character of the responsibilities of the secretary-general and the staff and shall not seek to influence them in the discharge of their responsibilities.
>
> The staff shall be appointed by the secretary-general under regulations established by the Assembly.
>
> Appropriate staffs shall be permanently assigned to the As-

sembly and the Council and, as required, to other organs of the Authority (Community). These staffs shall form a part of the secretariat.

The paramount consideration in the employment of the staff and in the determination of the conditions of service shall be the necessity of securing the highest standards of efficiency, competence, and integrity. Due regard shall be paid to the importance of recruiting the staff on as wide a geographical basis as possible (from within the region).

The Tribunal. The Latin American Seabed Draft Treaty includes a chapter on the settlement of disputes but does not specify any method. The manner of dispute settlement is left open, but the inclusion of a chapter on this subject should be taken as a sign of concern.

I would suggest that the Community establish an organ for the peaceful settlement of disputes, to be known as the Tribunal. The Tribunal would be composed of seven members of outstanding judicial standing appointed by the Council and ratified by the Assembly. No two members of a single state or dependency may serve at any one time on the tribunal.

Fiscal Measures

The preparation of an annual budget shall be the responsibility of the Council. The budget shall be submitted to the Assembly for approval.

It is anticipated that at the outset of establishing the Caribbean Community for Ocean Development, costs will be greater than revenues. During this period certain options will be available for raising the needed revenues. One method, previously discussed, would be the sale of stock in the Enterprise. It may be preferable, however, not to rely on this method at the outset when stock must be sold relatively cheaply on the promise of potential profit. It would seem advantageous to establish the profitability of developing the area's resources on a small scale and then issue stock in order to finance a larger scale of production.

A second method of gaining revenues to finance the initial costs of the organization would be to seek support from the United Nations Development Programme or other international funding source. A source such as the UNDP, however, is not to be relied on for the total financing of the organization. While the potential for attaining matching funds for a regional development program is probably good, it would be unrealistic to expect 100 percent support. Thus it would seem that there is probably no alternative to the members of the Community making some direct investment in the organization at the outset.

The criteria for assessing contributions from among the membership should be given serious consideration. One alternative would be to assess each regular member on the basis of its GNP with a weighting factor for its GNP/capita. Thus if two states had an equal GNP, a higher assessment would be made of the state with a lower population (and therefore higher GNP/capita).

A second alternative would be to make assessments to states and dependencies on the basis of their uses of the Caribbean Sea, with a limit of not more than 1 percent of revenues from such activities as passenger shipping (on sales price of tickets); freight (cargo-miles); military uses of the Caribbean Sea (ship-days); off-shore oil; desalination and in-solution mining; recreation (on the basis of tourist tax); dumping; industrial and domestic waste; cables (on the price of messages).[4] The assessment for usage could also be combined with a weighting factor for GNP/capita.

The alternative of assessing for area usage would be advantageous in setting a precedent for assessing non-Community members equally for their uses of the Caribbean. Compliance could be enforced by refusing access to landing, repair, and fueling facilities.

Certain contributions could also be made to the Community in the form of facilities and services. The contribution of university space for the Caribbean Ocean Institute is an example.

Interim Procedure

In order to move toward the establishment of the Caribbean Community for Ocean Development, a preliminary convention must be held. This convention, which could be called by one or all of the signatory states to the Latin American Seabed Draft Treaty, should bring together representatives from all independent nations in the Caribbean. The constituting body of the regional organization would thus consist of Mexico, Cuba, Jamaica, Haiti, Dominican Republic, Barbados, Trinidad and Tobago, Venezuela, Colombia, Panama, Costa Rica, Nicaragua, Honduras, and Guatemala. The primary purpose of the convention would be to create a charter for the regional organization that would be acceptable to all parties involved. Within the confines of this general directive, a number of specific decisions would need to be made.

First, a decision would have to be taken on the scope of regular membership in the organization. Are the dependencies to be included? If so, under what conditions? If the suggestion put forward in this article, that dependencies be admitted only if they can guarantee their right to local

---

[4]These suggestions on taxation were developed by Elisabeth Mann Borgese in her article, "A Mediterranean Council to Combat Pollution."

autonomy in regional matters, is accepted, what are the criteria for this guarantee to be? A decision will also need to be made on the inclusion of the states and dependencies with close ties to the area but not actually bordering on the Caribbean—that is, the Bahamas, El Salvador, French Guiana, Guyana, and Surinam. Are these entities to be offered regular membership in the organization?

Once decisions on regular membership are made, the convention must consider the problem of voting in the Assembly. Is an attribute-based voting scheme acceptable? If so, are population and shoreline in the region acceptable attributes on which to allocate votes? Once the criteria for a voting scheme are agreed to, it will be necessary to reach agreement on the scaling techniques and criteria for establishing cutoff points between, for example, population sizes.

One further aspect of the Assembly procedure should be considered by the convention. This relates specifically to the selection of representatives to the Assembly. I have suggested that the the Assembly be chosen by national parliaments and include, in addition to parliamentary representatives, representatives of science and industry nominated by the science and industry associates in that state. I consider this aspect of my proposal crucial to the success of the regional organization. That is, I consider it crucial that representatives of science and industry be given a decisional role in the organization rather than simply technocratic advisory or consultative functions. The inclusion of representatives of science and industry in the Assembly is designed to broaden the base of Community decision-making to include expertise in problems of ocean development, including knowledge of potentially hazardous side effects of proposed projects.

With the foregoing agreed on, the next agenda item for the constituting body should be to reach some accord on criteria for associate membership in the organization. I would suggest that the criteria allow for associations and organizations with transnational as well as national membership to be awarded associate status. When criteria for associate membership have been established, the convention should solicit membership applications from national and transnational scientific and industrial associations and organizations in the region. The convention should have the authority to approve applications in order that associate members will be able to make nominations for the first Community Assembly.

The next decision to be reached by the convention relates to the necessary funding for the establishment of the Caribbean Community for Ocean Development. This could be accomplished by working out a budget sufficient to convene the first Assembly and council, provide supportive staff from the secretariat, and establish the institute. All of this could be accomplished for a budget of between $500,000 and $750,000. This would mean that if assessments are weighted by GNP as a percentage of regional GNP and by GNP/capita, the organization could be founded on contributions ranging from $10,000 to $100,000 by the founding members of the Community.

Questions related to the distribution of revenues, when they become available, should be deferred to the Community Assembly for decision. The convention could, however, consider laying down charter guidelines with regard to the allocation of revenues. I would suggest the following three principles in accord with applying the common-heritage principle at the regional level. First, all revenues should be applied to programs of development. Second, it would seem appropriate that revenues be distributed in accord with intraregional need; that is, an attempt should be made to close the "progress gap" within the region and bring all regional entities up to agreed-upon primary developmental levels. The third principle would be the funding of pilot projects with regionwide applications in developmental areas such as health, education, and nutrition. Some examples of regional programs of interest to developing countries are listed in a United Nations report by the Secretary-General issued in 1971.[5] They include:

> Educational programs designed to supply the skills required for the implementation of economic development plans in developing countries.
>
> Development of labor-intensive technology which might be more appropriate for the industrial requirements of developing countries.
>
> Surveys of natural resource availability in developing countries, which could be brought into use to promote development.
>
> Comprehensive programs for the development of infrastructure services—transportation, energy, communications, water, etc.

A final area which the convention should take under consideration and build into the charter of the organization, in addition to those touched on in other sections of this article, is the relationship of the regional organization to the global Ocean Regime to be established. I have listed among the functions of the Community that it "coordinate on all matters of common concern with the appropriate organs of the global authority." This could

[5]"Possible Methods and Criteria for the Sharing by the International Community of Proceeds and Other Benefits Derived from the Exploitation of the Resources of the Area beyond the Limits of National Jurisdiction," A/AC.138/38, June 15, 1971.

entail the undertaking of joint ventures in the area involving the regional and global Enterprises. It could also entail the use by the regional organization of the global judicial system, perhaps eliminating the need for the regional judicial apparatus. One final aspect of coordination which should certainly be involved is the sharing of information between regional institutes.

The final product of the constituting convention should be a charter for the Caribbean Community for Ocean Development prepared in treaty format open for signature by states and dependencies designated as regular members.

Conclusion

Two major themes resonating through our time are the need for development and the recognition of the oceans as the common heritage of mankind. These themes join together along the shores of the Caribbean Sea and suggest an unprecedented experiment in regional cooperation among the developing countries to achieve developmental goals. I have sought in this chapter to provide impetus and a tentative form for this experiment by pointing out the applications of the Latin American Seabed Draft Treaty to a regional organization for ocean development in the Caribbean. At this point, there is nothing unusual in the concept of regional organization for development. The uniqueness of the Caribbean experiment would lie first, in its organization around ocean space for community development of ocean resources and second, in the self-reliance of a developing area on its own ability to develop its resources.

Critics will undoubtedly raise questions as to what possible interest Cuba could share with Barbados or Haiti with Costa Rica. The answer can be found only in the common concern of these nations for development and the efficient exploitation of the wealth to be derived from the Caribbean Sea. Presumably none of the nations in the area would prefer to see a vast source of wealth sit unexploited or be exploited by others.

Regional organization for exploitation of Caribbean resources offers the promise of increased wealth. We should not fool ourselves, however, that this wealth will be immediately forthcoming. It most likely will not be, as it will certainly require exploration and possibly technological advances as well to achieve. One fact I think we can be reasonably sure of, however, is that the wealth is there. At a minimum, proper planning in mariculture could supply the area with much needed protein to make up current nutritional deficiencies.

Future limits on deriving wealth from the seas will most probably be limitations of human imagination, and as these limitations are slowly eroded, great sources of wealth will become available for development. The question confronting the nations of the Caribbean is whether they will be organized and prepared to exploit the wealth of the Caribbean Sea, the semi-enclosed sea to which all are linked, as it becomes increasingly possible to do so.

PART V

SCIENTIFIC RESEARCH
IN THE OCEANS

The conduct of scientific research in the oceans raises two major clusters of problems, both interconnected. One concerns the *participation of scientists* in the decision-making processes of the ocean institutions. Given the fundamental importance of science for any economic or political decision on the uses of ocean space and resources, we need institutional arrangements which *promote synergy* between economics, science, and politics. The other problem cluster concerns the *freedom of research* in the oceans.

Theoretically, freedom of research is of equal interest to all people and all nations. Science is the common heritage of mankind par excellence, and it should be managed by all nations cooperatively for the benefit of all. Furthermore, science in the oceans is at the vanguard of all sciences, in two ways. First, the new understanding of marine geology is revolutionizing our understanding of the geology and history of the earth. Second, the very nature of ocean research makes it mandatory, due to the nature of the world ocean itself, that this research be carried out internationally. The nation that opts out of this science in fact opts out of modern civilization, opts out of development.

This, however, is theory. *Practically* there can be no doubt that the industrialized nations have a far greater immediate return from unrestrained scientific research in the oceans than do the developing nations, who are not equipped to participate in, and often, even to evaluate, the results of the research. There can be no doubt that in the developed nations, scientific research is inextricably linked with both industrial and military interests. The line between "pure" and "basic" research, commercially valuable exploration and military reconnoitering, is impossible to draw. Publication of the results is not an adequate answer if what is "published" is undecipherable to the developing nations along whose coasts the research is carried out. The case of the developing nations that want to control and restrict such research is as ironclad as the case of the developed nations demanding freedom of research.

A solution might be found in the *internationalization* of research by means of the establishment of a "scientific enterprise," that is, an international ocean research institute in whose management and policy-making both developed and developing nations would participate and which would be under the control of the governing organs of the international ocean regime. Such an institute would guarantee that ocean research be pure. It would interpret data; it would serve as a training center for scientists from the developing nations; and it would accelerate the transfer of knowledge and technologies. Only science channeled through such an International Ocean Institute should be free and unrestricted. Developing nations would be justified in keeping their defenses up against national research not so channeled.

Such a "scientific enterprise" would be the linchpin between the two sets of problems here indicated: It would provide both for *participation of scientists* in decision-making and for *freedom of research.*

In Part V, Professor Fye reports the difficulties he has experienced as a representative of a developed nation, because of the erosion of the concept of freedom of research. Professor Wooster gives an analysis of various atti-

304

tudes taken by various countries with regard to this problem. In conclusion, we present a *declaration* adopted by Pacem in Maribus II aimed at a resolution of these issues.

Dr. Fye is director of the Woods Hole Oceanographic Institution. Warren Wooster, formerly of Scripps Oceanographic Institution, is now at the University of Miami, Florida.

CHAPTER 18

Scientific Research in the Ocean

PAUL M. FYE

As one who spends at least a portion of his time at the operating end of this ocean business and as head of an oceanographic laboratory which operates ships on a worldwide scale, I can assure you that it is indeed getting progressively more difficult to carry out scientific investigations at sea. This is due in part to the increasing costs of operating ships and the accompanying difficulty of raising money to support these costs, in part to the increased sophistication of the research techniques being used, and perhaps most of all, due to the complexity of the questions being asked of nature about the oceans.

I shall limit my remarks to the artificial restrictions being imposed with distressingly increasing frequency on the scientist whose natural curiosity has impelled him to ask these questions about the oceans. Unfortunately, the restrictions are often imposed by states unnecessarily and unwisely, for reasons having little to do with the value, or even the necessity, of conducting the particular scientific research in question. This is being done partly because of a lack of understanding of the value of the scientific work to the nation imposing the restrictions, also perhaps because of a general devaluation of scientific endeavors, but mostly because of a concern that the information will be used to benefit others or for reasons completely unrelated to the scientific questions, for example, national pride, propaganda, or protection of national rights.

I remember nostalgically the first scientific expedition on which I was chief scientist, more than 25 years ago. Our plans took us into the territorial waters of a friendly nation and clearance was accomplished by a single letter

306

from Columbus Iselin, then the distinguished director of the Woods Hole Oceanographic Institution, to the head of that government, together with a letter in my hand indicating my credentials as chief scientist. Not only did this provide the necessary clearance, it also resulted in a grand reception at the Governor's Palace for the entire crew of the *Atlantis*.

I have no illusions that the present director could cut red tape so neatly today. Not only would a letter from me be ineffective in many parts of the world, but my own government would be distressed that I had taken matters into my hands, which they felt could be better left to Washington.

Perhaps I might give a few examples of difficulty or failure in obtaining clearance for basic scientific research to be conducted within areas restricted in one way or another by national action that have come to my attention.

The first illustration was a case when I was chief scientist again for a portion of the cruise. In this case, there was private correspondence with scientists in the nation concerned and with high government officials, with a long lead time of over a year before the cruise was to take place. Also, official requests had been filed through governmental channels. We were given every reason to believe that clearance was forthcoming, even as late as the leaving of the last port of call. However, for reasons never stated and which I suspect may have been entirely political, the request was denied, and at a time so late that I had no choice but to direct the captain to proceed through contested waters claiming the right of innocent passage but with all scientific equipment (even the fathometer) turned off.

Within recent months and on two different occasions, we found it necessary to cancel plans concerned with the study of "upwelling." Upwelling is a phenomenon whereby bottom waters rich in nutrients are brought to the surface by upward-flowing currents. Since all life in the sea, just as on the land, is supported by the photosynthetic process which takes place only in the sunlit surface layers, this process is nature's way of refertilizing the ocean. Areas of upwelling are generally areas of good fishing. Since the physical phenomenon producing the upwelling in both these cases was the movement of surface water away from the shore caused by offshore winds, the phenomenon occurred close to the beach and in part within the territorial waters of the coastal states. Our scientists were disappointed in not being able to carry out their scientific plans. However, I would submit that the coastal state was by far the greater loser. Any fishery based on such work would be under its control and benefit its people more than others.

I should note here that in these cases, as in any work from our institution conducted in waters adjacent to that of another state, we invite scientists of that state to participate in the cruise, give them copies of relevant data, and publish the results in open scientific literature available to the entire world. In fact, we send more than 1,000 copies of our collected reprints to libraries and scientists around the world each year.

I should probably add that in one of these cases the fault was partly our own, in that the request was only forwarded a few months in advance, and perhaps this was insufficient to process it through all the bureaucratic red tape. But this requirement of long lead times is also an impediment in conducting scientific research.

Nations do have legitimate reasons for concern about research vessels operating in their waters; yet I submit that the interest of the entire international community, including the coastal state concerned, is preserved. Ambassador Pardo has pointed this out much better than I could, and I shall quote briefly from him:

> Scientific research is in modern times not undertaken merely to satisfy the curiosity of a few scientists about the world in which we live. It is an essential prerequisite to technological advance: drafting of rational regulations to control ocean pollution is impossible without continuing research; only through research are we able to locate seabed areas likely to contain mineral deposits; management of living resources of the seas is inconceivable without intense and continuing scientific research. Scientific research in short is the condition *sine qua non* for the development of the oceans for the benefit of mankind. It must consequently enjoy maximum freedom.

Surely no intelligent person today would suggest that scientific curiosity should cease as the scientist proceeds from deep water into the shallow waters of the continental shelf; everyone will agree that many oceanographic studies can best be carried out when we have international cooperation; almost everyone would agree that many scientific questions can be answered only by exploring our natural world without restrictions imposed by national boundaries or national claims.

Some of my scientific colleagues have expressed grave doubts that sufficient freedom can be preserved so that the science of the seas can continue to flourish. I am not quite so pessimistic. It seems likely that wise men will work together, as for example in the Sea-Bed Committee, and out of their collective wisdom will come a variety of supranational regimes: regimes for the deep seabed, for the control of ocean pollution, and for international cooperative measures of many types. These regimes will necessarily require information that can be supplied only by continued scientific research. How can they get the necessary information to wisely carry out their functions? I suppose they could attempt to buy it by contracting with existing laboratories and institutions; or they could set up organizations of their own to go out and conduct the appropriate investigations; or they could use some other device. I would hope, however, that those charged with the responsibility of these regimes would be wise enough (and I believe they will be) to realize that scientific research can flourish only in an atmosphere of complete freedom.

No government official, no head of business, indeed, no laboratory director is smart enough to know what information he will need in the future. Indeed, committees of scientists have demonstrated great ineptness (on occasion) in attempting to define scientific questions of highest priority.

As in all intellectual endeavors, whether it be composing a symphony, painting, or writing, the best we administrators can do is to let the perpetrators have free reign and hope—or even require—that they share the results with all of us. I am hopeful that such freedoms will be assured for all time.

CHAPTER 19

Conditions for Ocean Research

WARREN S. WOOSTER

The problem of limitations on scientific research in the ocean is of recent origin. Before 1958 scientific research was universally regarded as one of the freedoms of the high seas. Claims of national jurisdiction were reasonably restrained, and most of the ocean was "high seas"; there were no special provisions for the seabed. The 1958 Convention on the Continental Shelf initiated a major change whereby coastal state jurisdiction was extended over an ill-defined shelf and a consent requirement for research "concerning the continental shelf and conducted there" was imposed. At the same time, scientific research was conspicuously absent from the freedoms listed in the Convention on the High Seas. Thus began a period of increasing limitation of ocean investigation, subsequently accelerated by further unilateral extensions of coastal state jurisdictions.

The change in attitude toward scientific research was stimulated by an increased realization of the potential value of seabed resources. The suspicion arose that a distinct advantage in resource exploitation accrued to the advanced countries that were conducting oceanographic research. The distinctions between research, exploration, and exploitation became blurred. Subsequent debates in the new seabed committee and elsewhere have revealed little understanding of the nature of scientific research or its role in development, management, and preservation of the ocean resource. Meanwhile, the possibilities of working at sea have been considerably and steadily reduced.

The Intergovernmental Oceanographic Commission in 1969 attempted to reverse the trend by its resolution (VI-13) promoting fundamental scientific research, in which a procedure was established to facilitate obtaining coastal state permission for such research. Implementation of this resolution has been bitterly opposed by several states, and to my knowledge, the procedure has never been successfully used.

Many of us hoped that the General Assembly would include specific endorsement of the freedom of scientific research in its Declaration of Principles Governing the Sea-Bed and Ocean Floor (Res. 2749/XXV). But the only mention (principle 10) concerns international cooperation in peaceful scientific research through participation in international programs, international dissemination of results, and strengthening of research capabilities of developing countries. Even this inoffensive statement was accompanied by a legal disclaimer. The US Working Paper goes little further, merely adding: "Each Contracting Party agrees to encourage, and to obviate interference with, scientific research." It is hard to accept such statements as ironclad guarantees, ringing endorsements, or even reassuring steps toward facilitating scientific research.

In an attempt to clarify the issues the US National Academy of Science's Committee on Oceanography proposed the establishment of an international working group to evaluate the need for freedom of scientific research in the ocean and the obligations implied by that freedom, and to examine the consequences for scientific research of the various alternative ocean regimes. The proposal was made to the Scientific Committee on Oceanic Research (SCOR), an international group of marine scientists which would be expected to concern itself with such a problem. SCOR accepted the proposal only in part and with some hesitation. The need for an objective evaluation of the question was clear. But some members believed that SCOR would become an adversary and by engaging in the controversy would weaken its scientific credibility. It was decided to restrict initial action to soliciting and compiling the views of individuals and national committees.

To initiate the inquiry, the following description of the issues was circulated:

Ocean investigations, whether called exploration or research, are conducted for both fundamental and applied reasons. The increased knowledge of ocean phenomena and processes resulting from fundamental research has made possible important uses of the ocean and its resources. Enhancement of the uses continues to depend on such research, not only in the case of extractive resources, but particularly in the cases of ocean forecasting and the control of pollution.

Important ocean phenomena do not, in general, correspond

in location with delimitations drawn on political grounds. The control of ocean research, however, is affected by such limits. Coastal states control research in ocean regions under their jurisdiction. These regions have expanded through international agreement and are being further extended by unilateral action. Beyond the limits of national jurisdiction, ocean research is at present restricted only by other uses of the ocean. However, this region is the subject of continuing international discussions; any regime established for its governance may include conditions for the conduct of research.

Restrictions on ocean research are justified principally on the grounds that such research will give special advantages in the exploitation of resources. National security and protection of the environment are also invoked. Although controls are first directed to applied research on selected problems (such as fisheries) or regions (such as the seabed), they tend toward coverage of all of ocean research, presumably because of the potential application of such research to practical problems.

Consideration of the conditions for conduct of ocean research should include (1) evaluation of the justification for control, (2) examination of alternative ways to meet problems implied by the justifications, and (3) estimation of the cost of various restrictions, including their effect on the rate of acquiring scientific knowledge. With reference to (2), special consideration should be given to ways of assisting developing countries to make effective use of the results of ocean research.

Attempts to reduce complex issues to simple statements are often unsuccessful, and this was no exception. Some correspondents considered it inappropriate for scientists to justify restrictions on research or to seek alternatives to such restrictions. The expression "cost of various restrictions" should have been replaced by "consequences." A more positive approach was called for by some.

By June 1971 formal replies had been submitted by six national committees, those of Australia, France, the Federal Republic of Germany, the United Kingdom, the United States, and the Soviet Union. A dozen individual comments have also been received, including those from scientists working in seven additional countries. Inadequate sampling, especially from developing countries, prevents any quantitative analysis of the replies, yet many of the key issues have been illuminated, and I will try to interpret these subjectively to better illustrate the nature of the problem.

The ideas can be summarized under the following questions: (1) What is scientific research? (2) What are its benefits? (3) Why does it need to be free? (4) Why and how is it being restricted? (5) What are the consequences of restrictions? (6) How should it be protected?

What Is Scientific Research?

The need to distinguish "fundamental scientific research" from other kinds of research is largely tactical. Scientists recognize that such a distinction has little real meaning and is extremely difficult to make in practice. At the same time, they sense a practical need to dissociate science from its military and commercial applications. This may reflect a pessimistic view that some minimum amount of freedom will be preserved only for research that has no obvious or direct application.

Operationally effective definitions of this sort have been made more difficult by continuing misuse. For example, although exploration has always been a key element in scientific investigations, "exploration and exploitation" have been so inextricably intertwined by the sea lawyers that the utility of the word has been destroyed.

The special-purpose definition required is to the effect that basic research is in the public interest and does not infringe the security of other nations nor give an unfair advantage in the exploitation of resources. Possible test criteria are the unrestricted circulation of data, rapid and complete publication of results, and participation of foreign scientists. Although such participations can be arranged in a variety of ways, it is most evident when the investigation is part of an international program or at least is a "declared national program" (that is, one in which there is a commitment for international data exchange). To many, some sort of international cooperation and coordination is considered highly diagnostic. Presumably this would include formal bilateral arrangements.

What Are Its Benefits?

The list of benefits should not be restricted to practical applications. Inquiry into the nature and behavior of the ocean is a vital part of man's culture, and the pursuit of knowledge should be considered a fundamental right. As noted in the report of the Pacem in Maribus Colloquium: "Scientists have viewed the ocean as a scientific resource and its investigation as a means for the expansion of the human spirit. At the same time, they have recognized the contribution that scientific understanding can make to the improvement of human conditions."

The goal of using the ocean and its resources for the maximum benefit of mankind seems to be generally accepted. This involves attaining the maximum sustainable yield of living resources, exploiting subsurface minerals and petroleum at minimum cost, protecting the ocean environment from excessive effects of man's activities, forecasting of ocean and atmosphere conditions, and so on. Achievement of these goals depends to a greater or lesser extent on the outcome of ocean research. A major educational task however, remains in demonstrating the relationship between ocean research and the economic development of the ocean.

Examples can be cited of exploitation that has not derived from previous scientific investigations. The major contribution of research is to elucidate the origin of resources, the nature of their environmental dependence, and, in the case of living resources, the dynamics of their replacement. Here science makes the difference between exploitation and responsible (and profitable) resource management. Science is the fundamental basis for the rational use of the ocean.

In addition, scientific research is the key to the preservation of the marine environment. To determine the effects and fate of pollutants is a scientific problem, the solution of which is essential to rational control of man's intervention.

Why Does It Need To Be Free?

In some ways, the need for freedom to conduct scientific research anywhere in the ocean is an article of faith among scientists, a basic assumption they do not think they have to prove. The assumption stems from the unity of the ocean and the vast extent of the processes operating therein, which have led to the unity and oceanwide character of marine science.

Important ocean events do not, in general, correspond in location with delimitations drawn according to political lines. The fluid itself, and most marine organisms, are highly mobile and ignorant of such boundaries. The need for free research is particularly clear in this continuous and interconnecting system and is most critical in the shallow regions where man's influence is greatest. But even on the relatively stationary sea floor, one must be able to examine the whole system, from ocean basin to continental shield, if there is to be adequate understanding.

Marine scientists can work effectively only if they are free to follow their objects of study wherever they extend or move. To exclude investigations from some parts of the sea because of proximity to land is likely to render inquiry superficial and results less valid and useful. Freedom of scientific research is essential to promoting the exploration and exploitation of the natural resources of the sea.

Scientific organizations such as SCOR have a responsibility to develop the positive arguments in favor of preserving and upholding the concept of freedom of scientific research, including demonstration of the scientific reasons why different kinds of investigations require such freedom of access. An attractive, but perhaps unrealistic, alternative is to argue that freedom of scientific research, as one of the traditional freedoms of the sea, should not be restricted unless an adequate case for such restriction is made.

Why and How Is It Being Restricted?

No justification for control of research has been submitted other than that connected with resource exploitation, national security, or protection of the environment. The fear that research itself will harm the ocean organisms or environment in any significant way is much exaggerated. Infringement of national security may be a factor in major power interactions or in some regions (for example, the Middle East), but does not appear to be the major consideration of coastal states in much of the developing world. States wish primarily to restrict research in order to protect information about offshore resources.

Restrictions on research appear to be most frequent in shallow seabed regions offshore from developing countries and in contiguous fishing zones. In such regions of limited national jurisdiction, the mildest (and most acceptable) restrictions take the form of a coastal state requiring advance notification, right of participation, and full access to results. The most satisfactory way for such restrictions to be accommodated appears to be through bilateral arrangements.

Beyond the limits of national jurisdiction, restrictions have been proposed, especially on the seabed, largely to protect the collective interests of the developing countries. No evidence has been presented of any positive benefits likely to result from such control, which would presumably be exercised by some international authority. The United Nations statement of principles referred to earlier implies that participation in international research programs would be a basis for gaining international approval. Such participation, if enforced, could constitute a significant restriction, especially if it entailed ponderous, complex, inflexible, and time-consuming intergovernmental arrangements.

What Are the Consequences of Restrictions?

The direct consequences of restrictions on the freedom to conduct scientific research are increased costs of doing such research and delays or prevention of its accomplishment. The economic effects appear to be negative for all concerned.

Nations that cut themselves off from research reduce their participation in the benefits therefrom. At the same time, they are less able to protect themselves from technological advances achieved elsewhere. No nation is unaffected by what other nations do. Those demanding extensions of restrictions on exploitation may lose more than they gain by applying such restrictions to research. The restrictions tend to stifle research, which depends on the ability to adapt quickly to changing conditions. Research is curtailed and the initiative is left to exploiters and those of limited interests. The protection of nature is better resolved by international cooperation in scientific research than by restrictions on the study of certain zones. Ultimately, scientists will work where they can find suitable conditions, thus depriving other regions of the increased knowledge and often of the educational opportunities that accompany participation in research programs.

How Should It Be Protected?

Although one can speak of protecting the freedom of scientific research in the ocean, a more constructive approach is to facilitate the acquisition of knowledge and understanding of the ocean and its resources. This will include the development of effective international cooperation in research and the effective transfer of scientific and technological information among all those concerned with the ocean. An essential consequence may be the transformation of the relevant institutions, one of several reasons why scientists must participate in the elaboration of future ocean regimes.

Restrictions on research result in part from lack of knowledge about the nature of scientific exploration and research. If scientific research is to serve the interests of all states in any direct and immediate way, there is a need to assure that these states have the capability to engage in the research and utilize its results themselves. Thus there must be increased and more effective efforts to assist the developing countries to acquire their own skills in marine science and resource development. The development of national programs to observe, document, and publish data on sea areas under national jurisdiction would strengthen such skills and benefit not only the coastal state but the community at large. To satisfy the apprehensions of the coastal states, we must convince them that free research does not impinge on their interests and that they have more to gain than lose from such research.

Scientists must learn to make their findings promptly and fully available. Methods of data exchange must be perfected and instruction offered in their use. In a more general sense, the making available of results cannot be distinguished from education and training.

This subjective interpretation of responses to the SCOR inquiry suggests to me some useful concepts and conditions on the freedom of scientific research that should be sought in the new law of the sea. Research of all kinds should be encouraged, with the greatest international support being given to that research whose results are made widely available and which can thus be considered in the best interests of mankind. International cooperation in ocean research should be strengthened in all its aspects. On the national, or even individual, level, one essential aspect of international cooperation is acceptance of the responsibility to conduct research in the best interests of mankind, including the promulgation of results in the most expeditious and effective manner. Institutions for international cooperation in ocean science should be strengthened and supported. These institutions should be so transformed that they have the mutual confidence of both scientists and governments, so that they can function as the agents of both in the acquisition and dissemination of scientific understanding of the ocean.

The restriction of scientific investigation serves no useful purpose unless the interests of states are protected thereby. It is important, therefore, to ensure that research does not endanger the interests of coastal states. These interests appear to be concerned largely with the economic potential of living and mineral resources. Then the important place to apply restrictions and controls is on the use of these resources, not on the research that makes the economic potential possible. Similarly, coastal states may have important concerns about their security or the condition of their environment. Then restrictions should apply directly to these matters. It is only through scientific research that we can learn to use effectively the ocean and its resources for the benefit of mankind. Therefore we must find ways to promote such research, not cripple it.

CHAPTER 20

Pacem in Maribus: Statement on Oceanic Research

Further rational development of the ocean and its resources, as well as protection of the marine environment, depends in large part on the outcome of vigorous and continuing programs of ocean research of all kinds. Thus it is in the interest of all states to facilitate ocean research in all possible ways and to promote effective implementation of the Long-Term and Expanded Programme of Ocean Exploration and Research.

Ocean research should in all cases be conducted so as not to interfere unduly with other uses or to cause significant harm to the environment. Nor should such research be considered to confer rights of sovereignty or exploitation. With these restrictions, there is a need to distinguish more precisely between the two classes of investigations often referred to in legal documents as "scientific research" and "exploration." The following new definitions are proposed as having the necessary operational value:

Open Research is that which is intended for the benefit of all mankind and is characterized by prompt availability and full publication of results. Where consent of a coastal state is required, participation by nationals of that state and availability of all data and samples should be provided.

Limited Exploration, in contrast to open research, is intended for the benefit of a limited group, as evidenced by restrictions on publication and availability of data and samples.

Investigations included in cooperative international scientific programs for peaceful purposes are among those classed as open research. Many other kinds of investigations can also be considered as open research.

In order to facilitate programs of investigation while protecting the interests of coastal states and the international community as a whole, the following approach to research is proposed for further consideration:

In territorial waters, both open research and limited exploration would require the consent of the coastal state. In zones of more limited national jurisdiction, coastal state consent would be required for limited exploration but not for open research. The latter should, however, involve significant participation from the coastal state, which would have full access to the results. In the international zone, investigations of all kinds would be encouraged.

As these proposals imply modification of international law regarding the continental shelf, the need is recognized for further study of this special problem.

Where consent is required it is essential that the request be acted on expeditiously. Effective research depends on flexibility in planning and the ability to take advantage of scientific opportunities as they arise. The efforts of international bodies such as IOC and ICES to facilitate these consent arrangements should be encouraged.

The problem of fully utilizing the results of ocean investigations is not solely one of data and information exchange but also requires the capability to conduct ocean research and analyze the results. This capability remains to be developed in many coastal states and is a central goal of education and training programs in marine science. International and other institutions concerned with this goal should be strengthened and made much more effective than they now are.

Other important aspects of facilitating ocean research such as port-calls and transfer of scientific staff and equipment are recognized as needing further study and positive action.

PART VI

AN OCEAN REGIME

Part VI, the final section of this volume, consists of statements presented at Pacem in Maribus IV, June 1973. The chapters in this section discuss the issues now before the United Nations Conference on the Law of the Sea and analyze and criticize the solutions thus far proposed in the drafts of various nations. Part VI concludes with the text of a "declaration" adopted by Pacem in Maribus IV, which attempted to bring the UN Declaration of Principles of 1970 up to date in accord with the technological and political requirements of today. The document was circulated to all delegations at the Caracas session of the Conference on the Law of the Sea.

Some fundamental changes have taken place in the four years since the UN Sea-Bed Committee came into existence. The extension of national jurisdiction over resource exploration and exploitation over a zone of 200 miles has become an irrefutable fact. Further claims, beyond the 200-mile limit—claims that are poorly defined and open-ended—are being advanced by many nations. This forces us to undertake an "agonizing reappraisal" of the concept of the "Sea-Bed Authority" as it was first proposed by the government of Malta in 1967. Restricted to an area without economic potential except for the extraction of manganese nodules, in which only a few highly developed nations and companies have a stake, such an authority would have little to do with the "common heritage of mankind." It would, in fact, be reduced to a cartel of a few mining companies. The real wealth of the oceans and the welfare of the oceans, would remain beyond its competence. The oceans would remain a free-for-all in which the small and weak nations could not compete against the powerful and rich, where conflict and pollution would continue to reign practically unchecked. The oceans would perish.

The only constructive response to the territorial expansion of national jurisdiction is the functional expansion of the competences of the international ocean regime. The concept of the common heritage of mankind must be extended from the seabed and its resources to ocean space and its resources. The developing nations, on which the success of the conference largely depends, have realized that their only hope is in a strong, operational seabed machinery. Instead of receding from this goal, which is now meaningless, they must proceed to the concept of strong, operational ocean space institutions. Merging wherever possible—in the Caribbean and in the Mediterranean—their "economic zones" into "integrated economic zones," they can create the basis for regional managerial regimes to articulate global law. Realizing, in legal and economic terms, the concept of the common heritage of mankind, they can determine a new development strategy. Advancing the synergy between politics, science, and economics at the international as well as the national level, they can hasten the process of transfer of science and technology.

All this amounts to a revolution in international relations—nothing less. It is an arduous task and will take time. It will not be completed in Caracas, nor in Geneva. If it is to be done well, it will take three years at least.

Other developments will take their course during this interval. The negotiations of the Conference on the Law of the Sea must be seen in this broader

322

context. They will be affected by this context, but they may affect it in turn. If we succeed in solving the basic, urgent problems of the oceans, we will have done more than save the oceans, important though this would be in its own right; we will have opened a new chapter in international relations and international organization. We will have laid a new foundation for development and for peace.

Dr. Arvid Pardo, formerly Ambassador of Malta to the United Nations, to the United States, and to the Soviet Union, is now director of the Marine Program of the Woodrow Wilson International Center for Scholars at the Smithsonian Institution in Washington. H. Shirley Amerasinghe is Ambassador of Sri Lanka to the United Nations and President of the Conference on the Law of the Sea.

CHAPTER 21

New Institutions for Ocean Space

ARVID PARDO

Since 1970 the debate of the UN has no longer revolved exclusively or even mainly around matters concerning the seabed but increasingly around matters concerning the seas and ocean space. Successive debates in the UN Committee on the Peaceful Uses of the Sea-Bed and Ocean Floor beyond the Limits of National Jurisdiction have revealed an increasing understanding that the law of the sea as we know it is rapidly becoming obsolete and therefore is no longer capable of providing an adequate legal framework for the multiplying activities of man in ocean space. In 1972 the General Assembly decided that an international Conference on the Law of the Sea, which will probably be one of the most important conferences in modern times, would be convened in November 1973 in New York and then meet again in Santiago* in 1974.

The March 1973 meeting of the Sea-Bed Committee was characterized by a new seriousness and determination to make progress in the negotiations and also by an explosion of national claims to ocean space and fierce clashes of interest. Particular importance was given in the debate to the question of the limits of national jurisdiction in ocean space; to the question of rights of coastal states, whether exclusive or preferential, to the exploitation of the living resources of the sea in the general vicinity of their coasts; and to navigation and freedom of passage through straits used for international navigation. Each of these questions, in turn, comprises a multitude of problems of great complexity. What has not yet been discussed are the

*The conference was transferred to Caracas (Ed.).

324

military uses of ocean space and the multiple, new uses of the sea from artificial islands to offshore airports and industrial zones.

The Geneva session of the Sea-Bed Committee, which will be the last session before the Conference on the Law of the Sea, will indeed be crucial. If no way is found to reconcile and accommodate the awakened interests and appetites of coastal states, the Law of the Sea Conference will fail, and if it fails, increasing conflict in ocean space is inevitable.

Yet I see little possibility of accommodating the interests involved and, at the same time, of creating a viable international regime for the ocean within the framework of present law. The dichotomy in ocean space between exclusive national sovereignty of the coastal state, on one hand, and total freedom, on the other, can only be accommodated temporarily by vastly expanded national sovereignty. But this, in turn, cannot produce a viable regime. It will only be a prelude to a division of the ocean among coastal states, with consequences for international order, the marine environment, and for vital international community interests such as navigation, which are likely to prove disastrous. These developments are *inevitable* in the framework of present law. *The only way to avoid a disastrous outcome is to set forth new concepts which transcend ideologies and the more parochial conception of national self-interest.*

The oceans involve the interests of all, and all must therefore work together to establish an equitable regime beneficial to all. Present law of the sea based on freedom and sovereignty is being rapidly eroded by technology and events and is, in any case, incapable of providing a lasting framework for the beneficial use of ocean space under present conditions. A new basis for a new regime must be created.

It appears that only the concept of the ocean space and its resources as a common heritage of mankind can provide a satisfactory framework for an equitable international order and, at the same time, insure the preservation of the marine environment and the management of living and nonliving resources in the interests of all. This concept has been accepted by the General Assembly with respect to the seabed beyond national jurisdiction. It must now be extended to the waters above the seabed, since the seabed and superjacent waters are inextricably interlinked. The concept of ocean space and its resources as the common heritage of mankind must necessarily be implemented through an international mechanism, or rather, an international institutional system which can fill the existing void in authority and resource management in ocean space beyond national jurisdiction. To fulfill this function the institution must receive the power to administer ocean space and manage its resources beyond national jurisdiction.

It would be a mistake, however, to conceive of ocean space only in terms of resources. The oceans are used with increasing intensity for an ever-greater variety of purposes, from waste disposal to navigation. Many of these uses, new and old, are being revolutionized by technology. They must be subject to international standards, both within and outside national jurisdiction if we are to avoid conflict and possibly irreparable harm to the marine environment. This is another function the new institution must undertake.

The concept of common heritage, however, cannot cover all activities in ocean space. There are many activities which, subject to international standards, states can and should freely undertake in their national jurisdiction. Other activities, on the other hand, are so vital to the international community that their exercise cannot be left to the sole discretion of the coastal state, even within its national jurisdiction. Among these activities are international navigation, which is vital to the economy of all countries; scientific research, which is equally vital to the continuing development of ocean space and for a better and wiser use of the ocean; and the laying of underwater cables. These activities are what I would call public international interests. Certainly they must be subject to international regulations, taking into account the security interests of the coastal states; but they must also be protected, both within and without national jurisdictions through a credible international machinery. Here again, international institutions have an essential regulatory and protective role to play. Finally, the new institutions for ocean space would not be complete without an impartial and flexible system for the settlement of disputes.

The idea of comprehensive ocean space institutions with the functions and powers which I have briefly outlined, is still very much a minority view in the UN Sea-Bed Committee, largely because there is no precedent for such institutions and because of national fears. Yet the world community does not really have any alternative to creating such institutions if the potential of the oceans is to be realized. No state, for example, can manage its fisheries within either a 3-mile or a 200-mile limit all by itself. Since fish unfortunately do not respect the artificial boundaries created by man, international cooperation is required both with neighboring states and on a regional basis. Regional fishery regimes, however, are seldom likely to be viable outside the context of a global, comprehensive regime, since so many other activities, for instance pollution or mineral exploitation, affect fish stocks. I could give other examples.

I submit that national fears of a comprehensive international institution are not justified. Comprehensive international institutions for ocean space do not contradict sovereignty but rather strengthen sovereignty and give to this concept a more contemporary interpretation. A nation whose ecological and economic base is determined by the decisions of others—and in the oceans this is increasingly true of all states and particularly true of small nations—has for all practical purposes lost control of much of its sovereignty. It can regain its sovereignty only through effective participation in the making of decisions that directly affect it. Far from restricting national sovereignty, comprehensive international ocean space institutions are the only way to safeguard and guarantee national sovereignty. Furthermore, for technologically less advanced countries, such institutions provide the only realistic route through which access can be gained to the advanced technology that will permit the national development of national ocean space.

The technological revolution, which has enabled man to penetrate, use, and exploit the ocean more and more intensively, cannot be halted. New opportunities in the oceans, unimaginable even a few years ago, are being offered to mankind. For the developing world, the oceans are truly its last realistic hope, yet the development of the ocean also offers mankind new motives for conflict, new means irrevocably to frustrate the hopes of the poor, and new possibilities of destroying an environment vital to man. There are signs that the international community, as represented in the UN, is beginning to appreciate the vital importance of the issues at stake. This process of understanding must accelerate, because technology and time do not wait. Within a few years at the most, the international community will have to make a momentous choice which may well determine the future of the world in which our children will live.

CHAPTER 22

Key Issues in the Third United Nations Conference on the Law of the Sea

H. SHIRLEY AMERASINGHE

The scope of the Third United Nations Conference on the Law of the Sea can be divided into two clearly identifiable sections: the drafting of a treaty for an international regime, with appropriate international machinery for the area of the seabed and the ocean floor beyond the limits of national jurisdiction; and a review and revision of the existing law of the sea.

Whether there is to be one omnibus convention covering both the question of the international regime and the other related issues of the law of the sea or separate conventions is a matter for the Conference to decide. I am inclined to think that the final shape of the new law, whether it be in one or more conventions, should be left to evolve.

The question of the international regime involves the drafting of new law. The rest of the task assigned to the Conference covers other related issues of the law of the sea which are affected by the proposed new law and which also were either not settled satisfactorily at the two earlier conferences of 1958 and 1960 or which require modernization to suit a changed and changing world. The principal issues are those related to:

The breadth of the territorial sea.
Straits used for international navigation.
The continental shelf and its precise limits.
The concept of an exclusive economic zone beyond the territorial sea,

including a fishery zone, where the coastal state would have exclusive rights.

The question of preferential rights and other nonexclusive jurisdiction of the coastal state over the resources beyond the territorial sea.

The preservation of the marine environment, including the question of the prevention of marine pollution.

The high seas.

Scientific research and the transfer of technology.

The peaceful uses of ocean space.

Problems of special interest groups, for example, landlocked and shelf-locked countries and their access to the sea and to a fair share in the common heritage of mankind.

Certain resolutions of the General Assembly, to which I shall refer later, assume a special importance in regard to the whole question. Each has given rise to conflicting interpretations and engendered—especially among the majority of nations, those who either had no part in the development of customary international law or have not acceded to the existing Geneva Conventions of 1958 relating to the law of the sea—a strong desire to change the law and the customs.

New concepts have been defined and claims asserted by some countries in pursuance of these concepts, such as the economic zone or the patrimonial sea. The positions of these countries are reflected mainly in three documents which have attracted special attention:

1. The Declaration of Santo Domingo approved by the meeting of Ministers of the Specialised Conference of the Caribbean countries on Problems of the Sea, held in June 1972.

2. The conclusions in the General Report of the African States Regional Seminar on the Law of the Sea, held in Yaounde in June 1972.

3. The Kenyan proposal on the Exclusive Economic Zone concept.

They have one point in common, which is that they assert the coastal state's right to extend its jurisdiction beyond the limits of its territorial sea to an area adjacent to its coast in which it will exercise sovereignty over the natural resources, living and nonliving, in the water and in the seabed and the subsoil of that area. In the Santo Domingo Declaration this area is called the patrimonial sea. In the Yauonde conclusions and the Kenya proposal it is called the exclusive economic zone. Both the Santo Domingo Declaration and the Kenya proposal limit the extent of the patrimonial sea or exclusive zone to 200 nautical miles, measured from the same baselines as the territorial sea. Both the Santo Domingo Declaration and the Kenya proposal accept a limit of 12 nautical miles for the territorial sea, whereas some participants in the Yauonde seminar had reservations about the fixing of a precise limit for the territorial sea. All recognized that the establishment of an exclusive economic zone or patrimonial sea would be without prejudice to the freedom of navigation, freedom of overflight, freedom to lay underwater cables and pipelines for all states without discrimination.

We have come a long way from Grotius and Selden—prominent landmarks have been erected along the route; the Truman Proclamation of September 1945; the Santiago Declaration of 1952 by Chile, Ecuador, and Peru; the four Geneva Conventions of 1958 on the Law of the Sea, which left many issues unresolved; President Johnson's pronouncement of July 1966; the imaginative initiative of Ambassador Pardo at the General Assembly session of 1967 to seek approval by the United Nations of a brave new concept, the reservation exclusively for peaceful purposes of the seabed and ocean floor and the subsoil thereof underlying the high seas, beyond the limits of present national jurisdiction and use of their resources for the benefit of mankind.

It might well be said that it all began with the Truman Proclamation of September 1945, which asserted the United States' exclusive right to exploit the mineral resources of its continental shelf beyond its territorial sea, a proclamation that was accompanied by a parallel statement in which the continental shelf was defined as the seabed extending roughly to the 200-meter isobath. The same right was, of course, to be recognized for all coastal states. This was a unilateral declaration of the type which affords an interesting insight into the manner in which customary international law evolves and which would appear to justify the Dickensian character's memorable, if rather impolite, verdict that the law is an ass.

The new era of international relations, with its progressive assertion of the right of self-determination of all peoples and of the principles of international social justice, must accept as its code of conduct, without reservation, the three main instruments in which the rights of man have been asserted, namely, the Charter of the United Nations, the Declaration of Principles of International Law concerning Friendly Relations and Cooperation among States in accordance with the Charter of the United Nations, adopted by the General Assembly on October 24, 1970, and the Declaration on an International Development Strategy for the Second Development Decade. Anything that is inconsistent with those instruments, repugnant to their substance, or at variance with their objectives must be rejected.

In this new era, equity must be the sole criterion by which the efficacy, value, and merit of any law or custom can be judged. It is ironic to hear powerful and affluent nations seeking equity from the weak in the matter of the law of the sea though such a demand may derive its inspiration from the fear that the Biblical prophecy will come true and the meek will inherit the earth.

I have made these observations at the very start in order to stress the need for all those who participate in the forthcoming Law of the Sea Conference to realize that if we are to have a stable and enduring law of the sea, the powerful maritime nations must refrain from issuing ultimatums or from seeking the entrenchment of rights which are exercisable by a minority without regard to the interests of the overwhelming majority of mankind. The acquisitive instincts and propensities of nations, corporations, and individuals must all be subordinated to the imperatives of international social justice, which alone can provide a stable foundation for peace and progress.

The Santiago Declaration of 1952 by Chile, Ecuador, and Peru, all countries not endowed with a continental shelf, was the inevitable riposte to the Truman Doctrine. From it grew the concept of the exclusive zone of a coastal state or that of the patrimonial sea.

President Johnson's pronouncement of July 1966 seemed to hold out new hope, expressed in more specific form in Ambassador Pardo's proposal:

> Under no circumstances, we believe, must we ever allow the prospects of rich harvest and mineral wealth to create a new form of colonial competition among the maritime nations. We must be careful to avoid a race to grab and to hold the lands under the high seas. We must ensure that the deep sea and the ocean bottoms are, and remain, the legacy of all human beings.

It was just a year later that Ambassador Pardo introduced his epoch-making proposal.

The next two major landmarks were the so-called moratorium resolution adopted by the General Assembly at its twenty-fourth session in 1969, Resolution 2574D (XXIV), and the "Declaration of Principles Governing the Sea-Bed and the Ocean Floor and the Subsoil Thereof beyond the Limits of National Jurisdiction," adopted by the General Assembly at its twenty-fifth anniversary session as Resolution 2749 (XXV). It was in conformity with these principles that the proposed international regime, including international machinery, was to be designed and the future law of the sea formulated. The grandiose concept of the "legacy of all human beings" envisaged by President Johnson was refurbished in a manner perhaps not intended by its author, and it appeared as the first article in the Declaration of Principles, which solemnly declared:

the seabed and ocean floor and the subsoil thereof beyond the limits of national jurisdiction, as well as the resources of the area, are the common heritage of mankind.

The moratorium resolution, introduced at the initiative of several developing countries, declared:

pending the establishment of an international regime for the area,
(a) states and persons, physical or juridical, are bound to refrain from all activities of exploitation of the resources of the area of the sea-bed and the ocean floor and the subsoil thereof beyond the limits of national jurisdiction;
(b) no claim to any part of the area of its resources shall be recognized.

The moratorium resolution was introduced because there was disturbing evidence that operational activities had already been initiated in the international area by states with advanced seabed technology, and it was feared that such operations were intended to and would forestall and thus jeopardize the efforts of the international community to establish international control over the exploitation of the resources of the area. The moratorium resolution—2574D (XXIV)—was further reinforced by the Declaration of Principles Governing the Sea-Bed and the Ocean Floor and the Subsoil Thereof, Beyond the Limits of National Jurisdiction—Resolution 2749 (XXV)—and Resolution 52 of the Third UNCTAD held in Santiago in 1972. These operations in the extra-jurisdictional area were held to be in violation of the principle of the common heritage of mankind accepted in the Declaration of Principles. The actual nature and location of the area, even if its limits were not precisely defined, established its international character; this was confirmed in the Declaration of Principles. The Declaration, as the only authentic, legal expression of the will of the international community on the matter, was deemed by the supporters of the moratorium to deny national authorities the power to regulate exploitation in the area or to grant licenses.

The countries opposed to the moratorium principle maintained, on the other hand, that it could not modify international law or deprive states of their rights in international law; that the Declaration of Principles did not constitute an interim regime and had no dispositive effect until the international regime had been agreed on and the area to which it was applicable defined; and further that the common heritage principle did not in any event mean the common property of mankind. The moratorium principle was regarded by this school of thought as an attempt to restrict technological progress and to limit experimental activities. There are many crusaders who march in the vanguard of technological and scientific progress who pay little heed to the will and interests of the overwhelming mass of mankind. Those who objected to a moratorium such as that proposed in regard to the exploitation of seabed resources had no objection to it, provided that at the same time a moratorium would also be applied with respect to the extension of the territorial sea, fishery zone, and the other economic zones beyond the 12-mile limit. The fears of these countries were not without foundation. Industrial research and prospecting for the recovery of hard minerals from the deep ocean floor continued, and in 1971 a United States firm announced that it was operating a pilot plant which successfully converted manganese nodules into commercially saleable metals with acceptable efficiency. Manganese nodules are most heavily concentrated in the Pacific Ocean in an area plus or minus 10 degrees of the Equator and about two-thirds of the way from San Diego, California, to Hawaii. They are located outside the continental margin and therefore in an area which indisputably falls outside national jurisdiction. Their commercial exploitation will be feasible by 1975. It is reported that an investment of $80 million has already been made by one financier in a project for the exploration and exploitation of these nodules.*

Bills have been introduced both in the United States Senate and in the House of Representatives (S.2801 and HR.11) to give the U.S. Secretary of the Interior authority to promote the conservation and orderly development of the hard mineral resources of the deep seabed, pending the adoption of an international regime for the area. The Senate bill, which provides for the issue of licenses by the Secretary of the Interior, recognizes rights "which shall be exclusive, as against all persons subject to the jurisdiction of the United States or of any reciprocating state, to develop the block designated in such license. . . ."

This legislation was criticized by several representatives from developing countries in the Sea-Bed Committee on the ground that it would encourage industrial exploitation inconsistent with the General Assembly's declaration in Resolution 2574D, without regard to the current efforts to set up an equitable regime for the seabed area beyond national jurisdiction. The senator who sponsored bill S.2801 is reported to have stated in an interview: "There has been no production beyond 200 meters on the US continental margin largely because of the condition the President inadvertently attached to such mineral development. He said that the right of US leases would be subject to a regime to be agreed upon. That condition was just too much of a risk for the industry to take."

There are many countries that consider the condition imposed by the

---

*This has already been surpassed by Howard Hughes adventure off the coast of Nicaragua, and his investment of a quarter of a billion dollars.

President as faithfully reflecting the feelings of the greater proportion of the international community as expressed in the "moratorium resolution," and indeed more explicitly set forth in several paragraphs, especially 3, 4, and 9 of the Declaration of Principles, which was adopted without dissent by the General Assembly at its 25th anniversary session: The text of these paragraphs is as follows:

3. No State or person, natural or juridical, can claim to exercise or acquire rights with respect to the area or its resources incompatible with the international regime to be established and the principles of this Declaration;

4. All activities regarding the exploration and exploitation of the resources of the area and other related activities shall be governed by the international regime to be established;

9. On the basis of the principles of this Declaration an international regime applying to the area and its resources and including appropriate international machinery to give effect to its provisions shall be established by an international treaty of a universal character generally agreed upon. The regime shall, *inter alia,* provide for the orderly and safe development and rational management of the area and its resources and for expanding opportunities in the use thereof and ensure the equitable sharing by States in the benefits derived therefrom, taking into particular consideration the interests and needs of the developing countries, whether land-locked or coastal.

The Soviet Union has declared that it would support the moratorium on exploitation provided it is balanced by a corresponding moratorium on unilateral extension of coastal state jurisdiction. China supports the moratorium. A modicum of patience is all the international community seeks.

The limits of the area will be the subjects of strenuous bargaining. The continental shelf, owing to the ambiguity of the exploitability criterion incorporated in the 1958 Convention, has by usage become synonymous and conterminous with the continental margin, which is the entire submarine extension of the land mass up to the border of the abyssal plain and includes, in addition to the continental shelf, those areas of the submarine extension that are described geologically as the continental slope and continental rise. If the continental shelf and continental margin are deemed synonymous and conterminous, approximately 25 percent of the sea area, which is roughly the proportion that falls within the continental margin, would be open to exploitation by coastal states with the technological and financial capacity to do so. The common heritage would therefore shrink to the area of the abyssal depths over which the international authority would exercise jurisdiction.

The maximum limit of the territorial sea is another key issue. The two previous international conferences of 1958 and 1960 failed to reach agreement on this issue. The trend among the developing countries is to treat this issue as distinct from that of coastal state resource jurisdiction, which is of paramount importance at least to the developing coastal states. It is widely held that the present law allows each state to determine the breadth of its territorial sea unilaterally, but there is a definite trend toward the acceptance of a maximum breadth of 12 miles of territorial sea. There are about 86 states whose territorial sea does not exceed 12 miles in breadth.

It is most likely that the developing countries will accept a maximum breadth of 12 miles of territorial sea provided their claim to an adequate area of exclusive resource jurisdiction, as expressed in the concept of an exclusive economic zone or a patrimonial sea, which they consider essential for their economic sustenance and growth, is satisfied.

At the present time a coastal state's claim to exclusive resource jurisdiction beyond its territorial sea is not universally acknowledged. Beyond the territorial sea of a coastal state lie the "high seas," which are, in the words of the Convention on the High Seas, "open to all nations," and no state may validly purport to subject any part of them to its sovereignty. The Convention further states that the "freedom" of the high seas comprises, among other things, (1) freedom of navigation; (2) freedom of fishing; (3) freedom to lay underwater cables and pipelines; and (4) freedom to fly over the high seas. Other freedoms are contemplated by the relevant article but not specified. The developing countries have taken the view that the "freedom" aspect of the high seas confers an undue advantage on states with the technological and financial capacity to exploit that "freedom." Consequently there has developed a trend toward the assertion of a coastal state's right to declare a zone of exclusive resource jurisdiction beyond its territorial sea where it would also have the power to regulate resource-exploitation activities and take conservation measures, as well as the right to exercise jurisdiction over offenders for the purpose of punishing any contravention of its rules.

The main areas in which such a zone of exclusive jurisdiction is contemplated are the adjacent waters for fisheries purposes and the adjacent undersea areas for exploitation of mineral resources.

The developing countries may be expected to support the right of a coastal state to exclusive jurisdiction over an adequate area beyond its territorial sea for both these purposes, namely fisheries and fishery conservation purposes, and exploration and exploitation of mineral resources.

The maximum breadth of this zone has to be negotiated, but a limit of 200 nautical miles, including the territorial sea, has been suggested.

In regard to the fishery zone, any historic rights of neighboring states to fish within the coastal state's exclusive zone should be safeguarded, as the Kenyan proposal envisages, so far as neighboring developing states are concerned. The Kenyan proposal also recognizes the need for taking into consideration the rights of developing land-locked and shelf-locked states and states with narrow shelves, including the right of access to the sea and the right of transit.

The United States, in an effort to accommodate the interests of the coastal state and those of the international community and to arrest the progressive nationalization of the ocean area and its resources, has proposed that the coastal state's exclusive jurisdiction over the national resources of its continental shelf be limited to the area falling within the 200-meter isobath but that the area beyond that limit and extending over the rest of the continental margin should be constituted as a trusteeship zone which would be administered by the coastal state subject to the international seabed authority's regulation and to the payment by the trustee to the international seabed authority of a minimum of 50 percent and up to a maximum of 66.66 percent of the revenue acquired from the exercise of the trust, this money to be used for international community purposes, including assistance to developing countries. This trusteeship zone proposal might have some attraction especially for developing land-locked countries whose interests might be best served if the area of the common heritage were as extensive as possible and the area of coastal state jurisdiction as narrow as possible, but it has its critics, not least because of the odious associations of the principle of trusteeship.

In the area beyond national jurisdiction, the international seabed authority's powers and functions would have to be defined again in respect to fisheries and the resources of the seabed and ocean floor and the subsoil thereof, that is, the mineral resources.

In regard to fisheries management, there seems to be a trend among the developing countries in favor of regional arrangements, with institutions empowered to allocate the catch and establish conservation rules based on biological factors. Another proposal that has been pressed is that in these international waters, coastal states which are developing countries and which cannot afford to maintain distant-water fishing fleets be given special treatment.

In regard to the resources of the seabed and the ocean floor and the subsoil thereof beyond the limits of national jurisdiction, the developing countries would want a regime conforming in substance to the Declaration of Principles which was adopted without a dissenting vote at the General Assembly's 25th anniversary session, a regime established by a treaty of a universal character, generally agreed upon and open to all states. The agreement should establish international machinery equipped with comprehensive powers. The main issues that will arise will be:

1. The scope and functions of the regime and machinery.
2. Who may exercise the right of exploration and exploitation.
3. Whether the machinery should also have the power to regulate prices so as to avoid disruptive effects on world market prices and which would, in turn, have adverse consequences for the economies of developing countries.

The machinery should also be empowered to promote and regulate scientific research and to promote the training of a personnel from developing countries and the transfer of technology to them, as well as to take measures for the protection of the marine environment.

There would appear to be a strong body of opinion in favor of a machinery with four main elements:

1. A plenary body comprising the entire membership.
2. An executive council of limited composition with equitable geographical representation and adequate representation for the technologically advanced countries.
3. A tribunal for settlement of disputes; whether its jurisdiction should be compulsory or not is a matter for negotiation.
4. A secretariat.

The developing countries would insist on the principle of one-state-one-vote for all decisions and would not favor a system of weighted voting.

There have been proposals for a system of voting by groups and for decisions to be taken on the basis of concurrent majorities within these groups. This would amount to a veto by a group or section, but the chief obstacle to its adoption is the definition of a "group." The accepted geographical groupings are by and large irrelevant with regard to law-of-the-sea matters.

The most controversial question will be whether the international machinery should itself have the power to undertake direct exploitation. The developing countries would want the international authority to have the power to undertake direct exploitation in addition to the power of granting licenses or entering into joint ventures. Whether it is to exercise the power of direct exploitation is a matter that should be left to its judgment and discretion.

The developing countries are also in favor of the international seabed authority's having the power to take measures to minimize the adverse economic effects that could be caused by fluctuations in prices of raw materials. For this purpose, it could act in collaboration with established institutions which now intervene to secure commodity price agreements such as UNCTAD.

The preservation of the marine environment would be an important function and responsibility of the international seabed authority. There must be internationally accepted standards and rules to prevent marine pollution, and offenders should be liable for damage caused by them. These provisions should be enforced by the international seabed authority.

In this regard, coastal states must be recognized as having special rights and responsibilities.

In the matter of scientific research, the developed countries, especially the Soviet Union and the United States, want scientific research, as opposed to industrial research, that is, research or prospecting for the purpose of industrial exploitation, to be free and unrestricted. The developing countries would want all research to be subject to certain rules which should, among other things, safeguard the security of coastal states and prevent pollution. A formula would have to be found to distinguish between scientific research and industrial research. The right of a developing coastal state to participate in scientific research conducted in its vicinity and to be kept informed of the results of such research would also be asserted.*

I have left to the last the question of straits used for international navigation. The Geneva Convention of 1958 on the Territorial Sea and the Contiguous Zone recognizes only the right of innocent passage of foreign ships through such straits.

The major maritime powers, and especially those with global strategic interests, fear that with the adoption of a maximum breadth of 12 miles for the territorial sea, straits used for international navigation which are not wider than 24 miles, would fall within the jurisdiction of the riparian states and become part of their territorial waters. They therefore claim the right of free and unimpeded transit. If such a right is claimed in the interests of the unimpeded movement of commerce, the existing right of innocent passage would be adequate to prevent unwarranted interference by the coastal state. But "free transit" seems to imply exemption of submarines from the present requirement that they should surface when entering territorial waters.

Indonesia and Malaysia, both of which claim a 12-mile territorial sea, have by their declaration of November 16, 1971—to the effect that the

*See the declaration on scientific research adopted by Pacem in Maribus II.

Straits of Malacca are not "international straits"—given rise to the apprehension that this would have grave implications of a military nature for states with powerful navies.

The question that is uppermost in the minds of us all is, what are the prospects for a successful conference?

A compromise will be necessary, and the principal elements of such a compromise will have to be:

1. The acceptance of the concept of an exclusive economic zone, but with considerable modification to allow for the application of certain international rules and standards within the zone and the assumption by coastal states of the responsibility for enforcing these rules and standards.
2. Agreement to no more than the right of innocent passage through straits falling within the territorial seas of opposite states.
3. An effective and equitable system of settlement of disputes by an independent tribunal.

It is in the interest of all that the conference, which will be one of the most important in the history of the United Nations, should succeed. Failure would create conditions in which international tensions would be exacerbated and the existing disparities between the affluent and the indigent widened. The international community faces one of its severest tests. We have to succeed only because we cannot afford to fail.

CHAPTER 23

A Constitution for the Oceans

ELISABETH MANN BORGESE

The economic potential is still largely unknown. For the next few decades, it is likely that the produce it may yield will not markedly affect world economy. This is borne out by the Secretary-General's report, "Possible Impact of Sea-Bed Mineral Production in the Area beyond National Jurisdiction on World Markets, with Special Reference to the Problem of Developing Countries; a Preliminary Assessment." How, then, can it be explained that hard-boiled and realistic national governments have lavished so much time, resources, and ingenuity on the devising of constitutional and institutional structures magnificent enough to administer the world as a whole, to cope with lands unknown quantitatively and qualitatively?

The disproportion between effort and object is so striking as to be unbelievable—*unless* one assumes that, consciously or unconsciously, nations are looking at the seabed not as an *object* but an *occasion;* an occasion to begin to think differently about the world of science and technology, of communications and development, a world as vulnerable as it is potent, as integrative as it is disintegrative; a world in which the international structures devised during the first half of the 20th century no longer fit.

If our minds were to remain fixed too long on the sea floor we would be lost, for the sea floor is fast eroding under the impact of the integrative-disintegrative forces around us. As we are striving to determine its boundaries, the disintegrative forces of misunderstood nationalism are pulling and pushing on them while uncontrolled macrotechnology is making a mockery of the entire issue.

We may well say: *No ship may trespass here, and the area under our national jurisdiction shall be closed to research and exploration, extraneous to our interest.* But while the ship stays out, satellites are moving in the freedom of space "beyond the limits of national jurisdiction" and uninterdictably doing the research the ship was interdicted from doing. The search for earth resources, including mineral deposits, soil with high growth potential, and fish at sea; the monitoring of such diverse phenomena as ice movements on the oceans, forest fires, mass insect movements on land; flood predictions, and similar worldwide collection of warning data, collision avoidance and distress relay and rescue—may all be achieved through the use of satellites. Fault structures extending from Swedish iron ore deposits into Finland and Norway were identified from about 1,000 miles up and are being explored for iron deposits. Photographs taken from about 125 miles up have assisted in Australian oil exploration. Much of the equipment used for gathering information about the moon is equally useful for earth.

Against this type of research, boundaries are of no avail.

We may well say that no oil rig may be erected here. This oil is ours, to enhance our national power, our wealth, our independence. But the world's fossil fuel-based economy is in trouble. All that has a beginning has an end. The post-industrial era into which we are rapidly moving will be based on other sources of energy, quite possibly, atomic fusion energy, with fuel drawn from the oceans, or solar energy. During a conference at the Center for the Study of Democratic Institutions, Dr. Richard Post, one of the greatest experts in the field of fusion energy, told me that (1) the scientific problems involved in the production of fusion energy will have been solved within eight to ten years; (2) the engineering and development phase might require a period of five to eight years thereafter, but it could be shortened if sufficient financial support were available, and much of the work could be carried out concurrently with the scientific work so that actual production could start in about 10 years; (3) the capital cost of fusion reactor plants will be lower than the capital required for the production of energy from other sources; (4) the fuel will be practically without cost and unlimited; (5) radiation and health hazards, in comparison with those connected with fission energy production, are about one to a million; and (6) atomic fusion energy cannot be diverted to atomic arms production, nor are fusion reactors vulnerable to sabotage, whereas every atomic fission breeder reactor is potentially a bomb factory.

Other experts may be less optimistic in their forecasts; but whether this development takes 10 or 20 or 50 years—what difference does it make?

The fact is that a world whose economy is based on new sources of energy will laugh at our squabbles over the boundaries of the continental shelf. An economy based on extracting minerals from the waters that know no boundaries, and only such an economy, is in fact capable of restoring to the planet ecological balance by a macrorecycling of productivity. Agricultural civilizations were ecologically balanced insofar as they were cyclical. Everything came from the earth and was restored to the earth. Industrial civilizations broke this cyclicity. They stripped, they exhausted, earth resources. They dumped, wasted, and polluted; most of the waste and pollution ended in the oceans, "the biggest hole in the ground." Post-industrial civilization, based on new sources of energy, may in fact heal the wounds of the planet before it is too late: taking from the oceans in multipurpose industrial complexes and restoring to the oceans through rivers and atmosphere.

The seabed, then, is a transitory concept, both real and unreal, an entity with which we can deal fruitfully only if we look beyond it. Thus we look at ocean space as a whole: a far more viable entity, geographically and ecnomically, than the seabed; a far better laboratory for the development of new and more rational methods of resource management, the control of macrotechnology and of science policy. In the post-industrial era ocean space may well become the fulcrum of world economy, just as each semi-enclosed or enclosed ocean basin (for example, the Mediterranean) will be, much more than in the past, the fulcrum of regional economic activities. What we are witnessing today is a shift from a heartland-continent-centered world view to an ocean-centered world view.

Ocean space may hold our attention much longer than the seabed, certainly for many years to come, yet some of the contradictions inherent in a seabed regime are inherent in an ocean space regime as well. The question of boundaries is still thorny, and complex issues arise whenever and wherever the functions of a system transcend its geographical area. Pollution controls in the oceans transcend these boundaries, involving rivers, land-based industries, and the atmosphere. Just as a "seabed authority" could function effectively only in the context of effective regimes for the multiple uses of ocean space, so an ocean space regime will eventually be able to function effectively only in the context of analogous regimes for the management of earth resources, energy, communications, and atmospheric processes.

But a beginning, a breakthrough, must be made; a model must be created somewhere. The seabed was ideal for this purpose. It was the most creative myth in the history of international organization. What is of lasting value in the seabed literature, however, lies not so much in the detailed technical provisions applicable to the seabed and to the seabed only, but in the structural concepts transcending technological innovation and changeable geographical contours, concepts which, although using the seabed as an occasion or test-application or model, come to grips with the basic problems of international organization in the year 2000. Such concepts are contained in all of the drafts.

Boundaries

Deterred by the controversial nature of the boundary problem and aware of the interdependence of the territorial delimitation, on one hand, and the structure and functions of the seabed or ocean space regime on the other, most of the UN draft treaties simply leave the boundary question open. The US draft, the draft of the landlocked nations ("Seven-Power Draft") and the Maltese Draft, are exceptions. Each proposes different criteria.

On the whole, there has been an unmistakable trend toward enlarging claims and pushing boundaries seaward, as well as a concurrent shift from an exclusive emphasis on the geographic location of boundaries to greater attention to the question of the content of jurisdiction within the boundaries, wherever they are located. This can be noted in the American and Maltese drafts; it is observable even with regard to the Latin American states that had been most adamant in their territorial claims. This shift seems inevitable, since the impact of "national" activities on international interests grows with the expansion of territorial claims and the concurrent advance of the technological revolution. What a nation does with its more powerful means within its enlarged boundaries thus must be tempered by consideration of the consequences of these activities beyond the boundaries. This recognition has undoubtedly contributed to a softening of the issue, which, in spite of all difficulties, appears more soluble than it did even a year ago.

I should like to add here another consideration. International boundaries are boundaries *between nations.* Their function is to safeguard territorial integrity and national sovereignty against intrusions or exploitations by another nation or nations or their citizens. The Geneva Conventions fixed the criteria (insofar as they went) for the establishment of international boundaries of precisely this sort—*between nations,* or, more precisely, between each nation and all other nations. It did not fix, nor touch on, the problem of boundaries *between nations and an international ocean organization* which did not exist and whose existence was not contemplated at that time.

When the Geneva Conventions are reopened for revision, the problem will have to be considered in the context of the establishment of an international authority or system. It is my contention that this changes the problem qualitatively. The boundary issue will now have to be divided into two parts:

(1) boundaries *between nations*
(2) boundaries *between nations and the international system.*

Boundaries *between nations* will have an unaltered function, albeit in an altered setting. Qualitatively, they will not be different from boundaries between nations anywhere else.

On the whole, national boundaries on land tend to decrease in importance with the increase and intensification of communications. Although they are strictly territorial in nature, functional factors tend to impinge on them (for example, customs controls are no longer located exclusively at frontier posts but at airports or anywhere within the nation space). Border disputes tend to be submitted to international arbitration or the jurisdiction of international courts.

It is not likely that international boundaries at sea will have to "recapitulate" the evolution of boundaries on land: from fortified geophysical boundaries to essentially political and administrative boundaries; from boundaries derived from bilateral agreement and subject to national control to boundaries agreed on and guaranteed internationally (as in the Charter of the UN).

History does not move by "recapitulating." "Phase-skipping" predominates, and boundaries in the oceans may take up the trend of land boundaries at a far more advanced stage. In the present state of technological and economic development, it is in fact essential that boundaries be fixed by international agreement and, once agreed upon, be guaranteed by the charter of the international ocean space regime.

The point I want to stress, however, is that they are now, and remain, boundaries *between nations,* that they are *territorial,* and that they do *not affect directly the relations between nations and the international regime.* For example, a fishing boat from another nation may be stopped at an international boundary. Whether a situation would ever arise in which a ship of the international ocean space institutions would be stopped there is a qualitatively different question. Boundaries between nations and the international community, of which these nations are part, in this sense, *cannot exist.*

There are no territorial boundaries between California and the United States (although the federal government recognizes the state boundaries between, say, California and Nevada), the Ukraine and the Soviet Union, Serbia and Yugoslavia, or France and the European Common Market. The boundaries between a state or republic or sovereign nation and the more comprehensive political or economic or economic/political unit of which it is part are not territorial, they are functional.

The question—in the relations between a nation and the international, supranational, or transnational organization it has freely decided to join—is not where the geographic boundaries of that nation are located. It is (1) whether laws, regulations, norms, or decisions in the framing of which the nation has had its full part are directly binding on that nation or its citizens; and (2) in which *functional areas* such laws, regulations, norms, or decisions would be so binding.

One could conceive of *boundaries between functional areas,* within which decision-making would have to be based on various degrees of consensus. The area of technical cooperation—for example, in setting standards for pollution controls, safety standards, a mining code—might be governed by decisions based on majorities, including a majority of the technical experts and "operators" in the area. Economic interests of nations would have to be safeguarded by decision-making based on a consensus, including the consensus of the parties most directly affected. Matters vital to the interest of nations, including military matters, might require consensus.

Once a decision had been made on the agreed-upon basis of consensus, however, it would be applicable to the *oceans as a whole* (or, depending on the case, to an ocean region or basin), *regardless of the territorial boundaries of nations.* Decisions regarding coal and steel production, once adopted by the European Community, are applicable across national boundaries. Decisions regarding the oceans, once adopted by the ocean community, apply equally across national boundaries.

These considerations, displacing the issue from one of determining territorial boundaries to determining functional boundaries, would seem to be in line with the above-mentioned trend to shift attention from the geographic location of boundaries to the content of jurisdiction.

Common Heritage of Mankind

The basic concept of all drafts is that of the common heritage of mankind. Adopted formally by the Twenty-Fifth General Assembly, it has since been spelled out and embodied in treaty articles and institutional structures.

Of all the documents before the United Nations, only two avoid the term. Neither the Soviet nor the Japanese draft contains the words "common heritage of mankind." But if they do not call it by its name, they nevertheless accept it in its legal and economic characteristics. And what's in a name?

There are four basic characteristics:

The first is that the common heritage of mankind is not appropriable. The "area" and its resources cannot be appropriated by states or persons by any means. This is recognized in Article 5 of the Soviet Draft and Article

7 of the Japanese draft—as it is, of course, recognized by all the drafts that have explicitly adopted the phrase "common heritage of mankind."

The second characteristic is that it requires benefit-sharing. It must be managed for the benefit of mankind as a whole, with particular consideration for the needs of developing nations. This, too, is recognized in all of the drafts, including the Soviet (Article 8) and the Japanese (Articles 1 and 42).

Benefit-sharing may be interpreted as the passive receipt of profits, or it may mean active participation in the management of the common heritage. On this point there is a marked division, not between the socialist and the free-enterprise nations, as one should have expected, but between developed and developing nations. The drafts of the developed nations (US, USSR, Japan) and the working papers of the UK and France reduce benefit-sharing to profit-sharing, not including a sharing of managerial prerogatives, nor do they provide in great detail for the sharing of skills and technologies. The drafts of the developing nations (Tanzania, the Latin American countries, the landlocked nations) stress the sharing of managerial prerogatives and decision-making power. Of course, this division is not sharp. The Maltese draft remains fairly equidistant from both extremes, establishing most precise criteria for profit-sharing and providing for rather comprehensive participation of the developing nations in general decision-making, but its provisions for planning and managing are minimal. The regime is conceived primarily as a regulatory, not as an operational, system. But explicitly or implicitly, the drafts of the developed nations project a control by the industrialized nations in active managing, even if conceivably the developing nations might control the organ entrusted with the distribution of profits.

The real question, however, does not hinge on the distribution of voting power as much as it depends on the nature of the regime. There can be no active participation in management if there is no management except in the hands of the individual developed nations. The real question is whether the regime is conceived as a "night watchman" type of government or as an economically active system. Here the distinction between the approaches of developed and developing nations is even clearer. The Tanzanian, the Latin American, and the landlocked-nations drafts project ocean institutions that are operational, that is, they themselves are production-managing enterprises. No such provisions are to be found in the drafts of the developed nations.

We shall later return to the structural implications of this. What I wish to stress here is that *the active concept of benefit-sharing implies not only participation in decision-making. It implies an active concept of governance.*

The third characteristic of the common heritage of mankind is that it can be used for peaceful purposes only. Here again, there is unanimity in the acceptance of the principle but wide differences in interpretation. In this instance, however, the alignment shifts and the socialist nations are closer to the developing nations in giving the most inclusive interpretation to the demilitarization of the "area." This is borne out not only by the texts of the drafts but by the debates preceding their introduction. The strongest statements in favor of total disarmament of the seabed in the perspective of total and general disarmament all come from the socialist and developing nations.

The US draft (Article 4) and the Japanese draft (Article 8) contain nothing beyond the acknowledgment of the principle. The British and French working papers contain nothing. The Soviet draft, on the other hand, goes far beyond the provisions of the Treaty on the Prohibition of Emplacement of Nuclear Weapons on the Seabed by stipulating that "the use of the sea-bed and the subsoil thereof for military purposes shall be prohibited" and imposing the obligation that "states parties to this Treaty undertake to conclude further international agreements as soon as possible." The Tanzanian draft (Article 17) empowers the authority "to conduct its activities in accordance with the principles of the UN to promote peace and international cooperation and, in conformity with policies of the UN furthering the establishment of safeguarded worldwide disarmament and in conformity with any international agreement entered into pursuant to such policies," and contains other provisions for maintaining peace and ensuring security. The Maltese draft (Article 84) stays in line with the Treaty on the Prohibition of the Emplacement of Nuclear Weapons on the Seabed and the Test Ban Treaty. It goes further than these Treaties by authorizing, in Article 127, the Council to "undertake such functions with regard to the military uses of ocean space or to the regulation of armaments in ocean space as may be conferred upon it by a unanimous vote of members in category A referred to in Article 110."

The important fact, however, is that the concept of the common heritage of mankind, named or unnamed, forms the basis of all drafts and working papers, all of which spell out, in various ways, its legal and economic characteristics and implications.

In all except the Maltese draft, the application of the concept is still restricted to the seabed and its resources. They do not touch on the other dimensions of ocean space and its multiple uses. Following the path marked by the Maltese draft, however, world opinion seems to be moving rather rapidly in the direction of considering ocean space as a whole. Thus a study prepared by the Secretary-General, the *Uses of the Sea* (E/5120, 28 April 1972) stresses the need "not only to consider the establishment of relevant sets of priorities but also to establish a basis for *ocean management systems* which would ensure the most rational development of resources and mini-mize potential conflicts," and it invites governments "to examine the varied, interrelated activities in ocean space" and calls for "bold and innovative concepts, not the least of which will be a new spirit within the United Nations system and action to supplement practical sectorial requirements and activities with over-all guidance according to modern management principles."

The basis for such management systems can only be an expanded concept of the common heritage of mankind, applicable to ocean space as a whole and to its resources.

Structure

If an ocean management system as envisaged by the Secretary-General requires a broadly based concept of common heritage, the common heritage concept, in turn, requires a system of management, and this is its fourth fundamental characteristic. It is in this area that most of the work is yet to be done. Several of the drafts do not provide for a management system at all. The British and French working papers propose to parcel it out to the nations, thus mutilating the principle of common heritage. The Soviet draft does not contain formulations regarding issues relating to licenses for industrial exploration and exploitation of seabed resources and the distribu-tion of benefits, but merely notes the existence of these issues (Articles 9 and 14). The Japanese and US drafts contain elaborate (perhaps too elaborate, considering the rapid rate of change!) provisions for licensing, but the Seabed Authority's function is strictly regulatory and supervisory, not plan-ning, operational, or managerial. The same (or almost) applies to the Mal-tese draft.

Interesting starting points are offered by the Tanzanian draft. Here the Authority is in fact empowered "to explore the International Area and exploit its resources for peaceful purposes by means of its own facilities, equipment and services, or such as are procured by it for the purpose" (Article 16 (1)). The draft of the land-locked nations likewise provides in Article 11 that "the Assembly may upon recommendation of the Council decide to establish a body charged with direct exploration, exploitation, and marketing (including the direct licensing of a private or public enterprise, joint ventures and service contracts) of a specified part of the international area." The direct licensing of enterprises is another interesting feature of this draft, conducive to the kind of relationship between the Authority and the producing enterprises that fits the base of the common heritage of mankind.

The Tanzanian draft also empowers the Authority "to establish oceanographic institutions on a regional basis for the training of nationals of developing countries in all aspects of marine science and technology" (Article 18 (9)). Perhaps it would be even more purposive if these institutions dealt with "ocean affairs" rather than oceanography and included the study of resource management, planning, and the legal/political dimension of ocean affairs. Other original features of the Tanzanian draft relating to the problem of management are the proposed "distribution agency" and "stabilization board." Between these two, the planning of seabed production, in the context of world production, might at least begin to emerge, although (1) it may be impractical that this germinal planning is splintered between two organs; (2) price-fixing and quantity-fixing belong to the regulatory rather than the planning function; (3) the criteria for benefit-sharing may turn out to be too rigid, and therefore not benefit-maximizing; and (4) while inadequate in terms of general economic planning, the provisions may in fact be too elaborate if applied only to the resources of the seabed, which for many years to come are not likely to cause fluctuations in prices, will hardly need to be restrained in quantity, and will not markedly raise the per capita income in the developing nations.

Like the Tanzanian and the land-locked nations' drafts, the Latin American draft empowers the Seabed Authority "to undertake exploration of the area, and exploitation of its resources as well as all activities relating to production, processing, and marketing" (Article 14 (c)). More specifically, however, the draft establishes the "Enterprise," which by itself or in joint venture with private or public corporations ("juridical persons duly sponsored by States"), engages in operational activities. Relations between the "Enterprise" and the Assembly are indicated in Article 24(h)—the Assembly is to "approve the report of the Enterprise, submitted through the Council"; relations with the Council are sketched in Article 32(m). There is no indication of any relation of the Enterprise with the Planning Board, which is briefly described in Article 25, and the questions relating to the structure and functions of the Enterprise are not dealt with—and this, of course, is the crux of the matter.

If the Enterprise is to correspond to the concept of the "common heritage of mankind," it would have to meet a number of conditions.

First, adequate measures must be taken to prevent its being controlled by private interests. This could be done by stipulating that at least half its capital must be provided by the Seabed or Ocean Space Authority; at least half its directors must be appointed or elected by the Assembly; and that a number of them must come from the developing nations. In this case the Enterprise would really be a shortcut not otherwise available, leading to the active participation of the poor nations in the industrial exploitation of ocean resources.

Second, if the economic and efficiency-oriented activities of the Enterprise are to be controlled and regulated by the political and equity-oriented organs of the Ocean Regime, such control and regulation can best, or only, be achieved through *participation*. That is, the Enterprise must be represented on the Planning Board and, in a suitable way, in the deliberative and policy-making organs of the regime.

The underlying concepts of the common heritage of mankind and of participation thus politicizes, to a certain extent, the Enterprise, just as it economizes the political organs of the regime. It is this new form of merger of the economic and the political that gives rise to new structures of the kind broadly envisioned by the Canadian government in its working paper: "It is clear that the nature of the task [the international machinery] is to perform is so radically different from anything now being undertaken in the UN system that this new institution will require a new approach not tied to traditions and practices intended for wholly different purposes. In a sense, this machinery may be more like an enterprise than the ordinary UN agency."

Third, if the Enterprise (or Enterprises) is (or are) structured and integrated into the system in this way, there is, of course, no reason whatsoever why it should operate exclusively in "the international area." It should operate wherever such operations are most beneficial, according to general consensus, including, of course, the consensus of the country on whose territory the operation is to take place. This may not be relevant with regard to manganese nodule production. A maritime mining corporation incorporated in the ocean regime may indeed prevalently operate on the "international seabed," but it would be quite relevant for a maritime oil corporation.

It is very likely that weaker nations will prefer, near their shores, the operation of the Enterprise in whose management and planning they have an active role, to the operations of an extraneous private enterprise, yielding royalties but no other benefits. It is indeed likely that the operation of the Enterprise will exert a competitive influence on the international style of the big, private, multinational corporations and may eventually bring them into an analogous relationship with the Regime, on one hand, and with the developing nations on the other.

Thus the impact of the common heritage concept on the *structure* of the regime is beginning to be felt, but it has not yet been fully spelled out. On the whole, the drafts still tend to perpetuate the structure of international organization devised during the first half of this century—an Assembly of all member states; a Council of a limited number of presumably leading states; a certain number of commissions, also based on states but leaning on experts and nongovernmental organizations; a secreteriat of international civil servants; and an international court or tribunal—and to stretch it and twist it to fit the totally new basis that has been created with the concept of the common heritage of mankind.

The drafts reflect *political* changes. They project, in various ways, the decline of the West, even though valid attempts to balance this trend are made by the US draft, which practically assures to the six industrially most advanced nations a veto over whatever the majority of developing nations might try to do; and, in a different way, by the Maltese draft through an ingenious method for weighting the vote. The drafts of the developing nations seem to take it for granted that the Council will be dominated by them, inasmuch as the Council is elected without further specifications by the Assembly, in which, in turn, they hold a safe majority. The Soviet draft allots one-fifth of the votes to the West. If one were to assume an interest coincidence between the socialist and the developing nations, the West could come off badly indeed. The way it would work out, however, would be cooperation between the highly developed socialist nations of eastern Europe and the West; a cooperation between the developing nations of Africa and Latin America; with "Asia," divided between a highly developed Japan and a China, espousing the cause of the developing nations, holding the balance.

Thus while the draft treaties reflect, and in various ways structuralize, *political* change, while they reflect (indeed, they are all inspired by) the underlying changes in the economic, technological, and scientific order, they do fail, to various degrees, to structuralize these changes. This would imply a departure from the model of international organization inherited from the first half of our century. The new model, while not by any means negating the reality of the nation state, would embody an active concept of sharing in the common heritage, in an operational system bringing together government, science, and production. It would be so structured as to (1) plan and control technological development through a new science policy emerging from joint decision-making between the political and the scientific communities; (2) plan and control economic development and its impact on the total environment through a new industrial management policy emerging from joint decision-making between the political and the industrial communities; (3) reconcile the conflicts between ecological-economic units of management and political units by a shift from a territorial to a functional perspective; (4) reconcile the disparate claims of governments and people, rulers and ruled, public sector and private sector, owner and nonowner, based on new forms of participation by peoples in the conduct of world affairs (without which democracy cannot survive in any form) and on the concept of the common heritage of mankind which transcends these dualisms.

The beginnings of all this are clearly recognizable, explicit or implicit, in one or another or all of the drafts, as are a number of other innovations in international law (for example, the acknowledgment of national responsibility beyond the limits of national jurisdiction or the acknowledgment of the need for peaceful settlement of conflicts) that would have been unthinkable only a few years ago. It is indeed amazing how many new concepts and approaches have been pullulating during the short span of four years and have found their way into the drafts.

If the oceans are indeed man's last frontier on this old earth of scarcity and competition to which we have reduced our common heritage, the law of the seas is the advance post on the long march toward a new world of science and technology, of abundance and cooperation which we have set out to achieve.

CHAPTER 24

Recommendations from Pacem in Maribus IV to the United Nations Committee on the Peaceful Uses of the Sea-Bed

At the end of the Pacem in Maribus IV convocation, the prevailing view was that the success of the forthcoming Law of the Sea Conference is vitally important to all nations and to mankind as a whole, that the Declaration of Principles adopted by the United Nations in 1970 should not only form the basis for a future international regime for the seabed, ocean floor, and subsoil thereof beyond the limits of national jurisdiction, but should be supplemented to conform to contemporary technological conditions and to the aspirations of the international community today.

Since the manner in which the objectives and principles are defined may be decisive for the success of the conference, it was felt that these objectives and principles should adequately reflect the persuasive evidence produced in the discussions within the UN since the initial text was adopted, to the effect that the seabed, ocean floor, and subsoil thereof beyond the limits of national jurisdiction must be considered as *part of ocean space* which is an ecological whole, that man's multiple uses of ocean space intersect and interact, that activities in the water column may affect the seabed and vice versa, that activities in the areas under national jurisdiction may affect international areas and vice versa, that the conservation of the marine environment and the rational management of its resources are essential to the survival of humanity.

Therefore, the UN Committee on the Peaceful Uses of the Sea-Bed might consider the following points as a possible basis for the UN Conference on the Law of the Sea.

Ocean Space as a Whole

1. Ocean space and the air column above it are an ecological unity. Increasing world industrialization, multiplying populations, coastal congestion, increased world use of chemicals, and many other factors are subjecting the marine environment to unprecedented pressures, particularly in the vicinity of highly industrialized countries. No one state alone can cope with the situation. Minimum worldwide standards are thus required with regard to the avoidance of pollution in the marine environment.

2. Rapidly advancing technology is enabling man to change significantly the state of the marine environment through diversion of important rivers and marine currents, weather modification, and other means. Use of technology which can seriously affect the natural state of the marine environment over large areas must be subjected to international control.

3. The development of supertankers, liquefied natural gas carriers, submarine navigation, ships with nuclear propulsion, and other developments are creating new hazards to the marine environment and to the safety of navigation. Minimum international standards must be elaborated through global marine institutions with comprehensive functions which can take into account the interaction between major peaceful uses of the sea.

4. Ocean space is becoming an economic unity, in that the uses of the surface of the sea, of the water column, and of the seabed are becoming increasingly interconnected. International law must recognize this fundamental fact by consolidating existing legal regimes for different activities.

5. The rapid increase of man's multiple activities requires the management of the seas and their resources to a much larger extent than has been the case in the past. Present realities make it mandatory that control and management of the oceans must be shared between coastal states and the international community in accordance with the principle of the common heritage of mankind.

Ocean Space within National Jurisdiction

6. Precise overall limits to national jurisdiction are required.

7. Navigation, overflight, scientific research, the laying of submarine cables, and perhaps some other activities are vital public international interests and as such must be internationally protected within the limits of national jurisdiction.

8. Due to technological advance and increasing fishing effort, intolerable pressures are developing on desirable fish stocks in some parts of the world. Global minimum standards of biological and economic management

must be elaborated to be implemented through regional bodies and marine institutions for ocean space with comprehensive functions.

9. Special international protection must be accorded to slowly reproducing marine species such as sea mammals.

10. Coastal states have obligations as well as rights in the area of ocean space within their jurisdiction. These obligations extend not only to the protection within the jurisdiction of such activities as may be considered public international interests, but also to management of the environment and of living resources in a manner conforming at least to minimum international standards.

11. States which do not possess the financial or technical capability to attain minimum international standards must receive the assistance needed through comprehensive institutions for ocean space.

Ocean Space beyond National Jurisdiction

12. It is strongly recommended that not only the seabed but also ocean space and its resources beyond national jurisdiction be considered a common heritage of mankind and that appropriate treaty articles embodying this concept be included in any draft treaty.

13. It is believed that only through the adoption and subsequent implementation by the international community of the basic concept of common heritage of ocean space beyond national jurisdiction can the future beneficial use of ocean space and its resources by all states be assured and, indeed, expanded in contemporary conditions of intensive exploitation accompanied by increasingly powerful technology.

14. *The concept of a common heritage of mankind of ocean space and its resources beyond national jurisdiction must form the basis of future international law of the sea* and be given expression in an international treaty or treaties generally agreed upon by the international community, which harmonize the rights of states with the emerging world interest.

15. The treaty or treaties to which reference has been made must include provision for a machinery balanced so as to insure that the decisions of the machinery reasonably reflect the wishes of the majority of the population of the world, giving due weight to the needs of the developing nations and to the economic dependence of states on ocean space.

16. Landlocked and shelf-locked countries must be assured access to ocean space, must be given the opportunity on an equal basis with coastal states to take part in the exploitation of resources beyond national jurisdiction, and must participate in the sharing of benefits derived from the exploitation of ocean resources beyond national jurisdiction.

The International Machinery

17. The international machinery must perform, among other things, the following functions:

(a) provide a general forum for the discussion, negotiation, and accommodation of national interests in ocean space;

(b) set general and nondiscriminatory standards and regulate them with respect to major peaceful uses of ocean space;

(c) manage and conserve biologically and economically the living resources of the sea beyond national jurisdiction and conservation and management, in cooperation with the coastal state, of living resources which migrate between ocean space under national jurisdiction and ocean space beyond national jurisdiction;

(d) explore and exploit the nonliving resources of ocean space beyond national jurisdiction either directly or in participation with states or through a system of licenses;

(e) provide for an equitable sharing of benefits derived from the exploitation of the living and nonliving resources of ocean space beyond national jurisdiction, which includes a contribution from coastal states with respect to benefits derived from the exploitation of resources in areas of ocean space under their jurisdiction; such a contribution appears justified in view of the benefits that would be derived by the coastal state from the management of resources outside its jurisdiction;

(f) protect and generally regulate such activities in the oceans exclusively for peaceful purposes as may be considered to be of vital international public interest;

(g) provide a mechanism for the access of technologically less developed countries to advanced marine technology relevant to their needs and for the transfer of such technology;

(h) promote scientific research in ocean space and establish an effective mechanism for associating scientifically less advanced countries in such research;

(i) provide for the international community such services in ocean space as may be considered necessary or desirable, including sail vessels for rescue and scientific or other international community purposes.

18. Many of the proposed functions of the international institutions could, it is believed, be appropriately undertaken through regional bodies.

19. It is believed that it is of great importance either to consolidate existing UN bodies primarily dealing with questions concerning ocean space into the future international institutions for ocean space or at least to coordinate their activities through the institutions in order to avoid

bureaucratic proliferation, duplication of activities, and inadequate or excessively complex coordination machineries at the international level.

20. The international regime should provide machinery for interdisciplinary discussion and decision-making, involving, as far as is possible, all users of ocean space and resources and including, in particular, science, industry, and the service sector.

21. It is considered very important to stress that international law and practice concerning the legal responsibility of states and of the persons under their jurisdiction with regard to culpable activities which cause damage to other states in the marine environment must be considerably expanded and made more precise; in particular, a course of action must be given to the international community through the international institutions with regard to deleterious activities in ocean space beyond national jurisdiction.

22. It is scarcely necessary to stress that no institutional system for ocean space would be complete without appropriate machinery for the compulsory settlement of disputes.